Browns 10/12 £34.99

10635058

4 Rei
20
L

DYSLEXIA AND LITERACY

WD.

Learning Resources Centre
Middlesbrough College
Dock Street
Middlesbrough
TS2 1AD

Do not W/D. On
reading list -
2014-15

m
middlesb
college

Middlesbrough College

00093920

Middlesbrough College

Learning Resources Centre

Class No 371·9144 Rei

Accession 093920

Location L

DYSLEXIA AND LITERACY

Theory and Practice

Edited by

Gavin Reid

Faculty of Education, University of Edinburgh, UK

and

Janice Wearmouth

Faculty of Education and Language Studies, The Open University, UK

Learning Resources Centre
Middlesbrough College
Dock Street
Middlesbrough
TS2 1AD

JOHN WILEY & SONS, LTD

Copyright © 2002   John Wiley & Sons Ltd, The Atrium, Southern Gate, Chichester,
West Sussex PO19 8SQ, England

Telephone   (+44) 1243 779777
Reprinted January 2003 and June 2004, August 2005, June 2006, September 2008

Email (for orders and customer service enquiries): cs-books@wiley.co.uk
Visit our Home Page on www.wileyeurope.com or www.wiley.com

All Rights Reserved. No part of this publication may be reproduced, stored in a retrieval
system or transmitted in any form or by any means, electronic, mechanical, photocopying,
recording, scanning or otherwise, except under the terms of the Copyright, Designs and
Patents Act 1988 or under the terms of a licence issued by the Copyright Licensing Agency
Ltd, 90 Tottenham Court Road, London W1T 4LP, UK, without the permission in writing of
the Publisher. Requests to the Publisher should be addressed to the Permissions Department,
John Wiley & Sons Ltd, The Atrium, Southern Gate, Chichester, West Sussex PO19 8SQ,
England, or emailed to permreq@wiley.co.uk, or faxed to (+44) 1243 770571.

This publication is designed to provide accurate and authoritative information in regard to
the subject matter covered. It is sold on the understanding that the Publisher is not engaged in
rendering professional services. If professional advice or other expert assistance is required,
the services of a competent professional should be sought.

Other Wiley Editorial Offices

John Wiley & Sons Inc., 111 River Street, Hoboken, NJ 07030, USA

Jossey-Bass, 989 Market Street, San Francisco, CA 94103-1741, USA

Wiley-VCH Verlag GmbH, Boschstr. 12, D-69469 Weinheim, Germany

John Wiley & Sons Australia Ltd, 33 Park Road, Milton, Queensland 4064, Australia

John Wiley & Sons (Asia) Pte Ltd, 2 Clementi Loop #02-01, Jin Xing Distripark, Singapore
129809

John Wiley & Sons Canada Ltd, 22 Worcester Road, Etobicoke, Ontario, Canada M9W 1L1

British Library Cataloguing in Publication Data

A catalogue record for this book is available from the British Library

ISBN 978-0-471-48633-6 (HB)
ISBN 978-0-471-48634-3 (PB)

Typeset in 10 / 12 Palatino by Techbooks, New Dekhi, India

CONTENTS

ABOUT THE EDITORS

Gavin Reid

Gavin Reid is a senior lecturer in the Faculty of Education, University of Edinburgh. He is an experienced teacher, educational psychologist, researcher and university lecturer. He has made over 200 keynote presentations throughout the UK and at conferences worldwide, including United States, Eastern and Western Europe, Scandinavia, New Zealand and Hong Kong. He is the author of a number of books on dyslexia and learning styles including *Dyslexia: A Practitioner's Handbook* (1998) and is co-author of *Dyslexia in Adults: Education and Employment* (2001), both published by Wiley.

He is in the course team which developed the joint Open University/University of Edinburgh course on Identifying and Addressing Difficulties in Literacy Development and has also a number of research and consultancy interests, including assessment, early literacy and dyslexia in adults.

Janice Wearmouth

Janice Wearmouth is a lecturer in the Faculty of Education and Language Studies at The Open University in the UK. She is an experienced teacher, researcher and author in the area of special educational needs and difficulties in literacy development. Her research interests include pupil self advocacy, the development and organisation of special and/or additional provision for pupils who experience difficulties in learning in mainstream schools, and home–school literacy partnerships.

She is co-chair of the course team which developed and produced the Open University course E801 Difficulties in Literacy Development in collaboration with the University of Edinburgh.

Learning Resources Centre
Middlesbrough College
Dock Street
Middlesbrough
TS2 1AD

ABOUT THE CONTRIBUTORS

Dirk J. Bakker is a Professor Emeritus of the Free University, Department of Child Neuropsychology, Amsterdam, Netherlands. He researches the etiology, classification and treatment of developmental dyslexia. He is past-president of the International Neuropsychological Society (INS).

Bob Burden is Professor of Applied Educational Psychology at the University of Exeter School of Education and Lifelong Learning, where he established the Masters level professional training programme in 1971. He is a former President of the International School Psychology Association and a former Chair of the Division of Educational and Child Psychology of the British Psychology Association. He is currently Chair of the British Dyslexia Association's Accreditation Board.

Tony Cline is Head of the Centre for Education Studies in the University of Luton. The starting point for his interest in dyslexia and bilingualism was experience as an educational psychologist in London and a researcher on the experiences of ethnic minority children.

Margaret Crombie is manager of the Special Educational Needs support team of teachers in East Renfrewshire in Scotland. She has researched into the effects of dyslexia on the learning of modern languages in school, and is currently researching policy and practice for dyslexia at the early stages.

Fidelma Healy Eames lectures in Literacy Education and is Director of fhe Education & Training Consultants, Co. Galway, Ireland. A former primary school teacher (Ireland and US), her current work includes observing and evaluating the teaching practices of beginning teachers. Her doctoral research probed understandings and approaches to the teaching of writing in Ireland. With a strong interest in pupils with dyslexia and learning difficulties, she frames her work against a holistic understanding of pupils' total needs.

Linnea C. Ehri is Distinguished Professor at the Graduate Center of the City University of New York. She studies how beginners learn to read and spell words. She was on the National Reading Panel and was president of the Society for the Scientific Study of Reading.

John Everatt is a Senior Lecturer within the Department of Psychology, University of Surrey, UK. He researches in the areas of dyslexia, reading ability and visual attention. He is an executive editor for the journal *Dyslexia*.

Angela J. Fawcett is a Senior Research Fellow in Psychology at the University of Sheffield. Her theoretical research on dyslexia, with Rod Nicolson provides direct evidence of cerebellar impairment in dyslexia and fed into the construction of best-selling screening tests for dyslexia from cradle to grave.

Uta Frith is Professor of Cognitive Development at the University of London and Deputy Director of the UCL Institute of Cognitive Neuroscience. She has carried out research in dyslexia and autism over the past 30 years.

Janet Hatcher is a member of the Centre for Reading and Language at the University of York. She is an educationist who is currently research co-ordinator for the Dyslexia Institute.

George Hunt is a lecturer in language and education at the University of Edinburgh. Previously he was a primary school teacher in London and a teacher educator in Reading and the Commonwealth of Dominica.

George W. Hynd is Research Professor of Special Education and Psychology, University of Georgia, and Clinical Professor of Neurology, Medical College of Georgia. He is also the Associate Dean for Research Development and Outreach within the College of Education.

Deborah F. Knight is an Assistant Professor at the University of Delaware in the US. Prior to her current position, she served as the Director of the Tennessee Center for the Study and Treatment of Dyslexia. Her research interests include dyslexia, spelling, and reading comprehension.

Lindsay Peer is Education Director of the British Dyslexia Association and is a widely recognised authority in the field of dyslexia and mainstream education. Her field of experience covers teacher training, research and the teaching of both mainstream students and of those with Specific Learning Difficulties/Dyslexia, from pre-school through to adult education.

Rea Reason is Senior Lecturer in Education at Manchester University. She is best known for her practical publications in the field of literacy learning and difficulties. She was chair of the British Psychological Society working party that published the report entitled *Dyslexia, Literacy and Psychological Assessment*.

Jean Robertson is an independent psychologist, who works primarily with dyslexic children and adults. Her background in dyslexia stems from her work within specialist support services for dyslexic children. Until recently she was a researcher and lecturer within the dyslexia field at the Metropolitan University in Manchester and worked extensively with teachers undertaking specialist qualifications in teaching dyslexic children and adults within Further and Higher Education.

Gerry Shiel is a research fellow at the Educational Research Centre, St Patrick's College, Drumcondra, Dublin, Ireland. He is involved in the design and implementation of international and national surveys of reading, literacy, and in the appraisal of interventions for students with learning difficulties.

Chris Singleton is Senior Lecturer in Educational Psychology, University of Hull. He is best known for his research on the early identification of dyslexia, which resulted in the development of several computer-based assessment systems now in use in many schools.

Margaret J. Snowling is a member of the Centre for Reading and Language at the University of York. She holds a personal chair in Psychology.

Janet Tod is a Reader in Education at Canterbury Christ Church University College and Director of their Special Needs Research and Development Centre. She is a chartered educational and clinical psychologist, qualified speech therapist, and is actively involved in teacher education at undergradute and postgraduate levels. She has managed two DfEE-funded research projects, one concerning dyslexia, the other Individual Education Plans (IEPs), and has published books and articles in these areas.

Keith Topping is director of graduate Educational Psychology and the Centre for Paired Learning at the University of Dundee. He develops and researches methods for parent- and peer-assisted learning, behaviour management and social competence, electronic literacy and computer-aided assessment.

David Wray is Professor of Literacy Education at the University of Warwick. He has published over 30 books on aspects of literacy teaching and is best known for his work on developing teaching strategies to help pupils access the curriculum through literacy.

INTRODUCTION

This book aims to provide the reader with an understanding of recent theoretical positions in dyslexia and literacy and how these may be applied in practice. At first glance one might question why we have separated 'dyslexia from 'literacy' as, clearly, there is considerable overlap between them. However, there are many examples of good practices in literacy not yet fully penetrating the dyslexia field. Until fairly recently this field has been preoccupied with the decoding, bottom-up aspects of literacy, and has been immersed in debate and controversy, some aspects of which will be discussed in Part I of this book.

In both Part I and Part II of this book there are many examples of research and practice which has yet to penetrate classroom interventions designed for students with dyslexia. Similarly, the field of dyslexia has made considerable breakthroughs both in research and practice, certainly over the last ten years. Much of this has still not reached, nor impacted upon, the practices of the classroom teacher. Some of this has training implications. A key role, therefore, can be identified for staff development within the area of dyslexia, linking it to the best practices in literacy development. This volume has been compiled to support all education professionals, in particular practising teachers, to re-appraise their thinking about theoretical and practical aspects of dyslexia and its relationship with literacy practices. This is crucial at a time when literacy acquisition is a focus of interest and intervention by governments in many countries. The editors hope, therefore, that this volume goes some of the way to satisfying the demand and the need to view practice within a theoretical framework and also provide the vehicle to link the good practices in the fields of literacy and dyslexia.

OVERVIEW OF THE BOOK

The book is divided into two parts. Part I focuses on theory and Part II on practice.

The opening chapter by Angela Fawcett focuses on the key issues for research and how these issues may impact on policy and practice. She considers the potential causes of some of the confusion in dyslexia research and practice and outlines the

---

Dyslexia and Literacy: Theory and Practice. Edited by Gavin Reid and Janice Wearmouth.
© 2002 John Wiley & Sons, Ltd.

progress which has been made over the past decade in theoretical understanding of dyslexia and also in diagnosis, support and policy. This chapter is followed by one from Deborah Knight and George Hynd who outline a basic explanation of brain function and go on to describe morphological, imaging and genetic studies of dyslexia.

The causal modelling framework as a model for explaining and understanding literacy acquisition has been well quoted and is referred to in several chapters in this book. The model (Frith and Morton 1995) is explained in the context of literacy difficulties in the chapter by Uta Frith. Other models of explaining literacy difficulties are more fully developed in the following four chapters. The phonological representation model is explained in the chapter by Janet Hatcher and Margaret Snowling. In this chapter the authors assess the extent to which this hypothesis is able to account for the behaviour of people identified as 'dyslexic' and discuss its implications for assessment and practice. The following chapter by John Everatt looks at visual processes, describes the historical viewpoints relating to visual deficits as a cause of dyslexia and then analyses current theories relating problems associated with dyslexia to a particular visual pathway which extends through the brain's visual system. He discusses the viewpoints relating to over-sensitivity to light and also those views concerning the magnocellular pathway deficit hypothesis. This chapter is followed by one by Jean Robertson and Dirk Bakker on the Balance Model of Reading which classifies readers as either P-type, that is those who use perceptual strategies, and L-type, linguistic strategies. In this chapter Robertson and Bakker explain the background to the theory and how it relates to the reading process and to developmental dyslexia. They also discuss their research on neuropsychological intervention approaches and the practical implications of these approaches. This is succeeded by a chapter on cognitive processes by Chris Singleton. He is concerned with the impact of variation in different cognitive abilities on literacy acquisition in general, and on dyslexia in particular. He also discusses the issue of whether cognitive measures can facilitate the identification of dyslexic children as early as possible and enable teachers to provide them with education appropriate to their needs.

Gerry Shiel provides an overview from national and international research of the factors that affect literacy practices. He discusses the outcomes of international studies of reading and related skills including the Reading Literacy Study and the Progress in International Reading Literacy Study from the IEA (International Association for the Evaluation of Educational Achievement). The chapter also refers to national assessments of literacy in Ireland and the U.K. and recognises that this type of data can offer information on standards of literacy and also on the factors associated with achievement in reading.

Part II of the book focuses primarily on practice, although it should be noted that it is not our intention to separate theory and practice because both are inextricably linked. This will be clear in some of the chapters in this part of the book. This part begins with a chapter by Janice Wearmouth and Gavin Reid on the issues for assessment and planning of teaching and learning. This chapter discusses and comments on some of the debates on models of assessment and encourages readers to be aware of the broad range of assessment strategies to assess the individual pupil in different contexts. The role of metacognitive assessment is one example of this which is discussed in relation to understanding the learning process of the student with dyslexia. The role of learning styles in the learning context is also discussed as well as pupils' and parents' perspectives. Next follows Linnea Ehri's chapter on reading processes and their instructional implications. In this chapter she focuses on the learner rather than on teaching methods and analysis and discusses the processes as a means of identifying teaching methods. As well as the reading process the author discusses reading models and stages in the acquisition of literacy and reading–spelling relationships.

Utilising the causal modelling framework outlined earlier, Rea Reason in the next chapter discusses the concept of dyslexia and the debates on assessment and intervention, debates which formed the basis of the Division of Educational and Child Psychology of the British Psychological Society report Dyslexia, Literacy and Psychological Assessment (BPS 1999). The author addresses the concept and the implications of a working definition of dyslexia as well as the practice of assessment and discusses the processes in which she has engaged to analyse and audit different forms of phonic instruction. The chapter refers to aspects of the impact of the report in practice, such as the concept of 'noticing and adjusting' as a means of monitoring the progress of young children at risk of reading failure. It concludes with a summary of key implications for practice.

Tony Cline in the following chapter picks up the theme of assessment from the perspective of children whose first language is other than English. He looks at some of the key underlying issues on how literacy skills in English develop normally in most children learning English as an additional language and then provides an overview of reading difficulties. Cline also outlines the nature of access to specialist provision and the 'serious concern' of this when viewed from both a historical perspective and the current definition of 'institutional racism.' In addition, this chapter discusses issues in the assessment of reading abilities, strategies for intervention and the need for a literacy curriculum to empower rather than inhibit.

In the subsequent chapter Janice Wearmouth discusses the role of a learning support co-ordinator in facilitating the learning of pupils with difficulties in literacy development. She outlines the challenges facing those who seek to bring about change in educational institutions in order to develop and implement improved provision for students with difficulties in literacy, whilst simultaneously harnessing sufficient support for that change to be sustained. This is followed by Margaret Crombie's chapter which addresses ways of dealing with diversity in the primary classroom. Crombie discusses the two themes of diversity and challenge with reference to the early years, early identification, the issues of labelling, intervention and support, including learning styles and metacognition. Additionally, she refers to technology, subject choices and emotional factors. The number of key issues she discusses in this chapter is indicative of the range of challenges facing primary school teachers as they familiarise themselves with ways in which these elements can relate to dyslexia in the classroom.

In the following chapter the focus is on the secondary school. This chapter by Lindsay Peer and Gavin Reid takes a curriculum approach implying that all students including dyslexic students should be entitled to a broad and balanced curriculum and this can be achieved through planning, appropriate teaching approaches, staff development and the notion of whole school responsibility for all students, including those with literacy difficulties. One method of achieving this is through practices associated with Individual Education Plans. In the next chapter Janet Tod provides a detailed analysis of the principles and policies of IEP's as well as the research and theoretical perspectives in relation to IEP's and literacy difficulties. Tod describes key factors relating to IEP's, indicating that an IEP is both a 'process and a document', and in this chapter she discusses and describes the implications of this. She highlights the key principles for IEP policy development as well as teachers and OFSTED responses to the practice of using IEP's. Tod concludes the chapter with some key principles for effective practice in the use of IEP's such as clarity of purpose, the need for IEP's to be contextualised, the impact of an IEP on curriculum development, the enabling and empowering role of IEP's and the fact that they should reflect collaborative educational effort.

In the following chapter, Bob Burden highlights a cognitive approach to dyslexia by focusing on learning styles and thinking skills. He sets the context for the chapter by referring to the usage of the label dyslexia and discusses the various roles the term can assume including those of 'convenience' 'description' and 'comparative'. Burden in this chapter also shows how individual learners make sense of, and respond to, their growing awareness of their difficulties by referring to cognitive approaches to learning. He uses as an example Feuerstein's 'deficient cognitive functions' model and in particular the process of dynamic assessment as a means of obtaining a differential diagnosis of dyslexic type difficulties. Learner self-perception is an important element in success in any field and in this chapter Burden highlights this from a number of perspectives such as the constructivist perspective, motivational approaches and self-concept approaches including the 'myself-as-learner scale developed by the author. He also refers to factors relating to 'locus of control' and 'attribution' and suggests that we should broaden the perspective in dealing with dyslexia to include elements of thinking, learning and socio-cultural processes in order to understand and mediate the student's learning environment and learning experiences. The theme of 'thinking' as a means of accessing the curriculum and providing learning opportunities is continued by Keith Topping in the next chapter. In it Topping describes how thinking skills can be developed within the curriculum and acknowledges that much of the research on this is concerned with teacher directed instruction in thinking skills with much of it relating to higher education rather than schools. He describes some of the classroom orientated approaches in developing thinking skills such as Reciprocal Teaching, Traditional Strategies Instruction, Peer Assisted Learning Strategies and scaffolding 'discourse patterns' through 'guided peer questioning'. The principal part of Topping's chapter describes his own work in the area of paired thinking, the stages and activities involved in paired thinking, tips for tutors and detailed examples of differentiation and progression at different levels. He also provides examples of how to organise the classroom for paired thinking, how it relates to specific learning difficulties, resources useful for paired thinking and evaluation of the procedure and outcomes.

David Wray in the subsequent chapter also continues the theme of metacognition and relates this directly to literacy. Wray explains metacognition as 'having the capacity to self-monitor your own understanding of reading in order to spot and then respond to a difficulty'. He provides examples of how metacognition can be used with comprehension monitoring and in expressive writing. He also provides some insights into teacher modelling and strategies such as thinking aloud and reciprocal teaching. He suggests that a key to enhancing children's abilities in literacy is to develop their abilities to be more 'aware' of their literacy processes and that the teaching of literacy would benefit from the wider application of metacognitive-type approaches.

In the next chapter George Hunt looks at critical literacy and access to the lexicon by critically describing some of the traditional approaches to reading and then providing some insights into critical literacy. He describes critical literacy as a term which is used to subsume a number of instructional approaches which challenge assumptions that texts can ever convey 'objective meanings' or that literacy is an ideologically neutral tool. This means, according to Hunt, that teachers need to do more than simply train pupils to become skilled decoders. This view assumes that literacy is only empowering if informed by critical awareness and Hunt acknowledges that, in the classroom, texts can limit rather than liberate both teachers and students. The goal of literacy teaching is therefore the empowerment of the reader. Hunt suggests that more research is needed to investigate the effectiveness of critical literacy approaches.

In the final chapter of the book Fidelma Eames looks at the changing definitions and concepts of literacy and its implications for pedagogy and research. Eames shows how definitions of literacy have the power to drive the curriculum. It is important, therefore, that we seek a broad definition of literacy, particularly in view of the cultural and linguistic diversities which are increasingly evident in the classroom. To highlight her view that literacy is broader than reading she discusses the literacy journey children make by focusing on critical literacy, looking at oral language, reading, writing and the use of information and communication technology. Eames also addresses expressive writing and metacognition, focusing on dyslexic children and emphasising the need for dyslexic pupils to take responsibility for their own learning. The chapter also includes a discussion of literacy in the technological age, factors relating to measuring literacy performances, a critical analysis of literacy studies and an outline of some challenges for literacy educators.

Eames concludes her chapter by suggesting that literacy is an agent of change. This statement perhaps encapsulates the spirit of this book and its intention to inform and extend the thinking of education professionals about literacy and dyslexia in order to facilitate change in both the theoretical understanding of literacy and dyslexia and classroom practices. We hope this book achieves these aims and, as editors, we are deeply indebted to all the authors who contributed chapters.

Part I

THEORY

There are numerous research studies incorporating different research perspectives within the field of dyslexia and literacy. We have selected here for this part of the book chapters from those researchers who hold prominent theoretical positions or have an influential understanding of the theoretical and research implications inherent within dyslexia and literacy. One of the most influential of these is the causal modelling framework (Morton & Frith, 1995) which is described by Frith in Chapter 3. This model is influential because it explains both dyslexia and literacy from causal and behavioural perspectives. The three elements of this model, biological, cognitive and behavioural, can assist and justify explanations and interventions offered by researchers and practitioners. By helping to explain the underlying concepts in this manner this model can incorporate different and often conflicting theories of developmental disorders which can account for literacy failure. Indeed, in Chapter 11 of Part II of this book, Reason speaks of the causal modelling framework as one which underpinned much of the report from the British Psychological Society Working Party investigation into dyslexia and assessment. Using this framework, Reason indicated that the report "presented ten different theoretical accounts of dyslexia as alternative or complementary hypotheses to explain learning difficulties of a dyslexic nature". These theoretical hypotheses include phonological delay, temporal processing, skill automatisation, working memory, visual processing, syndrome hypothesis, intelligence and cognitive profiles, subtypes, learning opportunities and social context and emotional factors. These represent influential factors associated with dyslexia and literacy, and the reader will find some form of reference to all of these within this book. By using this framework some of the controversies evident in this field can at least be explained, if not reconciled. The causal modelling framework also incorporates the, often overlooked, environmental dimensions: provision of teaching, cultural attitudes and socio-economic factors.

Frith herself suggests that "words and labels have a life of their own. They readily become loaded with ideology while the concepts they refer to may be perfectly non-contentious". It is interesting to consider the example provided by Frith of two established theories, one postulating the phonological deficit, the other the magnocellular deficit, both as explanations of dyslexia. According to Frith these are not in conflict. A framework which offers explanations at different levels, the magnocellular at the biological level and the phonological at the cognitive, can make theories compatible. These particular positions are discussed in detail in Chapters 4 and 5 of Part I of this book. In Chapter 4 Hatcher and Snowling provide explanations of some of the key points in relation to the "cause and effect" aspects of dyslexia. This is particularly relevant to the area of phonological development. Hatcher and Snowling ask how we can be sure that the phonological deficits in dyslexia are a cause rather than a consequence of literacy problems. The authors provide research evidence to suggest some qualitative differences between the dyslexic group and the control group in their early language skills, such as speech errors and the use of syntax at two and a half years and object naming and phonological awareness at five years.

Everatt discusses the magnocellular theory in Chapter 5 within a more general approach and investigates a range of visual processes which can affect reading. However, he suggests that magnocellular theories are appealing because they attempt to explain the underlying causes from a visual/biological perspective. This is important because, as Everatt points out, of the "very diversity of visual deficits" which attempt to explain reading failure. Many of these perspectives are covered in this chapter.

The importance of research is that it can not only explain conditions and syndromes, but can provide pointers for practice. Robertson and Bakker in Chapter 6 show how the balance model of reading, which is essentially derived from the brain/biological perspective, has been translated into a manageable programme for practitioners. Using Morton and Frith's framework as an example, the balance model can be included at all three levels: biological, cognitive and behavioural.

Morton and Frith incorporate the environmental perspectives, including culture and teaching, into their model. It is crucial, therefore, to examine the lessons from other countries and the factors which have affected progress or otherwise in these countries. This aspect is tackled by Shiel in Chapter 8. He comments on The International Adult Literacy Study conducted in 24 countries between 1994 and 1998. Despite the controversies engendered by these types of comparative studies (the results were met with a negative reaction in some countries), data of this type can help with comparing the focus of literacy teaching and also raise questions about the meaning of "functional literacy". For example, Shiel reports on the study in which adults with low levels of literacy considered their lack of skills "did not present them with major difficulties, indicating instead that their lack of skills were sufficient to meet their everyday needs". At the same time he emphasises the need to examine data carefully and critically, especially international studies of the kind reported in this chapter. For example, in one study (IEA/PIRLS) reading is defined as a constructive and interactive process, but this can emphasise different aspects in the culture and also in the assessment framework. Some studies have pointed to the range of factors that need to be addressed, for example the association between reading gender and reading achievement and between socio-economic status and performance in reading. This can provide pointers for the development of literacy policies and practices.

Planning is also the theme of the opening chapter of this book, where Fawcett looks at the key issues for research in dyslexia and literacy. Fawcett talks about a co-operative spirit between all those involved in research and practice in this field, noted in the round table discussions at the fifth BDA Conference in April 2001, and outlines the challenge in transforming this co-operative spirit into policy and practice. As well as discussing the potential causes of confusion in the area and the progress that has been made in research and practice, Fawcett also provides targets for future research. One such target relates to interlinking of theories in order to achieve clarity and a greater understanding of some of the key areas mentioned by Fawcett, such as co-morbidity, multilingualism, early identification and intervention, investigation of new technology, and exploiting the strengths of dyslexic children and adults.

The field of dyslexia is broad and diverse. The editors of this book hope that Part I, in conjuction with Part II, will explain some of that diversity, clarify some of the confusion, and help to provide a more cohesive and enlightened understanding of the field of dyslexia and literacy.

Chapter 1

DYSLEXIA AND LITERACY: KEY ISSUES FOR RESEARCH

Angela J. Fawcett

INTRODUCTION

At the start of the new millennium, considerable progress has been made in identifying the causes of dyslexia and providing intervention to break into the cycle of failure. My brief in writing this chapter is to consider how best we might consolidate this progress by working together to influence policy and practice for dyslexia over the next decade. This is not an easy task, nor one to be undertaken lightly. However, I have been able to draw on two sources here in support of my position, to ensure that the approach I advocate is fruitful. Firstly, the call from Rod Nicolson at the Fifth BDA Conference to consider targets for dyslexia research for the next decade in terms of unity of purpose. Nicolson (2001) noted that "the stage is set for undertaking ambitious, multi-disciplinary, multi-perspective projects aimed at redefining the field of dyslexia and learning difficulties as the field of learning abilities". Secondly, and perhaps more significantly, the spirit of collegiality and consensus which emerged from the round-table discussions of causal theories, diagnosis and intervention, which concluded the conference. It was my task to act as discussant, drawing together comments from the causal theories round-table panel and the floor, summarising the issues arising to the satisfaction of all involved, and feeding back this information to the plenary session. This was a challenging task. Feedback from the three round-table sessions concluded that significant progress had been made in working together towards a common goal. Transforming this co-operative spirit into a reality, which can affect policy and practice, forms the new challenge for dyslexia research.

My plan for the chapter is threefold: first, to consider potential causes of confusion in dyslexia research and practice; secondly, to outline the progress that has been

Dyslexia and Literacy: Theory and Practice. Edited by Gavin Reid and Janice Wearmouth.
© 2002 John Wiley & Sons, Ltd.

made in theory, diagnosis, support and policy over the past decade; and finally, to develop a series of targets for the next decade. Throughout the chapter, I will give my personal view of how to make progress in dyslexia research, with the key here that clarity and unity of purpose lead to success. In my role as an academic I advocate an open approach, with all the dyslexia community pulling together and respecting each others' viewpoints. This is reinforced by my role as parent of a dyslexic child, which leads me to think that no one theory will account for all the manifestations of dyslexia. It is our role here to work together towards greater understanding of the range of manifestations and theories which represent the truth about dyslexia.

The function of this chapter is be an introduction to the rest of this book. I shall therefore introduce a series of themes, which will be returned to and discussed in greater depth in other chapters in this volume.

THE DYSLEXIA ECOSYSTEM (NICOLSON 2001)

This striking analogy emerged at the Fifth International BDA Conference, to critical acclaim from the audience. In his keynote address, Rod Nicolson described the pool of different perspectives involved in dyslexia research as an "ecosystem", a group with overlapping but often conflicting needs attempting to inhabit the same space. Inevitably, failure to recognise and respect the differences between these needs has led to something of an impasse. With an increased understanding of the role that each one plays, we now have the potential to unite the dyslexia ecosystem into a dyslexia world. The associated surge in power for dyslexia research could fuel our joint targets for the next decade.

DIFFERENT ROLES

One of the major tensions in dyslexia research has been the range of potentially conflicting viewpoints which we are trying to accommodate. These might include those of researchers and practitioners; parents and teachers; teachers and educational psychologists; schools and local education authorities; local education authorities and governments—all have different agendas, and much of the time these force them into opposition. Moreoever, in order to secure funding, it is common for researchers to emphasise the differences between their approaches rather than the commonalities among them. This is by no means the most fruitful approach, indeed uniting under a common banner has led to a surge in research funding in the US over the past two decades. We would like to advocate unity of purpose in adopting a broader perspective to the manifestations of dyslexia. In our view, such an approach has the potential for a "win-win" situation, whereby substantial funding is available to all to quantify the impact of the different theories and their application into practice. We might envisage the scenario where routine use of early screening tests detected problems pre-school, leading to proactive individual support, preventing the development of the reading deficits which characterise dyslexia. A similar approach might be adopted with adult dyslexia, with fuller screening and expert subsequent assessment, specifically for job-related goals. The net result would be greater awareness of the requirements for "dyslexia-friendly" practice, both in education and at work. These innovations would satisfy everyone involved in the dyslexia ecosystem—dyslexic people, support specialists, schools, educational psychologists, funding bodies and the government. Above all, we need to show that the costs of such a scheme would be far outweighed by the savings, linked to a successful, effective and cost-effective policy for dyslexia throughout the lifespan. Interestingly enough, the government have recently established that pre-school intervention can reduce the costs of support by a factor of 1:8 (Department of Health/Home Office, 2001). These are the factors on which we need to work if we are to influence both policy and practice.

DIFFERENT THEORIES

In scientific research one of the most important distinctions is between cause and description. Typically, a reasonably complete description of the facts is needed, which allows researchers to derive hypotheses which can account for these facts. The hypothesis is then evaluated against new data, and scientific progress is made towards the true explanation. Naturally enough, problems can arise if hypotheses are built on incomplete data, because any characterisation of the difficulties is only partial.

In our talks, we often use the "medical model" of abnormal development, which distinguishes between cause, symptom and treatment. An appropriate analogy here might be with allergies. The same allergy can lead to different symptoms in different people, and the mechanisms are poorly understood. It is therefore necessary to use further, more sensitive tests, administered by a trained specialist, to determine the true underlying cause, and thus the appropriate treatment. Of course, there are very wide differences in the motivation of different protagonists within the dyslexic ecosystem. Practitioners are primarily concerned with treatment, educational psychologists with symptoms, and theorists with the discovery of the underlying cause(s). It is clear that, despite these different perspectives, a full understanding demands the investigation and integration of these three aspects. For example, in order to develop an applied test for early diagnosis of dyslexia, it is necessary to build on theoretical insights into the predictors of dyslexia which lie outside reading. Otherwise, we have no option but to return to the system where we wait for children to fail to learn to read, with all the associated trauma and negative impacts on self-esteem, which can damage children for life.

A further important discrimination is between the three "levels" of theory: the biological, the cognitive and the behavioural levels (Frith, 1997, and see Chapter 3 by Frith). Symptoms such as poor reading or rhyming deficits represent the behavioural level. Theories are explanations at the cognitive level; these might include deficits in working memory, phonological awareness, automatisation, and slow processing speed. Finally, the underlying brain mechanism lies at the biological level, with abnormalities in cortical language areas, magnocellular pathways, and the cerebellum. It should be recognised that these levels are different, that none is intrinsically "better" than another, and indeed that any complete explanation must include all three, with the cognitive level providing a necessary link between brain and behaviour.

Finally, let us consider development in terms of Thelen's "ontogenetic landscape" approach (Thelen & Smith, 1994), drawing on themes from developmental cognitive neuroscience. Here we need longitudinal studies of individual children, rather than the cohort approach which has been common in psychology, in order to see how underlying differences in the brain and cognition interact with the environment over time to produce the symptoms of dyslexia.

In summary, in order to develop a mature theory of dyslexia, we need to take on board all these different perspectives, and integrate them within a rich multidisciplinary framework, with specialists in all areas working together towards a common understanding.

DYSLEXIA OR READING DISABILITY?

One of the most contentious issues from an educational perspective is the concept of the dyslexic child as in some way "special" and deserving different treatment from the equally disadvantaged reading-disabled child. Many educationalists rightly stress the need for equal treatment for non-dyslexic children with special needs (Siegel, 1989). It is by no means clear whether dyslexia is a syndrome, like obesity (Ellis, 1993), or a collection of sub-types (Boder, 1973; Castles & Holmes, 1996) or based on a common "core" deficit (such as phonology). In Miles' (1994) terminology, a debate has arisen between the "splitters" and the "lumpers".

In the 1980s, US dyslexia researchers changed the focus to "reading disability" rather than "learning disability", thus concentrating resources on a painstaking analysis of the reading process rather than of the learning processes which underlie reading. Inevitably, this has led to divisions between researchers trying to find the causes of dyslexia and those trying to find the causes of the reading problems. In line with the analysis above, it should now be clear that both approaches are needed for a mature theory of dyslexia.

THE SITUATION IN 1990

In 1990, when we published our early work on automatisation (Nicolson & Fawcett, 1990), the dominant theoretical framework was the phonological deficit, derived from seminal research in the UK by Bradley and Bryant (1983) and by Snowling (1986, and see Chapter 4 in this volume), and in the US by researchers such as Stanovich (e.g. 1988). Indeed, in the US this consensus among dyslexia researchers was instrumental in generating substantial long-term funding via the NICHD Learning Disabilities Program. Phonological awareness deficits, based on abnormalities in the language-processing areas of the brain, were posited as the key to the deficits in grapheme–phoneme translation which characterised dyslexia. The natural solution lay in intensive training in phonological awareness, and research focused almost exclusively on identifying the cause of the phonological difficulties.

By contrast, as the parent of a dyslexic child, I was aware that the deficits in dyslexia included, but extended far beyond, these phonological deficits. Indeed, I had noticed that there were subtle differences in the fluency with which children with dyslexia performed on all tasks, including those in which their performance was to all intents and purposes normal. Crucially, many of these skills were not related to literacy, with motor skills in particular featuring strongly in the work of Augur (1985) and Haslum (1989). Working with Rod Nicolson, whose theoretical background was in theories of learning, it was natural for us to consider all these varied manifestations of dyslexia. We therefore formulated and tested the automatisation deficit hypothesis (DAD)—that dyslexic children have problems in becoming automatic in any skill, whether or not it is related to reading. The most stringent test of the theory was in a domain as far away from language as possible, and so we chose balance. Somewhat to our surprise, and precisely as predicted by the DAD hypothesis, we found that the dyslexic children whom we tested did show problems in balance, especially if they were prevented from concentrating on balancing by having to perform another task at the same time. Interestingly enough, phonological skills are built up in precisely the same way (without explicit instruction) over several years, and therefore this explanation could also be applied to phonological deficits. We argued that the automatisation deficit could provide a broader framework for dyslexia research, integrating the phonological deficits within mainstream theories of learning.

We were somewhat dismayed by the negative attitude of some dyslexia researchers towards our hypothesis. Naively, we had assumed that they would share our excitement at this new perspective, which we hoped would be fruitful for dyslexia research. Eventually, we realised that many researchers had mistakenly assumed that we were advocating training in balance to overcome these automatisation problems in dyslexia. This interpretation had not even entered our minds! By contrast, many practitioners and parents of dyslexic children resonated strongly with our automatisation hypothesis—often with the reaction "That's our Johnny" (Miles, 1983).

However, in 1992 we talked to many influential dyslexia researchers and practitioners for our international survey (Nicolson et al., 1993) on screening for dyslexia in adults. The project involved a literature survey of adult literacy and diagnosis of dyslexia, interviews with UK experts on theoretical and applied aspects of dyslexia, and finally an international questionnaire study with a wide range of dyslexia practitioners and researchers. Most pleasingly, the survey established a clear consensus in the dyslexia community that was particularly impressive given that the respondents were specialists whose opinions spanned the spectrum of approaches to dyslexia and adult literacy. Respondents agreed that testing procedures that do not need a trained clinician could be carried out cost-effectively in adult literacy centres, units for young offenders or job centres. However, they also agreed that a second-stage testing procedure must be available, and that the screening should be integrated within a support framework. This survey strongly influenced our subsequent three-stage Screening–Assessment–Support proposal outlined below.

However, if we screen and support children proactively, this "stitch in time" approach could prevent reading failure, and lead to a situation where the child would no longer be diagnosable as dyslexic. It is important to recognise that dyslexia still exists at the biological and cognitive levels even when these literacy-based symptoms have been remediated. Consequently, we need to move away from just examining the symptoms to examine the brain and cognition in dyslexia. This requires the development of a range of new tools and techniques.

PROGRESS 1990–2000

I shall consider progress in terms of policy, theory, diagnosis, and support.

Policy

This is the area in which the most consistent progress has been made, moving from a position where dyslexia was not recognised to one where the 1994 Code of Practice for Children with Special Educational Needs made it the responsibility of schools to identify and support children with dyslexia and other learning disabilities. A series of stages and procedures was introduced to ensure that children received appropriate and effective support, and interestingly, these were very much in line with our own recommendations (see Figure 1.1 below).

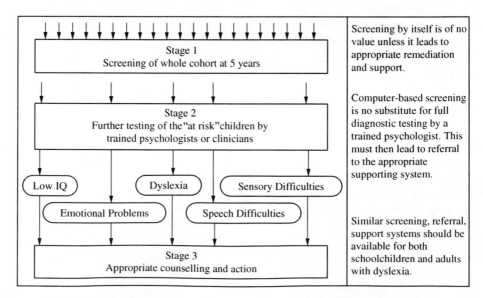

Figure 1.1 Objective: Introduction of systematic screening, diagnosis and support. This diagram is taken from our early-screening project, but our objective is to provide similar facilities at all ages—pre-school, junior school, secondary school and adult dyslexia (adapted from Fawcett & Nicolson, 1999)

The Code considered dyslexia specifically under the heading of "Specific learning difficulty (for example, dyslexia)" when considering criteria for making a Statutory Assessment (§3.60–3.63). A key requirement is that

> "...there is clear, recorded evidence of clumsiness, significant difficulties of sequencing or visual perception; deficiencies in working memory; or significant delays in language functioning" (§3:61iii).

At the time of writing this chapter, a new Code of Practice has been produced and will be available in early 2002.

In short, the school situation for the dyslexic child in the UK is currently one of the best in the world, well in advance of the US, where policy is fragmented between different states. Moreover, the situation for adults is improving, with the 1998 Disability Act now applied in education as well as employment, and the Moser Report (Moser, 2000) on adult literacy launching a well-funded programme of government support.

Theory

New techniques in neuroscience, brain imaging and genetics have led to outstanding progress in theoretical dyslexia research. Following Frith (1997) I shall classify theories at the biological level, the cognitive level and the behavioural level.

Biological Level

In our search for an underlying cause which was capable of handling the pattern of difficulties in dyslexia, namely, problems in balance, speed and phonological skill (Nicolson & Fawcett, 1994) we developed the cerebellar deficit hypothesis. It had always been known that the cerebellum was involved in speed, in learning and in becoming automatic in motor skill. However, new evidence coming from the US, completely independent of dyslexia research, suggested that the cerebellum might be involved in language dexterity, via rich interconnections with the language areas of the brain, in particular Broca's area. This made cerebellar deficit a prime candidate for the underlying cause of dyslexia. We tested this hypothesis indirectly, with a range of clinical tests of muscle tone and stability (Fawcett et al., 1996), and found strong evidence for previously unsuspected abnormalities in cerebellar function. Then we tested our hypothesis directly, in a PET scan study of motor learning (Nicolson et al., 1999a), known to activate the cerebellum. Exactly as we predicted, the adults with dyslexia showed reduced activation in the cerebellum, with only 10–20% of the expected level of activation compared with adult controls. This provides convincing direct support for the cerebellar deficit hypothesis, leading to a complete causal chain for dyslexia (see Figure 1.2).

In summary, the magnocellular deficit (Stein, 1997) and cerebellar deficit (for a review see Nicolson et al., 2001; Fawcett, 2000), both theories at the biological level suggest more widespread problems in addition to the phonological deficit. Further research is now needed on these theories; in particular, we need to establish the "prevalence" of the different sub-types implied by these accounts (see Chapter 2

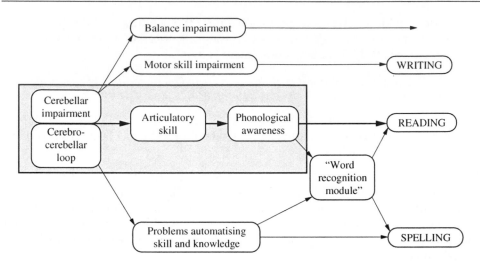

Figure 1.2 An ontogenetic causal chain for dyslexia from birth to age 8 (adapted from Nicolson & Fawcett, 1999)

by Hynd and Knight for an overview of neurological and biological factors, and Chapter 5 by Everatt on visual factors in dyslexia).

Cognitive Level
As well as the automatisation deficits and the phonological deficits account, the "double deficit" hypothesis (Wolf & Bowers, 1999) suggests that dyslexic children suffer from a processing speed deficit, in addition to their phonological deficits. A further perspective on learning from our laboratory suggests that there may also be abnormalities in fundamental learning processes such as classical conditioning, habituation, response "tuning" and error elimination. Our analysis of how dyslexic children learn (Nicolson & Fawcett, 2000) suggests performance can become automatic, but strikingly, our "square root rule" suggests that this takes longer by a factor of the square root of the time normally taken to acquire a skill. So, a skill that normally takes four sessions to master, would take a dyslexic child eight sessions, whereas if a skill normally took 400 sessions, it would take the dyslexic child 8000 sessions! This suggests that it is important to monitor learning in small, easily assimilated steps for dyslexics, providing theoretical support for existing good practice, and distinguishing dyslexia support from that necessary for other poor readers. Naturally, further research is needed to address these issues.

Behavioural Level
Dyslexic children show impairments in a wide range of skills, including sensory deficit (flicker, motion sensitivity, rapid auditory discrimination), motor (bead threading, balance) and cognitive (phonological, working memory, speed). Dyslexic children may also show strengths in non-verbal reasoning, vocabulary and problem-solving. However, it is not clear whether these patterns relate to different sub-types, and again, further research is needed to establish how distinct dyslexia is from other learning disabilities.

SCREENING AND DIAGNOSIS

Screening

Naturally, I focus here on our own screening tests—the Dyslexia Early Screening (4.5 to 6.5 years), the Dyslexia Screening Test (6.5 to 16.5), the Dyslexia Adult Screening Test (16.5 to 65) and the Pre-school Screening Test (3.5 to 4.5). Note also, however, Singleton's COPS computer-based screening tests for school-age children and adults, together with a wide range of phonological tests (see Chapter 7 by Singleton).

Each of these tests was explicitly designed to form the first stage in the systematic Screening–Assessment–Support procedure outlined in Figure 1.1. Our aim here was to satisfy the various needs of groups within the dyslexia ecosystem, particularly teachers who would be "empowered" to undertake the tests themselves, and produce understandable profiles related to their teaching objectives. Our aim was to produce tests that appealed to schools because they were quick, cheap, effective, and fitted into the Code of Practice; tests that appealed to the dyslexia community because they provided all the "positive indicators" for dyslexia; and tests that appealed to the children, in that they were fun, varied, and non-threatening. Our primary aim was to develop an early screening test for dyslexia that could be administered in a child's first year at school (from 4.5 years upwards) and that was a valid predictor of subsequent reading difficulty. In other words, we wanted to intervene before children fail!

Our key insight here was that really all the members of the dyslexia ecosystem are on the same side—they would all like a quick, simple, cost-effective test to check whether a child needs help. We believe that we have succeeded in this apparently impossible task.

Figure 1.3 illustrates the operation of the test with a 6-year-old child whom we tested. The child was very slow to name the 24 common objects on a card; 87 seconds falls within the bottom 10% for the norms for the age, which is why it has a double-minus label. The "sound order" test was 15 out of 15, which merits a 0 (average, between 25th and 75th percentiles), which suggests that the auditory magnocellular system is fine. Recognition of digits (7 out of 7) again is normal (0). The "−" band represents performance in the 11–25th percentile band, an "at risk" score, but not as serious as the double minus. The combination of "at risk" scores on the individual sub-tests (6 at double minus, 2 at minus) leads to a total "at risk" score of 14 (6@2 + 2@1), and an "at risk quotient" (ARQ) of 1.4 (dividing by 10, the number of tests used). An ARQ of 0.9 or more is "clear risk of dyslexia", and so the 1.4 ARQ indicates that the child needs extra support via the Code of Practice.

Interestingly enough, if we had measured only phonological skills, we would have noticed that the deficits here were precisely those predicted by the phonological deficit hypothesis. If we had not tested bead threading, balance (postural stability) and rapid naming, we would not have realised that this was in fact what we would consider a typical dyslexic profile, with problems in phonology, speed and motor skills. The teaching implications of problems in the right-hand five tests are

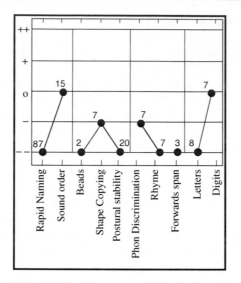

Figure 1.3 Illustrative DEST profile and at-risk quotient (ARQ) for child aged 6 years 2 months. Outcome: 6@– –, 2@–; hence ARQ = 1.4

clear—one teaches the appropriate skills. By contrast, most of the left-hand tests are purely diagnostic, rather than diagnostic/remedial. They suggest that the child is dyslexic, and therefore that standard teaching may have to be modified, as we discuss below.

Diagnosis

Until recently, diagnosis was available only for formal/legal purposes (formal diagnosis), rather than for personal development/treatment purposes (support diagnosis). At one time, as our adult screening survey showed, most diagnosticians tried to combine both functions, by starting with a structured interview, then moving to formal diagnostic tests, then ending with specific problems. More recently, the work of the Access centres in the UK has systematically addressed the issue of technical support, but it is still fair to say that there is no set approach to support diagnosis, and therefore I will focus on formal diagnosis.

In the traditional discrepancy definition of dyslexia, both reading and IQ were tested. The cut-off method takes a criterion such as "IQ of at least 90, and reading age at least 18 months behind chronological age" and the regression method takes "reading age that is at least 1.5 standard deviations below that expected on the basis of the child's IQ". The key difference is that the regression method takes account of the child's IQ (so a child with an IQ of 130 and reading standard score of 100 (exactly normal) may turn out to be dyslexic). By contrast, a child of IQ 92 with a reading standard score 90 would be classified as dyslexic using the cut-off method but not the regression method.

However, it has recently been argued that there is no point in trying to differentiate poor readers without discrepancy from dyslexic children. This is largely because in the USA poor readers without discrepancy (i.e. those with low IQ) show phonological problems just like poor readers with discrepancy (dyslexic poor readers); in other words, they are both poor readers. The recommendations of the Working Group of the BPS Educational Section also take up this point. However, Nicolson (1996) presents an alternative viewpoint. Again, this brings us back to confusion between the three issues: cause, symptom and treatment. Although the symptoms are similar, we lose focus if we lump the groups together when there may be different underlying causes. Similarly, there may also be differences in the optimal method of support, which may be lost if the groups are concatenated.

Support

Dyslexic children and adults have struggled with their literacy difficulties for many years, and often this is the last thing they wish to focus on. In fact, there are many areas of life in which they need support, particularly as adolescents and adults, and the key here is motivation. Thus, it is useful to differentiate between literacy and life support.

Life Support

Strikingly, literacy deficits in adolescence and adulthood are often accompanied by poor presentation of work, and deteriorating performance under time pressure. Moreover, problems in dynamic working memory make it difficult for adults with dyslexia to hold information in mind whilst they manipulate it, thus leading to a further range of difficulties. We have used the analogy of driving in a foreign country—it is possible, but it takes greater resources, and for dyslexic adults it may be as if they continually live in a foreign country! Some of the strongest general problems lie in organisational skills and in the ability to check work. These are natural consequences of the reduced mental "resources" caused by limitations in working memory, by slow speed of processing, and by difficulties in skill automatisation (Nicolson & Fawcett, 1990). McLoughlin et al. (1994) argue strongly that an even higher-level difficulty—a failure to understand one's own strengths and weaknesses, and in particular to predict the effects that dyslexia will have on one's performance—could be the most basic problem, which should be tackled as soon as possible. When this error-prone work is accompanied by the over-focused tunnel vision which can characterise dyslexia, it is hardly surprising that some dyslexic adults can appear to be surly. The creativity which leads them to work from first principles (West, 1991) may become a further irritant. Couple this with difficulties in picking up implicit knowledge of the work culture, and a dyslexic adult can easily become an outsider. A diagnosis of dyslexia can provide an explanation for a wide range of difficulties which even dyslexic adults themselves may not have appreciated are associated with dyslexia. A key requirement for life support is therefore to establish the major goals for each individual, and draw up an individual support plan tuned to these specific goals.

A similar analysis holds for dyslexic children, It is not enough to provide literacy support, because many children are scarred by their difficulties, with devastating consequences—emotional trauma, loss of self-esteem, and family difficulties. Few children emerge unscathed, and many resort to clowning or disruption to mask their difficulties. Here it is important to differentiate between two forms of coping: problem-solving coping and emotional coping. An ideal approach will include a combination of analysis and listening tailored to the needs of the individual child. One area which has been largely overlooked in the literature is the impact which support of this type can have on overall performance, and we advocate using effect-size analyses for comparison with alternative interventions as outlined below.

Literacy Support

The methods traditionally recommended for dyslexia intervention are typically based on overlearning, and it can become difficult for children to maintain their motivation, given their relatively slow progression. Moreover, despite recent advances in the UK in terms of the Literacy Hour, which is meant to ensure that children progress through the stages in reading in a sequence based on established good practice, it is not clear that the teaching methods used are best tuned to the teaching of dyslexic children.

What is needed is a method of evaluating different interventions, using effect sizes, a technique for comparing relative improvement across studies. In order to evaluate interventions, we need evidence from controlled studies of the comparative effectiveness of different methods for teaching reading, especially for dyslexic children. I illustrate this with some short-term intervention studies we have recently undertaken (see Nicolson et al., 1999b; Fawcett et al., 2001 for full details). Our main aim was to inform policy decisions on providing cost-effective support for dyslexic children, and we investigated two issues: first, how much improvement could be achieved with a low-cost intervention; and second, whether such an approach was suitable for dyslexic children. From the viewpoint of policy, the important question is: how can we best use resources so as to achieve the maximum benefit per unit cost? Surprisingly, research had not assessed cost-effectiveness, nor noted that the longer the intervention, the more effect it is likely to have.

In our studies, we took children in infant and junior schools, identified those at risk of reading problems, gave them reading-related support in groups of three for two 30-minute sessions per week for 10 weeks, and monitored how much they improved on standard tests of reading and spelling over that period. Naturally, we also used matched control groups in matched schools who did not have an intervention, so that we could establish the relative improvement. In all studies the intervention group made significantly more progress than the control group, as measured by mean literacy standard scores. However, from the viewpoint of educational policy the key indicator is cost-effectiveness rather than just effectiveness. For cost-effectiveness one must divide the benefits (effect sizes) by the costs (teacher hours per child). The fact that our interventions took place in small groups for relatively short times (10 hours per group) means that both of our interventions were very much more cost-effective than interventions which focus on the early stages, such as Reading Recovery.

Finally, we considered the results relating to dyslexia. In fact, in all studies there were children who did not improve much. Of these, almost all had "at risk" scores on the DEST (infant) or DST (junior) tests. We concluded that the results confirm the importance and cost-effectiveness of early intervention in a child's initial school years—the "stitch in time" approach. While cost-effective improvements in reading can be achieved at junior school, a significant proportion of junior-school children will fail to achieve lasting benefits from a relatively short intervention of this type. These children are likely to be dyslexic.

THE FUTURE

In pointing the way towards future developments in dyslexia research, I have benefited from insights derived from the round tables on causal theory, intervention and policy, and the subsequent plenary session at the Fifth International Conference of the BDA. I present here a synopsis of the findings, before drawing up some targets for dyslexia research.

Let us first consider causal theories. It may well be that, if a consensus can be reached on the need to investigate major causal theories more systematically, we can present a united front which will influence policy and practice. Certainly, identifying the causes of dyslexia can improve the timing of any intervention that might be delivered.

Emerging Consensus on Causal Theories

An emerging consensus was found that it was important to consider the biological level in addition to the cognitive/behavioural level. Further investigation is needed of all the major hypotheses, from underlying cerebellar deficits and/or magnocellular deficits to the overarching symptoms of phonological deficit, and to the double-deficit hypothesis. Systematic high-quality research is needed, based on comparative analyses of the incidence and severity of these deficits in different populations. Marker tasks for theories of dyslexia should be produced, to aid early identification. In order to establish how the theories interlink, a non-adversarial approach was advocated, based on listening to other theoretical viewpoints while maintaining stimulating dialectical processes.

Comorbidity

The need to examine commonalities and differences between dyslexia pure and plus ADHD, Specific Language Impairment (SLI) and dyspraxia was emphasised. Profiling of the developmental disorders would facilitate the translation of advances in theory into practice, in individually designed interventions.

Language

All aspects of language, including orthography, morphology and vocabulary, should be addressed in addition to phonology. Transparency and regularity in different languages should be addressed.

Genetics

Further research is needed on the interplay between genes and the environment, in relation to early and late plasticity in development. Particular reference should be made to the interaction between genetic endowment and deprivation.

Multilingualism

Further research is needed on the impact of the linguistic environment on the expression of dyslexia.

The Ontogenetic Causal Chain

A key requirement here is understanding the expression of dyslexia between birth and diagnosis. This involves two main areas; infancy and early intervention.

Infancy
Investigating learning in infancy is needed in terms of language and motor skills, in order to unravel the ontogenetic causal chain from infancy to school age. Family studies of dyslexia, and the impact of low birth weight should be examined. Marker tasks for sub-types of dyslexia should be produced.

Early Intervention
The need for early intervention was emphasised. An open-minded approach was advocated to the effects of complementary therapies, recognising the pain that dyslexic people suffer. This was coupled with the need for stringently controlled evaluations of intervention techniques.

The Brain

The potential of new tools such as fMRI, PET, EP, MEG and TMS in providing direct evidence of differences in brain organisation was emphasised, in order to provide converging evidence towards theoretical causal chains in dyslexia.

Strengths

Further attempts to investigate the strengths of dyslexia and work to these are recommended.

In the final section that follows I highlight where further research is needed to enrich our understanding of dyslexia, building on these insights derived from the conference round tables, in conjunction with those from Nicolson (2001). There are striking overlaps here, which in my view are indicative of a move towards a consensus within the dyslexia ecosystem. In this section, I focus on how to instantiate the insights derived from the round-table discussions.

Theory

Large-scale Quantitative Studies on Skills Across the Board
Aim: to identify the most extreme deficits, using a profile of deficits (including effect sizes), to complement the small-scale studies already completed, and establish how representative these data are for the general dyslexia population.

Quantitative Data on Prevalence and Comorbidity
Aim: to establish whether dyslexic children show one, two or more of the key indicators of phonological deficit, sensory deficit, speed deficit, and cerebellar deficit, based on a large-scale study using standardised tests that cover the range of the above skills to assess the relative incidence and overlap (comorbidity) of the possible different sub-types.

Quantitative Data on Dyslexia and Other Learning Disabilities
Aim: to investigate the unexpectedly high comorbidity between dyslexia and ADHD, SLI, dyspraxia, and generalised learning difficulty, including intriguing evidence of cerebellar abnormality in all of the specific disorders including ADHD (Berquin et al., 1998; Mostofsky et al., 1998).

Integrated Accounts at the Biological, Cognitive and Behavioural Levels
Aim: to establish how the various symptoms develop as a function of genes, brain and experience.

Screening and Diagnosis
There are now good screening tests available that can be used by a teacher or adult specialist to identify a profile of strengths and weaknesses and form the basis of an initial individual development plan. These can even be undertaken before a child starts school.

Need to Maintain Discrepancy Definitions
Key issues need to be resolved, before it would be appropriate to consider abandoning the discrepancy criteria, in particular because we have not yet clearly established whether there are different causes for dyslexia and more generalised learning disabilities.

Need for Positive Indices of Dyslexia
We need an index of dyslexia which is independent of reading, to cover the situations where a child has learned to read, and may no longer be classified as dyslexic,

despite their clear dyslexic profile in terms of speed of processing, learning and magnocellular deficit. This might include an analysis of learning ability.

Need for Clarity Regarding Diagnosis Relative to Other Learning Disabilities
We need a battery of fundamental tests which examine all aspects of performance, so that the diagnosis a child receives is not so dependent on the type of specialist to whom they are referred.

Need for Diagnosis in Multilingual Children
A key issue is identifying dyslexia in children whose first language is not English. The battery of fundamental tests above might clarify this issue.

Need for Diagnosis in Non-English-speaking Countries
We need cross-linguistic research, to identify commonalities between dyslexia in different languages, in order to advance the search for fundamental positive indicators of dyslexia.

Support
Turning to support, there has been considerable progress in teaching, but there remains a need for knowledge on a number of issues.

Dyslexia-friendly Teaching
We need carefully controlled evaluation studies aimed at identifying the cost-effectiveness of different support methods for different groups of children with reading problems. This will allow us to check whether the standardised pace of the Literacy Hour is appropriate for dyslexic children. We need to develop fluency and knowledge as well as phonological skills. Finally, we need to establish whether the same techniques are appropriate for dyslexic and non-dyslexic poor readers, as well as normal readers.

New Technology
Our research suggests that the computer provides a good method to maintain motivation, while developing automaticity in skills, and we now need to see the computer, the teacher and the learner as a team.

Exploiting Strengths
We need to remember that good learning builds on strengths rather than weaknesses.

Policy
The record of UK governments in this area is outstanding. There are further changes in hand at all stages: pre-school policy will concentrate on the development of learning in the pre-school years, in terms of a series of targets for nursery provision similar to the National Curriculum; a policy of inclusion for children with special needs will be implemented (see Peer & Reid, 2001 for further information); and finally issues of adult literacy will be addressed following the Moser report. Large

amounts of funding have been dedicated to implement these policies across the age range. We need to ensure that these advances in provision can build towards a dyslexia-friendly policy, based on a comprehensive and united research programme aimed at a complete and inclusive analysis of dyslexia theory, diagnosis and support.

CONCLUSIONS

In conclusion, the breadth of perspectives addressed in a book such as this, makes it very clear that considerable progress has been made in dyslexia research. However, dyslexia research has now reached a crossroads. In my view, we can best move forward by linking our research to the needs of policy and the government, providing the opportunity for a cohesive approach, based on partnership and moving towards a new strategy for dyslexia.

REFERENCES

Augur, J. (1985). Guidelines for teachers, parents and learners. In M. Snowling (Ed.). *Children's written language difficulties*. Windsor: NFER Nelson.

Berquin, P. C., Giedd, J. N., Jacobsen, L. K., Hamburger, S. D., Krain, A. L., Rapoport, J. L., & Castellanos, F. X. (1998). Cerebellum in attention-deficit hyperactivity disorder—A morphometric MRI study. *Neurology, 50*, 1087–1093.

Boder, E. (1973). Developmental dyslexia: a diagnostic approach based on three atypical spelling–reading patterns. *Developmental Medicine and Child Neurology, 15*, 663–687.

Bradley, L., & Bryant, P. E. (1983). Categorising sounds and learning to read: A causal connection. *Nature, 301*, 419–421.

Castles, A., & Holmes, V. M. (1996). Subtypes of developmental dyslexia and lexical acquisition. *Australian Journal of Psychology, 48*, 130–135.

Department of Health/Home Office (2001) Valuing people: a new strategy for learning disability for the 21st century. Cm 5086. London: HMSO.

Ellis, A. W. (1993). *Reading, writing and dyslexia: A cognitive analysis*. (2nd edn). Hove: Erlbaum.

Fawcett, A. J. (Ed.) (2001). *Dyslexia: Theory and good practice*. London: Whurr.

Fawcett, A. J., & Nicolson, R. I. (1999). Systematic screening and intervention for reading difficulty. In N. Badian, *Preschool Prediction and Prevention of Reading Failure*. York Press.

Fawcett, A. J., Nicolson, R. I., & Dean, P. (1996). Impaired performance of children with dyslexia on a range of cerebellar tasks. *Annals of Dyslexia, 46*, 259–283.

Fawcett, A. J., Nicolson, R. I., Moss, H., Nicolson, M. K., & Reason, R. (2001). Effectiveness of reading intervention in junior school. *Educational Psychology, 21*, 299–312.

Frith, U. (1997). Brain, mind and behaviour in dyslexia. In C. Hulme & M. Snowling (Eds.), *Dyslexia: Biology, cognition and intervention*. London: Whurr.

Haslum, M. (1989). Predictors of dyslexia? *Irish Journal of Psychology, 10(4)*, 622–630.

McLoughlin, D., Fitzgibbon, G., & Young, V. (1994). *Adult dyslexia: assessment, counselling and training*. London: Whurr.

Miles, T. R. (1983). Dyslexia: *The Pattern of Difficulties*. Oxford: Blackwell.

Miles, T. R. (1994). A proposed taxonomy and some consequences. In A. J. Fawcett & R. I. Nicolson (eds.) *Dyslexia in Children: Multidisciplinary Perspectives*. London: Harvester Wheatsheaf.

Moser, C. (2000). *Better basic skills—Improving adult literacy and numeracy*. London: Department for Education and Employment.

Mostofsky, S. H., Reiss, A. L., Lockhart, P., & Denckla, M. B. (1998). Evaluation of cerebellar size in attention-deficit hyperactivity disorder. *Journal of Child Neurology, 13,* 434–439.

Nicolson, R. I. (1996). Developmental dyslexia; Past, present and future. *Dyslexia: An International Journal of Research and Practice, 2,* 190–207.

Nicolson, R. I., (2001). Developmental dyslexia: Into the future. In Fawcett, A. J. (Ed.). *Dyslexia: Theory and good practice.* London: Whurr.

Nicolson, R. I. , & Fawcett, A. J. (1990). Automaticity: a new framework for dyslexia research. *Cognition, 30,* 159–182.

Nicolson, R. I., & Fawcett, A. J. (1994). Comparison of deficits in cognitive and motor skills among children with dyslexia. *Annals of Dyslexia, 44,* 147–164.

Nicolson, R. I., & Fewcett, A. J. (1999). Developmental dyslexia: the role of the cerebellum. *Dyslexia, 5,* 155–177.

Nicolson, R. I., & Fawcett, A. J. (2000). Long-term learning in dyslexic children. *European Journal of Cognitive Psychology, 12,* 357–393.

Nicolson, R. I., Fawcett, A. J., & Miles, T. R. (1993). *Feasibility study for the development of a computerised screening test for dyslexia in adults (Report OL176).* Sheffield: Employment Department.

Nicolson, R. I. Fawcett, A. J., & Dean, P. (2001). Developmental dyslexia: the cerebellar deficit hypothesis. *Trends in Neurosciences, 24:* 506–509.

Nicolson, R. I., Fawcett, A. J., Berry, E. L., Jenkins, I. H., Dean, P., & Brooks, D. J. (1999a). Association of abnormal cerebellar activation with motor learning difficulties in dyslexic adults. *The Lancet, 353,* 1662–1667.

Nicolson, R. I., Fawcett, A. J., Moss, H., Nicolson, M. K., & Reason, R. (1999b). An early reading intervention study: Evaluation and implications. *British Journal of Educational Psychology, 69,* 47–62.

Peer, L., & Reid, G. (2001). *Dyslexia: Successful Inclusion in the Secondary School.* London: David Fulton.

Siegel, L. S. (1989). IQ is irrelevant to the definition of learning disabilities. *Journal of Learning Disabilities, 22,* 469.

Snowling, M., Goulandris, N., Bowlby, M., & Howell, P. (1986). Segmentation and speech perception in relation to reading skill: A developmental analysis. *Journal of Experimental Child Psychology, 41,* 489–507.

Stanovich, K. E. (1988). The right and wrong places to look for the cognitive locus of reading disability. *Annals of Dyslexia, 38,* 154–177.

Stein, J., & Walsh, V. (1997). To see but not to read; The magnocellular theory of dyslexia. *Trends in Neurosciences, 20,* 147–152.

Thelen, E., & Smith, L. B. (1994). *A dynamic systems approach to the development of cognition and action.* Cambridge, MA: MIT Press.

West, T. G. (1991). *In the mind's eye: Visual thinkers, gifted people with learning difficulties, computer images, and the ironies of creativity.* Buffalo, NY: Prometheus Books.

Wolf, M., & Bowers, P. G. (1999). The double-deficit hypothesis for the developmental dyslexias. *Journal of Educational Psychology, 91,* 415–438.

Chapter 2

THE NEUROBIOLOGY OF DYSLEXIA

Deborah F. Knight and George W. Hynd

INTRODUCTION

Reading words is a complex act involving the processing of sensory, phonological, orthographic, and semantic information. Various theories about each of these areas have been offered as explanations for dyslexia. Investigation of the anatomical, functional, and genetic differences in individuals with dyslexia can offer insights to some of the theories and questions we have about dyslexia. The fields of genetics and neurobiology have only begun to inform our understanding of this reading disability, but there are a few things we know. The brains of individuals with dyslexia look different and function differently from typical readers' brains. There is substantial behavioral and molecular genetic information to indicate that at least some reading abilities appear to be inherited, and that certain patterns of inheritance result in reading disability. Just as the cognitive and behavioral studies reveal that reading words involves a complex interaction of processing sensory, phonological, orthographic, and semantic information, so do the neurobiological studies reveal that a sophisticated integration of a number of brain subsystems is involved in reading words. In this chapter, we begin with a basic explanation of brain anatomy designed to facilitate the reader's understanding of the studies described. Following this basic neuroanatomy are descriptions of the morphological, imaging, and genetic studies of dyslexia.

THE ANATOMY OF THE BRAIN

The human brain consists of the brainstem, the cerebellum, and two cerebral hemispheres joined by a bundle of fibers known as the corpus callosum. Each cerebral hemisphere is divided into four lobes, which are roughly associated with particular functions. Visual processing is found in the occipital lobes; receptive language

Dyslexia and Literacy: Theory and Practice. Edited by Gavin Reid and Janice Wearmouth.
© 2002 John Wiley & Sons, Ltd.

(particularly auditory perception and language comprehension) is associated with the temporal lobes; movement, orientation, and spatial relations are associated with the parietal lobes; and higher-order thinking and planning are believed to occur in the frontal lobes.

The cortex, which consists of four to six layers of gray matter (brain cells), makes up about 80% of the human brain. In order to increase the size of gray matter and still fit within the skull, the human brain folds in on itself. These folds are known as sulci; the surfaces between the folds are known as gyri. Although the sulci and gyri in each human brain differ, the principal sulci and gyri are found in all typical brains. Beneath the cortex and just in front of the brainstem is the thalamus, which serves as a switching station for sensory information.

DO THE BRAINS OF INDIVIDUALS WITH DYSLEXIA LOOK DIFFERENT?

The study of dyslexia has historically focused on specific areas of the brain. Study of the brain anatomy correlated with dyslexia has been accomplished through post-mortem analysis and through imaging techniques, one of the more recent being magnetic resonance imaging (MRI). A significant contribution to understanding the neurobiology of dyslexia was made by Galaburda and colleagues who studied the brains of four male (Galaburda et al., 1985) and three female (Humphreys et al., 1990) deceased adults with dyslexia. In addition to dyslexia these men and women had co-morbid diagnoses, including attentional problems, language delay, and in one case seizure. Two principal findings emerged from these autopsied brains. First, a number of misplaced cells (ectopias) were found in all of the brains. Specifically, these ectopias had migrated to the outer layer of cortex, which is typically cell-free. They were found predominantly in the left hemisphere in areas associated with language (the perisylvian language areas, the superior temporal gyrus containing Wernicke's area and the inferior premotor and prefrontal cortex containing Broca's area (Galaburda & Rosen, 2001)). It has been hypothesized that these cells migrated beyond their intended destinations and quite possibly formed atypical connections to other regions of the brain (Sherman et al., 1990).

A more recent finding from the post-mortem studies revealed that dyslexic brains have smaller neurons or a larger number of small neurons in the lateral geniculate nucleus (LGN) and medial geniculate nucleus (MGN) of the thalamus. These nuclei connect to primary visual and auditory cortex, where differences in neurons and patterns of cellular symmetry were also found (Galaburda & Rosen, 2001). These thalamic changes could conceivably provide a neural explanation for some of the visual and auditory sensory and perceptual difficulties that some researchers propose are a deficit of dyslexia (e.g., Eden et al., 1996; Fitch et al., 1997; Zeffiro & Eden, 2000). Reading is a complex act involving multiple sensory systems and brain networks. The implication of both low-level sensory systems and high-level cortical systems in both visual and auditory modalities is not surprising, although a controversial issue in the field. Pennington (1999) contended that it is unlikely that a local change would remain local, and that one change would result in additional changes distributed throughout the brain. One question that arises is whether the changes in the thalamus cause changes in the cortex or whether it is the other way around. Galaburda proposed that the sensory-level changes found in the thalamus might be secondary to the cortical changes that most likely occurred first in development. Because there is evidence that the cortical ectopias occur earlier in development than the changes in the thalamus, Galaburda speculated that the cortical ectopias cause the cells in the thalamus to develop differently.

Another major finding of the post-mortem studies is the lack of asymmetry in the planum temporale in all of these brains. This asymmetry was not a result of a smaller left planum but rather of a larger right planum. One possible explanation for this larger planum on the right is that there was insufficient cell death (pruning) in the right planum during fetal development, leaving an excess of cells in the right planum to make atypical connections.

The development of MRI permitted comparisons of the images of brains of living individuals with and without dyslexia. Therefore, more extensive investigation of the hypothesis that the planum temporale in the brains of people with dyslexia was either symmetrical or larger in the right hemisphere was possible. Although initial studies confirmed the results of the post-mortem studies by Galaburda and colleagues, later studies were less conclusive (see Hynd and Semrud-Clikeman (1989) and Filipek (1996) for reviews). Hynd and Semrud-Clikeman (1989) cite variation in samples (age, sex, co-morbid pathology, handedness) and in measurement techniques as the possible source for these inconsistencies. As researchers more carefully controlled sample characteristics, some interesting findings emerged. Larsen et al. (1990) examined the planum temporale in 37 eighth-graders, 19 carefully selected dyslexic students and a strictly matched control group. In general, the students classified as dyslexic showed symmetry in their plana. One particularly interesting finding was that the students with the most severe phonological decoding problems showed symmetry of the plana. Those students with dyslexia who demonstrated the least severe phonological problems had asymmetrical plana. In contrast, Leonard (2001) found that individuals with language impairment showed symmetry of the plana, but those with phonological dyslexia did not.

Although the planum temporale has received the most attention in neuroanatomical studies, other areas of the brain have been studied, for example, the corpus callosum (Duara et al., 1991; Hynd et al., 1995) and the insula (Hynd et al., 1990; Pennington, 1999). However, results reporting the size and/or symmetry of various structures have been inconsistent. One recent direction has been to look at the pattern of sulci and gyri. Clark and Plante (1998) found extra sulci in a frontal area of individuals with developmental language disabilities. Leonard et al. (1993; 2001) found marked leftward asymmetry of the sylvian fissure in individuals with dyslexia, and duplicated Heschl's gyrus. In a carefully selected sample, Hiemenz and Hynd (2000) discovered that a specific sulcal morphology appears to be related to specific language abilities, but was not directly related to a diagnosis of dyslexia. They emphasized the need to distinguish those individuals with developmental dyslexia who have concurrent language delay from those who do not. These studies have made the need to study clearly defined samples of individuals apparent.

Increasingly, brain morphology and brain activity are associated with specific language abilities rather than a clinical diagnosis (e.g. dyslexia or specific language impairment) that may not be consistently defined across samples.

Although there are inconsistencies in the findings of brain anatomy studies of dyslexia, there are trends that certainly suggest a biological basis for this reading disability (i.e. increased symmetry; more variability within the group, including ectopias, dysplasias, and gyral morphology; and cellular differences in the thalamus). These differences most likely occur during prenatal development. In addition, there is some recent evidence that there may be differences between males and females (Lambe, 1999; Shaywitz et al., 2000). Leonard (2001) suggested that there is a cumulative effect of these anatomical risk factors, and that identification of one structure as the explanation for dyslexia is not likely. Reading is a complex process involving a number of areas of the brain that are connected to one another.

Recent advances in technology now permit observation of the functional interaction of the structures identified as different in the brains of individuals with dyslexia.

DO THE BRAINS OF INDIVIDUALS WITH DYSLEXIA FUNCTION DIFFERENTLY?

How Are the Brain Functions of Readers Studied?

Recent advances in technology have made it more possible to explore the brain's activity while processing language. The studies described in this section used three neuro-imaging techniques: positron emission tomography (PET), functional magnetic resonance imaging (fMRI), and magnetoencelphalography (MEG). PET and fMRI assess brain activity by measuring either blood flow or oxygenation during experimental tasks, resulting in good spatial resolution (Demb et al., 1999). MEG, a variation of EEG, measures changes in a magnetic field, resulting in good temporal resolution (Hoien & Lundberg, 2000).

While exciting strides have been made in understanding the relationship between language and neural activity, these techniques, particularly fMRI, are in their infancy. Using an evolving technology to understand a process as complex as reading, even word reading, is complicated. Grigorenko (2001) and Demb et al. (1999) noted some of the complications. Brain functions are highly interactive, making it difficult to determine just what activation is directly related to the task of interest. For example, when reading a list of words, certain areas may be activated generally for object recognition and others specifically for orthographic processing of a word. So, one area may be activated whether a person is looking at the letter k or at a fixation point. Another area may only be activated if the person is processing the features of the letter k, that is, the activation is specific to linguistic stimuli. For this reason, one commonly used method of studying brain activation is the subtraction method. In the example above, the researcher would subtract the activation present during looking at a fixation point from the activation of looking at a letter. The presumption is that what is left relates specifically to visually processing a letter. To accomplish the goal of identifying what activation is associated with what task, the researcher must design tasks that represent a process as purely as possible. Considering the complexity of reading-related tasks, this is a challenge, to say the least.

The complexities of isolating a task and the corresponding activation are further complicated by several other methodological challenges. The apparatus used in studies varies somewhat, making interpretation across studies difficult. In addition, one must design a series of subtraction tasks with a theory of how the reading brain works in mind. This theory must necessarily assume reading involves a sequential and linear process, otherwise it would not be possible to subtract the activation associated with one task from the next (Pennington, 1999). If the flow of processing during reading is more recursive, a very real possibility, activation will not occur in the sequential manner necessary to do subtraction, making identification of specific sites of activation associated with tasks difficult. Another factor influencing interpretation is that some neuro-imaging techniques have good spatial resolution, but not temporal resolution (e.g. fMRI and PET). Therefore, it is difficult to evaluate the sequence of a process. Other techniques such as MEG and EEG have good temporal resolution but poor spatial resolution. Looking at a combination of techniques will provide a more complete understanding of the activation patterns observed.

Demb et al. (1999) suggested there are three additional reasons that studying individuals with dyslexia is complicated. First, if an individual with dyslexia fails at a task, activation patterns may reflect the failure rather than the effort associated with the task. One way to control for this is to design tasks that can be successfully completed by both the typical readers and the readers with dyslexia. Second, some literature indicates that there may be subtypes of dyslexia. If this were the case, participant selection would need to reflect these differences. Third, one must be cautious about making generalizations about children who are acquiring reading skills from studies using adult readers. Imaging techniques such as PET have not been considered safe for children. With the advent of fMRI, children can now participate in more neuro-imaging studies, and they can participate in repeated studies. The increasing number of children's studies will continue to shed light on differences between the processing of developing versus mature readers.

In spite of the caveats explained above concerning functional imaging of reading, promising findings have emerged from recent studies. The functional imaging studies seek to understand what areas of the brain are involved in reading single words, how these areas interact, and if these areas function differently in readers with dyslexia. To observe the brain activity involved, researchers have generally designed tasks to evaluate three putative areas related to reading, that is, phonological, orthographic, and semantic processing. What follows is a summary of selected studies that illustrate what is hypothesized about processing single words in the brains of typical readers and in readers with dyslexia.

What Parts of the Brain Are Involved in Reading Words and How Do They Function?

To read words, we integrate information about the sound (phonology) and patterns (orthography) of words. Competence in each of these areas appears to follow a developmental trajectory, with a phonological stage preceding an orthographic stage (Frith, 1986). At some point in the reader's development, it is likely that the phonological representation is bonded to an orthographic representation of a word. If this bonding has not occurred, the reader has a lower-quality representation of words in memory, which cannot take advantage of the redundancy available in phonological and orthographic information. Therefore, the reader fails to develop rapid, efficient lexical access (Ehri, 1991).

Assuming the above account is accurate, one question that brain imaging studies can address is whether phonological and orthographic processing are represented in different areas of the brain. It turns out that much of the brain is involved in the seemingly simple task of reading words. Because the brain is a neural network, it is unlikely that any initial change would remain a local change. Rather the initial change will have a downstream effect on other areas of the brain involved in the process of reading words. Because this activity is likely to be distributed throughout the brain, it is difficult to map specific areas involved (Pennington, 1999).

In an attempt to determine the localization of processes, researchers using neuro-imaging have developed specific tasks designed to isolate phonological and ortho-graphic processing. It is very difficult to create orthographic tasks that do not also involve phonological processing. Rumsey and colleagues (1997) have used some of the purest tasks in their PET study of typical adult male readers. Rumsey and colleagues contrasted phonological and orthographic processing in these readers with a set of four tasks, two phonological and two orthographic. Participants were asked to read pronounceable pseudowords (phonological task) and irregular words (orthographic task). They were also asked to determine whether two pseudowords sounded like a real word (e.g. *baip* or *baik*, phonological task) and which word was a real word (e.g. *hoal* or *hole*, orthographic task). There was considerable overlap of activation in all conditions, making it difficult to differentiate phonological and orthographic activation. Rumsey et al. proposed that their findings were most con-sistent with a connectionist theory of word reading. Although phonological and orthographic processes may be different processes, they may not be localized in the brain. The same neural circuits may be processing both phonological and ortho-graphic information found in words. These findings could also be interpreted as consistent with Ehri's (1991) theory, which emphasizes that phonological and or-thographic processes are bonded to one another. The pattern in beginning readers may look quite different, of course.

Although they cannot be neatly divided into phonological and orthographic re-gions of the brain, there do appear to be some major circuits involved in reading words. Pugh et al. (2000b) summarized three major circuits. A left hemisphere pos-terior system involves two circuits. A ventral circuit involves extrastriate cortex and an inferior occipito-temporal area. This area appears to be involved in reading words and pseudowords and may be word-specific, that is, the extrastriate cortex may be involved in analyzing orthographic regularity (Petersen & Fiez, 1993). An-other posterior dorsal circuit includes the angular gyrus, supramarginal gyrus, and the superior temporal gyrus (Wernicke's area). The angular gyrus is believed to be involved in integrating visual and phonological information. The third circuit is an anterior circuit located around Broca's area in the inferior frontal gyrus. This area has been implicated in recoding phonological information of visually presented information.

How Do the Brains of Individuals with Dyslexia Function when Reading Words?

It appears that the competent word reader uses both the anterior and posterior systems described above to read words. Compared to the typical reader, the reader with dyslexia appears to overactivate the anterior circuit and underactivate the posterior circuits. This result has been found consistently across neuro-imaging techniques. In the Rumsey et al. (1997) PET study described above, readers with dyslexia demonstrated reduced activity in the posterior regions of the brain whether reading silently or aloud. Salmelin et al. (1996) compared readers with and without dyslexia reading real words and pseudowords silently using magnetoencephalograpy (MEG). They found three differences between the groups. First, the typical readers showed an early response to reading pseudowords in the ventral circuit of the posterior region of the brain. The readers with dyslexia showed no early response in this area. Second, the readers with dyslexia did demonstrate an earlier response in the inferior frontal gyrus, suggesting greater activity in the anterior circuit. Finally, the readers with dyslexia demonstrated a later response in posterior language regions. This study using MEG, which permitted analysis of the reading process over time, supported the finding that readers with dyslexia overactivate anterior circuits with an early response to stimuli and underactivate posterior circuits with a late response.

In a review of functional neuro-imaging studies of reading and dyslexia, Pugh et al. (2000b) discussed the findings of their research group. In an attempt to focus on patterns and relations among regions of the brain involved in language, they developed a series of tasks with demands on visual, phonological, orthographic, and semantic systems. Working from the hypothesis that dyslexia is primarily the result of phonological processing difficulties, they designed five tasks with increasing phonological demands: line orientation judgment task (Do \\V and \\V match?), tapping visual/spatial but not orthographic processing; letter case judgment (Do *bbBb* and *bbBb* match?), tapping orthographic processing; single letter rhyme (Do *T* and *V* rhyme?), requiring orthographic to phonological translation; nonword rhyme (Do *leat* and *jete* rhyme?), making additional demands on phonological processing; and semantic category judgment (Are *corn* and *rice* in the same category?), requiring additional semantic demands. Converging with the findings of studies described above, Shaywitz et al. (1998) found readers with dyslexia demonstrated greater activation than typical readers in anterior regions and less in posterior regions. This pattern was amplified as the orthographic to phonological demands of the tasks increased.

In addition to a different pattern of activation in the anterior and posterior circuits of the brain, readers with dyslexia demonstrate underactivation in areas connecting these circuits. Paulesu et al. (1996) conducted a PET study of five typical college readers and five college readers with dyslexia whose reading tested in the average range. They were asked to complete two phonological and two visual tasks. The first phonological task required the participants to determine if two letters rhymed (e.g. b/d versus b/r). The matching orthographic task was to determine if two Korean letters were similar. The second phonological task required participants to determine if a single letter they were shown was present in a string of letters presented subsequently. The matching orthographic task involved searching for a Korean letter. Although both groups performed the tasks accurately, different patterns of activation were present. Although both groups activated posterior and anterior (Broca's) areas of language, the group with dyslexia failed to activate insular cortex, which connects the two areas. Paulesu et al. interpreted this to mean that there was a disconnection between the anterior and posterior language regions in individuals with dyslexia, even those who have learned to read. Horowitz et al. (1998) reanalyzed the data in the Rumsey et al. (1997) study described above, examining the correlation between the activated anterior and posterior areas and the angular gyrus. Readers with dyslexia demonstrated a significantly lower correlation between activity in the angular gyrus and activity in language areas in the frontal, temporal, and occipital lobes. The angular gyrus is located at the juncture of the occipital, parietal, and temporal lobes and is important in linking the visual word recognition system to the phonological word system. The studies of Horowitz and Rumsey and colleagues, therefore, suggested that the angular gyrus is disconnected from these language areas in readers with dyslexia.

Following up on the Horowitz et al. (1998) study of the connectivity of the angular gyrus to language areas, Pugh et al. (2000a) examined the relation of the angular gyrus to anterior and posterior regions using the tasks described above. They found the same disconnection of the angular gyrus as Horowitz et al., but only for those tasks requiring orthographic to phonological assembly. In a related finding, they discovered that homologues in the right hemisphere appeared to function in a compensatory manner. Specifically, the angular gyrus and the middle temporal gyrus demonstrated greater activation in the right hemispheres of the readers with dyslexia, the opposite pattern to the typical readers.

In all of these studies, there is a tendency for individuals with dyslexia to overactivate frontal areas in the anterior region of the brain and underactivate posterior language regions in the left hemisphere. In addition, there is evidence for a failure of these regions to communicate effectively with one another.

An additional line of inquiry has focused on the visual processing of readers at a sensory level. As noted above, neurons in the lateral and medial geniculate nuclei of the thalamus are smaller in the brains of individuals with dyslexia. Some researchers have investigated the possible functional implications of this morphological difference. In an fMRI study, Eden et al. (1996) looked at two conditions, having participants look at either stationary or moving dots. The moving dots are believed to activate the magnocellular system, a system that responds to fast-moving, low-contrast images. In the control sample, the magnocellular system was activated bilaterally for moving dots but not for stationary dots. There was no activation in the individuals with dyslexia in either condition. Eden et al. concluded that there is a magnocellular deficit in individuals with dyslexia, quite possibly an indication of a more pervasive temporal processing disorder. Demb et al. (1999) replicated the findings of Eden and colleagues. They found reduced activation in their readers with dyslexia in the magnocellular pathways. Interestingly, they found a strong correlation between activity in the magnocellular pathways and reading speed both in their participants with and without dyslexia. Habib and Demonet (2000) suggested that future studies carefully differentiate samples of individuals with dyslexia by subtype, identifying those with phonological difficulties. If these readers have reduced activation in the magnocellular pathways in the visual system, one possible conclusion would be that such a result would indicate a more pervasive sensory deficit for processing rapidly presented information. This conclusion would be consistent with the temporal processing theory of Tallal and colleagues (e.g. Tallal et al., 1997), who have investigated rapid auditory processing.

A recent direction of imaging studies has been to look at the effects of intervention on brain activity. Most of these studies are too recent to be in publications and results are preliminary. None the less, the initial findings are encouraging. Shaywitz and Shaywitz (Cannell et al., 2001) reported that their research group found increased activity in posterior regions of the brain that are typically underactive in children with dyslexia one year after intervention. In a research symposium at the International Dyslexia Association (2001), a number of researchers reported changes in activation patterns in the brains of participants with dyslexia following interventions. For example, Berninger and colleagues (Lyon, 2001; Richards et al., 2000) found that the activation patterns of the typical reader participants and the participants with dyslexia did not differ significantly following treatment.

In spite of the complexities of functional imaging, there are converging findings from these studies. Pugh et al. (2000b) have proposed a model of the word reading of individuals with dyslexia. Anterior regions of the brain, especially the inferior frontal gyrus including Broca's area, show increased activity in the brains of individuals with dyslexia. This region is hypothesized as processing phonological information, especially articulatory recoding. Posterior areas demonstrate decreased activity in the brains of individuals with dyslexia. Two regions are involved. A dorsal region is hypothesized to be responsible for integration of orthographic, phonological, and semantic information. A ventral region is believed to involve remembering word forms and to contribute to fluent reading in typical readers. The implication is that readers with dyslexia struggle with phonological analysis and integration of this information with orthographic and semantic information, a hypothesis supported by decreased activity in dorsal posterior regions of the brain. Without adequate development of this system, automatic word recognition will not take place, a hypothesis supported by decreased activity in ventral posterior regions. To compensate for this decreased activity, readers with dyslexia show increased activity in anterior regions responsible for pronunciation of words in an attempt to support phonological analysis of words. In addition, increased activation in right hemisphere homologues of the posterior system may indicate an attempt to use visual information to support word reading. This model of the brain's functioning in readers with dyslexia is consistent with the cognitive mechanisms suggested by behavioral data.

IS DYSLEXIA INHERITED?

It is largely accepted that dyslexia runs in families. The fact that a trait runs in families does not necessarily imply that it is inherited, however. Speaking English runs in families, but no one claims that it is inherited. The challenge when investigating a trait that is familial is to determine its heritability, the percentage of that trait that can be attributed to inheritance as opposed to the environment. Heritability (h^2) is a statistic that measures the genetic contribution to differences in individuals.

The heritability of reading disabilities has been studied in Colorado through comparing the genetic and environmental contributions to reading in fraternal and identical twins in third through twelfth grade. In one group, at least one of the twins has a reading disability. This twin is known as the proband; the other twin is referred to as the co-twin. A smaller sample of twins with no reading disability has also been studied. Twin studies make an important contribution to behavioral genetics. Identical twins come from one egg and therefore share the same genes; fraternal twins come from two eggs and therefore share only half of their genes on average. If dyslexia is genetic, the likelihood of both twins being dyslexic would be greater in identical twins than in fraternal twins. Presumably twins raised together are sharing the same environment. Assuming a shared environment, any difference between the concordance (the proportion of twins that show the same trait) in identical and fraternal twins can be attributed to genes or to nonshared environment. In fact, twin studies indicate that if one identical twin is dyslexic, the likelihood that the other twin will be dyslexic is 68%; the risk for fraternal twins is 38% (Plomin & DeFries, 1998). This difference of concordance between identical and fraternal twins is evidence for the genetic contribution to dyslexia.

Concordance rates work well for diseases that are categorical, that is, one either has the disease or does not. However, for conditions that are continual, identification often rests on the judgment of the severity of the case. Dyslexia is regarded as a condition that exists on such a continuum. Some researchers suggest that dyslexia represents the most severe reading problems found in the tail end of a continuum (Shaywitz et al., 1992). DeFries and Fulker (as reported in Plomin & DeFries, 1998) have developed a statistical technique to capture the quantitative nature of disorders that vary along a continuum. In the case of dyslexia, they assess the twins on a number of reading measures rather than looking for a shared diagnosis. This technique permits a more quantitative analysis of the reading behaviors that the twins share. Using this technique, one would expect that a fraternal co-twin would be more like a typical reader than an identical co-twin would. In other words, the co-twin of a fraternal pair would demonstrate greater regression to the mean because there is less genetic influence. DeFries et al. (1997) reported that identical twins were indeed more similar on a reading/spelling measure than fraternal twins. The mean discriminant score of the probands of an identical twin pair was –2.72; the score for the co-twin was –2.51. In the case of fraternal twins, the proband score was –2.65 and the co-twin score was –1.71. By calculating the amount of regression to the mean, DeFries and colleagues determined that more than one-half of the reading performance of the probands is due to heritable factors.

The nature of this heritability varies somewhat by age and subskill. DeFries et al. (1997) determined that word recognition was 64% heritable in the younger (age 8–11.5) group and 47% heritable in the older (age 11.5–20.2) group. Conversely, spelling was 52% heritable in younger children and 68% heritable in the older group. These results are consistent with other studies that find that compensated adults with dyslexia have persistent spelling problems (e.g. Bruck, 1990). The fact that word recognition is less heritable in the older group indicates that environment clearly plays a role in dyslexia. The fact that spelling difficulties, a hallmark characteristic of dyslexia, persist into adulthood is evidence for the role of genes in dyslexia.

Because the Colorado group's analysis of genetic influence is accomplished through analysis of performance on reading measures rather than a categorical diagnosis, they are able to determine the heritability of specific reading skills. As stated above, both phonology and orthography appear to be heritable. In contrast, the genetic influence on reading comprehension is smaller than it is on single word reading skills. The Colorado group found that the genetic contribution to phonological decoding and orthographic skills was highly heritable, 0.59 and 0.56 respectively. The environmental contribution was calculated to be 0.29 for phonological decoding and 0.27 for orthographic skills. In contrast, group reading comprehension weaknesses appeared to be less genetically influenced (0.27) and more environmentally influenced (0.52). The researchers hypothesized that the world knowledge necessary to understand text depended more on the home and school environment (Olson et al., 1999).

The behavioral genetic studies offer an insight into another issue. A cornerstone of the concept of reading disability has been the existence of a discrepancy between IQ and reading achievement. More recently, some people are questioning the importance of determining discrepancy, maintaining that the same core difficulty exists whether or not there is a discrepancy (e.g. Siegel, 1992; Stanovich, 1991). Interestingly, Olson and colleagues have found that heritability of word recognition difficulties increases as IQ increases. These data would suggest that IQ does in fact play a role in reading disability, or at least its heritability. Whether the intervention changes as a result is another question.

Behavioral genetics studies consistently indicate that dyslexia is heritable. What does it mean to inherit dyslexia? Is there a dyslexia gene? Probably not. It is not likely that dyslexia *per se* is inherited, but rather factors place an individual at risk for dyslexia. Pennington (1999) makes a case that dyslexia is most likely inherited through multiple genes that increase one's susceptibility to dyslexia. Dyslexia has heterogeneous manifestations, hence the extensive literature on subtypes of dyslexia. In addition, Pennington and his colleagues have found heritability for normal variations in reading that are not clearly different from dyslexia. If these two observations are accurate and dyslexia is on a continuum, then the same genes may explain exceptionally good reading and dyslexia. Certain alleles (different versions of a marker on a gene) on specific genes may make an individual susceptible for dyslexia, with environmental factors determining the extent to which this predisposition is manifested.

In linkage analyses, several markers associated with dyslexia have been identified as co-occurring in families with dyslexia. Markers are not a specific gene. They are, however, regions that are close to genes that are responsible. These regions tend to be inherited together (Olson et al., 1999). Pennington (1999) and Grigorenko (2001) have reviewed the results of the molecular genetic studies of dyslexia. To date, various laboratories have identified two sites that have been replicated. The first gene markers for dyslexia were found on chromosome 15 by DeFries and colleagues in the Colorado laboratory. This site has been replicated by Grigorenko's laboratory. Gene markers have also been identified on the short arm of chromosome 6 by both DeFries' laboratory and Grigorenko's laboratory. The linkage to chromosome 6 appears to be strong for individuals with deficits in phonological decoding, phoneme awareness, and orthographic coding (Olson et al., 1999).

CONCLUSIONS

Genetic, morphological, and functional imaging studies have offered evidence that there are significant differences in the brains of individuals with dyslexia. Still, there remain a number of unanswered or partially answered questions about dyslexia. Are there subtypes of dyslexia? How do individuals with dyslexia process phonological and orthographic information? What processes do readers with dyslexia use for reading words? To what extent are the factors interfering with reading in dyslexia sensory? To what extent are they linguistic? Are there fundamental differences in the functional organization of the processing of phonological information in men and women? What interventions are most effective? Studies investigating the structure and function of the brain have contributed information making it more possible to address these questions. These studies make it possible to test the neural substrates of specific hypotheses about dyslexia, thereby advancing understanding of this reading disability. With increased understanding of how the dyslexic brain reads comes the promise of more effective identification, diagnosis, and instruction.

One of the most exciting preliminary findings is that the brains of readers with dyslexia look more like the brains of typical readers after effective instruction. It appears the influence and responsibility of teachers extends to changing the actual neural processing of the brains of their students with dyslexia. At the very least, genetic and neurobiological studies contribute to our understanding. They also hold the promise of improving our early identification, diagnosis, and instruction of children with dyslexia.

REFERENCES

Bruck, M. (1990). 'Word-recognition skills of adults with childhood diagnoses of dyslexia'. *Experimental Psychology, 26*, 439–454.
Cannell, S. J., Shaywitz, B. A., & Shaywitz, S. E. (2001). 'Making connections: Stories, science, and policy'. Paper presented at the International Dyslexia Association, Albuquerque, NM.

Clark, M. M., & Plante, E. (1998). 'Morphology of the inferior frontal gyrus in developmentally language-disordered adults'. *Brain and Language, 61*, 288–303.

DeFries, J. C., Alarcon, M., & Olson, R. K. (1997). 'Genetic aetiologies of reading and spelling deficits: Developmental differences'. In C. Hulme & M. Snowling (Eds.), *Dyslexia: Biology, cognition, and intervention*. London: Whurr.

Demb, J. B., Poldrack, R. A., & Gabrieli, J. D. E. (1999). 'Functional neuro-imaging of word processing in normal and dyslexic readers'. In R. M. Klein & P. McMullen (Eds.), *Converging methods for understanding reading and dyslexia* (pp. 245–287). Cambridge, MA: MIT Press.

Duara, R., Kushch, A., Gross-Glenn, K., Barker, W. W., Jallad, B., Pascal, S., Lowenstein, D. A., Sheldon, J., Rabin, M., & Levin, B. (1991). 'Neuroanatomical differences between dyslexic and normal readers on magnetic resonance imaging scans'. *Archives of Neurology, 48*, 410–416.

Eden, F. F., Vanmeter, J. W., Rumsey, J. M., & Zeffiro, T. A. (1996). 'The visual deficit theory of developmental dyslexia'. *Neuroimage, 4*, S108–S117.

Ehri, L. C. (1991). 'Development of the ability to read words'. In R. Barr, M. L. Kamil, P. B. Mosenthal, & P. D. Pearson (Eds.), *Handbook of reading research* (Vol. 2, pp. 383–417). New York: Longman.

Filipek, P. (1996) 'Structural variations in measures in the development disorders'. In R. Thatcher, G. Lyon, J. Rumsey, & N. Krasnegor (Eds.), *Developmental neuroimaging: Mapping the development of brain and behavior* (pp. 169–186). San Diego, CA: Academic Press.

Fitch, R. H., Miller, S., & Tallal, P. (1997). 'Neurobiology of speech perception'. *Annual Review of Neuroscience, 20*, 331–353.

Frith, U. (1986). 'A developmental framework for developmental dyslexia'. *Annals of Dyslexia, 36*, 69–81.

Galaburda, A. M., & Rosen, G. D. (2001). 'Neural plasticity in dyslexia: A window to mechanisms of learning disabilities'. In J. L. McClelland & R. S. Siegler (Eds.), *Mechanisms of cognitive development: Behavioral and neural perspectives* (pp. 307–323). Mahwah, NJ: Erlbaum.

Galaburda, A. M., Sherman, G. F., Rosen, G. D., Aboitiz, F., & Geschwind, N. (1985). 'Developmental Dyslexia: Four consecutive patients with cortical anomalies'. *Annals of Neurology, 18*, 222–233.

Grigorenko, E. L. (2001). 'Developmental dyslexia: An update on genes, brains, and environments'. *Journal of Child Psychology and Psychiatry, 42*, 91–125.

Habib, M., & Demonet, J. (2000). 'Dyslexia and related learning disorders: Recent advances from brain imaging studies'. In J. C. Mazziotta, A. W. Toga, & R. S. J. Frackowiak (Eds.), *Brain mapping the disorders* (pp. 459–482). San Diego, CA: Academic Press.

Hiemenz, J. R., & Hynd, G. W. (2000). 'Sulcal/gyral pattern morphology of the perisylvian language region in developmental dyslexia'. *Brain and Language, 74*, 113–133.

Hoien, T., & Lundberg, I. (2000). *Dyslexia: From theory to intervention*. (Vol. 18). Dordrecht, Netherlands: Kluwer.

Horowitz, B., Rumsey, J. M., & Donohue, B. C. (1998). 'Functional connectivity of the angular gyrus in normal reading and dyslexia'. *Proceedings of the National Academy of Science USA, 95*, 656–667.

Humphreys, P., Kaufman, W. E., & Galaburda, A. M. (1990). 'Developmental dyslexia in women: Neuropsychological findings in three cases'. *Annals of Neurology, 28*, 728–738.

Hynd, G. W., Hall, J., Novey, E. S., Eliopulos, D., Black, K., Gonzales, J. J., Edmonds, J. E., Riccio, C., & Cohen, M. (1995). 'Dyslexia and corpus callosum morphology'. *Archives of Neurology, 52*, 32–38.

Hynd, G. W., Semrud-Clikeman, M., Lorys, A. R., Novey, E. S., & D., E. (1990). 'Brain morphology in developmental dyslexia and attention deficit disorder and hyperactivity'. *Archives of Neurology, 47*, 919–926.

Hynd, G. W., & Semrud-Clikeman, N. (1989). 'Dyslexia and brain morphology'. *Psychological Bulletin, 106*, 447–482.

Lambe, E. K. (1999). 'Dyslexia, gender and brain imaging'. *Neuropsychologia, 37*, 521–536.

Larsen, J. P., Hoien, T., Lundberg, I., & Odegaard, H. (1990). 'MRI evaluation of the size and symmetry of the planum temporale in adolescents with developmental dyslexia'. *Brain and Language, 39*, 289–301.

Leonard, C. M. (2001). 'Imaging brain structure in children: differentiating language disability and reading disability'. *Learning Disability Quarterly, 24(3)*, 158–176.

Leonard, C. M., Eckert, M. A., Lombardino, L. J., Oakland, T., Kranzler, J., Mohr, C. M., King, W. M., & Freeman, A. (2001). 'Anatomical risk factors for phonological dyslexia'. *Cerebral Cortex, 11*, 148–157.

Leonard, C. M., Voeller, K. K. S., Lombardino, L. J., Morris, M. K., Hynd, G. W., Alexander, A. W., Andersen, H. G., Garofalakis, M., Honeyman, J. C., Mao, J., Agree, O., & Staab, E. V. (1993). 'Anomalous cerebral structure in dyslexia revealed with magnetic resonance imaging'. *Archives of Neurology, 50*, 461–469.

Lyon, G. R. (2001). 'How successful interventions improve reading behavior and change the brain'. Paper presented at the International Dyslexia Association, Albuquerque, NM.

Olson, R. K., Datta, H., Gayan, J., & DeFries, J. C. (1999). 'A behavioral-genetic analysis of reading disabilities and component processes'. In R. M. Klein & P. McMullen (Eds.), *Converging methods for understanding reading and dyslexia* (pp. 133–151). Cambridge, MA: The MIT Press.

Paulesu, E., Frith, U., Snowling, M., Gallagher, A., Morton, J., Frackowiak, R. S. J., & Frith, D. D. (1996). 'Is developmental dyslexia a disconnection syndrome? Evidence from PET scanning'. *Brain, 119*, 143–157.

Pennington, B. F. (1999). 'Toward an integrated understanding of dyslexia: Genetic, neurological, and cognitive mechanisms'. *Development and Psychology, 11*, 629–654.

Petersen, S. E., & Fiez, J. A. (1993). 'The processing of single words: studies with positron emission tomography'. *Annual Reviews of Neuroscience, 16*, 509–530.

Plomin, R., & DeFries, J. C. (1998). 'The genetics of cognitive abilities and disabilities'. *Scientific American*, May 1998.

Pugh, K. R., Mencl, W. E., M. W., Shaywitz, B. A., Shaywitz, S. E., Fulbright, R. K., Constable, R. T., Skudlarski, P., Marchione, K. E., Jenner, A. R., Fletcher, J. M., Liberman, A. M., Shankweiler, D. P., Katz, L., Lacadie, C., & Gore, J. C. (2000a). 'Task specific differences in functional connections within posterior cortex'. *Psychological Science, 11*, 51–56.

Pugh, K. R., Mencl, W. E., Jenner, A. R., Katz, L., Frost, S. J., Lee, J. R., Shaywitz, S. E., & Shaywitsz, B. A. (2000b). 'Functional neuro-imaging studies of reading and reading disability (developmental dyslexia)'. *Mental Retardation and Developmental Disabilities Research Reviews, 6*, 207–213.

Richards, T. L., Corina, D., Serafini, S., Steury, K., Echelard, D. R., Dager, S. R., Marro, K., Maravilla, K. R., Abbot, R. D., & Berninger, V. W. (2000). 'The effects of a phonologically driven treatment for dyslexia on lactate levels as measured by proton MRSI'. *American Journal of Neuroradiology, 21*, 916–922.

Rumsey, J. M., Nace, K., Donohue, B., Wise, D., Maisog, J. M., & Andereason, P. (1997). 'A positron emission tomographic study of impaired word recognition and phonological processing in dyslexic men'. *Archives of Neurology, 54*, 562–573.

Salmelin, R., Service, E., Kielila, P., Uutela, K., & Salonen, O. (1996). 'Impaired visual word processing in dyslexia revealed with magneto-encephalography'. *Annals of Neurology, 54*, 1481–1489.

Shaywitz, B. A., Pugh, K. R., Jenner, A. R., Fulbright, R. K., Fletcher, J. M., Gore, J. C., & Shaywitz, S. E. (2000). 'The neurobiology of reading and reading disability (dyslexia)', in: *The handbook of reading research, third edition* (pp. 229–249).

Shaywitz, S. E., Escobar, M. D., Shaywitz, B. A., Fletcher, J. M., & Makuch, R. (1992). 'Evidence that learning disabilities may represent the lower tail of a normal distribution of reading disability'. *New England Journal of Medicine, 326*, 145–150.

Shaywitz, S. E., Shaywitz, B. A., Pugh, K. R., Fulbright, R. K., Constable, P., Fletcher, J. J., Katz, L., Marchione, K. E., Lacadie, C., Gatenby, C., & Gore, J. C. (1998). 'Functional disruption of the organization of the brain for reading in dyslexia'. *Proceedings of the National Academy of Science USA, 95*, 2636–2641.

Sherman, G. F., Stone, J. S., Press, D. M., Rosen, G. D., & Galaburda, A. M. (1990). 'Abnormal architecture and connections disclosed by neurofilament staining in the cerebral cortex of autoimmune mice'. *Brain Research, 529*, 202–207.

Siegel, L. S. (1992). 'An evaluation of the discrepancy definition of dyslexia'. *Journal of Learning Disabilities, 25*, 618–629.

Stanovich, K. E. (1991). 'Discrepancy definitions of reading disability: Has intelligence led us astray?' *Reading Research Quarterly, 26*, 1–29.

Tallal, P., Miller, S., Jenkings, B., & Merzenich, M. (1997). 'The role of temporal processing in developmental language-based learning disorders: Research and clinical implications'. In B. A. Blachman (Ed.), *Foundations of reading acquisition and dyslexia* (pp. 343–356). Mahwah, NJ: Erlbaum.

Zeffiro, T., & Eden, G. (2000). 'The neural basis of developmental dyslexia'. *Annals of Dyslexia, 50*, 3–30.

Chapter 3

RESOLVING THE PARADOXES OF DYSLEXIA

Uta Frith

INTRODUCTION

The definition and explanation of dyslexia have long been problematic. A causal modelling framework involving three levels of description—behavioural, cognitive and biological—can solve some seemingly intractable problems and confusions. Dyslexia can be defined as a neuro-developmental disorder with a biological origin and behavioural signs which extend far beyond problems with written language. At the cognitive level, putative causes of the behavioural signs and symptoms of the condition can be specified. These hypothetical deficits are subject to debate, but serve as a basis for testable predictions at both the behavioural and biological levels. At all three levels, interactions with cultural influences occur. These influences have a major impact on the clinical manifestation of dyslexia, the handicap experienced by the sufferer, and the possibilities for remediation. When all these factors are considered together, paradoxes disappear and a satisfactory definition of dyslexia can be achieved.

THE THREE-LEVELS FRAMEWORK

Words and labels have a life of their own. They readily become loaded with ideology while the concepts they refer to may be perfectly non-contentious. This is true for the term "dyslexia", but the common ground between different ideas can be hard to see. Drawing a few lines on the back of an envelope while talking to colleagues can make all the difference to mutual understanding. John Morton and I have developed a notation for just this purpose. Our aim was to create a neutral framework within which to compare different theories of developmental disorders

Dyslexia and Literacy: Theory and Practice. Edited by Gavin Reid and Janice Wearmouth.
© 2002 John Wiley & Sons, Ltd.

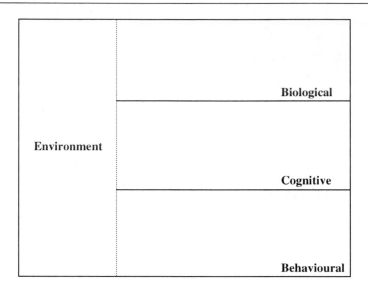

Figure 3.1   The three-levels framework

(Morton & Frith, 1993; 1995). Figure 3.1 shows the rudiments of this framework. The graphic schema acts as a reminder and a map for the causal modelling of these disorders. In unknown territory this map is largely white, but it will soon be filled in by intrepid explorers.

If we wish to construct and compare causal models of dyslexia, we need to connect the various elements of this framework. There are three levels of description, the biological, the cognitive and the behavioural; there is also a space for environmental influences which interact at any or all of these levels. We can start at a point of agreement: Difficulties in learning to read and write are characteristic features of dyslexia. These observations are facts that can be situated at the behavioural level. This means that whenever we talk about poor reading progress, either in a particular child or in a whole group of children, we can place the data in the appropriate space. We are not as yet saying anything about the causes of the poor performance.

However, we know that a large number of conditions can cause poor reading performance. We can start putting some hypotheses about possible causes into the space marked for environmental factors, others into the space labelled "cognitive". Yet others can be put into the space labelled "biological". As regards environmental causes, provision of teaching, cultural attitudes and socio-economic factors might be considered. Biological causes may include genetic contributions and neuro-anatomical factors. The sorts of causes that qualify for the label "cognitive" have to do with information-processing mechanisms. How such mental mechanisms work can be specified in computational language, in principle. In practice, these mechanisms and their faults are still extremely sketchy, yet they are sufficient to make testable predictions. Theoretical propositions include difficulties in speech processing, in visual or auditory perceptual processing, and in motor or temporal processing.

We can see the advantage of the framework when we compare different causal models. Such comparisons often involve a confusion of levels. This is not an unusual state of affairs and no reason to feel dispirited. On the contrary, to be able to identify a confusion of levels is usually a first step in reconciling ideas that at first glance seem to be rival positions. Let us take an example: There are currently two well known theories postulating respectively a phonological and a magnocellular deficit. The question is: Are these hypotheses in conflict with each other and mutually exclusive? By using the framework we can see that the answer is no. The phonological deficit theory stakes a claim at the cognitive level of explanation. It assumes that abnormality in speech processing is the immediate cause of reading difficulties in dyslexia. The magnocellular deficit theory stakes a claim at the brain level. It assumes that an abnormality in the anatomy of the magnocellular system is a remote cause of reading difficulties, possibly affecting speech problems as well. Hence the two theories are compatible with each other.

Causal Modelling as Linking Levels

The framework can be applied readily to the idea of dyslexia as a syndrome. Starting with the *biological level*, we can assume that dyslexia is a condition with a genetic origin and a basis in the brain. The evidence for this assumption is increasingly compelling. Recent reviews have been provided by Grigorenko (2001) and DeFries et al. (1997). There is also a substantial amount of evidence of physiological brain dysfunction in people with dyslexia while reading or doing reading-related tasks (Rumsey et al., 1992, 1997; Shaywitz et al., 1998; Brunswick et al., 1999; McCrory et al., 2001; Paulesu et al., 2001).

If dyslexia is to be represented as a neuro-developmental syndrome with a basis in the brain, should explanations be confined to the biological level? Absolutely not. They may start, but should not stop, there. The framework reminds us that there is a vast gap between brain and behaviour, and that external influences will enter into the clinical picture. Facts about the biology of dyslexia gained through genetic studies, post-mortem anatomical studies, and *in vivo* brain imaging, are quite separate from the behavioural facts, and links tend to be very tenuous. My claim is that they are less tenuous if the cognitive level is used as a bridge. If there is an abnormality at the neurological level in a specific brain system, then an abnormality in the mental processes subserved by this system would be expected. Of course, such a consequence is not inevitable—there may be protective factors. There is a certain amount of brain plasticity, and there may be sufficient redundancy in the cognitive system to avert any further consequences.

The framework can also represent a very different view. Here dyslexia is represented not as a syndrome but as a type of reading difficulty. In particular, there is no claim about a biological cause. The question is whether this type of explanation can be confined to the *behavioural level*. Again, emphatically not. The observations are not by themselves informative. They need to be interpreted. One danger is that observations and their interpretation tend surreptitiously to slide into one another. After all, the tests we use carry labels of psychological functions (e.g. working memory; phoneme awareness; retrieval speed) purporting to give us a direct line to underlying mental abilities and processes. However, labels can be deceptive, and there is always a difference between what tests actually measure and what they are intended to measure. For example, tests of working memory, phoneme awareness or retrieval speed often also involve other abilities that are not mentioned in the label, e.g. auditory discrimination, orthographic knowledge and attention to specific stimulus characteristics.

Behavioural measures must be seen as the outcome of the interaction of a great many factors. Test results reflect not only an underlying target skill, but also noise due to unwanted influences. The attitude, the mood and alertness of the subject at the time of testing, the events preceding the test, can all be powerful temporary determinants of behaviour. A poor score on the test can have a number of different causes, and so can a good score. A good score can give a distorted picture of the underlying ability, for instance, if it is due to unusual effort that cannot be sustained outside the laboratory, or if it is due to intensive training. If there are doubts, it will be necessary to clarify test performance by giving further tests. This could be a never-ending process, unless the tests are selected so as to adjudicate between alternative theories.

Theories to explain poor test performance are plentiful. Mostly they either postulate a *cognitive deficit* or blame *environmental* factors. If dyslexia is to be represented as a neuro-developmental disorder, explanations should not be confined to one particular level. Thus, cognitive theories need to take into account biological and environmental risk factors as well. One common danger with cognitive theories is that they can be circular, by postulating deficits which are merely re-statements of behavioural phenomena. For instance, slow naming speed is only a shorthand label, and does not in itself carry much of an explanation. Is the slowness due to poor access to representations of words? Is it due to representations themselves being poor? Is it part and parcel of slowness in other aspects of language processing? Is the slowness due to a socially conditioned attitude of caution? Cognitive theories need to make novel predictions in all directions of the diagram. This means they have to be anchored within current knowledge of brain function. At the same time they have to systematically take account of environmental factors that influence behaviour. In this context ideas about cognitive causes should act as a vital bridge in causal models and should lead to ideas for remediation.

The examples of causal modelling of different theories described below illustrate the weakness of focusing on one level of the framework only. Thus, a definition of dyslexia at the biological level is by no means better or more desirable than a definition at the cognitive level. The notation illustrated in Figure 3.2 shows that causal links are indicated by the convention of arrows. Clearly, when talking about causal links we are not talking about deterministic causes, only probabilistic ones.

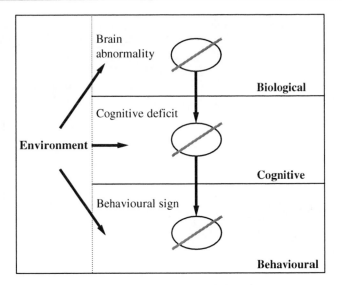

Figure 3.2   General causal model of a developmental disorder

The crossed-out fields in Figure 3.2 symbolise assumed dysfunction. We talk about "dysfunction", "deficit", "abnormality" and "impairment" without prejudice to value, but merely with reference to normative function, i.e. what is shown by the majority of people in the same cultural context. The reason that terms such as abnormality, deficit and dysfunction are prominent in causal modelling is that we are discussing possible causes of persistent impairments that have an impact on the daily life of the affected person. In the theories that we consider, causes tend to be phrased in terms of dysfunction. At the same time, these theories allow one to think about ways of ameliorating or removing the dysfunction. To talk about normal development requires a somewhat different notation (see Morton & Frith, 1995). In this case it is more sensible to talk of prerequisites rather than causes, and of contingency modelling rather than causal modelling, since the numerous possible causes of normal development are difficult to trace exhaustively. Mostly what we can talk about here is that the development of some abilities is contingent on the development of other abilities. For example, explicit phonological awareness does not emerge until the child has attained a minimum level of mastery of the alphabet (Morais et al., 1979; Wimmer et al., 1991).

REAL DYSLEXIA AND PSEUDO DYSLEXIA

One simple test of the causal modelling notation is whether it allows us to discriminate between extreme cases, as illustrated in Figures 3.3 and 3.4.

Figure 3.3 illustrates the case of a dyslexic individual with excellent scores on literacy tests. More economically than I can do it in words, I can use the diagram to declare just what I assume has happened. This particular individual no longer shows clinical signs on standard reading and writing tests. This is because of successful

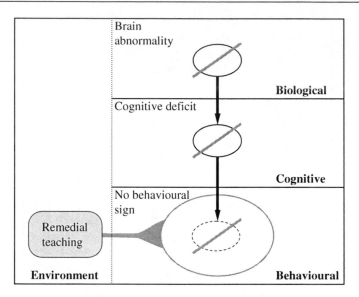

Figure 3.3   A causal model of compensation in developmental disorders

reading remediation. Nevertheless, the underlying condition has persisted. The claim of persistence would of course have to rest on other evidence, not illustrated in the diagram. For example, reading and spelling might be slow while accuracy and comprehension were good.

In contrast, in Figure 3.4 illustrates the case of an individual with reading difficulties, but no other signs of dyslexia. The diagram reminds us that reading difficulty can have other explanations than dyslexia. Perhaps the causes of the reading

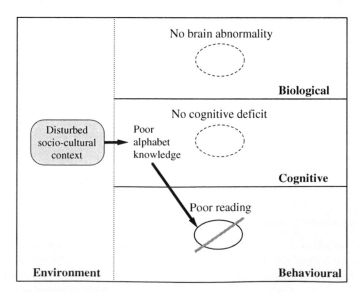

Figure 3.4   A causal model of poor reading: not dyslexia

problem were social-emotional problems of environmental origin. Again this claim will stand and fall with the evidence. For instance, improving the teacher/pupil relationship should result in fast catch-up in reading and writing skills.

PROBLEMS WITH BEHAVIOURAL DEFINITIONS

The two examples show that on the one hand, the absence of reading difficulties can be seen to be compatible with dyslexia; on the other hand, the presence of reading difficulties may have nothing to do with dyslexia. A definition of dyslexia purely in terms of performance on reading tests would get the diagnosis hopelessly wrong. So, it is possible to overcome some of the confusion that exists between "reading difficulties" and "dyslexia". I propose that we use the term "dyslexia" only when we refer to the neuro-developmental disorder, not when we refer to reading problems. A neuro-developmental disorder implies a complex causal chain from biology to behaviour. In contrast, when we talk about reading difficulties we are not at that point committed to any cause. The cause *may* be the neuro-developmental syndrome of dyslexia. But other causes too have to be considered. These may be purely environmental, for instance, inadequate teaching. Often, of course, the causes will be a complex interplay of external and internal factors: a pre-existing cognitive weakness may be aggravated by fear of failure.

Before accepting the proposed definition, it is useful to consider the alternatives. The definition of dyslexia as unexpected reading failure is a possibility, but has been widely criticised (e.g. Siegel, 1992). It remains a definition at the behavioural level, with all its attendant problems. However, it is important to acknowledge that it was originally extremely helpful. Thus dyslexia research was given impetus by the idea that dyslexia can be identified operationally in terms of a discrepancy between reading and general intelligence. Objectively measurable performance on standardised tests and the use of relevant regression equations made dyslexia scientifically respectable. It transformed dyslexia from an unspecified complaint in the mind of the beholder to a reality that can be seen by everyone. One point that critics have made is that for a discrepancy to be found, the child has to have a relatively high IQ test score, since differences at the lower end of the scale become necessarily smaller (Miles & Haslum, 1986). With a low IQ score it is difficult to show an even lower reading test score. This introduces a bias against diagnosing dyslexia in less able children.

One well-known paradox arises from this problem. How is it possible for dyslexia to target the able child while sparing the less able one? Does it in fact do so? The discrepancy concept gives no option in this matter and therefore cannot test whether the assumption is true. In a sense, it does not allow this question to be asked, for fear of losing objective ground. This suggests a deep scepticism about the concept of dyslexia itself. At a time when the genetic risk factors of the syndrome of dyslexia are being unravelled, this lack of confidence is inappropriate.

Perhaps the main paradox inherent in purely behavioural definitions is that the diagnosis will not be stable. Furthermore, the definitions will not be applicable to all languages. For instance, a specified discrepancy between reading and general ability which qualifies for dyslexia, may be present at one point in time, but not at another. Typically, as reading improves with age, the behavioural criteria are harder to fulfil. Yet, individuals with dyslexia claim that their problems persist. Meanwhile, it has become apparent that reading level, measured in terms of reading accuracy, is not a sensitive index of reading achievement. In particular, it may overestimate achievement as it does not take into account time taken to read. Most importantly, there are problems that extend beyond literacy which persist even when reading improves.

Another alternative is to define dyslexia as an impairment in non-word reading or exception word reading. One robust finding is that groups of dyslexic children, when matched with younger children on their ability to recognise words, are less able to recognise non-words than these controls (Rack et al., 1992). Poor non-word reading certainly suggests that a child has not achieved competence in the alphabetic strategy. Dyslexics may have problems in acquiring this strategy and never reach sufficient mastery to move on to a mature orthographic strategy which enables them to access a word's meaning as quickly as the word's sound (Frith, 1985). However, the reverse does not hold. Poor alphabetic knowledge may have other causes than dyslexia. For instance, a very complex and irregular orthographic system could, under certain circumstances, put off a child from learning to use an alphabetic strategy. Conversely, some dyslexic children may receive highly effective training in decoding non-words. In other words, as with all behavioural tests used for diagnosis, false positives as well as false negatives can occur. Therefore, non-word reading is not a shortcut to diagnosis, but needs to be part of a systematic assessment which includes information about teaching and remedial help.

Not all poor readers are abysmal at reading regular non-words, but some have excessive difficulties with irregular words. This has been taken as a basis for defining subtypes of dyslexia (Castles & Coltheart, 1993; Manis et al., 1996). Clearly, it is of interest to describe such subtypes, and it would be important to show that they remain stable over time in individual children. However, the significance of behaviourally defined subtypes in terms of underlying causes is not self-evident. The causes might be linked to particular teaching methods. Thomson (1999) demonstrated that error types taken to be indicative of subgroups in a group of 58 dyslexic children changed markedly after two years of tuition. It may be that different causes for subtypes can be specified at the cognitive and biological levels; for instance, there may be visual problems in one case and auditory problems in another. A third possibility is that behavioural subtypes reflect the interaction of general factors with one and the same underlying cognitive deficit, which is present to different degrees of severity (Stanovich, 1998).

One interesting problem thrown up by using different types of words and non-words in diagnostic tests, is that they are specific to English orthography. In Italian and German, for example, irregular words are rare, and non-word reading is far less of a problem than it is in English (Frith et al., 1998). Italian people with dyslexia are perfectly accurate when reading words or non-words. However, they are much slower than their peers (Paulesu et al., 2001).

INDIVIDUAL VARIABILITY

A great challenge for cognitive theories is that they have to explain the diversity of dyslexia as it manifests itself in different people. Most cognitive theories are not designed to cope with individual variation. They address the prototypical case instead. The behaviour patterns characteristic of the prototypical case are distilled from many individual cases, and it is this distilled information that is usually the target of explanation.

This is not necessarily a limitation. It is reasonable to assume that individual variation can be explained in the same way as individual variation in the normal population, namely by a range of internal and external influences. These other factors are not strictly relevant to the cause of the disorder. They are important, however, in that they aggravate or ameliorate the basic clinical picture. Age, sex, ability, motivation, personality, social support, physical resources, instructional systems, the nature of the language and orthography—these all play a role. Another attempt to account for individual variation is the notion of subgroups. However, here again idealised subtypes are the target of explanation, each with their own individual variation.

The field is still wide open as to potential sources of individual variability in clinical disorders, and likewise in normal development. Inevitably, practitioners who are overwhelmed daily by individual differences between children will be dissatisfied by current cognitive theories. However, they may find the causal modelling framework useful because it carries a reminder that the behaviour in question always has multiple determinants. Thus, individual differences might have explanations that lie entirely outside the factors responsible for the disorder.

INFLUENCES FROM CULTURAL AND CONSTITUTIONAL FACTORS

As everyone would agree, dyslexia concerns literacy, a supremely cultural phenomenon. Yet we now know that dyslexia has a biological basis. This creates a paradox: biology and literacy seem to belong to different domains altogether. After all, the brain did not evolve for the use of an alphabetic writing system. Reading failure can be reasonably explained as a result of cultural deprivation or lack of teaching. It is obvious what to do—teach reading in a context where literacy is valued. At first glance it seems outlandish to think that reading problems are primarily due to brain problems. The idea seems implausible since it appears to presume the brain is innately hard-wired for "reading". It also is unpalatable, since it implies that the problems cannot be treated.

This paradox can be resolved. Of course, the ability to read in an alphabetic or any other script does not have an innate basis. However, the ability to read depends crucially on an ability which may well be innate. This prerequisite ability is likely to reflect processing of spoken words. Second, it is wrong to equate the contrast between cultural and biological causes with the ability to do something about the condition. It may be no more difficult to treat a neurologically caused disorder, than it is to treat a disorder caused by cultural deprivation.

The incompatibility between cultural and biological factors disappears when we look at their interaction. One possible scenario is that genetically influenced peculiarities in brain anatomy, present in a minority of people, preclude a certain type of information processing. This need not be a disadvantage in daily life. However, it could turn into one, if a particular writing system was strongly reliant on the type of information processing in question. Those individuals born without this special facility would have a hard time learning written language. They would suffer especially where there is a premium on literacy, and even more, where they have to learn a complex orthography. This thought experiment explains why dyslexia can be of very little consequence in one country and constitute a major handicap in another.

While it may be difficult to disentangle cultural effects, it is even more problematic to disentangle factors situated inside the individual which have an influence on the clinical picture without actually causing the condition. Two of the most obvious points to make are that there are degrees of severity, and that the picture changes with age. Common experience suggests that reading and writing skills improve whatever the remedial scheme. Personality factors are rarely mentioned, but it seems plain in everyday life that some people can cope with their problems more easily than others. This is even evident with illnesses, such as the common cold. While one person has to take to bed and take numerous medicines, another can continue to work. Different needs and demands are counterbalanced by differences in supply. High general ability, which can be seen as an internal resource, and remedial teaching programmes, which can be seen as an external resource, in combination can mitigate the symptoms of dyslexia. People who so benefit often seem to exhibit mild forms of the disorder. However, mildness usually refers to the overall clinical picture, which includes the effects and efforts of compensation. This picture may actually conceal the severity of the cognitive deficit.

NEURO-COGNITIVE CAUSES OF DYSLEXIA

A number of neuro-cognitive causes have been proposed to date, and these can readily be modelled in the three-level framework. Two directions can be distinguished in these proposals. One is to assume that the deficit is specific rather than all-pervasive. In this case the approach is to identify the specific neuro-cognitive component that is responsible for the core symptoms and to demonstrate that everything else is working perfectly. The other direction is to assume that the deficit is more general, and that it should not be assumed that everything else is working perfectly. In this case the approach is to look for problems in many different mental functions. Both these directions have been taken, and it is as yet unknown just how general or specific the neuro-cognitive deficit is. In addition, it is clear that even a highly specific deficit would have effects on areas that are not directly related to written language. Specific deficits in critical cognitive processes may have domino effects, delaying the development of other functions (Frith & Happé, 1998). The possibility of investigating these exciting questions makes dyslexia a key disorder, which may help unlock the architecture of the mind.

While different cognitive deficits have been proposed as causes of dyslexia, one idea has become particularly dominant: that learning difficulties in written language are intimately connected with learning difficulties in spoken language (Shankweiler et al., 1979; Brady & Shankweiler, 1991). Language does not represent a global function. Language processes can be broken down into a number of quite specialised functions. One well-accepted division distinguishes phonology (processing of information contained in speech sound), syntax (processing of information contained in relationships between words) semantics (processing of information contained in the meaning of words) and pragmatics (processing of information contained in the use of language for communication). The processing of speech sounds has been targeted as the critical link between spoken and written language (Bradley & Bryant, 1983). If the preschool child has difficulties in the ability to process the sounds of speech, then difficulties in the acquisition of reading will follow. It is the elucidation of this "phonological" component, therefore, that remains a crucial step in the explanation of dyslexia as a "phonological" deficit.

The importance of phonology in learning to read is asserted by all current models of cognitive psychology (e.g. Wagner & Torgesen, 1987; Goswami & Bryant, 1990; van Orden et al., 1990; Snowling & Nation, 1997; Snowling, 2000). Briefly, the alphabet is based on the notion that speech can be represented by small units, the phonemes, which are represented by letters. The main task that a child has to master, when learning to read in an alphabetic system, is to understand how to represent speech sound by letters, and how to translate precisely between written and spoken language in the given mappings of a particular language. Syntax, semantics, pragmatics, the other—hugely important—components of language processing, do not come into this task in the first instance. Only phonology does. However, since phonology is a bottleneck in language processing, it is possible that the other components will be subtly affected "downstream".

How children normally develop phonology and acquire alphabetic literacy in an almost effortless way is still a matter of debate, and many theorists have addressed this problem. By age five or so, children approach the task of learning to read with thousands of word "names" at their disposal. They have to make a big leap in learning how these word sounds relate to letter sounds. This leap is easy to make for those with a well-functioning phonological system, but hard for those who have some weakness in this system. Difficulties in learning to read would be the result of such a weakness. Snowling and Hulme (1994), for instance, propose that poorly specified phonological representations prevent the precise learning of phoneme-to-grapheme mapping that is necessary for alphabetic systems. In contrast, sufficiently well-specified phonological representations are normally available by age five, the age at which many children start to acquire decoding skills. The idea that people with dyslexia may have less distinct representations of the sounds of words has been widely accepted (e.g. Elbro, 1996; Snowling, 2000; Goswami, 2000).

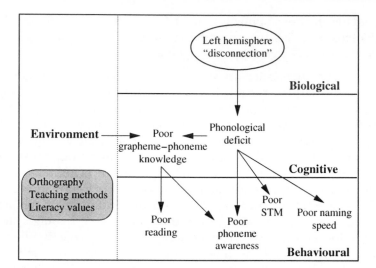

Figure 3.5   A causal model of dyslexia as a result of a phonological deficit

An Illustration of the Hypothesis of a Phonological Deficit

Figure 3.5 illustrates the theory that dyslexia is caused by a deficit in phonological processing (see Snowling, 2000 for a comprehensive and authoritative review).

If there is a cognitive deficit in the phonological system, then this deficit should also be noticeable in spoken language. The answer from a large number of studies is that individuals with dyslexia do show impairments in speech processes. They implicate accuracy of information processing as well as speed (Bowers & Swanson, 1991; Wolf, 1991). They implicate listening as well as speaking. Tasks that have been used include speech sound discrimination (Adlard & Hazan, 1998), word production (Stackhouse & Wells, 1997), word repetition (Miles, 1993; Snowling et al., 1988), picture naming (Swan & Goswami, 1997), and verbal short-term memory, which depends on subvocal rehearsal (Nelson & Warrington, 1980). None of these tests involve written language. Miles (1993) drew attention to the fact that poor performance on certain items of the Bangor Dyslexia test (in particular, saying the months of the year forwards and backwards, reciting multiplication tables) involve short-term verbal memory and can also be attributed to impaired phonological processing. This can also be said about a characteristic profile on the Wechsler test, with relatively poor performance on the subtests of Arithmetic, Coding and Digit span, shown by many people with dyslexia. All these tests involve short-term verbal memory.

The diagram in Figure 3.5 shows a subset of impairments that are all consistent with the idea of a phonological deficit. The brain basis of the phonological deficit is thought to lie in the peri- and extra-sylvian areas of the left hemisphere of the brain. Post-mortem neuro-anatomical studies (see Galaburda, 1993, for a review) have shown that exactly these brain regions are abnormal in dyslexic brains. The abnormalities are subtle and take the form of cell migrations in certain layers of the cortex. They are also associated with greater symmetry of the planum tempo-rale in both hemispheres than is found in normal brains. A number of functional brain-imaging studies have demonstrated that compensated adults with dyslexia show atypical neural activity in the left hemisphere language system during both phonological and reading tasks (Flowers et al., 1991; Rumsey et al., 1992, 1997; Shaywitz et al., 1998; Brunswick et al., 1999). Since no one has shown actual lesions in the brains of individuals whose dyslexia is of developmental origin, a possible hypothesis is disconnection between the various and distributed systems that are involved in speech processing (Paulesu et al., 1996; Brunswick et al., 1999; Paulesu et al., 2001).

However, an intact brain is not enough for learning to read. As the diagram shows, the acquisition of reading is mediated through cultural factors. The grapheme–phoneme knowledge that the reader has to acquire is primarily a cultural gift and is dependent on the provision of schooling.

What about other theories that postulate different deficits? Unless they provide evidence against the relationship between learning to read and phonological capacity, they too need to incorporate an explanation of a phonological deficit. However, they might postulate more general deficits, for instance, deficits in processing fast-moving temporal sequences, from which a phonological deficit might be derived. In addition, as discussed earlier, this argument does not preclude the existence of non-dyslexic reading-disabled children who do not have phonological problems.

An Illustration of Comorbidity

There is no reason to assume that a phonological deficit can only occur when there is no other problem. Instead, comorbidity is a common occurrence in developmental disorders. We can illustrate the case of attention deficit co-existing with dyslexia. Since both disorders are fairly frequent, their co-occurrence may be no more than what would be expected by chance. On the other hand, brain anatomy may reveal other reasons for a common effect on systems involved in phonology and in executive functions. Executive functions are thought to be compromised in attention deficit disorder. Figure 3.6 shows how such comorbidity might be represented in the causal framework.

It is easy to see that a problem in the attention system, possibly caused by some minor anomalies affecting the development of the frontal parts of the brain, could affect the learning of spoken and written language. Attention deficits are problems precisely when new skills have to be learned. Therefore, the attention deficit would result in poor learning and poor achievements in a whole range of school subjects, not just reading. It would also result in poor performance on tasks specifically designed to tap executive functions subserved by the frontal lobes (Shallice & Burgess, 1991). If there were an additional phonological deficit, this would make learning to read even more problematic. Certain learning strategies applied to reading and writing which might help the child with an attention deficit (e.g. fast stimulus presentation) might not be very effective for the child who is also dyslexic. Dyslexia

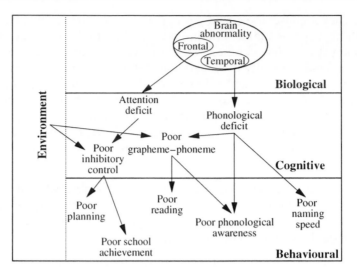

Figure 3.6   A causal model of dyslexia with attention deficit disorder

in the presence of persistent impairments of attentional strategies is probably a frequent occurrence. This is suggested by the problems most frequently raised by people with dyslexia in tertiary education. These students tend to complain of difficulties with planning essays, talks, timetables and projects in general. Whether or not these problems should be thought of as executive function problems is a question that deserves further study.

Illustrations of Dyslexia as an Abnormality of the Magnocellular System and as a Cerebellar Anomaly

Several theories are at present trying to derive the phonological deficit from some even deeper underlying problem or consider the possibility of the phonological deficit as an additional problem superimposed on other difficulties. Two examples are illustrated in Figures 3.7 and 3.8.

The theory illustrated in Figure 3.7 is based on the finding that the magnocellular system of the brain is anatomically and functionally abnormal in people with dyslexia (Livingstone et al., 1991; Lovegrove, 1994; Eden et al., 1996). In line with the notion that the magnocellular system is implicated in the detection of fast movements, dyslexic people have been found to have a higher threshold in perceiving fast-moving objects (e.g. Cornelissen, 1998). One important question to ask is how an impairment in magnocellular-based functions can give rise to reading and writing problems. Stein & Walsh (1997) proposed that the causal link might involve problems in eye-movement control, visuo-spatial attention and peripheral vision. All these functions clearly play a role in the reading process. Another theory, proposed by Nicolson & Fawcett (1990), is illustrated in Figure 3.8. Here an impaired cerebellar system is proposed as a distal cause of dyslexia. Both the magnocellular and cerebellar theories are potentially compatible. If expressed at the

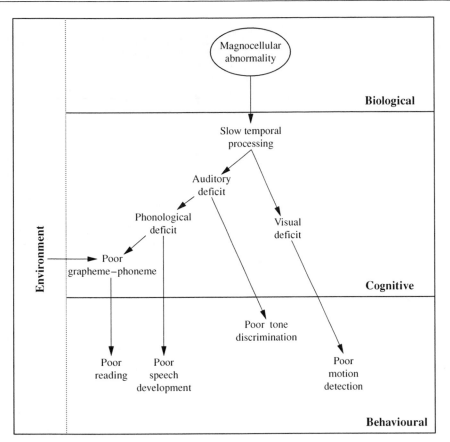

Figure 3.7   A causal model of dyslexia as a result of a magnocellular abnormality

cognitive level, both theories may imply a temporal processing deficit. Fast temporal processing may be a basic characteristic of all perceptual systems, visual as well as auditory, object-based as well as speech-based. Slower than normal perceptual processing might well compromise the development of a phonological system.

An important explanation of specific language impairment (SLI), a neurologically based disorder of which dyslexia may well be a mild form, has been proposed by Tallal (1980) and Neville et al. (1993). This theory postulates a sequential processing difficulty within basic sensory processes, primarily acoustic but possibly visual as well. A difficulty with identifying temporal order at ultra-fast speeds is thought to impinge on speech processing, which might lead to a phonological deficit. This idea can be seen as highly compatible with the diagrams in Figures 3.7 and 3.8. The theory proposes that intervention at the sensory level can remediate a number of downstream deficits (Tallal et al., 1996).

All these theories appear to acknowledge the bottleneck presented by phonological impairment. This impairment matters above all when it is necessary to acquire grapheme–phoneme knowledge. The theories differ in the range of additional predictions they make about signs and symptoms in dyslexia. They also differ in their

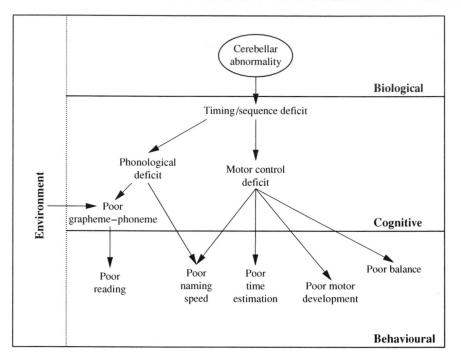

Figure 3.8   A causal model of dyslexia as a result of a cerebellar abnormality

suggestions for diagnosis and remediation. Whatever specific questions they are addressing, all current theories have to grapple with the following theoretical problems: How exactly are literacy difficulties related to phonological difficulties? How exactly are phonological difficulties related to lower-level perceptual difficulties? What is the nature of the processing mechanisms that appear to be faulty? What is their basis in the brain?

PITFALLS IN TESTING PHONOLOGICAL AND LITERACY COMPETENCE

While the distal causes of dyslexia are at present conceptualised in different ways, the proximal cognitive cause, common to all accounts, is a phonological deficit. How can we best measure phonological skills? This is a difficult question even though there are currently a number of standardised tests available for this purpose. These tests do well in discriminating groups, but their sensitivity and specificity in individual cases remain to be established. One such battery of phonological tests (Frederickson et al., 1997) is illustrated in Figure 3.9.

In the diagram, general ability and phonological processing competence are assumed to be independent. Nevertheless, test performance will be influenced by the general ability factor 'g', because it is in the nature of 'g' to determine in part performance on any achievement test. The diagram makes explicit that some

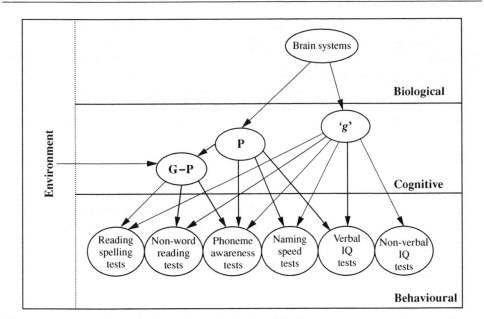

Figure 3.9 A sketch of the hypothetical relationships between tests tapping grapheme–phoneme knowledge (G–P), phonological processes (P) and general ability (*g*)

of the phonological tests can be solved by virtue of being a proficient reader (indicated by their dependence on grapheme–phoneme knowledge (G–P). This has implications for diagnosis. It is possible to become a proficient reader by an abnormal route, that is, without an intuitively grounded phonological ability. Such a reader would acquire explicit knowledge of phonology, rather like an art critic can acquire knowledge of art without having artistic competence. This reader would be likely to obtain high scores on several of the tests in the battery.

We need to bear in mind that, like other skills, phonological skills can be achieved in different ways and may mean different things. Performance on phonological awareness tasks, in particular, is greatly aided by practice in alphabetic literacy (Morais et al., 1979). Whether or not a person can delete the initial or final sound from a word depends greatly on whether that person has experienced schooling. It remains to be seen to what extent other phonological skills, such as naming speed and verbal short-term memory, are similarly affected by literacy practice. Again, it is useful to be reminded that behavioural tests alone will not allow an inference about the causes of impairments.

The diagram in Figure 3.9 allows us to see what pattern to expect when a phonological deficit is present. It can be seen that such a deficit may occur in the presence of either high or low scores on verbal and non-verbal IQ tests. Slow digit naming would be especially interesting in a child with high general ability, where one would assume high information-processing speed for other non-verbal tasks. Poor performance on reading and spelling tests, non-word reading tests and phoneme-awareness tests alone would not be sufficient to infer the presence of phonological problems. Good performance, on the other hand, could be a result of extra training on the test words. Performance on these tests will always be highly influenced by environmental variables. If we can assume only advantageous environmental influences, then poor results on these tests are suggestive of a specific problem. This simplified analysis of patterns of performance on a test battery shows how difficult it is to diagnose phonological deficits in the presence of environmental disadvantage and low 'g'. In this case poor test performance is overdetermined. It could be due to a number of different factors. However, it should not be overlooked that one of these factors might be a phonological deficit.

Standardised tests measuring literacy achievement also need to be included in a diagnostic assessment. Spelling, being a more demanding task, is a more sensitive test and is likely to reveal dyslexia more readily than reading. Speed measures of word recognition are also a sensitive measure, but normative data at different ages are scarce. A score, regardless of whether it is within the normal range or not, is only a pointer. In all diagnostic procedures that are based on behavioural criteria, clinical judgement—that is, a good hypothesis—is needed.

While the task of finding reliable and valid diagnostic tests of dyslexia is still incomplete, it would be a mistake to think that we should doubt that dyslexia exists, or doubt that a cognitive deficit in phonological processing is a critical bottleneck in the explanation of the syndrome. The existence of a specific deficit has been shown in well-controlled group studies proving it to be early emerging (Scarborough, 1990), persistent (Pennington et al., 1990) and universal (Landerl et al., 1997; Paulesu et al., 2001). It is the strong empirical support that has given the hypothesis such a central position in dyslexia research.

In individual cases a phonological deficit may be severe or mild, or else camouflaged. It may not always be easy to reveal. Take the case of Edmund B., a 17-year old student who was re-assessed for dyslexia. He had had early difficulties in learning to read. He had largely overcome these difficulties but remained a slow reader. During the assessment Edmund scored surprisingly well on a spoonerism test ("Chuck Berry" becomes "Buck Cherry" by exchanging the initial phonemes). The educational psychologist also found that Edmund's spelling was not as bad as that of the other dyslexic pupils in his school. However, she found that he was reading and writing extremely slowly. His short-term verbal memory was middling, but his visual memory was excellent. Edmund reported that he was able to get a strong visual image of the words in the spoonerism test, which had enabled him to do it easily. He was also able to memorise spellings in this way. The psychologist recommended that Edmund B., because of his partially compensated dyslexia, should be allowed extra time in his exams.

This case illustrates how under certain circumstances a cognitive deficit may not manifest itself at the behavioural level in the expected way. Some individuals may be protected by compensation and may not show adverse effects that, in other less favourable circumstances, they would certainly show. This is why diagnosis is such a fraught and complex business, and why clinical intuition, rightly, plays an important part.

TOWARDS A DEFINITION OF DYSLEXIA IN A CULTURAL CONTEXT

It is a fact that behaviour changes over time. The behavioural signs of dyslexia improve with learning and compensation, even when the underlying problem which had given rise to the difficulty in the first place still persists. It is therefore unlikely that behavioural criteria alone will ever be adequate to the job of defining dyslexia. We have to grasp the nettle of definition by admitting a theory-driven approach. I have argued that we should define dyslexia as a neuro-developmental disorder, existing from birth, with different manifestations over the lifetime of an individual. Dyslexia is thus not synonymous with reading failure. To define dyslexia in terms of reading test performance is rather like defining 'flu as an increase in body temperature. Raised temperature, however, is merely a sign of the infection, not the illness itself. Decreasing the temperature is usually a good thing, but it does not cure the illness. All the knowledge accumulated in dyslexia research indicates that dyslexia is not a disease which comes with school and goes away with adulthood. It is not a temporary childhood affliction; it is a lifelong burden. Nor can it be cured simply by improving reading and writing skills. Of course, such improvement is highly desirable, but it needs to be recognised as a symptomatic treatment rather than a cure.

The precise identification of the underlying neuro-cognitive information-processing abnormality is a task for the future. However, we will not be far wrong if we define dyslexia as a condition with a phonological deficit. As a rough estimate we can assume that 80% of children who are potentially dyslexic would show phonological deficits on testing. This estimate is based on a study with an unselected group of children currently diagnosed by educational psychologists as suffering from specific learning disability (Frederickson & Frith, 1998). What about the 20% of children who did not show phonological impairments? Since a great many factors went into the procedure to "statement" the children in terms of special educational needs, the reasons for the classification are difficult to pin down. Some children may be cases with mild or camouflaged phonological deficits, others may have serious intellectual or socio-emotional problems which interfered with learning. In addition, there would be cases of "specific learning difficulty" which do not represent a neuro-cognitive syndrome. Finally, there may be cases with other neuro-developmental disorders, including Attention Deficit Disorder, also leading to difficulties in written language learning, but which do not necessarily implicate phonological impairments. These cases would be missed out by the phonological deficit definition, and this is a pity. Clearly, it would be of great value to investigate putative cases and to develop appropriate diagnostic tests.

Focusing on a phonological deficit in dyslexia leaves open the possibility that other, more primary causes in auditory, visual or temporal processing might be found as well. Regardless of these primary causes, phonological processing can be seen as a critical bottleneck. A phonological deficit causes a whole range of signs and symptoms, not only literacy problems. In fact, in the historical context, literacy problems have to be seen as relatively peripheral. Phonological impairment exists in different languages, but literacy problems differ. A phonological deficit, but not of course "dyslexia" as we know it, should exist even in pre-literate societies. Nothing illustrates more poignantly the radical change in the conceptualisation of dyslexia over the past fifty years.

Over and above cognitive factors, it is cultural factors that shape the clinical picture and time course of dyslexia. They determine the degree of handicap that the disorder may impose on the sufferer. This can range from none at all to a serious burden. Alphabetic writing systems make very high demands on phonological ability. Other writing systems that do not use small units of speech sounds as a basis for written symbols, but use whole syllables or whole word sounds or meanings, should therefore be easier to acquire for people with phonological impairments. In support of this notion, there is the case of a dyslexic boy, bilingual in English and Japanese, whose reading and writing difficulties were confined to English only (Wydell & Butterworth, 1999).

While cognitive factors are more important in the causation of dyslexia, environmental factors are more important in its remediation. The single most important factor in the remediation of dyslexia is, without doubt, the protective influence of culture. This is not only through the fostering of positive attitudes towards written language and the provision of schools and teachers trained specifically in the art of teaching children with dyslexia. Culture also influences the outcome of dyslexia through the writing system it offers. A complex and inconsistent orthography is often a result of historical forces, for example different languages being amalgamated, as in English. The more complex the system, the more difficult it is to acquire for normally developing and for dyslexic children alike. Not all languages are equal in terms of the complexity of their phonology or their grammar either. The influence of this aspect of cultural heritage on the development of language has hardly been explored. Considering all these factors together, it is possible that dyslexia-friendly languages will be found, as well as dyslexia-friendly writing systems. It is yet another question whether such languages and writing systems would present problems for other sections of the population.

Cultural tools give us power to mitigate the symptoms of neuro-cognitive deficits. It may well be that the deficit itself is best left alone and instead the effort might go towards circumventing it. The use of computer spellcheckers, for example, a prime tool of the future of literacy, has dramatically improved dyslexic writing within one generation, within the same language and without change of instructional methods. This does not mean giving up the idea of ever treating the neuro-cognitive basis of dyslexia directly. Consider how the use of spectacles has been a boon for people with myopia for a long time, and contact lenses made the defect invisible to others. Laser surgery of the lens may become an option in the future, treating the immediate cause of short-sightedness.

It is often said that, happily, diagnosis itself is the first therapeutic step in an otherwise misunderstood and misinterpreted pattern of problems. A better understanding of dyslexia in the future should mean an earlier diagnosis. This could have very practical benefits. At the very least, the humiliating feeling of school failure might be prevented if potential difficulties in literacy acquisition were anticipated and explained to child and teacher. In this way the much feared spiral of educational failure and social maladjustment might be avoided.

CONCLUSIONS

We may disagree about the nature of the biological or non-biological origin of a particular cognitive deficit and its behavioural consequences. We may disagree about the nature of the particular deficit. We may also disagree about the meaning of the behavioural data. The beauty of the visual notation is that we can tell where the disagreement lies and how it could be resolved by further testing (Morton & Frith, 1993).

Defining dyslexia at a single level of explanation, biological, cognitive, or behavioural, will always lead to paradoxes. For a full understanding of dyslexia we need to link together the three levels and consider the impact of cultural factors which can aggravate or ameliorate the condition. The consensus is emerging that dyslexia is a neuro-developmental disorder with a biological origin, which impacts on speech processing with a range of clinical manifestations. There is evidence for a genetic basis and there is evidence for a brain basis, and it is clear that the behavioural signs extend well beyond written language. There may be many different kinds of genes and different kinds of brain conditions that are ultimately responsible for the dyslexia syndrome, but in each case the symptoms have to be understood within the relevant cultural context. The influence of cultural factors is such that in some contexts the condition causes hardly any handicap in affected individuals, but in others it can cause a great deal of suffering. The behavioural signs and the clinical impairments of the syndrome show great variability within and between individuals. In spite of this variability, theories situated within the three-levels framework have the potential to unify ideas on the causation and remediation of this fascinating condition.

(This chapter is based on a paper that first appeared under the title: Paradoxes in the definition of dyslexia, in *Dyslexia*, Volume 5, issue 4, 192–214 (1999).)

REFERENCES

Adlard, A. & Hazan, V (1998) Speech perception abilities in children with developmental dyslexia. *Quarterly Journal of Experimental Psychology: Section A.*, 51A, 153–177.

Bowers, P.G. & Swanson, L.B. (1991) Naming speed deficits in reading disability: multiple measures of a singular process. *Journal of Experimental Child Psychology*, 51, 195–219.

Brady, S. & Shankweiler, D. (1991) *Phonological Processes in Literacy.* New Jersey: Lawrence Erlbaum.

Bradley, L. & Bryant, P. (1983) Categorising sounds and learning to read: A causal connection. *Nature*, 310, 419–421.

Brunswick, N., McCrory, E., Price, C., Frith, C.D. & Frith, U. (1999) Explicit and implicit processing of words and pseudowords by adult developmental dyslexics: a search for Wernicke's Wortschatz? *Brain*, 122, 1901–1917.

Castles, A. & Coltheart, M. (1993) Varieties of developmental dyslexia. *Cognition*, 47, 149–180.

Catts, H. (1989) Speech production deficits in developmental dyslexia. *Journal of Speech and Hearing Disorders*, 54, 422–428.

Cornelissen, P. (1998) Magnocellular visual function and children's reading. In: C. von Euler, I. Lundberg, & R. Llinas (Editors) *Basic Mechanisms in Cognition and Language*, Amsterdam: Elsevier, pp. 19–48.

DeFries, J.C., Alarcon, M. & Olson, R.K. (1997) Genetic aetiologies in reading and spelling difficulties. In: C. Hulme and M. Snowling (Editors) *Dyslexia: Biology, Cognition and Intervention*. London: Whurr.

Eden, G.F., Van Meter, J.W., Rumsey, J.M., Maisog, J.M., Woods, R.P. & Zeffiro, T.A. (1996) Abnormal processing of visual motion in dyslexia revealed by functional brain imaging. *Nature*, 382, 66–69.

Elbro, C. (1996) Early reading abilities and reading development: a review and a hypothesis about distinctness of phonological representations. *Reading and Writing*, 8, 453–485.

Flowers, D.L., Wood, F.B. & Naylor, C.E. (1991) Regional cerebral blood flow correlate of language processes in reading disability. *Archives of Neurology*, 48, 637–643.

Frederickson, N. & Frith, U. (1998) Identifying dyslexia in bilingual children: A phonological approach with Inner London Sylheti Speakers. *Dyslexia*, 4, 119–131.

Frederickson, N., Frith, U. & Reason, P. (1997) *Phonological Assessment Battery*. Windsor: NFER Nelson.

Frith, U. (1985) Beneath the surface of developmental dyslexia. In: M. Coltheart, K. Patterson, & J. Marshall (Editors) (1985) *Surface Dyslexia*. London: Lawrence Erlbaum.

Frith, U. & Happé, F. (1998) Why specific developmental disorders are not specific; on-line and developmental effects in autism and dyslexia. *Developmental Science*, 1, 276–282.

Frith, U., Wimmer, H. & Landerl, K. (1998) Differences in phonological recoding in German- and English-speaking children. *Scientific Study of Reading*, 2, 31–54.

Galaburda A.M. (1993) Neurology of developmental dyslexia. *Current Opinion in Neurobiology*, 5, 71–76.

Goswami, U. (2000) Phonological representations, reading development and dyslexia: towards a cross-linguistic theoretical framework. *Dyslexia, An International Journal of Research and Practice*, 6, 133–151.

Goswami, U. & Bryant, P.E. (1990) *Phonological Skills and Learning to Read*. London: Lawrence Erlbaum.

Grigorenko, E.L. (2001) Developmental dyslexia: an update on genes, brains and environments. *Journal of Child Psychology and Psychiatry*, 42, 91–123.

Landerl, K., Wimmer, H. & Frith, U. (1997) The impact of orthographic consistency on dyslexia. A German–English comparison. *Cognition*, 63, 315–334.

Livingstone, M.S., Rosen, G.D., Drislane, F.W. & Galaburda, A.M. (1991) Physiological and anatomical evidence for a magnocellular defect in developmental dyslexia. *Proceedings of the New York Academy of Sciences*, 88, 7943–7947.

Lovegrove, W. (1994) Visual deficit in dyslexia: evidence and implications. In: A. Fawcett and R. Nicolson (Editors) *Dyslexia in Children*. Hemel Hempstead, UK: Harvester Wheatsheaf.

Manis, F.R., Seidenberg, M.S., Doi, L.M., McBride-Chang, C. & Petersen, A. (1996) On the bases of two subtypes of developmental dyslexia. *Cognition*, 58, 157–195.

McCrory, E., Frith, U., Brunswick, N. & Price, C. (2000) Abnormal functional activation during a simple word repetition task: A PET study of adult dyslexics. *Journal of Cognitive Neuroscience*, 12, 753–763.

Miles, T.R. (1993) *Dyslexia: The Pattern of Difficulties* (Second Edition). London: Whurr.

Miles, T. (1994) A proposed taxonomy and some consequences. In: A.J. Fawcett & R.I. Nicolson (Editors) *Dyslexia in Children: Multidisciplinary Perspectives*. Hemel Hempstead, UK: Harvester Wheatsheaf.

Miles, T.R. & Haslum M. (1986) Dyslexia: anomaly or normal variation. *Annals of Dyslexia*, 36, 103–117.

Morais, J., Cary, L., Alegria, J. & Bertelson, P. (1979) Does awareness of speech as a sequence of phones arise spontaneously? *Cognition*, 7, 323–331.

Morton, J. & Frith, U. (1993) What lesson for dyslexia from Down Syndrome? Comments on Cossu, Rossini & Marshall. *Cognition*, 48, 289–296.

Morton, J. & Frith, U. (1995) Causal modelling: A structural approach to developmental psychopathology. In: D. Cicchetti & D.J. Cohen (Editors) *Manual of Developmental Psychopathology* (pp. 357–390). NY Psychological Assessment of Dyslexia: Wiley.

Nelson, H.E. & Warrington, E.K. (1980) An investigation of memory functions in dyslexic children. *British Journal of Psychology*, 71, 487–503.

Neville, H.J., Coffey, S.A., Holcomb, P.J. & Tallal, P. (1993) The neurobiology of sensory and language processing in language-impaired children. *Journal of Cognitive Neuroscience*, 5, 235–253.

Nicolson, R.I. & Fawcett, A.J. (1990) Automaticity: A new framework for dyslexia research? *Cognition*, 35, 159–182.

Paulesu, E., Frith, U., Snowling, M., Gallagher, A., Morton, J., Frackowiak, R.S.J. & Frith, C.D. (1996) Is developmental dyslexia a disconnection syndrome? Evidence from PET scanning. *Brain*, 119, 143–157.

Paulesu, E., Démonet, J.-F., Fazio, F., McCrory, E., Chanoine, V., Brunswick, N., Cappa, S.F., Cossu, G., Habib, M., Frith, C.D. & Frith U. (2001)Dyslexia—cultural diversity and biological unity. *Science*, 291, 2165–2167.

Pennington B.F., Van Orden G.C., Smith S.D., Green P.A. & Haith M.M. (1990) Phonological processing skills and deficits in adult dyslexics. *Child Development*, 61, 1753–1778.

Rack, J.P., Snowling, M. & Olson, R.K. (1992) The nonword reading deficit in developmental dyslexia. *Reading Research Quarterly*, 1, 71–83.

Rumsey, J.M., Andreason, P., Zametkin, A.J., Aquino, T., King, C., Hamburger, S.D., Pikus, A., Rapoport, J.L. & Cohen, R. (1992) Failure to activate the left temporal cortex in dyslexia: an Oxygen 15 Positron Emission Tomographic study. *Archives of Neurology*, 49, 527–534.

Rumsey, J.M., Nace, K., Donohue, B., Wise, D., Maisog, M. & Andreason, P. (1997) A positron emission tomographic study of impaired word recognition and phonological processing in dyslexic men. *Archives of Neurology*, 54, 562–573.

Scarborough, H.S. (1990). Very early language deficits in dyslexic children. *Child Development*, 61, 207–220.

Schulte-Körne, G., Deimel, W., Bartling, J. & Remschmidt, H. (1998). Auditory processing and dyslexia: evidence for a specific speech processing deficit. *NeuroReport*, 9, 337–340.

Shallice, T. & Burgess, P. (1991) Higher-order cognitive impairments and frontal lobe lesions in man. In: H.S. Levin, H.M. Eisenberg & A.L. Benton (Editors) *Frontal Lobe Function and Dysfunction*. Oxford: Oxford University Press, pp. 125–138.

Shankweiler, D., Libermann, I.Y., Mark, L.S., Fowler, C.A. & Fischer, F.W. (1979) The speech code and learning to read. *Journal of Experimental Psychology: Human Learning and Memory*, 5, 531–545.

Shaywitz, S.E., Shaywitz, B.A., Pugh, K.R., Fulbright, R.K., Constable, R.T. et al. (1998) Functional disruption in the organization of the brain for reading in dyslexia. *Proceedings of the National Academy of Sciences, USA*, 96, 2636–2641.

Siegel, L.S. (1992) An evaluation of the discrepancy definition of dyslexia. *Journal of Learning Disabilities*, 25, 618–629.

Snowling, M.J. (1995) Phonological processing and developmental dyslexia. *Journal of Research in Reading*, 18, 132–138.

Snowling, M.J. (1998) Dyslexia as a phonological deficit: Evidence and implications. *Child Psychology and Psychiatry Review*, 1, 4–11.

Snowling, M.J. (2000) *Dyslexia*. Second edition. Oxford: Blackwell.

Snowling, M. & Hulme, C. (1994) The development of phonological skills. *Philosophical Transactions of the Royal Society, London B*, 346, 21–27.

Snowling, M. & Nation, K. (1997) Language, phonology and learning to read. In C. Hulme & M. Snowling (Editors) *Dyslexia: Biology, Cognition and Intervention* (pp. 153–166). Gateshead, Tyne and Wear, UK: Athanaeum Press Ltd.

Snowling, M., Goulandris, N., Bowlby, M. & Howell, P. (1986) Segmentation and speech perception in relation to reading skill: a developmental analysis. *Journal of Experimental Child Psychology*, 41, 489–507.

Snowling, M., Wagtendonk, B. & Stafford, C. (1988) Object naming deficits in developmental dyslexia. *Journal of Research in Reading*, 11, 67–85.

Stackhouse, J. & Wells, B. (1997) Children's speech and literacy difficulties: the psycho-linguistic framework. London: Whurr.

Stanovich, K.E. (1998) Refining the phonological core deficit model. *Child Psychology and Psychiatry Review*, 1, 17–21.

Stein, J. & Walsh, V. (1997) To see but not to read: the magnocellular theory of dyslexia. *Trends in Neurosciences*, 20, 147–152.

Swan D. & Goswami, U. (1997) Picture naming deficits in developmental dyslexia: The phonological representations hypothesis. *Brain and Language*, 3, 334–353.

Tallal, P. (1980) Auditory temporal perception. phonics, and reading disabilities in children. *Brain and Language*, 9, 182–198.

Tallal, P., Stark, R., Kallman, C. & Mellits, D. (1981) A reexamination of some nonverbal perceptual abilities of language-impaired and normal children as a function of age and sensory modality. *Journal of Speech and Hearing Research*, 24, 351–357.

Tallal, P., Miller, S.L., Bedi, G., Byma, G., Wang, X. et al. (1996) Language comprehension in language-learning impaired children improved with acoustically modified speech. *Science*, 271, 81–84.

Thomson, M.E. (1999) Subtypes of dyslelxia: a teaching artefact? *Dyslexia: an International Journal for Research and Practice*, 5, 127–137.

Wagner, R.K. & Torgesen, J.K. (1987) The nature of phonological processing and its causal role in the acquisition of reading skills. *Psychological Bulletin*, 101, 192–212.

Wimmer, H., Landerl, K., Linortner, R. & Hummer, P. (1991) The relationship of phonemic awareness to reading acquisition: more consequence than precondition but still important. *Cognition*, 40, 219–249.

Wolf, M. (1991) Naming speed and reading: The contribution of the cognitive neurosciences. *Reading Research Quarterly*, 26, 123–140.

Wydell, T.N. & Butterworth, B. (1999) A case study of an English–Japanese bilingual with monolingual dyslexia. *Cognition*, 70, 273–305.

Chapter 4

THE PHONOLOGICAL REPRESENTATIONS HYPOTHESIS OF DYSLEXIA: FROM THEORY TO PRACTICE

Janet Hatcher and Margaret J. Snowling

INTRODUCTION

The most common explanation for dyslexia is that it stems from an underlying phonological deficit—a difficulty in processing the speech sounds of the native language (Snowling, 2000; Stanovich, 1994). Dyslexia is considered a specific disorder of development because phonological processing is selectively impaired in dyslexic people while other aspects of their language, for instance their vocabulary and grammatical skills, are normal (Goulandris et al., 2000). In this chapter we consider the "phonological representations hypothesis" of dyslexia and assess how well this hypothesis can account for the behaviour of dyslexic people (their signs and symptoms). We then discuss implications of the hypothesis for assessment and practice.

WHAT IS A PHONOLOGICAL REPRESENTATION?

It is commonplace for psychologists to use the term "representation", yet its meaning may be obscure to the teacher or practitioner. Representation is in fact an abstract concept. It refers to a kind of brain "image" or memory trace that captures the individual's knowledge and experience, perhaps of a particular task, an aspect of language or of an episode in their lives. During language acquisition, it is possible to imagine that the child gradually accumulates a store of knowledge about the attributes of words: their meanings, their sounds, how they are used in sentences

Dyslexia and Literacy: Theory and Practice. Edited by Gavin Reid and Janice Wearmouth.
© 2002 John Wiley & Sons, Ltd.

and the connotations they evoke for that individual. Arguably, knowledge of these attributes is organized in a system of representations that are activated during spoken word recognition and that have to be retrieved for the purpose of language production.

The language processing system that the child brings to the task of learning to read can be thought of as comprising different sub-systems. The phonological processing system (phonology) is concerned with how speech sounds are perceived, coded and produced. This is the system with which we will primarily be concerned in the present chapter because it is highly relevant for learning to read.

Typically, dyslexic children have been found to have difficulties that primarily affect the phonological domain of language processing. An extremely influential hypothesis in recent years has been that their difficulties can be traced to problems at the level of phonological representations (Fowler, 1991; Hulme & Snowling, 1992; Metsala, 1997; Swan & Goswami 1997a). But how should this difficulty be conceptualized? Snowling and Hulme (1994) suggested that children create phonological representations by mapping the speech they hear on to the speech they produce, and vice versa. Gradually over development, the specification of spoken words built up through this process becomes more and more detailed as the child's proficiency with speech increases.

Although the nature of the representational deficit in dyslexia is not yet well understood, a widely held view is that the detail in these representations is less well specified than in the phonological representations of normally developing children who do not have reading difficulties. A specific version of this hypothesis is that their representations are coarse-grained, perhaps coding rhyme-sized units (e.g. -oat; -ine), whereas the representations of normal readers are coded at the level of the individual speech sound or phoneme (e.g. -[o] [t]; [I] [n]).

What are the Signs of Difficulties at the Level of Phonological Representation?

The idea that the problems of dyslexic people can be traced to the way in which their brains code phonology was put forward as a way of integrating what were, on the face of it, disparate signs and symptoms of dyslexia. The most consistently reported phonological difficulties found in dyslexia are limitations of verbal short-term memory. These can be seen in the classroom as problems following instructions, memorizing lists, carrying numbers and in keeping up with dictation. It has been known for some years that the storage and maintenance of verbal information over short periods of time depends upon speech-based codes (see Hulme & Roodenrys, 1995, for a review). The problems of dyslexic people are, therefore, probably due to problems at the level of phonological representation. Interestingly, there is some evidence from brain-imaging studies, that the brain regions that are usually highly active in normal readers during short-term memory tasks, show lower levels of functional activation even in highly literate dyslexic readers (Paulesu et al., 1996).

There is also evidence that dyslexic children have trouble with long-term verbal learning. This problem may account for many classroom difficulties, including problems memorizing the days of the week or the months of the year, mastering multiplication tables and learning a foreign language. Perhaps connected to this long-term learning problem are difficulties with the retrieval of phonological information from long-term memory. Word-finding difficulties are often seen in children who in other respects have good oral vocabularies (Snowling et al., 1988).

Possibly most noticeable to teachers who work with individual dyslexic children are the problems they have with phonological awareness. Dyslexic children typically can perform as well as expected for their reading level on tests that require them to segment or manipulate the "larger" units of spoken words (syllables and rimes), but they have difficulty accessing "smaller" units or phonemes (Marshall et al., 2001; Swan & Goswami, 1997b). It seems likely that these basic deficiencies are strongly implicated in the reading and spelling problems that ensue from problems at the level of phonological representation. It is interesting to note here, however, that the persistent difficulties with phonological awareness associated with dyslexia are not a universal phenomenon. Rather, they appear to be specific to children learning to read in irregular or "deep" orthographies, such as English.

Why are Phonological Representations Important for Literacy Development, and What Goes Wrong in Dyslexia?

Studies of normal reading development offer a framework for considering the role of phonological representations in learning to read, and for understanding the problems of dyslexia. The task of learning to read in an alphabetic system entails learning to associate letters with their sounds, and reaching an understanding of how sounds can be put together to make words (blending). Conversely, learning to spell requires the child to be able to pull the sounds of spoken words apart (segmentation) and to associate the relevant letters (or spelling patterns) with them. At a fundamental level, therefore, learning to read requires the child to establish a set of mappings between the letters (graphemes) of printed words and the speech sounds (phonemes) of spoken words. These mappings between orthography and phonology need to be made at a fine-grained level to ensure that novel words that have not been seen before can be decoded.

The initial mappings between orthography and phonology are not just important in the early stages of learning to read but also provide a critical foundation for the development of more automatic reading skills and hence reading fluency. In English, they also provide a scaffold for learning multi-letter (e.g. ough, igh), morphemic (-tion, cian) and inconsistent (-ea) spelling–sound correspondences. Deficits at the level of phonological representation constrain the reading development of dyslexic children (Snowling, 1998). Thus, although dyslexic children can learn to read words they have been taught, they code the correspondences between the letters of these words and their pronunciations at a coarse-grained level (imagine chunks rather than grapheme–phoneme mappings). A consequence is that dyslexic children have difficulty generalizing this knowledge, and therefore one of the most robust signs of dyslexia is poor nonword reading (Rack et al., 1992). Since the semantic skills of dyslexic readers are, by definition, within the normal range, some dyslexic children can get around their decoding difficulties to some extent by relying on the semantic and syntactic facilitation that is offered by reading in context (Nation & Snowling, 1998). None the less, it is unusual for such a compensatory process to be able to get around the difficulty fully. Hence reading often remains slow, and the use of global reading strategies is not conducive to spelling which usually remains poor across the lifespan (Hatcher et al., 2002).

In short, learning to read is an interactive process to which the child brings all of his or her language skills. However, it is phonological processing that is most strongly related to the development of reading, and a deficit in phonological representation that is the source of most dyslexic problems in reading and spelling.

HOW CAN WE BE SURE THAT THE PHONOLOGICAL DEFICITS IN DYSLEXIA ARE A CAUSE RATHER THAN A CONSEQUENCE OF LITERACY PROBLEMS?

We have seen that the phonological representations hypothesis of dyslexia provides a good account of the range of behavioural symptoms of the disorder, and is compatible with theories of normal literacy development. However, it has been argued that literacy experience is crucial for the development of phonological awareness (Morais et al., 1979). Furthermore, there is some evidence that exposure to alphabetic literacy may have an effect on functional brain processes (Castro-Caldas et al., 1998). It follows that the phonological deficits that are marked among dyslexic readers of English may be a consequence, as much as a cause, of their failure to learn to read.

The best way to address this issue is to investigate the development of dyslexic children before they fail to read. The only way of doing this is to follow the progress of children at high risk of dyslexia before they go to school, and then to conduct retrospective analyses to assess the validity of the claims about causation. In a pioneering study of this type, Scarborough (1990) followed the development of children aged 2 to 7 years who were "at risk" of dyslexia by virtue of having a dyslexic parent. When the children were 7 years old and their reading skills could be assessed, they were classified as dyslexic or normal readers; it was then possible to compare, retrospectively, the pre-school data of children who went on to become dyslexic and of children who did not develop reading difficulties.

An important difference between the reading-disabled and normal reader groups lay in their early language skills. Although the dyslexic children used as large a range of vocabulary as their non-dyslexic counterparts at 2:6 years, they made more speech errors and their use of syntax was more limited. At 3 years, the dyslexic children had more difficulty with object naming and at 5, their difficulties extended to problems with phonological awareness. Their emerging literacy skills were also poorer; they were less familiar with the letters of the alphabet and worse at matching pictures with print.

In a study following Scarborough's approach, we have been exploring the early language precursors of dyslexia in a longitudinal study of children from 4 to 8 years at genetic risk by virtue of having a first-degree affected relative (Gallagher et al., 2000). Preliminary findings indicate that more than 60% of the high-risk group develop literacy problems. Children with significant reading impairments at 8 years showed slow speech and language development in the pre-school years and poorly developed phonological awareness shortly after school entry. Interestingly, at an early stage in literacy development, at the age of 6 years, both groups of high-risk children had poorer alphabetic knowledge than controls and were worse at decoding words and at spelling them phonetically. This difficulty applied equally to those who did not go on to develop reading problems as well as to those who did.

Whilst the pattern of poorly developed decoding skills was to be expected for the dyslexic children, it is intriguing that the unaffected children were also impaired in their use of "phonological" reading skills. These findings suggest that the inherited tendency in dyslexia may be a slowness in establishing mappings between orthography and phonology. It remains an issue whether these unaffected children will develop literacy problems at a later stage in their development.

CAN THE HYPOTHESIS ACCOUNT FOR INDIVIDUAL DIFFERENCES?

As we have seen, the phonological representations hypothesis suggests that children with dyslexia approach the task of learning to read with poorly specified phonological representations. As a result, they have difficulty in establishing the connections between the letter strings of printed words and the phonemic sequences of spoken words, and difficulty in generalizing this knowledge when they meet new words.

All children do not learn to read in the same way. Children approach the reading task differently because of varying combinations of cognitive skills and individual styles of processing. For example, one child may have severe phonological deficits but good visual memory skills, whilst another child may have weak phonological skills and slow speed of processing. These differing combinations of underlying skills mean that children will bring differing strengths and weaknesses to developing their literacy skills. Furthermore, in addition to these individual sets of problems, children may have varying accumulations of print knowledge and varying degrees of exposure to print. They may also have experienced differing forms of reading instruction.

Given these variations in children's reading processes and skills, can the phonological representations hypothesis account for these individual differences? The hypothesis applies well to those children who are referred to as developmental *phonological* dyslexics (Castles & Coltheart, 1993); they clearly have an impairment in the ability to establish mappings between letter strings and phonology. Phonological dyslexics have a limited sight vocabulary, great difficulties with word attack and phonic analysis and synthesis, and rely on a visual strategy for reading words. However, what about those dyslexic children who *can* use alphabetic skills in reading and spelling? These children have been referred to as developmental *surface* or *morphemic* dyslexics (Colheart et al., 1983, Seymour, 1986). In single-word reading, *surface* dyslexics can map from letters to sounds, though they may read slowly. However, they rely heavily on this phonic strategy, and as a result they often pronounce irregular words as though they were regular words.

Research indicates that it is in fact difficult to classify dyslexic children into subtypes, as there is always a substantial majority of the children who remain unclassified. More importantly, it cannot be assumed that, because developmental surface dyslexics have the ability to apply the alphabetic principle, they have no problem whatsoever with phonological processing. In studies by Manis et al. (1996) and Stanovich et al. (1997), surface dyslexics performed as well as reading-age controls on phonological awareness and phonological coding tasks, but their level of performance was still substantially below that of their chronological-age peers. Most dyslexic children do have some kind of phonological processing problem (Griffiths & Snowling, 2002).

Rather than different patterns of performance reflecting different types of dyslexia, it may be the severity of children's phonological difficulties that influences their developing reading and spelling profile. Snowling et al. (1994) reported a series of single-case studies comparing the phonological processing of children with different reading profiles. In general they found that it was the children with the more severe phonological processing impairments who showed the most significant impairments in their decoding skills and in their ability to spell phonetically. More recently, Griffiths and Snowling (2002) showed that phonological skills, as measured by verbal short-term memory, nonword repetition, phoneme deletion and the rate at which words could be articulated (speech rate), were significant predictors of nonword reading ability in a large group of dyslexic readers. In other words, those who did well on the phonological tasks were better at decoding than those who performed poorly.

The phonological representations hypothesis, therefore, provides a basis for accounting for individual differences in the way that children learn to read and spell. The severity and the extent of the phonological processing deficiencies determine the nature of the reading and spelling strategies available to the dyslexic child, and they dictate the course of reading and spelling development that the child follows. However, children will also have other strengths that they can draw on to support their reading behaviour, such as visual abilities and the use of meaning in text reading. It is therefore differences in the severity of phonological deficits, interacting with other cognitive skills and ameliorated by compensatory resources, that determine differences in children's reading and spelling behaviour.

HOW DO WE ASSESS PHONOLOGICAL REPRESENTATIONS?

The status of a child's representation of spoken words determines the ease or difficulty with which they learn to read. How then can we assess the quality of the phonological representations, to discover whether they are well specified, "fuzzy" or unspecified?

A major difficulty in attributing the problems of dyslexic people to the level of phonological representations is that such representations cannot be assessed directly. We can say or read a word such as *cat*, and know that it is made up of the three phonemes /c/, /a/, /t/ but we may find it difficult to describe the precise nature of the phonological representation of the sounds.

Nevertheless, several phonological processing tasks tap various aspects of underlying phonological representations. For example, phonological awareness tasks can measure whether or not specific sounds are represented, whilst production tasks are sensitive to whether phonological representations are accessible. There are complications, however, in that these tasks are not of equal level of difficulty. Some easier tasks can be completed by children before they have started reading, whilst others are only attainable by children once they have started the process of learning to read. Also, the tests always tap different underlying abilities. It is therefore important to have an understanding of the phonological level of the tasks, in order to present them appropriately and interpret them correctly.

Adams (1990) reviewed various phonological tasks and was able to identify at least five levels of difficulty:

- *Knowledge of nursery rhymes* involves only an ear for the sounds of words.
- *Awareness of rhyme and alliteration* requires both sensitivity to the sounds and an ability to focus on certain sounds.
- *Blending of phonemes and splitting of syllables to identify phonemes* demands an awareness that words can be subdivided into smaller sounds.
- *Phoneme segmentation* requires a thorough understanding that words can be analysed into a series of phonemes.
- *Phoneme manipulation* requires a child not only to understand and produce phonemes, but also to be able to manipulate them by addition, deletion or transposition.

The size of the unit tested (whether it be at the word, syllable, onset-rime or phoneme level) and the type of task set (an awareness, recognition or production task) are therefore important considerations.

Tasks that will Provide an Indication of a Child's Underlying Phonological Representations

Phonological Awareness Tasks
- Rhyme recognition and detection tests can assess the ability of a child to identify rhyme in words. For example, which picture goes with <u>bell</u>? ball; hen; shell
- The rhyme oddity task presents the child with a set of three or four spoken words and requires the child to identify which is the one that "does not belong". For example, sun; <u>rub</u>; fun; bun
- Alliteration tests assess the ability to isolate initial sounds in words. For example, which word has the same beginning sound as <u>sun</u>; sock; cow; chip

Phonological Production Tasks

- Rhyme production requires that the child understands the nature of rhyming words and is able to produce a rhyming word. For example, which words rhyme with play?
- Syllable blending requires the child to be able to assemble segments of words that have been presented to them. For example, which picture goes with [snow] – [man]; [win] – [dow]?
- Phoneme blending measures the child's ability to blend a sequence of sounds into words. For example, /d/ /o/ /g/; dog.
- In word completion tasks the child has to be able to isolate the final phoneme in order to be able to complete a partial word. For example, tab-[le]; fi-[sh].
- Phoneme segmentation assesses a child's ability to segment words into separate sounds. For example, sand; /s/ /a/ /n/ /d/.

Phonological Manipulation

Words can be manipulated by adding, deleting or transposing sounds. The phoneme deletion task assesses the child's ability to isolate a single phoneme, remove it from a word and thereby produce a new word, (e.g. 'mice' without the /m/ is 'ice'). The phoneme transposition test requires the child to isolate each phoneme in a word, and to reverse the order of those phonemes to produce a new word, (e.g. pat → tap, kiss → sick). The spoonerisms test assesses a child's ability to segment words and to synthesize the segments to produce a new word. For example, exchanging the beginning sounds of the words 'gold/coat' would become 'cold – goat'.

Access to Phonological Representations

Naming speed and fluency tests assess the speed of phonological production. This involves retrieval of phonological coding at the whole-word level. If an item is weakly represented it may be irretrievable, retrieved incorrectly or remain at the tip of the tongue. Short-term memory tasks are also sensitive to the accessibility of phonological representations.

Letter Knowledge

Children need to be able to connect their ability to segment words into sounds with their knowledge of letter names and sounds. It is therefore fundamental that letter knowledge is assessed and monitored.

A number of commercially produced assessment batteries are now available, which include a range of phonological-awareness and phonological-processing tests. The Phonological Assessment Test, *PAT* (Muter et al., 1997) is a standardized test that can be used with children between the ages of 4 and 7 years. It is useful as a screening measure, for identifying children at risk of reading difficulties. It can also be used diagnostically with older children experiencing reading difficulties, in order to assess the nature and extent of their phonological weaknesses.

The Phonological Assessment Battery, *PhAB* (Frederickson et al., 1997) is standardised for children aged 6 to 14:11 years. It is designed to assess phonological processing. It contains tests of phonological awareness, phonological production and speed.

The Sound Linkage Test of Phonological Awareness (Hatcher, 2000) includes tests of rhyme, sound blending, phoneme deletion and transposition. It can be used as a criterion-referenced test, and is also standardized to the end of Year 3. It can be used for identifying young children at risk of reading failure and those children whose reading delay may be attributable to limited phonological skills.

The choice of assessment tool used should be guided by the purpose of the assessment. Whatever that purpose is, the assessment should provide an opportunity for the analysis of a child's strengths and weaknesses in order to inform future teaching and learning.

WHAT DO WE NEED TO HAVE IN A TEACHING PROGRAMME TO ADDRESS DIFFICULTIES WITH PHONOLOGICAL REPRESENTATION?

We understand many of the elements of effective instruction for children who find it difficult to learn to read (Snowling, 1996; Torgesen et al., 2001). Teaching needs to be intensive and explicit and should provide systematic instruction in word-level skills appropriate to the stage of reading that the child has reached.

Obviously, older children in remediation programmes will require different learning tasks from beginning readers at risk of reading failure or younger children in early intervention programmes. However, all teachers of reading need to know about the basic building blocks of learning to read. Firstly, children need to develop grapheme knowledge. They must memorize the upper- and lower-letter case shapes and learn how these letters work. They must also develop phoneme knowledge by learning how, either singly or in combination, the letters symbolize the phonemes in words. Children need to be able to segment words into phonemes, and to do this they need to be aware of the invisible seams in flows of speech, and then to be able to analyse and manipulate the separate sounds. Harder still, they must then access both their grapheme and phoneme knowledge to "get inside" the phonological structure of words, so as to be able to attach the written spellings of words to their phonological representations. Later they will need to draw on their knowledge sources in memory, so that they can read and write multi-letter units and spelling patterns.

Understandably, those children who have been assessed as having poorly specified or degraded phonological representations are going to find these tasks difficult. Effective teaching therefore needs to combine structured teaching instruction with phonological training (Hatcher et al., 1994).

Phonological awareness training should follow the pattern of normal development, with activities aimed at extending the child's level of phonological skill.

- *Rhyme activities* require the child to discriminate between rhyming and non-rhyming pairs of words, or pick out the word that does not rhyme from a short

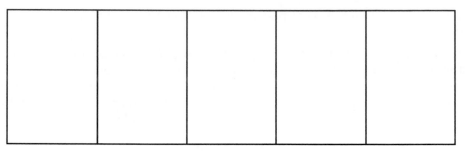

(a)

Figure 4.1a   Diagram of Boxes Used for Pushing Counters Whilst Segmenting Sentences or Words
Source: Sound Linkage (Hatcher, 2000)

list of spoken words. For example, encouraging the child to finish a simple verse: "I'll give you a clue, My colour is bl—".

- *Identifying words as units within sentences* can be achieved through activities such as pushing counters into a line of rectangles marked on a card (see Figure 4.1a), to coincide with the words in a simple spoken sentence, or matching (and saying) words to a simple written sentence, such as "The dog began to bark".
- *Onset–rime activities* might initially be organized around words with the same rime unit, such as *tin, pin, fin*, and involve splitting words orally into onset and rime and then making links with the written word.
- *Syllable awareness activities* progress from blending syllables into words (for example, *scare-crow* to *scarecrow, ex-ter-min-ate* to *exterminate*), to segmentation of words into syllables using counters, and manipulation of syllables within words (for example, deleting the word *bow* from *rainbow* to leave the word *rain*).

Phoneme awareness is a relatively advanced phonological skill, but is the facility required to be able to penetrate speech processes. Children need to be helped to become aware that words contain phonemes. However, some phoneme tasks are easier than others. It is usually easier to be able to identify or discriminate between phonemes in words, before the harder tasks of blending and segmentation. Children can also usually identify beginning sounds in words (for example, indicating which pictures have the same sound at the beginning, see Figure 4.1b) before the final or medial sound. In sound blending the child is asked to produce a word from a string of sounds, such as *p-i-n* or *c-l-o-w-n*. Early sound-blending tasks may require the child to choose the picture that shows the word that the teacher is trying to say, for example *boy* rather than *sea* when the teacher articulates *b-oy* (see Figure 4.1c). Phoneme segmentation can normally be accomplished at about the same time as the development of early reading skills. It requires the child to be aware of all the sounds in a word and to break the word up into its constituent sounds. For example, for the word *sack*, a child would say *s-a-ck* slowly whilst simultaneously pushing three counters into the boxes marked on the card, as illustrated in Figure 4.1a. More advanced phonemic work, like deletion, substitution and transposition, demands good phonological skills and develops later as reading skill increases.

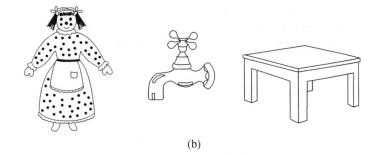

(b)

Figure 4.1b   Pictures for Discriminating Two of Three Words (*doll, tap, table*) with the Same Initial Sound.
Source: Sound Linkage (Hatcher, 2000)

It is insufficient to train phonological skills in isolation. It is important to establish links between sounds and the written forms of words. This can be done in a number of ways: using plastic letters, in writing activities (using boxes for sound segments or "stretching" a word to be able to hear its sounds), using letters as clues in text reading, and playing with words.

Programmes of specific activities to promote phonological awareness include *Sound Linkage* (Hatcher, 2000), *The Lindamood Phoneme Sequencing Program for Reading, Spelling and Speech* (Lindamood & Lindamood, 1998), *Sound Practice* (Layton et al., 1997), and *Earobics* (Cognitive Concepts, Inc., 1999).

Suggestions for phonological activities can be found in many teacher texts such as Townend and Turner (2000), *Active Literacy Kit* (Bramley, 1998), and *Jolly Phonics* (Wernham & Lloyd, 1993).

What Evidence is There That Such Programmes Work?

There is a good deal of evidence that the most effective teaching method for children who have poorly specified phonological representations is one which combines reading instruction with phonological awareness training. Whilst some intervention programmes have aimed to prevent reading failure, other studies have investigated how best to teach reading to children who have already failed.

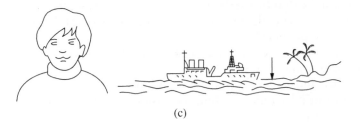

(c)

Figure 4.1c   Pictures for Blending of Sounds into Words
Source: Sound Linkage (Hatcher, 2000)

Lundberg et al. (1988) found that children who had received pre-school training in phonological awareness performed better in reading at school than an untrained group. Bradley and Bryant (1983) worked with 6-year-old children identified as at risk of reading failure. The children received two years of intervention. The two experimental groups who received training in sound categorization (phonological awareness) made more gains than the two control groups, one trained in semantic categorization and the other an unseen control. Of the two experimental groups the one that made the most significant progress was the group who had been taught letter–sound correspondences in the context of phonological training, rather than the one who had received phonological training alone.

In an intervention study for children who had already failed at learning to read Hatcher et al. (1994) found that the children who received a programme of Reading and Phonological Awareness training made the most progress in reading and spelling. The children who received only the phonological awareness training made gains in acquiring phonological skills, but did not make as much progress in learning to read or spell. Phonological training alone was therefore not as effective in promoting reading as the training that linked reading with phonology.

In order for readers to be able to make sense of text, however, a large proportion of words should be familiar and easily read. Reading text at the easy level (with at least 95% accuracy) provides children with the opportunity to practise newly acquired sight words in as many different contexts as possible, and helps to develop fluency and phrasing. On the other hand, whilst reading text at 90–94% accuracy children can be helped to learn new skills and to acquire strategies for reading unfamiliar words by decoding. A teaching programme should provide reading experiences at both levels. Children should also be encouraged to write; writing reinforces their ability to segment words and helps to develop their knowledge of the alphabetic system.

The Sound Linkage programme (Hatcher, 2000) is a highly structured reading programme with activities to promote and link phonological awareness to reading and writing. The programme provides a teaching framework within which a teacher can assess a child's strengths and weaknesses and monitor their progress through graded levels of text, writing and phonological-linkage activities. The sequence of activities in the programme is:

- Re-reading a familiar book, to consolidate reading strengths
- Reading a book introduced at the end of the previous session. During this section the teacher helps the child to work on one or two new skills or strategies, and monitors the "book level".
- Letter identification, if required, using a multi-sensory approach
- Phonological training activities
- Writing a story; the teacher supports the child in writing a short story, by helping the child to acquire an initial spelling vocabulary and write phonetically complete spellings of words
- Cutting up the story, where necessary, to consolidate one–one correspondence between spoken and written words
- Introduction to, reading and shared reading of a new book.

CONCLUSIONS

The phonological representations hypothesis provides a parsimonious account both of what needs to be in place for reading to develop and of why reading development goes wrong in dyslexia. It also accounts for a range of other symptoms that dyslexic people show across the lifespan. Moreover, since the theory makes predictions about why dyslexic children have difficulty learning to read, it therefore prescribes methods of assessment. An important corollary of the theory is that training in phonological skills should promote reading development. Whilst there is some support for this claim, and certainly boosting phonic skills helps children to read, there is a growing body of evidence that to read effectively, children must also use language skills beyond phonology. Moreover, interventions that rely exclusively on training in phonological awareness are less effective than those that combine phonological training with making connections between print and meaning, in the context of sentences in text.

REFERENCES

Adams, M. J. (1990). *Beginning to Read—Thinking and Learning about Print*. Cambridge, MA: MIT Press.

Bradley, L. & Bryant, P. E. (1983). Categorising sounds and learning to read—causal connection. *Nature, 301*, 419–421.

Bramley, W. (1998). *Active Literacy Kit; Essential Foundations for Literacy*. Cambridgeshire: LDA.

Castles, A. & Coltheart, M. (1993). Varieties of developmental dyslexia. *Cognition, 47*, 149 – 180.

Castro-Caldas, A., Petersson, K. M., Reis, A., Stone-Elander, S. & Ingvar, M. (1998). The illiterate brain. Learning to read and write during childhood influences the functional organization of the adult brain. *Brain, 121*, 1053–1064.

Cognitive Concepts Inc. (1999). *Earobics*.

Coltheart, M., Masterson, J., Byng, S., Prior, M. & Riddoch, J. (1983). Surface dyslexia. *Quarterly Journal of Experimental Psychology, 35*, 469–495.

Fowler, A. (1991). How early phonological development might set the stage for phoneme awareness. In S. A. Brady & D. P. Shankweiler (Eds.), *Phonological Processes in Literacy: A Tribute to Isabelle Liberman* (pp. 97–117). New Jersey: Erlbaum.

Frederickson, F., Frith, U. & Reason, R. (1997). *The Phonological Abilities Battery*. London: NFER-Nelson.

Gallagher, A., Frith, U. & Snowling, M. J. (2000). Precursors of literacy-delay among children at genetic risk of dyslexia. *Journal of Child Psychology and Psychiatry, 41*, 203–213.

Goulandris, N., Snowling, M. J. & Walker, I. (2000). Is dyslexia a form of specific language impairment? A comparison of dyslexic and language impaired children as adolescents. *Annals of Dyslexia, 50*, 103–120.

Griffiths, Y. M. & Snowling M. J. (2002). Predictors of exception word and nonword reading in dyslexic children: The severity hypothesis. *Journal of Educational Psychology, 94*, 34–43.

Hatcher, J., Snowling, M. J. & Griffiths, Y. M. (2002). Cognitive assessment of dyslexic students in higher education. *British Journal of Educational Psychology, 72*, 119–133.

Hatcher, P. J. (2000). *Sound Linkage* (Second Edition). London: Whurr.

Hatcher, P. J., Hulme, C. & Ellis, A. W. (1994). Ameliorating early reading failure by integrating the teaching of reading and phonological skills: The phonological linkage hypothesis. *Child Development, 65*, 41–57.

Hulme, C. & Roodenrys, S. (1995). Practitioner review: Verbal working memory development and its disorders. *Journal of Child Psychology & Psychiatry, 36*, 373–398.

Hulme, C. & Snowling, M. (1992). Deficits in output phonology: An explanation of reading failure? *Cognitive Neuropsychology, 9*, 47–72.

Layton, L., Deeny, K. and Upton, G. (1997). *Sound Practice; Phonological Awareness in the Classroom.* London: David Fulton.

Lindamood, P. & Lindamood, P. (1998). *The Lindamood Phoneme Sequencing Program for Reading, Spelling and Speech.* Austin, TX: PRO-ED.

Lundberg, I., Frost, J. & Petersen, O. (1988). Effects of an extensive program for stimulating phonological awareness in pre-school children. *Reading Research Quarterly, 23*, 263–384.

Manis, F. R., Seidenberg, M. S., Doi, L. M., McBride-Chang, C. & Petersen, A. (1996). On the bases of two subtypes of developmental dyslexia. *Cognition, 58(2)*, 157–195.

Marshall, C. M., Snowling, M. J. & Bailey, P. J. (2001). Rapid auditory processing and phonological processing in dyslexic and normal readers. *Journal of Speech, Hearing and Language Research, 44*, 925–940.

Metsala, J. L. (1997). Spoken word recognition in reading disabled children. *Journal of Educational Psychology, 89(1)*, 159–169.

Morais, J., Cary, L., Alegria, J. & Bertelson, P. (1979). Does awareness of speech as a sequence of phones arise spontaneously? *Cognition, 7*, 323–331.

Muter, V., Hulme, C. & Snowling, M. J. (1997) *The Phonological Abilities Test.* London: Psychological Corporation.

Nation, K. & Snowling, M. J. (1998). Individual differences in contextual facilitation: Evidence from dyslexia and poor reading comprehension. *Child Development, 69*, 996–1011.

Paulesu, E., Frith, U., Snowling, M., Gallagher, A., Morton, J., Frackowiak, F. S. J. & Frith, C. D. (1996). Is developmental dyslexia a disconnection syndrome? Evidence from PET scanning. *Brain, 119*, 143–157.

Rack, J. P., Snowling, M. J. & Olson, R. K. (1992). The non-word reading deficit in dyslexia: a review. *Reading Research Quarterly, 27*, 29–53.

Scarborough, H. S. (1990). Very early language deficits in dyslexic children. *Child Development, 61*, 1728–1743.

Seymour, P. H. K. (1986). *A Cognitive Analysis of Dyslexia.* London: Routledge.

Snowling, M. J. (1996). Annotation: Contemporary approaches to the teaching of reading. *Journal of Child Psychology and Psychiatry, 37(2)*, 139–148.

Snowling, M. J. (1998). Reading development and its difficulties. *Educational and Child Psychology, 15(2)*, 44–58.

Snowling, M. J. (2000). *Dyslexia* (Second Edition). Oxford: Blackwell.

Snowling, M. J. & Hulme, C. (1994). The development of phonological skills. *Philosophical Transactions of the Royal Society B, 346*, 21–28.

Snowling, M. J., van Wagtendonk, B. & Stafford, C. (1988). Object naming deficits in developmental dyslexia. *Journal of Research in Reading, 11*, 67–85.

Snowling, M. J., Goulandris, N., Bowlby, M. & Howell, P. (1986). Segmentation and speech perception in relation to reading skill: a developmental analysis. *Journal of Experimental Child Psychology, 41*, 489–507.

Snowling, M., Goulandris, N. & Stackhouse, J. (1994). Phonological constraints on learning to read: evidence from single-case studies of reading difficulty. In C. Hulme & M. Snowling (Eds.), *Reading Development and Dyslexia* (pp. 86–104). London: Whurr.

Stanovich, K. E. (1994). Does dyslexia exist? *Journal of Child Psychology and Psychiatry, 35(4)*, 579–595.

Stanovich, K. E., Siegel, L. S. & Gottardo, A. (1997). Progress in the search for dyslexia subtypes. In C. Hulme & M. Snowling (Eds.), *Dyslexia: Biology, Cognition and Intervention.* London: Whurr.

Swan, D. & Goswami, U. (1997a). Picture naming deficits in developmental dyslexia: The phonological representations hypothesis. *Brain and Language, 56*, 334–353.

Swan, D. & Goswami, U. (1997b). Phonological awareness deficits in developmental dyslexia and the phonological representations hypothesis. *Journal of Experimental Child Psychology, 60*, 334–353.

Torgesen, J. K., Alexander, A. W., Wagner, R. K., Rashotte, K. S. V. and Conway, T. (2001). Intensive remedial instruction for children with severe reading disabilities: Immediate and long-term outcomes from two instructional approaches. *Journal of Learning Disabilities*, *34(1)*, 33–58, 78.

Townend, J. & Turner, M. (Eds). (2000). *Dyslexia in Practice: A Guide for Teachers*. New York: Plenum.

Wernham, S. & Lloyd, S. (1993). *Jolly Phonics*. Chigwell, Essex: Jolly Learning.

Learning Resources Centre
Middlesbrough College
Dock Street
Middlesbrough
TS2 1AD

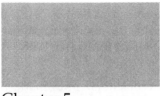

Chapter 5

VISUAL PROCESSES

John Everatt

INTRODUCTION

"Confuses b for d or vice versa"
"The letters go all blurry"
"I find it tiring to read for long periods of time"
"The words seem to move over each other"
"Is always looking out the window during lessons"

Teachers and other educational practitioners, researchers, even dyslexic people themselves have often cited examples such as the above statements when discussing experiences or phenomena related to dyslexia. Unsurprisingly, attempts to explain these particular perspectives on dyslexia have led theorists to consider one or more of the processes involved in vision as the underlying cause of such difficulties. The present chapter aims to provide a selective coverage of the theoretical viewpoints that have been derived from these perspectives. The chapter is divided into five areas. This is purely for ease of presentation, rather than to suggest any distinction between the views presented. Indeed, the reader will note that the classification combines theories that can be considered as quite distinct. Contrast Pavlidis (1990) and Stein et al. (1989), who are both subsumed under the area of eye movement deficits. In addition, some theoretical viewpoints cross several proposed categories: the recent grand theory of Stein (2001), for example, covers all five areas.

The following five sections will provide a selective coverage of the theories, evidence, and problems associated with each of the areas under consideration. The first area covers general visual recognition processes and will allow the chapter to start with a historical viewpoint of visual deficits as a cause of dyslexia. The theories subsumed within this section have often focused on visual memory in much the same way that phonological theories have considered phonological representations

Dyslexia and Literacy: Theory and Practice. Edited by Gavin Reid and Janice Wearmouth.
© 2002 John Wiley & Sons, Ltd.

as a cause of dyslexia. The argument proposed is that processes which access the representation of a letter or word, or the representations themselves, are inaccurate or faulty in some way, leading to difficulties identifying visual forms (see Willows et al., 1993).

From this general recognition viewpoint, the next section considers a more modern perspective on visual deficits. Theories considered in the second section argue that dyslexia-related problems are associated with a particular visual pathway which extends through the brain's visual systems. Differences between dyslexic and non-dyslexic people in how this pathway processes information lead to differences between these groups in tasks such as reading. The present chapter will focus on deficits in the processing of the transient (e.g. Lovegrove, 1996) or magnocellular (e.g. Stein, 2001) pathway, which a number of theorists now consider synonymous (for example, see discussion in Breitmeyer, 1993).

In the third section, another recent viewpoint is considered. This again argues for relatively specific recognition deficits, this time caused by over-sensitivity to light. Such an over-sensitivity is usually confined to certain wavelengths (or colours) of light and is sometimes referred to as Scotopic Sensitivity Syndrome (Irlen, 1991). The importance of this area is that it may be related to evidence presented for benefits of coloured filters, overlays or lenses (see Wilkins et al., 1994), a tool that has increasingly been incorporated into practitioners' remediation programmes and is said to alleviate reading problems. Although theories in this area are not well specified, they incorporate ideas associated with the magnocellular pathway deficit hypothesis and are therefore related to the views presented in the second section.

The next section is also related to the magnocellular pathway deficit viewpoints. This fourth section considers several different perspectives on the view that poor eye movement co-ordination or control is the underlying cause of poor reading skills amongst people with dyslexia (see Pavlidis, 1990; Stein et al., 1989). This view has been around for some time (e.g. Pavlidis, 1981) and has gained a revival with the magnocellular pathway deficits perspective (see Stein & Walsh, 1997). However, in each of their forms, eye movement deficit viewpoints have converted to arguing for a causal role of visual attention in reading difficulties, leading to the final area covered in the chapter. This is not surprising, given that movements of the eyes are considered connected to changes in visual/spatial attention (though see Underwood & Everatt, 1992) and attention has been viewed as vital for learning to read (Conners, 1990). As with eye movement hypotheses, visual attention deficit positions also have historical and modern counterparts (see Conners, 1990; Everatt, 1999) which in one case (Stein & Walsh, 1997) have led to a combination with the magnocellular pathway deficit hypothesis.

Prior to detailing the five proposed areas of deficits, the perspective of dyslexia from which they derive needs to be considered. The majority of visual deficit theories focus on explanations of reading difficulties. A large number of researchers working in these areas consider dyslexia synonymous with reading disabilities. Even if other features of dyslexia are studied, they may often be considered ancillary to the main task of identifying causes of, and supporting improvements in, reading difficulties. Similarly, when non-reading conditions are included in the research, they are usually incorporated as a method of assessing the accuracy of the predictions of the theory tested, rather than as a way of identifying problem areas for dyslexic individuals. Consequently, much of the present chapter will focus on studies of reading. It should be noted, however, that current theories are extending beyond the focus of reading (see Stein, 2001), although this extension usually requires the incorporation of additional areas of deficit beyond those of the purely visual and are outside the remit of the present chapter.

VISUAL RECOGNITION OR REPRESENTATION PROCESSES

Theories of reading impairment initially considered perceptual dysfunctions as being a major cause of reading problems (see, for example, the review of this area by Willows et al., 1993). This has a logical basis; if you cannot correctly perceive the text, you will not be able to read it. Indeed, one of the original investigators in the field, Morgan (1896), referred to specific deficits in reading as "word blindness". The argument also has a basis in the errors made by people with dyslexia, the most common cited being mirror-image or reversal errors, e.g. mistaking "b" for "d" or even "p"; writing "s" instead of "z"; reading "was" for "saw". One of the major visual-based explanations for such errors was provided by Orton in the 1920s/30s (Orton, 1937) who argued that the two hemispheres formed mirror-imaged representations of visual stimuli. In the non-dyslexic brain, the left hemisphere is dominant, leading to the correct representation of the letter/word being derived. However, in the dyslexic brain, the right hemisphere is dominant, leading to the image-reversed representation being processed. Because of increased understanding of the functions of the hemispheres that were incompatible with Orton's theory, this viewpoint has been rejected, although more recent theoretical perspectives have included aspects of Orton's ideas in their own causal explanations (see Geschwind, 1982).

This general visual recognition impairment viewpoint fell into disfavour in the 1970s and early 1980s. For example, in an authoritative review of individual differences in reading, Carr (1981) concluded that visual discrimination theories were "unique in that the factor supposed by many of them to underlie the entirety of dyslexia may not account for any of it" (page 75). Evidence for such a conclusion was derived from studies such as those of Mason and Katz (1976), who found that reading-disabled individuals could search for a shape in a set of other shapes as easily as good readers. Similarly, Ellis and Miles (1978) found that dyslexic subjects could match letters (i.e. "a a" are the same whereas "a b" are different) as easily as non-dyslexic controls. It was only when verbal correspondence was necessary ("A a" are the same, but "a B" are different) that the dyslexic group showed poorer performance than their non-dyslexic peers. These findings suggested that dyslexic people have the ability to search, locate, recognize and compare visual stimuli, and therefore cannot have a visual impairment of the sort outlined in theories such as Orton's. Evidence also indicated that reversal errors were common amongst non-dyslexic subjects, particularly beginning readers (see Vellutino et al.,

1972), which argues against this feature being a peculiarity of a dyslexia-specific trait.

As the emphasis moved away from recognition processes, it switched to consideration of the representations of visual forms in memory. Consistent with this possibility, dyslexic people show deficits compared to non-dyslexic individuals when required to name pictures or line drawings of familiar objects ("chair", "ball", etc.). However, the precise cause of these naming deficits is questionable, and may be due to phonological rather than visual representations in memory. A linguistic, rather than visual, interpretation is given credence by research such as that by Nelson and Warrington (1980) in which dyslexic subjects were found to differ from non-dyslexic controls only in those memory tasks involving linguistic coding of visual stimuli. We have found similar evidence in a series of tasks that involved the retention of sequences of visually presented stimuli (see Everatt et al., 1999b; Everatt et al., 2001). When linguistic labelling was required or enhanced performance (as in digit span tasks involving sets of visually presented digits), non-dyslexic subjects outperformed those with dyslexia. However, when phonological recoding was not important (as in tasks involving sequences of spatial locations indicated on a board or computer screen, or ordering previously presented abstract shapes), the dyslexic group performed at equivalent levels to the non-dyslexic group.

These findings suggest that people with dyslexia, in general, do not show evidence of deficits in the retention of visual-based information. However, data from single cases may indicate caveats to this conclusion. For example, Goulandris and Snowling (1991) discuss the case of a dyslexic university student with proficient letter–sound rules (i.e. they were able phonologically) but problems accessing lexical information potentially related to a visual memory deficit. This may be considered as a form of surface dyslexia, one of two subtypes of dyslexia (phonological versus surface) that are specifically based on the framework of the Dual Route Model of reading (see Castles & Coltheart, 1993). Whereas people with phonological dyslexia show evidence of deficits in recoding letters into sounds, those with surface dyslexia present evidence of being reliant on the relationships between letters and sounds. Hence individuals with surface dyslexia will show regularization errors (reading "pint" as though it rhymes with "mint"). This evidence has been used to argue that one route to reading/pronunciation involves the direct access of a word via its visual form. Visual deficits would obviously cause major problems for this process. However, studies that have directly associated any type of visual deficit with surface dyslexia are rare, and the rationale and procedures underlying the phonological/surface subtyping perspective have been criticized (see Manis et al., 1996; Stanovich et al., 1997; Zabell & Everatt, 2002).

Finally, in contrast to the above perspectives, visual memory processes have been identified by some theorists as mechanisms that can compensate for weak phonological skills (see Snowling, 2000). Other theorists have taken this a stage further and argued that visual-based talents are associated with dyslexia (see Aaron & Guillemord, 1993; West, 1991), although the evidence is inconclusive (see Everatt, 1997). Their use in compensatory strategies and their potential for enhanced skills makes *general* visual deficits unlikely as a basic feature of dyslexia.

MAGNOCELLULAR DEFICIT HYPOTHESIS

An alternative visual-based theory that has received recent research attention proposes that dyslexia may be the consequence of an abnormality in the neural pathways of the visual system. This pathway can be divided on anatomical bases into two streams, the parvocellular (P) and magnocellular (M) systems which, in turn, have been proposed as differentially sensitive to different types of stimuli; the parvocellular system seems to respond to slowly changing (low temporal frequency) information, to more detailed stimuli (i.e. higher spatial frequencies), and to colour, whereas the magnocellular system is more sensitive to gross (lower spatial frequency), rapidly changing (high temporal frequency) or moving information. Research has documented the poor performance of people with dyslexia on tasks assessing the functioning of the magnocellular pathway (see recent reviews in Chase, 1996; Hogben, 1997; Lovegrove, 1996), and conclusions from behavioural and psychophysical data have been given added credence by post-mortem studies (Livingstone et al., 1991) that have found abnormal cell size and organization in magnocellular layers of the visual system of individuals with documented reading disabilities.

The evidence for magnocellular pathway deficits has accumulated from several sources. For example, Lovegrove and colleagues (see Lovegrove, 1996, for a review) have consistently found longer visual persistence in reading-disabled compared to control subjects. Visual persistence is determined by varying the time gap between two visual stimuli to assess how long the gap has to be for an individual to be able to identify reliably gap from non-gap conditions. Basically, longer visual persistence means that dyslexic individuals require longer gaps. Similarly, it has been argued that dyslexic subjects have longer identification thresholds. Identification thresholds are based on tasks where subjects are required to identify a stimulus that is presented very quickly, followed immediately by a mask (the mask being some sort of random dot pattern, or a stimulus such as a hash, that should remove the stimulus from any short-term store). Thresholds are calculated by measuring how fast the item can be presented, yet still be identified. Reading-disabled individuals appear to require longer presentations to identify the item compared to control subjects (see Stanley & Hall, 1973; Williams et al., 1990). Both these phenomena relate to rapidly changing visual stimuli, implicating the processes of the magnocellular pathway.

Studies of dyslexic people's ability to process moving stimuli have provided the most consistent evidence for this theoretical position. Thresholds for the perception of coherent motion have been shown to be lower among dyslexic subjects than controls (Cornelissen et al., 1995; Everatt et al., 1999a). This task involves moving dots in which a proportion move coherently (i.e. in the same direction) while the remainder move randomly. A threshold is based on the smallest number of coherently moving dots that the individual can detect reliably. Additionally, functional magnetic resonance imaging (fMRI) data have indicated that dyslexic individuals present evidence of a lack of task-related activation in those areas of the cortex, V5/MT, hypothesized to be responsible for motion detection (Eden et al., 1996). Indeed, selective lesions of the magnocellular lateral geniculate nucleus (LGN) have been shown to result in a reduction of motion sensitivity in the cortical cells of area V5/MT (Maunsell et al., 1990).

However, not all dyslexic people present magnocellular pathway deficits, and some good readers (i.e. not dyslexic) show poor performance on tasks that have been used as evidence for the dyslexic person's magnocellular pathway deficits (see Hogben, 1997; Skottun, 2000). Additionally, Cornelissen et al. (1993) have argued that while abnormalities within the magnocellular LGN might well account for the observed visual deficits in dyslexia, such a conclusion becomes difficult to sustain at a cortical level where the strict anatomical and functional differentiation of the magnocellular and parvocellular streams becomes blurred. At this level, processes are typically mediated by input from both pathways. Our own data (see Bradshaw et al., 2001) are more consistent with this interactive viewpoint, rather than a strict magnocellular pathway deficit. Dyslexic and non-dyslexic adults were assessed on a motion-processing task (as in Cornelissen et al., 1993; Everatt et al., 1999a) in scotopic and photopic conditions. The former involves the perception of dim points of light in dark adaptation conditions, whereas the latter consists of the same task with brighter points of light in more normal lighting. Under these two conditions, the responses of magnocellular and parvocellular cells within the LGN are differentiated, with the magnocellular pathway being dominant under scotopic conditions and the visual cortex receiving input from both pathways under photopic conditions. As in the previous research using these tasks, in more normal photopic conditions, dyslexic subjects underperformed compared to the non-dyslexic controls—their motion processing was impaired. However, in scotopic conditions, which would be expected to enhance magnocellular pathway deficits, the groups did not differ. These findings suggest that differences between dyslexic and non-dyslexic individuals may only be evident when magnocellular and parvocellular pathways interact and are therefore inconsistent with a strong version of the magnocellular pathway deficit hypothesis that localizes deficits in visual processing purely within that pathway.

VISUAL SENSITIVITY AND COLOURED FILTERS

Another area of visual processing where magnocellular pathway deficits may play a vital role is in the processing of depth information. Despite evidence suggesting that few dyslexic people show deficits in this area (Everatt et al., 1999a), problems with processing depth have been associated with Scotopic Sensitivity Syndrome (Cotton & Evans, 1990), which has itself been considered as a feature of dyslexia and led to the use of visual filters to improve reading amongst those with dyslexia (Irlen, 1991). Research has suggested that visual filters (coloured lenses that are worn, or coloured overlays that are placed over the page, when reading) may be effective for alleviating (at least some) reading difficulties (see Wilkins et al., 1992; 1994). However, despite the research and practitioner evidence, the theoretical rationale for such visual filters requires specification. For example, the diagnosis of Scotopic Sensitivity Syndrome is controversial (see Lopez et al., 1994) and it is unclear what mechanism is responsible. Additionally, the practice of allowing dyslexic individuals to choose the filter that they feel improves their reading is open to placebo effects. Indeed, the one study that has attempted to control potential placebo effects (Wilkins et al., 1994) did not find reliable improvements in reading amongst the individuals provided with correct filters compared to a placebo filter. However, dramatic improvements have been claimed for this treatment and it is a pity that this is one of the weakest visual-based areas in terms of research and theory.

Interestingly, magnocellular pathway functioning may provide a theoretical frame-work for the use of coloured filters. For example, Breitmeyer and Williams (1990) present evidence that magnocellular pathway activity may be inhibited by red compared to white or green backgrounds. Also, in studies comparing red versus blue visual filters, and text presented on red versus blue screens, Williams and colleagues (see Lovegrove & Williams, 1993; Williams et al., 1992) found that reading-disabled subjects showed reduced performance in red conditions and better performance with blue. Similarly, in a study looking at the effectiveness of tinted glasses, Maclachlan et al. (1993) found that those dyslexic individuals continuing to wear tinted glasses appeared to prefer blue hues. These findings are consistent with the view that red decreases magnocellular pathway functioning, making things worse than they already are, while blue enhances magnocellular pathway activity, potentially alleviating the deficit. Although these findings are appealing, they are not in accord with the current practice of allowing dyslexic individuals to choose the coloured filter that best suits them. Under such procedures, they often select filters at the red end of the spectrum, which should reduce their reading ability.

EYE MOVEMENT CO-ORDINATION

Eye movements can be considered from two perspectives: (i) via measurements of eye movements themselves, referred to as *saccades*, which indicate the periods when the eyes are in motion across text, and (ii) via the period of time when the eyes are not in motion, but are fixed on a part of the text, referred to as a *fixation*. Evidence suggests that nearly all of the information about a scene is processed during fixations. Even gross changes of a scene that occur within the timespan of a saccade go unnoticed by the subject (see Latour, 1962). Therefore most research on text processing focuses on fixations. However, movements from one fixation to another are necessary; reading without eye movements is virtually impossible (see Rayner & Bertera, 1979).

The study of eye movements during reading has a long history, with research consistently indicating that reading-disabled individuals show erratic eye movement behaviours (Fischer & Weber, 1990; Just & Carpenter, 1987; Pavlidis, 1981; Rayner, 1986; Stanley, 1978). This is evident in both fixations and saccades: dyslexic individuals show more frequent and longer fixations, shorter saccades, and more frequent regressive saccades (eye movements from right-to-left back through a text). These findings have led to opinions that reading problems may stem from erratic eye movement behaviours (Pavlidis, 1981). There are, however, two problems with this view. Firstly, the severity of the reading problems shown by a particular dyslexic person may not be directly proportional to the abnormality of their eye movements. Some disabled readers do not diverge a great deal from normal patterns of eye movements, and yet show more severe reading impairment than other disabled readers whose eye movements patterns are less typical of normal readers (Rayner & Pollatsek, 1989). Second, even if the severity of dyslexia had a direct correspondence to eye movement abnormality, it does not mean that reading disability is caused by such behaviour. The main consensus is that reading dysfunctions produce abnormal eye movement behaviour as the individual tries to compensate for their reading problems. For example, long fixations on a word may simply indicate difficulties encoding or integrating the information fixated. Similarly, the abnormal eye movement behaviour (associated with some dyslexic subjects) of apparently moving in the opposite direction to normal reading (Pavlidis, 1981, has suggested that this might be a characteristic identifier of dyslexia) may not be due to problems with the saccadic system, but to the subject having to re-read parts of the text to aid integration of that text (see Kennedy, 1987). If eye movements are the cause of reading problems, then eye movement abnormalities should be apparent in contexts where reading is not required. However, the evidence is inconclusive; some studies have found evidence for abnormal eye movement patterns in dyslexic and reading-disabled subjects in non-reading tasks (Fischer & Weber, 1990; Lennerstrand et al., 1993; Pavlidis, 1981); others have not (Adler-Grinberg & Stark, 1978; Olson et al., 1983; Stanley et al., 1983). Obviously, there is a relationship between reading problems and non-typical eye movement patterns during reading, but whether poor eye movement control produces problems in reading, or problems in reading produce poor eye movement control, or whether both are caused by a third factor (such as attention) is still open to debate—see Pavlidis (1990).

An alternative eye movement control viewpoint has been proposed by Stein and colleagues. This started from a series of studies in which ocular dominance was measured under conditions in which the eyes were made to converge or diverge (see Stein et al., 1987; 1989). Most reading-able subjects tested under these conditions showed dominance in one eye across trials, whereas reading-disabled subjects showed alternating dominance between the left and right eye (though see Lennerstrand et al., 1993, for contradictory findings). This, Stein et al. (1989) argued, is related to an inability to converge or diverge the eyes, leading to the problem of the reading-disabled individual potentially "seeing double". In an intervention study, a group of reading-disabled children were given spectacles with a single lens covered with opaque tape that were to be worn during reading. Six months later half the children given the spectacles showed improvement both in vergence control and in reading, whereas control children, not given the spectacles, did not improve in either vergence control or reading ability. In explaining these findings, Stein et al. (1989) argued that the poor readers had an inappropriately functioning right hemisphere leading to responses analogous to a left-sided unilateral neglect (a condition associated with attentional difficulties—see Posner et al., 1984). Consistent with this latter argument, some 60% of the reading-disabled subjects tested by Stein et al. produced drawings of clocks with the left-hand side incomplete or incorrect in some way. Given that not all individuals presented these problems nor responded to treatment, Stein et al. argued that there are individuals with underlying phonological or linguistic problems which lead to reading problems, in addition to those with the identified visual deficits (though see Stein, 2001).

More recently Stein and Walsh (1997) have linked the eye movement control viewpoint with the magnocellular pathway deficit hypothesis, since the movements of the eyes may be controlled primarily by areas of the brain (such as the superior colliculus and the posterior parietal cortex) which receive input from the magnocellular pathway. Stein and Walsh (1997) suggest that impaired magnocellular pathway functioning might destabilize binocular fixation, given its dominant role in the control of eye movements. However, this theory requires further specification as it appears inconsistent with other research. Cornelissen et al. (1993) presented evidence that the magnitude of vergence errors made by a group of reading-able subjects was as large as those found amongst dyslexic subjects, and Everatt et al. (1999a) found poor vergence control to be rare amongst adults with dyslexia in a task that comprised the identification of images in random dot stereograms that required successive and precise convergence/divergence movements.

VISUAL ATTENTION

Fischer and Weber (1990) measured another feature of eye movement control, that of saccadic reaction time. In this study, subjects were required to fixate a central point and move their eyes to a target as quickly as possible when that target appeared. In certain trials, the subject was performing some attentional task at fixation, whereas on others they were simply waiting for the target. Fischer and Weber referred to the attentional system as being engaged and disengaged respectively during these two situations. They also argued that the attentional system has to be disengaged to allow a saccadic movement. Thus, if a target appears while in the engaged state, the time required to disengage the attentional system will increase the time taken to initiate a saccade. If the attentional system is already disengaged, then very fast saccadic movements (express saccades) will occur. Fischer and Weber argued that the number of express saccades an individual shows would be related to states of engaged and disengaged attention. In comparing dyslexic and control subjects' express saccades they found evidence that the former show larger numbers of express saccades, suggesting that dyslexic individuals show inappropriate handling of engaged/disengaged states and related insufficient eye movement control. Poor eye movement control is therefore produced by problems within the attentional system, which may lead to poor reading performance.

Although Fischer and Weber's findings are not without criticism (see Klein & D'Entremont, 1999), they suggest a relationship between reading difficulties and poor attentional control which has been proposed many times before. However, the most extreme view, that dyslexia is simply an attentional disorder, such as attention deficit hyperactivity disorder (ADHD), is incorrect. Research has identified individuals with the symptomatology of attention deficit disorder who do not show evidence of reading problems and, similarly, individuals with reading difficulties with no evidence of attentional deficit disorder (Ackerman & Dykman,

1990; Denckla et al., 1985; Dykman & Ackerman, 1991; Pennington et al., 1993; Shaywitz et al., 1994). Thus attentional problems (as diagnosed by measures of attentional deficit disorders) and reading problems (as a major characteristic of dyslexia) do not have a direct correspondence. In contrast, it is often difficult to find dyslexic subjects who do not show some symptomatology of attention deficit disorder (Dykman & Ackerman, 1991; Dykman et al., 1985). Similarly, research undertaken expressly to seek out attentional problems in individuals with reading problems has found that they are more susceptible to visual distracter stimuli within various tasks (Copeland & Wisniewski, 1981; Denney, 1974; Everatt et al., 1997; Hallahan et al., 1973; Lazarus et al., 1984; Pelham & Ross, 1977; Sabatino & Ysseldyke, 1972). For example, compared to control subjects, there is evidence for increased Stroop interference in learning-disabled (Lazarus et al., 1984), reading-disabled (Das, 1993) and dyslexic (Everatt et al., 1997) subjects. The Stroop effect (Stroop, 1935; see review by MacLeod, 1991) occurs when the subject is required to name the colour of the ink in which a colour word is printed (the word "red" written in blue ink, for example). In comparison to a neutral condition (a coloured rectangle is often used), the colour word slows down (i.e. interferes with) the naming of the ink colour. Given that the Stroop task measures the extent to which we can focus attention to one aspect of a stimulus (the colour) and ignore another (the word), this is consistent with dyslexic subjects presenting poorer focusing of attention.

The problem with interpretations that focus on attentional processes as the basis of dyslexia-related difficulties (as in the majority of eye movement theories: Fischer & Weber, 1990; Pavlidis, 1990; Stein & Walsh, 1997) is the lack of specification of the term "attention". This has been used to refer to a multitude of potentially disparate processes, from spatial selection and response inhibition, to executive control and resource allocation, to conscious and sustained effort, each of which has been used in theories discussing the basis of dyslexia (see Everatt, 1999). Additionally, references to attention do not dispel problems of assigning cause and effect associated with eye movement theories. Reading difficulties could lead to poor attention as much as a lack of attention might lead to poor reading skill. For example, Everatt et al. (1997) found increased Stroop interference amongst dyslexic subjects compared to chronological age-matched controls, but not compared to reading age-matched controls. Interference (argued as indicative of poor attention) was consistent with levels of reading experience.

CONCLUSION

This chapter has briefly reviewed theories and findings relating visual-based deficits and dyslexia. It has also covered the problems associated with these perspectives. Since these need to be addressed before any one theory can be considered complete, it is worth reiterating them in the conclusion:

1. The first difficulty for this area of work is the very diversity of visual deficits identified and varying explanations for them. We need to clarify between these different effects and specify whether the visual-based difficulties derive from

the same underlying cause. The magnocellular theories are the most appealing in this respect.

2. There is often a lack of specification of the way in which visual deficits cause dyslexia difficulties. Visual sensitivity theories are difficult to assess due to their lack of specification and eye movement/attention deficits, in particular, could easily be consequences rather than explanations of reading problems.

3. We also need to consider the evidence for potential positive or compensatory abilities that do not seem compatible with the general ethos of the visual deficits explanation—though see Stein (2001).

4. Not all of those diagnosed as dyslexic (and showing the usual characteristics of dyslexia) present visual deficits—theories need to consider how to accommodate these individuals.

5. Some non-dyslexic individuals present evidence of visual deficits analogous to those which are indicative of the dyslexia causal process—again, theories need to specify how this can happen in their causal pathways.

REFERENCES

Aaron, PG & Guillemord, J-C (1993). Artists as dyslexics. In DM Willows, RS Kruk & E Corcos (Eds), *Visual Processes in Reading and Reading Disabilities*. Hillsdale, NJ: Erlbaum.

Ackerman, PT & Dykman, RA (1990). ADD students with and without dyslexia differ in sensitivity to rhyme and alliteration. *Journal of Learning Disabilities*, 23, 279–283.

Adler-Grinberg, D & Stark, L (1978). Eye movements, scan paths, and dyslexia. *American Journal of Optometry and Physiological Optics*, 55, 557–570.

Bradshaw, MF, Hibbard, PB & Everatt, J (2001)."Interactions between processing streams revealed by performance of dyslexics and non-dyslexics on stereo and motion tasks under scotopic conditions". Paper presented to the British Dyslexia Association International Conference *Dyslexia: At the Dawn of the New Century*, University of York, UK, 18–21 April 2001. (Article in preparation.)

Breitmeyer, BG (1993). Sustained (P) and transient (M) channels in vision: A review and implications for reading. In DM Willows, RS Kruk, & E Corcos (Eds), *Visual Processes in Reading and Reading Disabilities*. Hillsdale, NJ: Erlbaum.

Breitmeyer, BG & Williams, MC (1990). Effects of isoluminant-background color on meta-contrast and stroboscopic motion: Interactions between sustained and transient channels. *Vision Research*, 30, 1069–1075.

Carr, TH (1981). Building theories of reading ability: On the relation between individual differences in cognitive skills and reading comprehension. *Cognition*, 9, 73–114.

Castles, A & Coltheart, M (1993). Varieties of developmental dyslexia. *Cognition*, 47, 149–180.

Chase, CH (1996). A visual deficit model of developmental dyslexia. In CH Chase, GD Rosen & GF Sherman (Eds), *Developmental Dyslexia: Neural, Cognitive and Genetic Mechanisms*. Baltimore, MD: York Press.

Conners, CK (1990). Dyslexia and the neurophysiology of attention. In GTh Pavlidis (Ed), *Perspectives on Dyslexia*, Vol. 1. Chichester: Wiley.

Copeland, AP & Wisniewski, NM (1981). Learning disability and hyperactivity: Deficits in selective attention. *Journal of Experimental Child Psychology*, 32, 88–101.

Cornelissen, P, Munro, N, Fowler, S & Stein, J (1993). The stability of binocular fixation during reading in adults and children. *Developmental Medicine and Child Neurology*, 35, 777–787.

Cornelissen, P, Richardson, A, Mason, A, Fowler, S & Stein, J (1995). Contrast sensitivity and coherent motion detection measured at photopic luminance levels in dyslexics and controls. *Vision Research*, 35, 1483–1494.

Cotton, MM & Evans, KM (1990). An evaluation of the Irlen Lenses as a treatment for specific reading disorders. *Australian Journal of Psychology*, 42, 1–12.

Das, JP (1993). Differences in cognitive processes of children with reading disabilities and normal readers. *Developmental Disabilities Bulletin*, 21, 46–62.

Denckla, MB, Rudel, R, Chapman, C & Krieger, J (1985). Motor proficiency in dyslexic children with and without attentional disorders. *Archives of Neurology*, 42, 228–231.

Denney, DR (1974). Relationship of three cognitive style dimensions to elementary reading abilities. *Journal of Educational Psychology*, 66, 702–709.

Dykman, RA & Ackerman, PT (1991). Attention deficit disorder and specific reading disability: Separate but often overlapping disorders. *Journal of Learning Disabilities*, 24, 96–103.

Dykman, RA, Ackerman, PT & Holcomb, PJ (1985). Reading disabled and ADD children: Similarities and differences. In DB Gray & JF Kavanagh (Eds), *Biobehavioral Measures of Dyslexia*. Maryland: York Press.

Eden, GF, VanMeter, JW, Rumsey, JM, Maisog, JM, Woods, RP, & Zeffiro, TA (1996). Abnormal processing of visual motion in dyslexia revealed by functional brain imaging. *Nature*, 382, 66–69.

Ellis, NC & Miles, TR (1978). Visual information processing in dyslexic children. In MM Gruneberg, PE Morris & RN Sykes (Eds), *Practical Aspects of Memory*. London: Academic Press.

Everatt, J (1997). The abilities and disabilities associated with adult developmental dyslexia. *Journal of Research in Reading*, 20, 13–21.

Everatt, J (Ed), (1999). *Reading and Dyslexia: Visual and Attentional Processes*. London: Routledge.

Everatt, J, Warner, J, Miles, TR, & Thomson, ME (1997). The incidence of Stroop interference in dyslexia. *Dyslexia: An International Journal of Research and Practice*, 3, 222–228.

Everatt, J, Bradshaw, MF & Hibbard, PB (1999a). Visual processing and dyslexia. *Perception*, 28, 243–254.

Everatt, J, McNamara, S, Groeger, JA & Bradshaw, MF (1999b). Motor aspects of dyslexia. In J Everatt (Ed). *Reading and Dyslexia: Visual and Attentional Processes*. London: Routledge.

Everatt, J, Groeger, J, Smythe, I, Baalam, S, Richardson, J & McNamara, S (2001). Dyslexia and deficits in short-term memory: phonological versus sequential explanations. Paper presented to the British Dyslexia Association International Conference *Dyslexia: At the Dawn of the New Century*, University of York, UK, 18–21 April 2001. (Article in preparation.)

Fischer, B & Weber, H (1990). Saccadic reaction times of dyslexic and age-matched normal subjects. *Perception*, 19, 805–818.

Geschwind, N (1982). Why Orton was right. *Annals of Dyslexia*, 32, 12–30.

Goulandris, N & Snowling, M (1991). Visual memory deficits: A plausible cause of developmental dyslexia. *Cognitive Neuropsychology*, 8, 127–154.

Hallahan, DP, Kauffman, JM & Ball, DW (1973). Selective attention and cognitive tempo of low achieving and high achieving sixth grade males. *Perceptual & Motor Skills*, 36, 579–583.

Hogben, JH (1997). How does a visual transient deficit affect reading?. In C Hulme & M Snowling (Eds), *Dyslexia: Biology, Cognition and Intervention*. London: Whurr.

Irlen, H (1991). *Reading by the Colours*. New York: Avery.

Just, MA & Carpenter, PA (1987). *The Psychology of Reading and Language Comprehension*. Boston: Allyn and Bacon.

Kennedy, A (1987). Eye movements, reading skill and the spatial code. In J Beech & A Colley (Eds), *Cognitive Approaches to Reading*. Chichester: Wiley.

Klein, RM & D'Entremont, B (1999). Filtering performance by good and poor readers. In J Everatt (Ed). *Reading and Dyslexia: Visual and Attentional Processes*. London: Routledge.

Latour, PL (1962). Visual threshold during eye movements. *Vision Research*, 2, 261–262.

Lazarus, PJ, Ludwig, RP & Aberson, B (1984). Stroop color-word test: A screening measure of selective attention to differentiate LD from non LD children. *Psychology in the Schools*, 21, 53–60.

Lennerstrand, G, Ygge, J & Jacobsson, C (1993). Control of binocular eye movements in normals and dyslexics. *Annals of the New York Academy of Science*, 682, 231–239.

Livingstone, MS, Rosen, GD, Drislane, FW & Galaburda, AM (1991). Physiological and anatomical evidence for a magnocellular defect in developmental dyslexia. *Proceedings of the National Academy of Science of the USA*, 88, 7943–7947.

Lopez, R, Yolton, RL, Kohl, P, Smith, DL & Sexerud, MH (1994). Comparison of Irlen Scotopic Sensitivity Syndrome test results to academic and visual performance data. *Journal of the American Optometric Association*, 65, 705–713.

Lovegrove, WJ (1996). Dyslexia and a transient/magnocellular pathway deficit: The current situation and future directions. *Australian Journal of Psychology*, 48, 167–171.

Lovegrove, WJ & Williams, MC (1993). Visual temporal processing deficits in specific reading disability. In DM Willows, RS Kruk & E Corcos (Eds), *Visual Processes in Reading and Reading Disabilities*. Hillsdale, NJ: Erlbaum.

Maclachlan, A, Yale, S & Wilkins, AJ (1993). Open trials of precision ophthalmic tinting: one-year follow-up of 55 patients. *Ophthalmic and Physiological Optics*, 13, 175–178.

MacLeod, CM (1991). Half a century of research on the Stroop effect: An integrative review. *Psychological Bulletin*, 109, 163–203.

Manis, FR, Seidenberg, MS, Doi, LM, McBride-Chang, C & Petersen, A. (1996). On the bases of two subtypes of developmental dyslexia. *Cognition*, 58, 157–195.

Mason, M & Katz, L (1976). Visual processing of nonlinguistic strings: Redundancy effects and reading disability. *Journal of Experimental Psychology: General*, 105, 338–348.

Morgan, WP (1896). Word blindness. *British Medical Journal*, 2, 1378–1379.

Nelson, HE & Warrington, EK (1980). An investigation of memory functions in dyslexic children. *British Journal of Psychology*, 71, 487–503.

Olson, RK, Kliegl, R & Davidson, BJ (1983). Dyslexic and normal readers' eye movements. *Journal of Experimental Psychology: Human Perception and Performance*, 9, 816–825.

Orton, ST (1937). *Reading, Writing and Speech Problems in Children*. New York: Norton.

Pavlidis GTh (1981). Sequencing, eye movements and the early objective diagnosis of dyslexia. In GTh Pavlidis & TR Miles (Eds), *Dyslexia Research and its Applications to Education*. London: Wiley.

Pavlidis GTh (Ed) (1990). *Perspectives on Dyslexia. Volume 1: Neurology, Neuropsychology and Genetics*. Chichester: Wiley.

Pelham, WE & Ross, AO (1977). Selective attention in children with reading problems: A development study of incidental learning. *Journal of Abnormal Child Psychology*, 5, 1–8.

Pennington, BF, Groisser, D & Welsh, MC (1993). Contrasting cognitive deficits in attention deficit hyperactivity disorder versus reading disability. *Developmental Psychology*, 29, 511–523.

Posner, MI, Walker, JA, Friedrick, FJ & Rafal, RD (1984). Effects of parietal injury on covert orienting of visual attention. *Journal of Neuroscience*, 4, 1863–1874.

Rayner, K (1986). Eye movements and the perceptual span: Evidence for dyslexic topology. In GTh Pavlidis & DF Fisher (Eds), *Dyslexia: Its Neuropsychology and Treatment*. New York: Wiley.

Rayner, K & Bertera, JH (1979). Reading without a fovea. *Science*, 206, 468–469.

Rayner, K & Pollatsek, A (1989). *The Psychology of Reading*. Englewood Cliffs, NJ: Prentice-Hall.

Sabatino, DA & Ysseldyke, JE (1972). Effect of extraneous "background" on visual-perceptual performance of readers and non-readers. *Perceptual and Motor Skills*, 35, 323–328.

Skottun, BC (2000). On the conflicting support for the magnocellular deficit theory of dyslexia. *Trends in Cognitive Sciences*, 4, 211–212.

Shaywitz, BA, Fletcher, JM & Shaywitz, SE (1994). Interrelationships between reading disability and attention deficit-hyperactivity disorder. In AJ Capute, PJ Accardo & BK Shapiro (Eds), *Learning Disabilities Spectrum: ADD, ADHA, and LD*. Baltimore, MD: York Press.

Snowling, MJ (2000). *Dyslexia*, Second Edition. Oxford: Blackwell.

Stanley, G (1978). Eye movements in dyslexic children. In G Stanley & KW Walsh (Eds), *Brain Impairment: Proceedings of the 1977 Brain Impairment Workshop*. Victoria, Vic.: University of Melbourne/Dominion Press.

Stanley, G & Hall, R (1973). Short-term visual information processing in dyslexics. *Child Development*, 44, 841–844.

Stanley, G, Smith, GA & Howell, EA (1983). Eye movements and sequential tracking in dyslexic and control children. *British Journal of Psychology*, 74, 181–187.

Stanovich, KE, Siegel, LS & Gottardo, A (1997). Progress in the search for dyslexia subtypes. In C Hulme and M Snowling (Eds), *Dyslexia: Biology, Cognition and Intervention*. London: Whurr.

Stein, JF (2001). The magnocellular theory of developmental dyslexia. *Dyslexia: An International Journal of Research and Practice*, 7, 12–36.

Stein, J & Walsh, V (1997). To see but not to read: The magnocellular theory of dyslexia. *Trends in Neuroscience*, 20, 147–152.

Stein, JF, Riddell, P & Fowler, MS (1987). Fine binocular control in dyslexic children. *Eye*, 1, 433–438.

Stein, JF, Riddell, P & Fowler, MS (1989). Disordered right hemisphere function in developmental dyslexia. In C von Euler, I Lundberg & G Lennerstrand (Eds), *Brain and Reading*. New York: Stockton Press.

Stroop, JR (1935). Studies of interference in serial verbal reactions. *Journal of Experimental Psychology*, 18, 643–662.

Underwood, G & Everatt, J (1992). The role of eye movements in reading. In E Chekaluk & KR Llewellyn (Eds), *The Role of Eye Movements in Perceptual Processes*. North-Holland: Elsevier Scientific Publishers.

Vellutino, FR, Steger, J & Kendal, G (1972). Reading disability: An investigation of the perceptual deficit hypothesis. *Cortex*, 8, 106–118.

West, TG (1991). *In the Mind's Eye*. Buffalo, NY: Prometheus.

Wilkins, A.J., Milroy, R., Nimmo-Smith, I., Wright, A., Tyrrell, R., Holland, K., Martin, J., Bald, J., Yale, S., Miles, T., & Noakes, T. (1992). Preliminary observations concerning treatment of visual discomfort and associated perceptual distortion. *Ophthalmic and Physiological Optics*, 12, 257–263.

Wilkins, AJ, Evans, BJW, Brown, JA, Busby, AE, Wingfield, AE, Jeanes, RJ & Bald, J (1994). Double-masked placebo-controlled trial of precision spectral filters in children who use coloured overlays. *Ophthalmic and Physiological Optics*, 14, 365–370.

Williams, MC, LeCluyse, K & Bologna, N (1990). Masking by light as a measure of visual integration time and persistence in normal and disabled readers. *Clinical Visual Science*, 5, 335–343.

Williams, MC, LeCluyse, K & Faucheux, AR (1992). Effective interventions for reading disability. *Journal of the American Optometric Association*, 63, 411–417.

Willows, DM, Kruk, RS & Corcos, E (Eds) (1993). *Visual Processes in Reading and Reading Disabilities*. Hillsdale, NJ: Erlbaum.

Zabell, C & Everatt, J (2002). Surface and phonological subtypes of adult developmental dyslexia. *Dyslexia: An International Journal of Research and Practice*, 8, 1–18.

Chapter 6

THE BALANCE MODEL OF READING AND DYSLEXIA

Jean Robertson and Dirk J. Bakker

The balance model of reading was first introduced some 30 years ago, in a period that showed prevalence of neuropsychological research into the lateral representation of functions in the brain. It was generally accepted already that language, both spoken and printed, is mediated by the left cerebral hemisphere and visual-spatial perception by the right cerebral hemisphere. However, it soon became apparent that the division of these functions does not run completely parallel with the left–right division in the brain. The prosody of spoken language, for example, appeared to show dependency on the right, rather than the left cerebral hemisphere, and text, when printed in an exotic fashion with adornment of the letters, proved to be primary matter for the right, not for the left hemisphere (Faglioni et al., 1969). Moreover, it is well established now that hemispheric side of language mediation is largely dependent on the age of language acquisition. This is illustrated by the case of immigrants who had mastered English as their second language. When this had happened early in life (age 1–3 years), the use of English later on appeared largely mediated by the left hemisphere, whereas the mediation appeared to be a matter for both hemispheres when mastering English had commenced at ages over 6 years (Barinaga, 2000; referring to the research of H. Neville).

THEORY

Learning to Read

The letter shapes that make up a text must be very puzzling for a novice reader as a number of learned strategies in the processing of forms are of little help when it comes to the processing of letters. A few examples may clarify the kind of difficulties

Dyslexia and Literacy: Theory and Practice. Edited by Gavin Reid and Janice Wearmouth.
© 2002 John Wiley & Sons, Ltd.

encountered. First, a letter printed upside down may have a different meaning from the same letter printed normally (*p* versus *d* /*m* versus *w*), whereas the shape of an apple always denotes an apple, irrespective of its position in space. Second, a letter may have different shapes and nevertheless be the same letter (*d* and *D*), but the forms of an apple and a pear refer to different objects. In view of these and other perceptual novelties the beginning reader is faced with, the balance model holds that early reading requires a lion's share of the right hemisphere in the processing of text (Bakker, 1979; 1990; 2002). Evidence is available in support of this assertion (e.g. De Graaff, 1995).

In view of the perceptual complexities encountered, it cannot be a surprise that the beginning reader usually reads slowly. The ultimate aim, though, is fluency of reading. At least two developments will facilitate fluency. First, the perceptual analysis of text features becomes an automatism and sinks below the level of consciousness (Fries, 1963). Second, the child gets more and more acquainted with syntactical rules, while at the same time the child's lexicon grows. As a result the child will not read letter by letter or syllable by syllable any more, but rather process large parts of a sentence in one act. The balance model holds that reading, guided by syntactical rules and linguistic experience, is predominantly mediated by the left cerebral hemisphere. The outcomes of a number of investigations are in support of this assertion (e.g. Goldberg & Costa, 1981).

Thus, in the normal case, early and advanced reading will predominantly be mediated by the right and left hemisphere, respectively (Licht et al., 1988; Waldie & Mosley, 2000).

DEVELOPMENTAL DYSLEXIA

Since the introduction of the balance model it was thought possible that some children may not be able to shift from right to left in the hemispheric mediation of reading. In a sense these children remain beginning readers in that they read slowly and in a fragmented fashion. They presumably stick to the perceptual features of text, in view of which they are classified as P-type dyslexic children (P for *perceptual*). It was also thought possible that some other children shift to left-hemispheric processing of text (much) too early. One can imagine how such children try to manage text: they read fast but, because they tend to overlook the perceptual features, they make many errors. In view of their efforts to use *linguistic* strategies these children were classified as L-type dyslexics. There certainly are dyslexic children who read slowly while producing many errors; these subjects have been denoted M-types (Masutto et al., 1994; Robertson, 2000).

Research has been devoted to the question of whether P- versus L-dyslexia does exist in reality: the validity question (Fabbro et al., 2001). The results of investigations do indicate that subjects with P- and L-dyslexia differ with regard to the lateral distribution of hemispheric activity elicited by words flashed in the central visual field, that is, in the field normally used to read a text (Bakker, 1986). The groups

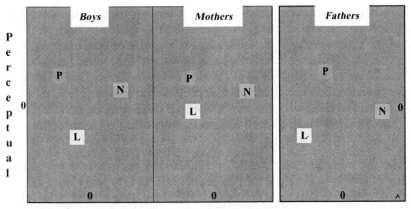

Figure 6.1 Positions of dyslexic (P and L) and normal (N) boys and their biological parents in a perceptual versus verbal–lingual factor space (after Van Strien et al., 1990)

also differ with regard to the speed of processing of reading-related information. P-types, for instance, are faster than L-types in deciding whether all letters in an array are the same or different, but P-types are slower than L-types when it comes to the question of whether a word is real or not (Licht, 1994). L-types, as recently demonstrated in another study (Van der Schoot et al., 2000) are less successful than P-types in the inhibition of an already initiated response, a finding which suggests that L-types share some of the difficulties suffered by ADHD children.

Finally, a most interesting study (Van Strien et al., 1990) included P- and L-dyslexic boys, normally reading boys, and the biological parents of all participating boys. They were administered a battery of cognitive tests which loaded on a verbal and a perceptual factor. The mean factor values are rendered in Figure 6.1.

The normally reading boys and their parents perform better verbally than the dyslexic boys and their parents. With the validity question in the back of one's mind, though, it is of particular importance to find that the P-dyslexic boys, as well as their fathers, perceptually outperform the L-dyslexic boys and their fathers (the P versus L difference is not significant for the mothers).

The outcomes of these and other investigations warrant the conclusion that the P/L classification of developmental dyslexia shows sufficient validity.

NEUROPSYCHOLOGICAL TREATMENT

As there is overwhelming evidence now that the brain is able to change capacities according to stimulation from the learning environment (Rosenzweig et al., 1972; Castro-Caldas et al., 1998; Eisenberg, 1995), one might think of stimulating the left cerebral hemisphere to improve the reading of P-dyslexic children and of stimulating the right hemisphere to improve the reading of L-dyslexic children. The balance model holds that P-dyslexic children, while learning to read, took the role of the left hemisphere somewhat for granted and that L-dyslexic children did so with regard to the right hemisphere; thus, stimulating one or other hemisphere seems appropriate. Hemisphere stimulation, as a treatment for P- and L-dyslexia, started more than 20 years ago (Bakker et al., 1981; Bakker & Vinke, 1985). The techniques that have been applied are: hemisphere-specific stimulation (HSS), either through the visual channel (HSS-vis), the tactile channel (HSS-tac), or, occasionally, the auditory channel (HSS-aud), as well as hemisphere-alluding stimulation (HAS) for P- or L-types.

- HSS-vis: the commercially available HEMSTIM programme provides for the flashing of words in the right (of P-types) or left (of L-types) visual field, in order to stimulate the left and right cerebral hemisphere, respectively (the relationship between visual fields and hemispheres is crossed). The flashing only occurs when central fixation is established.
- HSS-tac: the so-called Tactile Exploration Box provides for synthetic letters to be explored by the right hand of P-types and by the left hand of L-types, in order to stimulate the left and the right hemisphere, respectively (the relationship between hands and hemispheres is crossed).
- HSS-aud: words are spoken into the right ear of P-dyslexic children (left hemisphere stimulation), while the other ear is listening to non-vocal music, and to the left ear of L-dyslexic children (right hemisphere stimulation), while the other ear is listening to non-vocal music (the relationship between ears and hemispheres is mainly crossed).
- HAS: concerns the reading of phonetically and syntactically demanding text by P-types, in order to allude to predominant left hemispheric processing, and the reading of perceptually demanding text by L-types, in order to allude to predominant right hemispheric processing.

The HSS and HAS techniques have been used to treat dyslexic children within various language domains. Mentioning a few recent investigations using experimental designs, that is designs with controls, may suffice to illustrate the various treatment effects.

Russo (1993), in the USA, had L-type underachievers in reading who were treated either by stimulating the right cerebral hemisphere through HSS-vis and HSS-tac, or by applying an existing training programme (word games), whereas a third group was kept away from treatment. Treatment was given three times a week, 15 minutes per session, for some 14 weeks; the children of all groups received regular (remedial) teaching in the classroom during the project. Russo reported a gain of over 60% in accuracy of reading in the group which received specific stimulation of the right hemisphere, whereas the other two groups improved by less than 10%.

Van den Bungelaar and Van der Schaft (2000) in Holland treated L-type and P-type severely dyslexic children, by applying both the HSS and HAS techniques according to the guidelines of the balance model, whereas a group of equally disturbed L- and P-types served as controls who did not receive treatment. All other conditions were equal across groups. The experimental group was treated for six months, two

45-minute sessions per week. The variable of interest was the ratio of reading age and chronological age, which normally equals 1.00. The ratios for word reading rose from 0.33 pre-treatment to 1.24 post-treatment for the treated children and dropped from 0.31 pre-treatment to 0.18 post-treatment for the control children. With regard to text reading the ratios rose from 0.24 pre-treatment to 1.46 post-treatment for the treated children and from 0.22 pre-treatment to 0.75 post-treatment for the controls. Within and between group comparisons all revealed significant differences.

Other experimental, clinical, and educational research is completed or ongoing within a variety of language domains, including English (Robertson 2000a,b; Bodien, 1996; Kappers & Dekker, 1995; Goldstein & Obrzut, 2001), Italian (Lorusso et al., submitted 2002), Finnish (Neuvonen et al., 1992), and Dutch (Kappers, 1997; Struiksma & Bakker, 1996).

THE BALANCE MODEL AND CURRENT OUTCOMES OF DYSLEXIA RESEARCH

Much research on developmental dyslexia has been completed ever since the introduction of the balance model of learning to read and dyslexia. The availability of modern imaging techniques revealed neuroanatomical, neurophysiological and neuropsychological parameters to differ between dyslexic and normally reading individuals. The outcomes of psychological and educational investigations invariably point to problems with phonemic awareness and analysis in dyslexic readers. In view of this recent research one may ask the question: To what extent can the balance model account for the findings?

In a provisional effort to address this issue one should realise that linguistic deficits, such as difficulties in the processing of phonemes, do not necessarily result from inadequacies in the functioning of the left cerebral hemisphere. At some early point of the process of learning to read, it may be the right rather than the left hemisphere which takes the lion's share in enabling the transition from grapheme to phoneme. This idea is actuated by the results of at least one study. De Graaff (1995) longitudinally investigated normal elementary school children, covering Grade one through the beginning of Grade two. She administered a number of experimental tasks. In one such task a child had to find out whether a particular letter in a visual array of four letters was the same as or different from all the other letters. In the first part of this task a decision could be made on the basis of the letter shape alone (e.g. in 'aaBa'), while this was pretty impossible in the second part of the task. To conclude that 'A' and 'a' are the same in the array 'aaAa', one first has to couple a phoneme to the grapheme 'a'. Brain potentials evoked by both of these tasks demonstrated that the right cerebral hemisphere produced significantly more activity during task execution than did the left hemisphere. In view of this finding, it seems not impossible that a basic language capacity is a bilateral, rather than a unilateral brain affair, at least at some point in the mastering of text. Difficulties with learning to read could consequently result from deficiencies of the right hemisphere, the left hemisphere, or both hemispheres.

The work of Galaburda and his group (Galaburda, 1989) allows for a similar conclusion, as pointed out by Satz (1990). Galaburda's research concerned a post-mortem investigation of the brains of persons with a documented dyslexia. He found abnormalities, such as ectopias (clusters of neurons at the wrong place), on both sides of the brain but particularly in the left cerebral hemisphere. Presuming that such abnormalities cause reading problems and given that the abnormalities show up on both sides of the brain, one might think of at least two types of dyslexia. One type may stem from processing difficulties in the left hemisphere and another type from a similar stagnation in the right hemisphere. Satz (1990) accordingly tries to make a connection between the brain pathologies demonstrated by Galaburda and the balance model of dyslexia.

However, most recent research locates the evil-doer in the posterior part of the left hemisphere (Simos et al., 2000). If brain tissue that normally subserves a function gets damaged, then surrounding tissue or tissue of a homologous part in the other hemisphere is usually prepared to try to take over the subservience of that function. Depending on what actually happens, different types of dyslexia may develop.

At some point in the construction of the balance model it is said that some children may not be able to make the hemispheric shift in the predominant control of learning to read, for whatever reason. That reason may be damage to tissue and/or neuronal mechanisms, of the kind mentioned above or other types found in the literature. Such failures thus seem not necessarily to be at variance with the balance model of learning to read and dyslexia.

PRACTICAL IMPLICATIONS OF NEUROPSYCHOLOGICAL INTERVENTION APPROACHES

A strength of the neuropsychological approach is that allocation to sub-types is based largely on observation of pupil performance in the particular aspects of the reading process which are causing concern. The resulting intervention aims directly to adapt learning behaviour in line with the identified weaknesses in reading behaviour.

Thus the L-type learner needs to acquire perceptual care towards letters and symbols, whereas the P-type learner needs to acquire fluency for speedy access to print. In reality, skilled reading requires facility with both accuracy and speed and requires both the direct and the indirect routes to text to be available to the reader, depending on the text they are trying to access.

DUAL ROUTE THEORY

Many theories of reading and reading development exist, but one prevalent within the literature is the dual route model of Morton (1968). Though this model represents the reading system of the skilled adult reader, it is still useful in illuminating two different approaches to reading: the direct or lexical route and the indirect or sublexical route.

In the direct route to reading, the theory states that we recognise many words because we have encountered them so many times before that we know them. This repeated contact with the words has enabled "logogens" to be established (a logogen is a pictorial representation of the word, which includes all the letters or components within it). Once a logogen is established for a word, each time the sequence of letters within it is encountered the logogen will become active. Partial attention may be achieved for certain visually similar words; for example, if there is a logogen for the word "side", the words "hide" and "wide" will cause partial activation but only "side" fulfils all the criteria. When the logogen is fired or activated a message is sent to the semantic system to retrieve the meaning of the word. The next stage is for a message to be transmitted to the pronunciation store so that the word can be pronounced accurately. In this way the direct route processes words as gestalts or wholes and allows the meaning to be accessed.

This route is only effective when the logogens have been created, so this method cannot be used for unknown words or nonsense words. It is, however, a major component in establishing a basic sight vocabulary of words to which a speedy and accurate response can be made. Central here are the elements of speed and accuracy. The L-type dyslexic person may show an overuse of the direct route, as response to text will be speedy but will not be accurate in the absence of perceptual care. Thus there are many erroneous responses to the printed word. These errors are termed "substantive" errors and include word substitutions, additions, omissions and reversals. In fact they are "real" errors which impact on the accuracy scores of, for example, standardised reading tests such as the Neale Analysis of Reading Ability (NARA; Neale, 1989).

In contrast, the indirect or sublexical route (dealing with sub-word units) is the preferred approach for unknown words. In this process the symbols or letters are visually inspected and are mapped onto the knowledge of letter sounds and then blended to produce the correct pronunciation. It is only at this point that the meaning of the word can be accessed. Thus the indirect route cannot respond to whole words but first requires synthesis of the component parts or letters. This approach to text is the preferred approach of the P-type or perceptual dyslexic subject. Text (whether familiar or unfamiliar) is likely to be accessed via explicit grapheme–phoneme decoding and may use the same process for phonetically regular words which appear on the same page, for example the word "had". Errors for this group are "time-consuming" errors and include hesitations, repetitions and "spelling-like" reading. Impact here is on speed of reading, but in extreme cases also on reading comprehension as few attentional resources are available for comprehension if all resources are focused on decoding. The P-type dyslexic pupil raises important issues of identification as many reading assessments measure accuracy only, and even when measures such as the NARA also include norms for rate of reading they may not always be used. Yet speed of reading is an important factor in the repertoire of the skilled reader and is interestingly one which often remains affected for the remediated adult dyslexic subject (Hanley, 1997; Leong, 1999).

The sub-types are therefore identified on three levels. The first is the theoretical level concerning the hemisphere which appears to be the dominant one in the reading (L-types left versus P-types right). The second is the behavioural level concerning the preferred approach to text (L-types direct versus P-types indirect). The third level is the assessment level concerning the observed deficiency in reading compe- tence (L-types accuracy versus P-types speed and fluency).

Differential intervention needs to be able to respond to the demands of both accu- racy and fluency so that comprehensive reading competence can be attained, which affords the reader the flexibility to adapt the approach to the material. If material is unfamiliar or complex there may be a return to the phonological (or indirect) route as no entry is available in lexical memory. An example of this would be a layper- son reading medical terminology; the approach and usually the speed of reading would be different from accessing material in a newspaper. The important element is that the skilled reader can return to these earlier strategies when the occasion demands, whereas the challenge for the novice reader is to acquire the full range of strategies. Neuropsychological approaches can provide differentiated intervention to address these varied demands, and the utility of these within both clinical and experimental UK settings can be revealed with reference to the following studies.

Study 1: An Experimental Investigation into Hemisphere Alluding Stimulation (HAS)

Several other studies had reported positive results for dyslexic students follow- ing intervention via specially adapted text (Bakker & Vinke, 1985; Russo, 1993; Kappers & Hamburger, 1994; Kappers, 1997; Goldstein & Obrzut, 2001). This study aimed to investigate the effectiveness of HAS to P-type and L-type pupils in a UK setting. The study was a quasi-experimental methods study on 35 pupils and has been reported in detail by Robertson (2000a). Research evidence here suggests that, following intervention, L-types showed greater improvements in reading accuracy and made fewer substantive errors whereas P-types showed greater improvements in the fluency of word reading and made fewer fragmentation errors. The results of other studies have revealed that hemisphere stimulation did not improve the reading speed of L-types; on the contrary, reading became slower but with fewer errors, indicating an increase in reading efficiency and accuracy in processing text. Initial classification of the sample yielded one P-type and 21 L-type pupils only. A further 13 pupils were classified as M (Mixed) as these showed the characteristics of both sub-types. The final design for this study was that both L- and M-type pupils were randomly allocated to receive material designed to stimulate either the functionally inactive hemisphere (right for L-types and left for P-types) or the already functionally overactive hemisphere (left for L-types and right for P-types). The study thus became a challenge study where the validity of the Bakker theory and paradigms of treatment models could be evaluated.

This study involved the researcher and 15 teachers in three Local Education Author- ities (LEAs) within the UK. The sample comprised 21 L-type pupils aged between 8 and 13 years and 14 M-type pupils in the same age range.

Pupils for both this and the following study (HSS) were statemented as having Specific Learning Difficulties or Sp.L.D (legislative term for SDD in the UK under the Code of Practice for the Identification and Assessment of pupils with Special Educational Needs, Department of Education and Science, 1994.)

Method
Using Bakker's identification procedures (Bakker, 1990), based on pupils' oral reading of the NARA (Neale, 1989), pupils were initially classified as either L(inguistic) or P(erceptual). The detailed recording procedure of the NARA made it possible for reading errors to be categorised according to the Bakker (1990) theory. Substantive errors include omissions, reversals and substitutions; they are real errors and impact on reading accuracy scores. Fragmentation errors are hesitations and repetitions and impact on the time taken and the fluency of the reading. An L-type pupil was one who made more than the average number of substantive errors and fewer than the average number of fragmentation errors. A P-type pupil shows the reverse pattern. In the event a clear L-type sub-group only emerged. These L-dyslexic pupils were then randomly allocated to one of two treatment groups using either the semantic (theoretically for P-types) aspects of text (LP group) or the perceptual (theoretically for L-types) aspects of the text (LL group) for HAS training. Random allocation was achieved by listing subjects and assigning alternate pupils to the LL or the LP group. A similar procedure was followed for the M-type sub-group. In other respects pupils were similar, and for all pupils text was at a suitable age and interest level and was adapted according to the criteria stipulated by Bakker in 1990. They additionally received exercises theoretically designed to stimulate either the left or the right cerebral hemisphere. During training the LP and MP groups received texts to read in which, for example, words had been omitted. The deleted words could be found on the basis of rhyme or context. The LL and ML groups, on the other hand, received perceptually loaded text with different typefaces within words and with no illustrations. Random allocation was considered ethical as the design was experimental and aimed to ascertain whether teaching should stimulate the functionally deficient hemisphere or stimulate the already overactive hemisphere. A challenge study was therefore considered appropriate to explore the interactions between pupil sub-type and type of intervention.

Intervention was carried out once a week over a period of 12 weeks. Each session lasted for approximately 40 minutes: 25 minutes reading the adapted text and 15 minutes of exercises.

The Neale Analysis (1989) was selected to allow for the experimental results to be measured. This test allows reading comprehension and reading rate to be assessed, in addition to accuracy. By extending analysis of the graded reading passages to include the Bakker error categories, it also became suitable as a classification measure and allowed for reading errors to be evaluated qualitatively. This reduced any unnecessary assessment demands on pupils. The testing schedule was pre-testing, post-testing (time interval approximately 16 weeks) and follow-up testing (time interval 20 weeks approximately). Follow-up testing with the NARA was considered particularly important in allowing the retention of any improvements to be monitored. Both reading accuracy (as reflected in the number of errors for each respective NARA category) and reading comprehension were assessed on all occasions.

Rate of reading could not be analysed statistically as the amount of data appeared to be inconsistent over the three occasions of testing, but the available data could be included in the clinical analysis when exploring the differential results for individual pupils.

The differential effect of adequate (LL) versus challenging (LP) treatment validated the theoretically appropriate L-type treatment for the L-type dyslexic pupils. It is remarkable that the differential effect revealed itself after 12 treatment sessions, which is fewer than in other reported studies, which have a minimum of 16 treatment sessions.

Clinical Results and Observations
Results on differential pupil × group interventions on the various aspects of reading can be summarised as follows:

- L-type pupils matched with L-type materials (LL-group) all improved in reading accuracy (from 1:7 years to 1:11 years) whereas L-type pupils matched with P-type materials (LP-group) did not.
- Pupils from both LP- and LL-groups gained in reading comprehension, and for the LL-group the improvement in comprehension was in excess of 2:6 years for each pupil. This could reflect increasingly effective processing of text, which would impact on comprehension. The substantial increase in comprehension for the LP-group was not surprising. (P-type materials encourage semantic and syntactic interaction with the text.)
- The LL-group showed variable increases in the number of both substantive and fragmentation errors but still overall accuracy increased. This could reflect the scoring criteria of the NARA as most fragmentation errors would not count as errors, unlike the substantive ones, which would impact on scores.
- Results for the M-type pupils supported the differential results on the basis of pupil sub-type as neither type of material was revealed as being more effective for these pupils. The L-type materials, which aimed to improve the accuracy of response to the surface features of the text, were found to be as powerful as the P-type materials, which aimed to develop semantic and syntactic analysis. Thus for M-type dyslexic pupils only, this study suggests that the two interventions are equally effective or ineffective. The results of this study must be analysed with caution. Sample sizes were small and further studies are clearly required to test further the validity of the M-(ixed) category and the differential intervention hypothesis. It may be useful to extend this research by providing both L-type and subsequently P-type materials to a group of M-type pupils, in addition to providing materials as in the present study. The results of such studies may provide further support that sub-type theory may usefully inform teaching decisions.

Conclusions of the Study
It was interesting that initial classification of subjects revealed a different profile from studies reported in the Netherlands. This may be due to differences in the

categorisation, identification and assessment procedures used. In the UK the L-type pupil, who makes substantive errors, is readily identified by mainstream teachers. These errors impact on standardised assessment scores and reveal a discrepancy between chronological age and reading age. In contrast, the P-type pupil makes time-consuming errors but may ultimately decode the word accurately. Such errors are not reflected in standardised scores unless the time taken for reading is analysed, which is rare. P-type pupils also have superficial reading strengths with overt decoding ability and some knowledge of grapheme–phoneme conversion. These factors combine to mask the full extent of the reading difficulty and may result either in the pupil not being identified at all or in delayed identification.

The results of these studies yielded some evidence of sub-type × treatment inter-actions. The pupils in the LL-group showed an improvement in reading accuracy whereas those in the LP-group did not. Error analysis for these pupils may reflect a more analytic approach to text and could indicate the beginning of independent word-attack strategies. Results in this study are hemisphere-specific as stimulation of the right hemisphere improved reading accuracy. This would be consistent with the Novelty theory of Goldberg and Costa (1981) whereby the right hemisphere is more effective in processing novel stimuli (thereby generating new concepts and descriptive systems) and the left hemisphere is better equipped to process sym-bolic information (using existing systems). It is also consistent with theories of hemisphere-specific activation and reciprocal balance (Kinsbourne, 1989). The right hemisphere is primed by the nature of the tasks to enable effective processing of text to take place. This would not be so for the readers treated with the P-type ma-terials. Here the hemisphere primed would not be best suited to the initial reading so that the reciprocal balance between hemisphere and task could not be achieved.

Certain "factors beyond the method" may be in evidence, as even after intervention had ceased and during a long summer holiday the LL pupils continued to make reading gains. Although speculative in the absence of direct neurophysiological measures, this could indicate that a change of hemispheric involvement had taken place, as relapses in performance following holidays are well observed phenomena. It could also indicate that the pupils had learned how to learn and were more actively engaged with and more knowledgeable about the reading process.

Study 2: A Clinical Investigation Using Hemisphere-specific Stimulation (HSS)

The second study investigated the effectiveness of HSS (via the tactile modality). The study is a small-scale individual clinical study on six pupils. All studies to date (Grace, 1987; Bakker & Vinke, 1985; Kappers, 1997) showed the beneficial effects of right hemisphere stimulation in L-type dyslexic pupils. The current state of knowledge does not allow one to say with certainty whether treatment via the tactile or the visual half-field (via computer program) is most effective. Research evidence (Bakker et al., 1990) from P-type dyslexic children would indicate benefit from HSS using the tactile receptors of the right hand rather than HSS of the right visual field.

Study 2, involving the researcher and three teachers in two LEAs, was a check on the validity of Bakker's theorising and interventions on an English sample. In part, both studies were action research.

Using Bakker's identification procedures pupils were classified as either P-type or L-type. This was on the basis of reading errors from the NARA or, in the case of non-readers, followed the developmental trend. This was to provide initially L-type treatment to encourage perceptual care towards text.

Six pupils participated in this study, two P-type, three L-type and one M(ixed)-type dyslexic pupils (four boys, two girls; mean age 11.5 years). (The M-type pupil was classified thus as test scores showed almost equivalent substantive and frag-mentation errors.) In the case of this pupil it was decided to administer the in-tervention via the left hemisphere as the pupil showed the beginnings of reading accuracy.

Pupils were generally treated according to the theory, that is, P-type dyslexic chil-dren received specific stimulation of the left cerebral hemisphere, L-type dyslexic children of the right one. Pupils received haptic training via either the fingers of the left hand (L-types) or the right hand (P-types) in a tactile training box as devised by Bakker (1990). This was of wooden construction and allowed letters and words to be placed under a wooden shelf, out of the pupil's sight. Words and letters were palpated and "read" via the fingers of the hand. For both P- and L-type subjects the training included the palpation and ultimate reading of words and sentences, in addition to exercises theoretically designed to activate either the left or the right cerebral hemisphere. Exercises for the L-type children included reading imageable words or assessing whether pairs of words were the same or different. Exercises for the P-type children used low-imagery vocabulary and included missing letters or words or answering questions on the serial order of words in a sentence. These were again prepared according to the Bakker (1990) guidelines and were provided by the researcher for all subjects. It was intended that the existence of differential pupil responses could be explored.

Intervention again took place once a week over a period of 12 weeks. The NARA was again used to measure the impact of the intervention on reading accuracy, reading comprehension and reading rate for the six subjects. For this study there was an additional factor for sample inclusion, that of persistent reading failure. All pupils had reading ages with a discrepancy of at least 4.5 years against their chronological age. It was therefore considered appropriate that a very different approach from regular classroom teaching could be used.

Prior to the HSS intervention the pupils had all received specialist teaching at the school, in an effort to overcome their reading difficulties. This had comprised a mixture of teaching methods, including multi-sensory teaching, and had been de-livered over periods between two months and 2.5 years. According to statutory provision for all pupils, these programmes had to be continued during the inter-vention provided in the current treatment programme. The new element of the programme was that HSS was provided for one session per week, in addition to the ongoing multi-sensory training. It must be clear from the outset that, even though the multi-sensory sessions did not appear profitable, one has to be cautious with interpretation of any results of the current training; these probably, but not definitely, are caused by HSS. The likelihood that HSS was effective is enhanced if type × treatment effects emerge.

Main Results

Reading accuracy (NARA) improved over the sessions for all pupils. It is noteworthy that for three pupils, reading improved so that a measurable and standardised reading accuracy age could be obtained. Previously their scores had been below the level at which an age equivalent could be found on the standardised form of this measure. Clinically, beginning to score can be a significant finding as all of the pupils in this sample had experienced entrenched reading failure.

Reading comprehension scores (NARA) showed gains for five of the six pupils. As with reading accuracy, two pupils gained a reading comprehension age for the first time. Though results varied, gains for three pupils were in excess of one year.

The number of substantive errors showed some variability, with reductions for the L-type pupils but not for the P- and the M-type ones. This is a predicted type × treatment effect and signals improvement in accurate decoding of text.

The number of fragmentation errors showed variability, but five of the six pupils (including the L-type pupils) showed a substantial increase between occasions 1 and 2. This may again indicate a type × treatment effect as it demonstrates use of explicit decoding as a strategy when meeting unknown words.

When results were analysed there were qualitative differences according to both sub-type and the type of intervention received. This can be seen first by reference to the P-type pupils.

- Fluency and rate of reading had increased. This would be supported by the literature as HSS (tactile) for P-type pupils is intended to increase semantic and syntactic involvement with the text. This can contribute to increased fluency of reading style.
- In contrast, reading accuracy had increased only minimally, which would be supported by the literature as P-type intervention is not intended to impact on reading accuracy but rather on style and fluency of reading.
- There had been some gains in comprehension for both pupils and both now answered questions more confidently. Possibly this could be expected, as a decrease of spelling-like reading might be thought to improve the level of semantic involvement with the text.
- Interestingly, the pupils' approach to text had changed from a predominantly indirect route to reading to a more direct route, as evidenced by the number of substantive versus fragmentation errors. This would be supported by the literature, which describes such changes following P-type HSS (tactile) treatment for P-type pupils.

Marked differences were found when results for the L-type pupils were analysed and these were as follows:

- Reading accuracy had improved considerably. This would be supported by the literature as HSS (tactile) is intended to facilitate accurate decoding by specific involvement with the right hemisphere.
- Reading comprehension had increased. There is little evidence on results from experimental studies on the impact of HSS through the tactile modality on comprehension. It seems logical, however, that increased accuracy of response to text should facilitate greater involvement in the semantic aspect.
- The number of substantive errors had decreased. This would be supported by the literature and could indicate the presence of increased perceptual care to the text. It could also indicate a "rightening" of hemispheric involvement during the reading process. (In the absence of neurophysiological measures this is hypothetical.)
- There were now noticeable and successful attempts at independent word-building. Experimental evidence here is not available but could indicate ability to access reading by both the direct and the indirect route, which had previously not been possible for this pupil. This increased knowledge of grapheme–phoneme correspondence also revealed itself in a successful approach to the spelling of phonically regular words, which had previously been impossible for all pupils.
- Confidence in reading had increased, and the pupils were more willing to take risks with unknown words and to use effective self-correction strategies.
- Reading had increased in speed and fluency and yielded a standardised score for rate of reading by occasion 3. This would not be supported by the literature as HSS (tactile) is intended to increase reading accuracy rather than reading fluency.
- The number of fragmentation errors had increased. This would again be supported by results from other studies.
- These pupils also made substantial gains in reading accuracy and comprehension during a period of no intervention, which has interestingly also been reported in other studies. A possible hypothesis is that the pupils had in fact learned "how to learn".

In these cases results of the theoretically appropriate intervention would seem to have had positive, though different, impact on observed reading behaviour.

CONCLUSION

In conclusion it does seem possible that neuropsychological intervention may be seen as a useful addition to the repertoire of specialist teaching approaches available for dyslexic pupils. Overall both pupils and teachers were positive about the method. It was interesting that several pupils voluntarily commented on the impact derived from the method on their reading generally. This was particularly marked with the pupils who had received the perceptually demanding text, as many commented that the perceptually loaded text had made them approach all text with more care. Thus neuropsychological intervention does seem to hold some promise for certain pupils, though a challenge which must be confronted is to identify which pupils will derive maximum benefit from the approach. This is a dilemma of which teachers everywhere are all too aware, but one which we are sure merits ongoing work in this field.

REFERENCES

Bakker, D.J. (1979). Hemispheric differences and reading strategies: Two dyslexias? *Bulletin of the Orton Society, 29*, 84–100.

Bakker, D.J. (1986). Electrophysiological validation of L- and P-type dyslexia. *Journal of Clinical and Experimental Neuropsychology, 8*, 133.

Bakker, D.J. (1990). *Neuropsychological Treatment of Dyslexia*. New York: Oxford University Press.

Bakker, D.J. (2002). Teaching the brain. In A.Y. Springer, E.L. Cooley, & A.L. Christensen (Eds), *Pathways to Prominence in Neuropsychology: Reflections of 20th Century Pioneers*. Philadelphia, PA: Psychology Press.

Bakker, D.J. & Vinke, J. (1985). Effects of hemisphere-specific stimulation on brain activity and reading in dyslexics. *Journal of Clinical and Experimental Neuropsychology, 7*, 505–525.

Bakker, D.J., Moerland, R. & Goekoop-Hoefkens, M. (1981). Effects of hemisphere-specific stimulation on the reading performance of dyslexic boys: A pilot study. *Journal of Clinical Neuropsychology, 3*, 155–159.

Bakker, D.J., Bouma, A. & Gardien, C.J. (1990). Hemisphere-specific treatment of dyslexic sub-types: A field experiment. *Journal of Learning Disabilities, 23*, 433–438.

Barinaga, M. (2000). *Science, 288*, 2116–2119.

Bodien, P. (1996). Using scrambled text with an L-type dyslexic: A teaching case study. *Dyslexia Review, 7*, 20–23.

Castro-Caldas, A., Petersson, K.M., Reis, A., Stone-Elander, S. & Ingvar, M. (1998). The illiterate brain: Learning to read and write during childhood influences the functional organization of the adult brain. *Brain, 121*, 1053–1063.

De Graaff, M. (1995). *Hemispheric engagement during letter and word identification in beginning readers: An event-related potential study*. Doctoral dissertation, Vrije Universiteit, Amsterdam.

Department of Education and Science (DES) (1994). *The Code of Practice on the Identification and Assessment of Special Educational Needs*. London : HMSO.

Eisenberg, L. (1995). The social construction of the human brain. *American Journal of Psychiatry, 152*, 1563–1575.

Fabbro, F., Pesenti, S., Facoetti, A., Bonanomi, M., Libera, L. & Lorusso, M.L. (2001). Callosal transfer in different subtypes of developmental dyslexia. *Cortex, 37*, 65–73.

Faglioni, P., Scotti, G. & Spinnler, H. (1969). Impaired recognition of written letters following unilateral hemispheric damage. *Cortex, 5*, 120–133.

Fries, C.C. (1963). *Linguistics and Reading*. New York: Holt, Rinehart and Winston.

Galaburda, A.M. (1989). Ordinary and extraordinary brain development: Anatomical variation in developmental dyslexia. *Annals of Dyslexia, 39*, 67–79.

Goldberg, E. & Costa, L.D. (1981). Hemispheric differences in the acquisition and use of descriptive systems. *Brain and Language, 14*, 144–173.

Goldstein B.H. & Obrzut, J.E. (2001). Neuropsychological treatment of dyslexia in the classroom setting. *Journal of Learning Disabilities, 34*, 276–285.

Grace, G.M. (1987). *Brief Results of Pilot Study*. Unpublished manuscript, University of Victoria, BC, Canada.

Hanley, J.R. (1997). Reading and spelling impairments in undergraduate students with developmental dyslexia. *Journal of Research in Reading, 20*, 22–30.

Kappers, E.J. (1997). Outpatient treatment of dyslexia through stimulation of the cerebral hemispheres. *Journal of Learning Disabilities, 30*, 100–125.

Kappers, E.J. & Hamburger, H.B. (1994). Neuropsychological treatment of dyslexia in outpatients. In R. Licht & G. Spyer (Eds), *The Balance Model of Dyslexia : Theoretical and Clinical Progress*. (pp. 101–133). Assen, The Netherlands : Van Gorcum.

Kappers, E.J. & Dekker, M. (1995). Bilingual effects of unilingual neuropsychological treatment of dyslexic adolescents: A pilot study. *Journal of the International Neuropsychological Society, 1*, 494–500.

Kinsbourne, M. (1989). Neuroanatomy of dyslexia. In D.J. Bakker & van der Vlugt (Eds), *Neuropsychological Correlates and Treatment.* Amsterdam: Swets and Zeitlinger.

Leong, C.K. (1999). Phonological and morphological processing in adult students with learning/reading disabilities. *Journal of Learning Disabilities, 32,* 224–238.

Licht, R. (1994). Differences in word recognition between P- and L-type reading disability. In R. Licht & G. Spyer (Eds), *The Balance Model of Dyslexia: Theoretical and Clinical Progress* (pp 41–55). Assen, Netherlands: Van Gorcum.

Licht, R., Bakker, D.J., Kok, A. & Bouma, A. (1988). The development of lateral event-related potentials (ERPs) relted to word naming: A four year longitudinal study. *Neuropsychologia, 26,* 327–340.

Lorusso, M.L., Facoetti, A., Cazzaniga, I., Paganoni, P., Pezzani, M. & Moltini, M. (submitted 2002). Treatment of developmental dyslexia: Visual hemisphere-specific stimulation and speech therapy.

Masutto, C., Bravar, L. & Fabbro, F. (1994). Neurolinguistic differentiation of children with subtypes of dyslexia. *Journal of Learning Disabilities, 27,* 520–526.

Morton, J. (1968). *Grammar and Computation in Language Behaviour.* CR1113 Progress Report No. VI, University of Michigan.

Neale, M.D. (1989). *The Neale Analysis of Reading Ability (revised British edition).* Windsor: NFER-Nelson.

Neuvonen, M., Rekiö-Viinikainen, N., Ahonen, T. & Lyytinen, H. (1992). Tietokoneelle sovellettu Bakkerin tasapainomalliin perustuva lukemisen kuntoutus. (Hemisphere-specific stimulation via the visual half-fields.) *Kielikukko, 4,* 26–29.

Robertson, J. (2000a). Neuropsychological intervention in dyslexia: Two studies on British pupils. *Journal of Learning Disabilities, 33,* 137–148.

Robertson, J. (2000b). *Dyslexia and Reading: A Neuropsychological Approach.* London: Whurr.

Rosenzweig, M.R., Bennett, E.L. & Diamond, M.C. (1972). Brain changes in response to experience. *Scientific American, 226,* 22–29.

Russo, A.E. (1993). *Effects of the presence of pathological left handedness indicators on the efficiency of a neuropsychological intervention with low achieving readers.* Doctoral dissertation, Indiana University of Pennsylvania, Harrisburg, USA.

Satz, P. (1990). Developmental dyslexia: An etiological reformulation. In G. Th. Pavlidis (Ed.), *Perspectives on Dyslexia, Vol. 1* (pp 3–26). London: John Wiley.

Simos, P.G., Breier, J.I., Fletcher, J.M., Bergman, E. & Papanicolaou, A.C. (2000). Cerebral mechanisms involved in word reading in dyslexic children: A magnetic source imaging approach. *Cerebral Cortex, 10,* 809–816.

Struiksma, A.J.C. & Bakker, M.G. (1996). Dyslexiebehandeling op de grens van speciaal onderwijs en gezondheidszorg (Treatment of dyslexia on the borderline of special education and healthcare.) In K.P. van den Bos & D.R. van Peer (Eds.), *Dyslexie '96* (pp 85–96). Apeldoorn, Netherlands: Garant.

Van den Bungelaar, H.C.I. & Van der Schaft, A.J. (2000). Effecten van neuropsychologische behandeling van kinderen met een ernstige dyslexie (Effects of neuropsychological treatment in children with severe dyslexia.) *Tijdschrift voor Orthopedagogiek, 39,* 475–483.

Van der Schoot, M., Licht, R., Horsley, T.M. & Sergeant, J.A. (2000). Inhibitory deficits in reading disability depend on sub-type: Guessers but not spellers. *Child Neuropsychology, 6,* 297–312.

Van Strien, J.W., Bakker, D.J., Bouma, A. & Koops, W. (1990). Familial resemblance for cognitive abilities in families with P-type dyslexic, L-type dyslexic, or normal reading boys. *Journal of Clinical and Experimental Neuropsychology, 12,* 843–856.

Waldie, K.E. & Mosley, J.L. (2000). Developmental trends in right hemispheric participation in reading. *Neuropsychologia, 38,* 462–474.

Chapter 7

DYSLEXIA: COGNITIVE FACTORS AND IMPLICATIONS FOR LITERACY

Chris Singleton

INTRODUCTION

Literacy involves the integration of many complex cognitive skills, including those that enable human beings to input, store and process phonological, visual and kinaesthetic information, and to control movement of the eyes and the hands. It is unsurprising, therefore, that literacy attainment correlates with many cognitive measures, and also, more interestingly, that strengths and limitations in various cognitive skills can be used to predict those children who are likely to experience difficulties in literacy development. Of course, we can already anticipate a substantial proportion of children who are at risk of poor attainment in literacy. This group includes children who have low general ability, who are from disadvantaged socio-economic backgrounds, who have limited experience of the language in which they are learning to read and write, or whose home experiences have not prepared them well for a literate world nor motivated them to get the best out of education (see Stevenson et al., 1999). The educational needs of such children are considerable and by no means unimportant, but they are not the focus of this chapter. Here we are concerned with the impact of variation in different cognitive abilities on literacy acquisition in general, and on dyslexia in particular, and also whether cognitive measures can facilitate the identification of dyslexic children as early as possible and enable teachers to provide them with education appropriate to their needs.

The evidence regarding the relationship between certain cognitive abilities and dyslexia is consistent with two different theoretical perspectives. In the cognitive neuropsychological perspective, dyslexia is viewed as a genetically inherited neurological condition characterised by deficits (or differences) in certain cognitive

Dyslexia and Literacy: Theory and Practice. Edited by Gavin Reid and Janice Wearmouth.
© 2002 John Wiley & Sons, Ltd.

functions, although researchers are not entirely agreed which cognitive functions lie at the core of the condition. By contrast, the information-processing perspective maintains that all human beings differ on a wide range of cognitive information-processing dimensions, and that children who are at the lower tails of the distributions of certain of these dimensions will find particular learning tasks more difficult. Accordingly, dyslexia may be regarded as a form of learning difficulty arising out of specific combinations of cognitive limitations. Explicitly or implicitly, the cognitive neuropsychological perspective embraces a medical approach in which dyslexia is classed as one of a number of developmental disorders, and for practical reasons each of these needs to have clear diagnostic criteria. Since children with developmental dyslexia do not differ *qualitatively* from other children learning to read and write, the requirement for clear diagnostic criteria presents problems. There *are* no unequivocal diagnostic symptoms of developmental dyslexia, only quantitative ones (see Stanovich, 2000). Within the totality of children with literacy difficulties, where is the boundary line to be drawn around those who are to be labelled "dyslexic"? When assessing children who have literacy difficulties, educational psychologists are regularly faced with this challenge. Dyslexia is a condition that varies widely in severity. Some children show dyslexic features that are not quite severe enough for the psychologist to be confident about applying the label "dyslexia". The term "borderline dyslexia" may be applied in such cases, but this is not a satisfactory solution. Perhaps understandably, the response of some educational psychologists is to avoid using the label "dyslexia" at all (cf. Reason, 1999).

In reality, these two perspectives on dyslexia—cognitive neuropsychological and information-processing—are not quite as different as might first appear, because individual differences in cognitive processing are likely to have strong genetic links (see Johnson, 1997). An advantage of the information-processing approach, however, is that it shifts the focus away from the *label* that is applied to the child towards the *nature of the cognitive profile* underpinning the child's literacy difficulties and the implications which that has for teaching. Hence it more satisfactorily enables us to deal with cases that would otherwise have been classified as "borderline" and consigned to educational limbo.

PHONOLOGICAL PROCESSING AND WORKING MEMORY

Without question, the cognitive domain that has been most extensively researched in relation to reading and dyslexia is that of phonological skills. The literature on the relationship between phonological skills and reading is substantial (e.g. see Goswami, 1999; Lundberg & Hoien, 2001; Rack, 1997; Seymour et al., 1999; Snowling, 2000; Torgeson et al., 1997). There is also a well-established connection between reading and memory (for reviews see Baddeley, 1986; Beech, 1997; Brady, 1986; Jorm, 1983; Wagner & Torgesen, 1987). In general, it is argued that phonological processes underpin the development of a phonological recoding strategy in reading, and that working memory plays a significant role in this strategy. Distinctions may be drawn between "short-term memory" and "working memory". The former concerns the ability to retain information in short-term storage, while the latter implies that some additional processing is being carried out on the information when it is being held in short-term store (Gathercole & Baddeley, 1993a). Swanson (1994) found that although both short-term memory and working memory were significant predictors of reading comprehension for good as well as poor readers, working memory made the most important contribution to word recognition, accounting for 13% of the variance. In good readers, however, working memory was found to be more important than short-term memory for *both* word recognition and comprehension. The widespread underlying assumption is that working memory enables constituent sounds and/or phonological codes to be held in short-term store until these can be recognised as a word and its meaning accessed in long-term memory (Wagner et al., 1993). The two cognitive components—phonological processing and working memory—are interdependent, since working memory is one of the cognitive functions that subserve speech perception and production.

When groups of good and poor readers matched on intelligence are compared on various psychological measures, the most salient differences tend to be in phonological processing and short-term memory. In an intensive longitudinal study of reading development, Ellis and Large (1987) found that only three variables (out of a total of 44) reliably differentiated children with specific reading retardation from their better-reading peers when the groups were matched for intelligence. These variables were short-term memory, phonological segmentation (e.g. ability to detect rhyme and alliteration) and reading vocabulary. In a similar large-scale study, Jorm et al. (1986) reported comparable results. Bowers et al. (1988) found that when non-verbal intelligence was controlled in comparison between dyslexic and non-dyslexic subjects, the groups were found to differ mainly on verbal memory and rapid naming ability, the latter being a measure of lexical access speed, and a function of both phonological processing and memory.

The above studies suggest that phonological awareness and working memory are processes that underpin the acquisition of reading and hence have potential as early indicators of children who are likely to experience difficulty. However, studies in which groups are matched for intelligence may be criticised on the grounds that the participants are not equivalent in the amount of reading they have experienced, and this variable could account for the findings. The good readers will have had more practice in reading, which should have facilitated greater fluency in the cognitive functions (memory and phonological processes) that are under investigation. The poor readers, on the other hand, will have had limited experience of reading, and hence will have had fewer opportunities to practise and develop the cognitive processes on which reading depends. This is an example of the so-called "Matthew effect" noted by Stanovich (1986, 2000).

However, studies employing other methodologies provide strong confirmatory evidence that phonological and memory processes are key precursors of reading. Alternative approaches include comparison of groups of good and poor readers that have been matched on reading level, and prospective longitudinal studies of the literacy development of children whose cognitive skills have been assessed at an earlier stage. Studies employing reading-level controls rest on the assumption that such groups will be equivalent in reading experience. This methodology is not subject to the defect suffered by the IQ-match methodology, although the groups will inevitably be of different chronological ages. Several reading-match investigations have yielded findings that support the conclusion that phonological skills play an important role in reading development (for review see Snowling, 2000). One such study, by Nicolson and Fawcett (1995), involved groups of 8-year-old good readers and 12-year-old dyslexic children that had been matched for reading level, and groups of 12-year-old good readers and 16-year-old dyslexic students that had also been matched for reading level. The dyslexic subjects performed significantly worse than their reading-level matched groups on measures of phonological segmentation and rhyming.

Notable prospective longitudinal studies include that by Stanovich and colleagues (1984), who administered a variety of phonological awareness tasks to children aged 5–6 years, and assessed their reading ability one year later. All seven of the phoneme-awareness tasks employed in this study correlated significantly with later reading ability ($r = 0.4$ to 0.6), compared with a measure of intelligence, for which the correlation coefficient was only 0.25. In a regression analysis, IQ combined with a reading readiness measure accounted for 59% of the variance in reading ability. By comparison, the two best phonological measures were found to account for 66% of the variance in reading ability. Stuart and Coltheart (1988) reported on a longitudinal study involving phonological tests administered to children before they started school and repeated assessment of reading, letter-sound and letter-name knowledge over four subsequent years. The results showed a decreasing effect of intelligence and an increasing effect of phonological ability over the duration of the study. In a later study, Stuart (1995) found that scores on a battery of phonological tasks administered to children on school entry correlated significantly ($r = 0.7$) with reading ability one year later. Hagtvet (1997) reported on a longitudinal study of 74 children from the age of 4 to 9 years in Norway. The focus of the study was the oral language precursors of reading difficulties. Phonemic awareness at age 6 was found to be the strongest predictor of reading ability at both ages 8 and 9. However, the success rate for predicting poor reading was only 52%. The author suggests that these results do not detract from a phonological deficit hypothesis of dyslexia, but would also support the view that reading difficulties are linked with a broader spectrum of cognitive–linguistic deficiencies (Nicolson & Fawcett, 1995; Tunmer & Hoover, 1992).

Passenger and colleagues (2000) reported a detailed, longitudinal study in which 80 children were monitored during their first year of formal education. It was found that phonological awareness (alliteration, rhyme detection and rhyme production) and phonological memory (digit span and nonword repetition) both made significant contributions to early literacy. Specifically, results of factor analysis indicated that early phonological awareness predicts subsequent single-word reading, while early phonological memory plays an important role in the development of decoding strategies.

Grogan (1995) measured various cognitive abilities in a sample of young children at age 4.5, and then assessed the children's reading skills at age 7. Although phonological processing ability was not assessed in this study, after partialling out age and intelligence as factors in the analysis, auditory memory scores at age 4.5 were found to account for 13% of the variance in reading scores at age 7, with visual sequential memory accounting for a further 5%.

The association of phonological processing and reading ability can still be detected in adulthood. In a study of 76 adults, Gottardo et al. (1997) found that phonological processing ability was a consistent and unique predictor of reading. There is also evidence that phonological and working memory difficulties seen in dyslexic children persist into adulthood (e.g. Bruck, 1990; Pennington et al., 1990). This seems to hold true even for dyslexic adults who have literacy skills in the normal range or who are bright and have developed compensatory strategies for coping with high-level literacy tasks such as those encountered in higher education (e.g. Paulescu et al., 1996). Hanley (1997) compared the performance of 33 dyslexic university students with non-dyslexic students on several measures, and found that as a group the dyslexic students showed evidence of impaired phonological processing and working memory, the latter being based on the finding that the dyslexic group had significantly shorter digit span. Snowling et al. (1997) found that dyslexic students had significant difficulties in nonword reading, phoneme awareness, phonemic and semantic fluency. The dyslexic students were also found to have significantly lower memory span for nonwords, thus indicating a continuing difficulty with working memory.

The findings reported thus far should not be taken to mean that we have an unequiv-ocal understanding of how, exactly, phonological processes and memory contribute to reading development. There is an ongoing dispute about the precise nature of the causal pathways involved and, in particular, whether developmental growth proceeds from small phonological units (phonemes) to large phonological units (rimes) or vice versa (e.g. Duncan et al., 1997; Goswami, 1999; Seymour et al., 1999; Savage, 2001). There is also disagreement about which aspects of memory are most important to reading (see Beech, 1997; Gathercole & Baddeley, 1993b) and about the role of articulation rate in verbal memory tasks (Avons & Hanna, 1995; Hulme & Roodenrys, 1995; McDougall & Hulme, 1994). Several studies find phonological skills to account for a larger proportion of variance in reading development than that accounted for by memory skills. This is particularly the case when the children involved are very young. For example, in a three-year longitudinal study of 244 children starting at kindergarten age, Wagner et al. (1994) used test of memory span for digits and words, together with a battery of phonological tasks. They found that although both types of measures were significantly related to reading development, memory made a somewhat smaller contribution than phonological skills.

A simple interpretation of the evidence on relationships between working memory and reading development is that the processes involved in maintaining information in auditory short-term memory are less efficient in dyslexic readers. In other words, the problem is *memory-specific*. Evidence from studies by de Jong (1998) and Shankweiler and Crain (1986) lends support to this view. Awaida and Beech (1995) reported on a longitudinal study of 236 children aged 4 to 6 years, in which a range of phonological, memory and visual tasks were employed. Although reading quotients were *not* predicted by phonological memory, phonological memory at age 5 was found to predict nonword reading at age 6. The authors suggest that this implies an effect of phonological memory on sublexical processes (i.e. phonic decoding) in the development of early reading, rather than on lexical processes. An alternative view is that dyslexic children have impaired representations of phonological information, which restricts the amount of information that can be held in short-term memory. According to this view, the problem is not memory-specific, but, rather, a secondary effect of a phonological deficit on memory (see Hulme & Roodenrys, 1995; Snowling, 2000).

VISUAL MEMORY

Models of reading acquisition suggest that visual memory is particularly important in the earliest stages of learning to read, usually referred to as the logographic phase (e.g. Ehri, 1995; Frith, 1985). Young children typically show a preference for visual encoding of some information (see Palmer, 2000a). Conclusions reported by Passenger et al. (2000) from their study of pre-literate children during their first year at school lend some support for this view. Although their results implicate the specific contribution of phonological memory to the development of a phonological recoding strategy for reading and spelling, the association between pre-literate phonological memory ability measured at age 4 and single-word reading measured one year later was found to be rather weak. It is suggested that other factors, such as visual memory, would figure more importantly at this stage. Stuart et al. (2000) found that visual memory influences acquisition of sight vocabulary in 5-year-olds who displayed poor graphophonic skills (i.e. those who had not yet acquired the ability to segment words on the basis of their sounds and who displayed little or no knowledge of sound-to-letter mappings). There was a highly significant correlation between visual memory scores and single-word learning for the children with poor graphophonic skills ($r = 0.8$). For children with good graphophonic skills, however, no association between visual memory and word learning was found.

In general, the research literature suggests that dyslexic children tend to have good visual skills, including good visual memory. Ellis et al. (1996) reported that dyslexic children aged 10 years were significantly faster on some visual processing tasks (e.g. picture categorisation) than other groups, including reading age controls. Palmer (2000b) found that dyslexic teenagers significantly outperformed reading age controls on a measure of visuo-spatial memory span in three groups. This study also suggested that while all participants showed evidence of using phonological coding to remember pictures, only those in the dyslexic group used visual coding. Poor readers are also known to perform *better* than reading age controls on word recognition tasks when the words are paired with visually similar cues than when they are paired with phonologically similar cues (Holligan & Johnston, 1988; Rack, 1987). In other words, they display a less pronounced phonological similarity effect and a more pronounced visual similarity effect (Katz, 1986; Mann & Liberman, 1984). In adulthood, it has been observed that dyslexic individuals often incline towards careers in which visual skills are an advantage, such as architecture and design, engineering, and the graphic arts, suggesting a developmental continuity in visual strengths (see West, 1997). Of course, these trends might be due to factors other than underlying constitutional differences. For example, these individuals are likely to have relied on visual skills to a greater extent than other people, and so will have been able to develop those skills to higher levels.

A notable feature of approaching the problem of dyslexia from a cognitive perspective is that both strengths as well as deficits or weaknesses in various cognitive abilities can have implications for literacy development. If the ideal strategy for a given task is not an option for a child because the cognitive skills that underpin that strategy are not strong enough, the child may be forced to use an alternative strategy, and in so doing inadvertently develop the skills which subserve that strategy. For example, there is evidence that poor readers have a bias towards visual encoding of words. Johnston and Anderson (1998) reported that poor readers showed a preference for using pictorial rather than verbal information, which they suggest may arise from previous difficulties in learning to attach verbal labels to visual stimuli. Palmer (2000c) found that children who maintained a visual representation of words alongside a phonological representation after age 7, were significantly worse readers than those for whom the ability to switch strategies by inhibiting the visual representation had fully developed. Children with good visual memory but poor auditory verbal memory would not only be expected to find acquisition of an effective phonological recoding strategy in reading rather difficult, but also be inclined to rely for an longer period on visual strategies. This approach is liable to run into trouble as the child's education progresses and the number of new words with which the child is confronted steadily increases. Singleton and colleagues (2001) report a case in which this occurred, while Fawcett et al. (1998) discuss a case in which the opposite pattern was observed, i.e. poor visual memory but good verbal memory. In this latter case the child, who was very bright and had not long started school, was struggling to learn words by sight. His teachers were reluctant to adopt an alternative teaching approach, but when they appreciated his particular pattern of cognitive strengths and weaknesses they switched from this strongly visual approach to a more phonological and auditory approach, whereupon he began to make substantial improvement. His reading attainment is now well above average but, as might be expected, he continues to have problems in spelling irregular (exception) words, which rely on good visual memory. This pattern is comparable with the type of acquired dyslexia usually known as "surface dyslexia", in which patients are able to utilise a phonological recoding strategy, and therefore can read nonwords, but have poor ability to read exception words and tend to confuse homophones, e.g. *leek/leak*, *mare/mayor* (Marshall, 1984). A case of developmental surface dyslexia was described by Coltheart et al. (1983).

EARLY IDENTIFICATION OF DYSLEXIA BASED ON COGNITIVE MEASURES

The foregoing indicates the potential of using measures of cognitive abilities as predictors of reading difficulties and dyslexia. Since cognitive abilities are measurable

in children before they begin to learn to read and write, it is possible to anticipate which of them are likely to struggle in literacy (and in what manner they will
probably struggle) before they actually fail (see Singleton, 1987; 1988). To test this
hypothesis, Singleton and colleagues (2000) carried out a longitudinal study using
a computer-based system for cognitive assessment called "CoPS" (Cognitive Profiling System) that had been developed by Singleton et al. (1996; 1997). A total of
421 children were first assessed at age 5 on cognitive tests administered by computer and they were followed up over the next 3.5 years using conventional tests of
reading, spelling, phonic skills, verbal and nonverbal ability. The eight computer
tests in CoPS are presented in a game format, with colourful graphics, sound and
digitised speech.

The potential of computer-based assessment for diagnosis of reading difficulties
and identification of dyslexia has been explored by several researchers, including Seymour (1986), Hoien and Lundberg (1989), Singleton (1991; 1994), Singleton
and Thomas (1994) and Fawcett and Nicolson (1994). The principal advantages of
computer-based systems over conventional methods of assessment are that assessment of cognitive skills can be more precise, and that significant savings can made
in both time and labour (Singleton, 1997). Computerised assessment methods can
usually be administered more speedily than conventional tests (particularly if the
tests are adaptive) and as the scoring is generally automatic the results can be
immediately available (Singleton et al., 1999. Computer-based tests can also take
advantage of the capabilities of the technology to create items that include anima-
tion and speech. These features help to make the tests attractive to children and
hence more acceptable. Studies have shown that children and adults (particularly if
they feel that they might perform badly) tend to prefer computer-based assessment
to conventional assessment by a human assessor (see Singleton, 1997; 2001).

The intention in the CoPS suite of tests was to create tasks that young children would
readily engage with. Hence the test of auditory working memory, instead of using a
conventional digit span task (which can be unstimulating and therefore potentially
unreliable as a measure of short-term memory for young children), presents the
child with a task in which they have to remember animal names in sequence. In
this test, called "Races", the scenario is a race in which various animals (dog, fox,
cat, etc.) are competing. The child is told by the computer the order in which the
animals finish the race (although the child cannot see the outcome of the race) and
has to replicate that sequence by clicking on the pictures of the animals in the correct
order. The number of syllables in each sequence of names has been controlled so
that different "races" are equivalent in phonological memory load for a given level.
CoPS includes a four different tests of visual memory (two associative and two
sequential), which vary in their susceptibility to verbal labelling as a memorisation
strategy. The test called "Rabbits" assesses the child's short-term recall of spatial
and temporal position. The screen displays 10 "holes" which are meant to represent
rabbit burrows. A rabbit appears at different burrows in sequence and the task is
to replicate the sequence using the mouse. Verbal labelling is not a very suitable
strategy to use in this task. By contrast, another test of visual sequential memory
("Zoid's Friends") involves remembering sequences of colours (the children had
been checked for colour vision deficiencies in advance). In this test, Zoid (a cartoon

character) appears with different numbers of "friends", who are of identical shape but different colours (red, blue, green or yellow). The child has to remember the sequence of colours and replicate this by clicking on the appropriate colours on the screen, a task that is much more amenable to use of a verbal labelling strategy. CoPS also includes two tests of phonological abilities, one that assesses phonological awareness ("Rhymes") and one that assesses phoneme discrimination ("Wock"). In each item of the Rhymes test, the child has to identify which of four objects has a name that either rhymes or alliterates with the name of the target object. In the Wock test the scenario is that two of Zoid's "friends" are trying to learn English. The child has to "help" them by determining which of two alternative pronunciations of a name of an object is correct (e.g. *rock* versus *wock*). In both of these tests, each object is named aurally as well as presented pictorially.

The results of this longitudinal study indicated that cognitive assessment by means of computer-delivered tests is a valid and practical method for identifying children who are at risk of reading difficulties. The tests in the computer suite CoPS administered at age 5 correlated significantly with reading measures at ages 6 and 8 years. Tests of auditory verbal sequential memory (Races) and phonological awareness (Rhymes) yielded the highest correlation coefficients, but many other important correlations were found. Phoneme discrimination (Wock) was found to be a significant predictor of phonic skills and listening skills. Visual memory measures (Rabbits, Zoid's Friends) were also significantly correlated with later word and text reading. In general, correlations between CoPS measures and later reading attainment were found to be higher than those obtained with measures of general ability but not as high as those obtained with early reading measures. Regression analyses revealed that the CoPS tests given at age 5 accounted for 31% of the variance in reading scores at age 6, and 37% of the variance in reading scores at age 8. In these regression analyses, Races and Rhymes were the chief predictor variables. By comparison, a combination of conventional tests administered at age 6 (i.e. one year after the CoPS assessment), including measures of reading and general ability, accounted for a total of 67% of the variance in reading scores at age 8. In regression analyses general ability measures used alone perform less well than the cognitive measures as early predictors of reading attainment. Discriminant function analysis revealed that CoPS outperformed conventional tests on all counts in predicting poor readers at age 8. Levels of false positives and false negatives were low or at zero for the CoPS measures, while the conventional tests produced unacceptably high levels of false positives and moderate levels of false negatives. It was concluded that as components of a screening procedure for identifying children at risk of reading failure, the conventional tests employed in this study would be unsatisfactory and inferior to cognitive measures such as those in CoPS. These results are somewhat better than those of Hagtvet (1997), in which the success rate (true positives) for predicting reading at 8 from phonemic awareness at age 6 was only 52%. The correlation values with later reading attainment obtained by Singleton et al. (2000) for phonological processing and short-term verbal memory, compared with intelligence measures as predictors, are comparable with those of similar studies reported in the literature (e.g. Stanovich et al., 1984; Passenger et al., 2000) although a few studies have reported somewhat higher correlations for phonological processing (e.g. Stuart, 1995). In the study by Singleton et al. (2000) correlations between visual memory measures and single-word reading ($r \approx 0.3$–0.4) were not of the order reported by Stuart et al. (2000), which was described earlier in this chapter ($r = 0.8$). Nevertheless, the correlations were statistically significant. It should also be borne in mind that in the Stuart et al. (2000) study, the children had to learn to recognise words that were unfamiliar to them (e.g. *leopard*, *haddock*, *canoe*), whereas in the Singleton et al. (2000) study, the children were assessed on words that they had already acquired, and no distinction was made between children with good or poor graphophonic skills.

CONCLUSIONS

In spite of the ongoing debates in this field, there is broad agreement that children who have poor phonological abilities and/or poor short-term auditory memory skills would be expected to struggle in reading development, compared with children in whom these capabilities are in the average or above-average range. The findings of the study by Singleton et al. (2000) not only confirm the widely held view that phonological processing and short-term verbal memory are critical precursors of reading development, but also support the less widely held view that visual memory predicts important aspects of reading development. Furthermore, the results validate the use of computer-delivered tests to assess these cognitive abilities early in the child's education. Other computer-based systems have subsequently been developed to assess cognitive abilities in older children and adults and to utilise this information in the identification of dyslexia (see Horne et al., 1999; Thomas et al., 2000; Singleton et al., 2002). Individual differences in strengths and weaknesses on the various tests can also be examined ipsatively as a cognitive profile, a technique which confers even greater utility on this approach. Consistent with current models of reading development (e.g. Erhi, 1995), these results suggest that visual memory measures are likely to be most useful in predicting early acquisition of single-word reading, the mastery of visual strategies at the logographic stage of reading, and also ability to spell irregular (exception) words. Measures of phonological skills and verbal memory, on the other hand, will prove most useful in predicting acquisition of phonological decoding strategies at the orthographic stage of reading, and the abilities to spell regular words and read nonwords. To date, however, research has concentrated mainly on reading, with relative neglect of writing and spelling. One of the constraints has been the lack of satisfactory measures of writing ability, which has fortunately been addressed by the publication of the Wechsler Objective Language Dimensions (WOLD), developed by Rust (1995). There are some studies of dyslexic subjects that contribute to an understanding of cognitive factors in spelling. Several of these implicate deficits in visual memory in cases of older children and adults who could read fluently but had specific spelling problems, including difficulties with homophones (e.g. Goulandris & Snowling, 1991; Romani et al., 1999; Seymour, 1986).

Studies on cognitive factors in reading and dyslexia have a bearing on the debate about subtypes of dyslexia. Are there cognitive measures that might be used to identify different types of poor readers? In considering this issue, Stanovich et al. (1997) observed that the classic subtyping literature was not particularly encouraging in this regard, an outcome which they attribute largely to the fact that earlier studies were basically empirical and not grounded in information-processing theory. These authors concur with Castles and Coltheart (1993) that the search for subtypes should proceed from psychological mechanisms that closely underpin the word-recognition process. When examined in this way, developmental phonological dyslexia represents what Stanovich et al. (1997, p. 123) refer to as "true developmental deviancy", while developmental surface dyslexia resembles "a form of developmental delay". However, they stress that such parameters inevitably interact with experience of print. Individuals with surface dyslexia, having a milder form of phonological impairment conjoined with inadequate reading experience, make slow progress in literacy, but their prognosis is better than that for those with phonological dyslexia, who experience lifelong repercussions of their phonological deficits. The evidence on cognitive factors in dyslexia reviewed in this chapter suggests that developmental surface dyslexic subjects may have visual memory deficits that impair their acquisition of a sight vocabulary (especially in the earliest stages of learning to read), hinder their development of visual word-recognition strategies (especially for irregular words), hamper their spelling of exception words, and slow their speed of text reading.

Individual differences in cognitive abilities can be assessed before children begin to learn to read, thus making it possible to assess such abilities and predict at a relatively early age those who, as a result of particular profiles, are likely to encounter greater-than-normal difficulties in literacy development. This approach also makes it possible to instigate intervention much earlier than would otherwise be the case, without having to wait until the child shows evidence of failure. Cognitive weaknesses displayed by children that are likely to impact on their acquisition of literacy skills can be compensated for by differentiated teaching. If addressed sufficiently early, this can be dealt with in the ordinary classroom and does not necessarily require specialist teachers. Progress is enhanced because the child's motivation will not have been damaged by the experience of failure (see Miles & Varma, 1995; Riddick et al., 1997). Suitable teaching techniques differentiated according to cognitive profile have been outlined by Horne et al. (1999), Singleton et al. (2001) and Thomas et al. (2000). This strategy does not necessarily imply giving children training in cognitive skills that are found to be weak, although in some instances (e.g. phonological awareness) this may be desirable (e.g. see Lundberg et al., 1988; Hatcher et al., 1994). The key principle is that the teacher can select from a variety of techniques for teaching and learning that will provide the best fit to the child's cognitive profile—a philosophy that equates with the optimisation of teaching strategies to children's learning styles (see Carbo et al., 1986; Reid, 1998; Riding & Rayner, 1998). The most important outcome of research on cognitive factors in literacy and dyslexia is probably this: that intervention does not necessarily have to be predicated upon failure. The bitter fruits of prolonged humiliation in the classroom experienced by so many dyslexic children in the past, that have so often frustrated subsequent attempts to rectify the difficulties by remedial teaching and which typically sour their self-confidence into adulthood, are *not* inevitable.

REFERENCES

Avons, S. E. & Hanna, C. (1995) The memory span deficit in children with specific reading disability: is speech rate responsible? *British Journal of Developmental Psychology*, 13, 303–311.

Awaida, M. & Beech, J. R. (1995) Children's lexical and sublexical development while learning to read. *Journal of Experimental Education*, 63, 97–113.

Baddeley, A. D. (1986) Working memory, reading and dyslexia. In E. Hjelmquist & L. Nillsson (Eds) *Communication and Handicap: Aspects of Psychological Compensation and Technical Aids.* Amsterdam: Elsevier Science.

Beech, J. R. (1997) Assessment of memory and reading. In J. R. Beech & C. H. Singleton (Eds) *The Psychological Assessment Of Reading.* London: Routledge, pp. 143–159.

Bowers, P., Steffy, R. & Tate, E. (1988) Comparison of the effects of IQ control methods on memory and naming speed predictors of reading disability. *Reading Research Quarterly*, 23, 304–319.

Brady, S. (1986) Short-term memory, phonological processing and reading ability. *Annals of Dyslexia*, 36, 138–153.

Bruck, M. (1990) Word recognition skills of adults with childhood diagnoses of dyslexia. *Reading Research Quarterly*, 23, 51–69.

Carbo, M., Dunn, R. & Dunn, K. (1986) *Teaching Children to Read Through Their Individual Learning Styles.* Englewood Cliffs, NJ: Prentice-Hall.

Castles, A. & Coltheart, M. (1993) Varieties of developmental dyslexia. *Cognition*, 47, 149–180.

Coltheart, M., Masterson, J., Byng, S., Prior, M. & Riddoch, J. (1983) Surface dyslexia. *Quarterly Journal of Experimental Psychology*, 35, 469–495.

de Jong, P. F. (1998) Working memory deficits of reading disabled children. *Journal of Experimental Child Psychology*, 70, 75–96.

Duncan, L. G., Seymour, P. H. K. & Hill, S. (1997) How important are rhyme and analogy in Beginning Reading? *Cognition*, 63, 171–208.

Ehri, L. C. (1995) Phases of development in learning to read words by sight. *Journal of Research in Reading*, 18, 116–125.

Ellis, N. C. & Large, B. (1987) The development of reading. *British Journal of Psychology*, 78, 1–28.

Ellis, A. W., McDougall, S. J. P. & Monk, A. F. (1996) Are dyslexics different? I. A comparison between dyslexics, reading age controls, poor readers and precocious readers. *Dyslexia*, 2, 31–58.

Fawcett, A. J. & Nicolson, R. (1994) Computer-based diagnosis of dyslexia. In C. H. Singleton (Ed.) *Computers and Dyslexia. Educational Applications of New Technology.* Hull: Dyslexia Computer Resource Centre, University of Hull, pp. 162–171.

Fawcett, A. J., Singleton, C. H. & Peer, L. (1998) Advances in early years screening for dyslexia in the United Kingdom. *Annals of Dyslexia*, 48, 57–88.

Frith, U. (1985) Beneath the surface of developmental dyslexia. In K. E. Patterson, J. C. Marshall and M. Coltheart (Eds) *Surface Dyslexia.* Hove, Sussex: Erlbaum.

Gathercole, S. E. & Baddeley, A. D. (1993a) *Working Memory and Language.* Hove, Sussex: Erlbaum.

Gathercole, S. E. & Baddeley, A. D. (1993b) Phonological working memory: a critical building block for reading development and vocabulary acquisition? *European Journal of Psychology of Education*, 8, 259–272.

Goswami, U. (1999) Causal connections in beginning reading: the importance of rhyme. *Journal of Research in Reading*, 22, 217–240.

Gottardo, A., Siegel, L. S. & Stanovich, K. E. (1997) The assessment of adults with reading disabilities: what can we learn from experimental tasks? *Journal of Research in Reading*, 20, 42–54.

Goulandris, N. & Snowling, M. J. (1991) Visual memory deficits: A plausible case of developemntal dyslexia? Evidence from a single case study. *Cognitive Neuropsychology*, 8, 127–154.

Grogan, S. (1995) Which cognitive abilities at age four are the best predictors of reading ability at age seven? *Journal of Research in Reading*, 18, 24–33.

Hagtvet, B. E. (1997) Phonological and linguistic-cognitive precursors of reading disabilities. *Dyslexia*, 3, 163–177.

Hanley, J. R. (1997) Reading and spelling impairments in undergraduate students with developmental dyslexia. *Journal of Research in Reading*, 20, 22–30.

Hatcher, P. J., Hulme, C. & Ellis, A. W. (1994) Ameliorating early reading failure by integrating the teaching of reading and phonological skills. *Child Development*, 65, 41–57.

Hoien, T. & Lundberg, I. (1989). A strategy for assessing problems in word recognition among dyslexics. *Scandinavian Journal of Educational Research*, 33, 185–201.

Holligan, C. & Johnston, R. S. (1988) The use of phonological information by good and poor readers in memory and reading tasks. *Journal of Memory and Cognition*, 16, 522–532.

Horne, J. K., Singleton, C. H. & Thomas, K. V. (1999) *Lucid Assessment System for Schools, Secondary Version (LASS Secondary)*. Beverley, East Yorkshire: Lucid Creative Limited.

Hulme, C. & Roodenrys, S. (1995) Practitioner review: verbal working memory development and its disorders. *Journal of Child Psychology and Psychiatry*, 36, 373–398.

Johnson, M. H. (1997) *Developmental Cognitive Neuroscience*. Oxford: Blackwell.

Johnston, R. S. & Anderson, M. J. (1998) Memory span, naming speed and memory strategies in poor and normal readers. *Memory*, 6, 143–163.

Jorm, A. F. (1983) Specific reading retardation and working memory: a review. *British Journal of Psychology*, 74, 311–342.

Jorm, A. F., Share, D. L., Maclean, R. & Matthews, R. (1986) Cognitive factors at school entry predictive of specific reading retardation and general reading backwardness: a research note. *Journal of Child Psychology and Psychiatry*, 27, 45–54.

Katz, R. B. (1986) Phonological deficiencies in children with reading disability: evidence from an object naming task. *Cognition*, 22, 225–257.

Lundberg, I. & Hoien, T. (2001) Dyslexia and phonology. In A. Fawcett (Ed.) *Dyslexia: Theory and Good Practice*. London: Whurr, pp. 109–123.

Lundberg, I., Frost, J. & Petersen, O. (1988) Effects of an extensive program for stimulating phonological awareness in pre-school children. *Reading Research Quarterly*, 23, 263–284.

Mann, V. A. & Liberman, I. Y. (1984) Phonological awareness and verbal short-term memory. *Journal of Learning Disabilities*, 17, 592–599.

Marshall, J. C. (1984) Rational taxonomy of developmental dyslexias. In R. N. Malatesha & H. A. Whitaker (Eds) *Dyslexia: A Global Issue*. The Hague: Martinus Nijhoff.

McDougall, S. & Hulme, C. (1994) Short-term memory, speech rate and phonological awareness as predictors of learning to read. In C. Hulme and M. Snowling (Eds) *Reading Development and Dyslexia*. London: Whurr, pp. 31–44.

Miles, T. & Varma, V. (Eds) (1995) *Dyslexia and Stress*. London: Whurr.

Nicolson, R. I. & Fawcett, A. J. (1995) Dyslexia is more than a phonological deficit. *Dyslexia*, 1, 19–36.

Palmer, S. (2000a) Working memory: a developmental study of phonological recoding. *Memory*, 8, 179–194.

Palmer, S. (2000b) Phonological recoding deficit in working memory of dyslexic teenagers. *Journal of Research in Reading*, 23, 28–40.

Palmer, S. (2000c) Phonological recoding and literacy development. *British Journal of Developmental Psychology*, 18, 533–555.

Passenger, T., Stuart, M. & Terrell, C. (2000) Phonological processing and early literacy. *Journal of Research in Reading*, 23, 55–66.

Paulescu, E., Frith, U., Snowling, M., Gallagher, A., Morton, J., Fackowiak, F. S. J., & Frith, C. D. (1996) Is developmental dyslexia a disconnection syndrome? Evidence from PET scanning. *Brain*, 119, 143–157.

Pennington, B. F., Orden, G. C. V., Smith, S. D., Green, P. A. & Haith, M. M. (1990) Phonological processing skills and deficits in adult dyslexics. *Child Development*, 61, 1753–1778.

Rack, J. (1987) Orthographic and phonetic coding in developmental dyslexia. *British Journal of Psychology*, 37, 187–206.

Rack, J. (1997) Assessment of phonological skills and their role in the development for reading and spelling skills. In J. R. Beech and C. H. Singleton (Eds) *The Psychological Assessment of Reading*. London: Routledge, pp. 124–142.

Rack, J., Snowling, M. J. & Olson, R. K. (1992) The nonword reading deficit in developmental dyslexia: a review. *Reading Research Quarterly*, 27, 28–53.

Reason, R. (Chair) (1999) *Dyslexia, Literacy and Psychological Assessment*. (Report by a Working Party of the Division of Educational and Child Psychology of the British Psychological Society.) Leicester: The British Psychological Society.

Reid, G. (1998) *Dyslexia: A Practitioner's Handbook*. Second Edition. London: Wiley.

Riddick, B., Farmer, M. and Sterling, C. (1997) *Students and Dyslexia: Growing Up With a Specific Learning Difficulty*. London: Whurr.

Riding, R. & Rayner, S. (1998) *Cognitive Styles and Learning Strategies*. London: David Fulton.

Romani, C., Ward, J. & Olson, A. (1999) Developmental surface dyslexia: What is the underlying cognitive impairment? *Quarterly Journal of Experimental Psychology, Section A*, 52, 97–128.

Rust, J. (1995) *Wechsler Objective Language Dimensions (WOLD)*. London: Psychological Corporation.

Savage, R. (2001) A re-evaluation of the evidence for orthographic analogies: a rely to Goswami (1999). *Journal of Research in Reading*, 24, 1–18.

Seymour, P. H. K. (1986) *Cognitive Analysis of Dyslexia*. London: Routledge & Kegan Paul.

Seymour, P. H. K., Duncan, L. G. & Bolik, F. M. (1999) Rhymes and phonemes in the common unit task: replications and implications for beginning reading. *Journal of Research in Reading*, 22, 113–130.

Shankweiler, D. & Crain, S. (1986) Language mechanisms and reading disorder: a modular approach. *Cognition*, 24, 139–168.

Singleton, C. H. (1987) Cognitive models of dyslexia. *Support for Learning*, 2, 47–56.

Singleton, C. H. (1988) The early diagnosis of developmental dyslexia. *Support for Learning*, 3, 108–121.

Singleton, C. H. (1991). Computer applications in the diagnosis and assessment of cognitive deficits in dyslexia. In C. H. Singleton (Ed.) *Computers and Literacy Skills*. Hull, UK: Dyslexia Computer Resource Centre, University of Hull, pp. 149–159.

Singleton, C. H. (1994) Computer applications in the identification and remediation of dyslexia. In D. Wray (Ed.) *Literacy and Computers: Insights from Research*. Widnes, UK: United Kingdom Reading Association, pp. 55–61.

Singleton, C. H. (1997) Computerised assessment of reading. In J. R. Beech and C. H. Singleton (Eds) *The Psychological Assessment of Reading*. London: Routledge, pp. 257–278.

Singleton, C. H. (2001) Computer-based assessment in education. *Educational and Child Psychology*, 18, 58–74.

Singleton, C. H. & Thomas, K. V. (1994). Computerised screening for dyslexia. In C. H. Singleton, (Ed.) *Computers and Dyslexia. Educational Applications of New Technology*. Hull, UK: Dyslexia Computer Resource Centre, University of Hull, pp. 172–184.

Singleton, C. H., Thomas, K. V. & Leedale, R. C. (1996) *CoPS 1 Cognitive Profiling System* (Developmental version). Beverley, East Yorkshire, UK: Lucid Research Limited.

Singleton, C. H., Thomas, K. V. & Leedale, R. C. (1997) *CoPS Cognitive Profiling System* (Windows version). Beverley, East Yorkshire, UK: Lucid Research Limited.

Singleton, C. H., Horne, J. K & Thomas, K. V. (1999) Computerised baseline assessment of literacy. *Journal of Research in Reading*, 22, 67–80.

Singleton, C. H., Thomas, K. V. & Horne, J. K. (2000) Computerised cognitive profiling and the development of reading. *Journal of Research in Reading*, 23, 158–180.

Singleton, C. H., Thomas, K. V. & Leedale, R. C. (2001) *Manual for CoPS Cognitive Profiling System* (Second Edition). Beverley, East Yorkshire, UK: Lucid Research Limited.

Singleton, C. H., Horne, J. K. & Thomas, K. V. (2002) *Lucid Adult Dyslexia Screening (LADS)*. Beverley, East Yorkshire, UK: Lucid Creative Limited.

Snowling, M. (2000) *Dyslexia* (Second Edition). Oxford: Blackwell.

Snowling, M., Nation, K., Moxham, P., Gallagher, A. & Frith, U. (1997) Phonologial processing skills of dyslexic students in higher education: a preliminary report. *Journal of Research in Reading*, 20, 31–41.

Stanovich, K. E. (1986) Matthew effects in reading: some consequences of individual differences in the acquisition of literacy. *Reading Research Quarterly*, 21, 360–407.

Stanovich, K. E. (2000) *Progress in Understanding Reading*. New York: Guildford Press.

Stanovich, K. E., Cunningham, A. E. & Cramer, B. B. (1984) Assessing phonological skills in kindergarten children: issues of task comparability. *Journal of Experimental Child Psychology*, 38, 175–190.

Stanovich, K. E., Siegel, L. S. & Gottardo, A. (1997) Progress in the search for dyslexia subtypes. In C. Hulme & M. J. Snowling (Eds) *Dyslexia: Biology, Cognition and Intervention*. London: Whurr, pp. 108–130.

Stevenson, H. W., Lee, S. & Schweingruber, H. (1999) Home influences on early literacy. In D. A. Wagner, R. L. Venezky & B. V. Street, *Literacy: An International Handbook*. Bolder, CO: Westview Press, pp. 251–257.

Stuart, M. (1995) Prediction and qualitative assessment of five- and six-year-old children's reading: a longitudinal study. *British Journal of Educational Psychology*, 65, 287–296.

Stuart, M. & Coltheart, M. (1988) Does reading develop in a sequence of stages? *Cognition*, 30, 139–181.

Stuart, M., Masterson, J. & Dixon, M. (2000) Spongelike acquisition of sight vocabulary in beginning readers. *Journal of Research in Reading*, 23, 12–27.

Swanson, H. L. (1994) Short-term memory and working memory: do both contribute to our understanding of academic achievement in children and adults with learning disabilities? *Journal of Learning Disabilities*, 27, 34–50.

Thomas, K. V., Singleton, C. H. & Horne, J. K. (2000) *Lucid Assessment System for Schools, Junior Version (LASS Junior)*. Beverley, East Yorkshire, UK: Lucid Creative Limited.

Torgesen, J. K., Wagner, K. K., Rashotte, C. A., Burgess, S. & Hecht, S. (1997) Contributions of phonological awareness and rapid naming ability to growth of word-reading skills in second- to fifth-grade children. *Scientific Studies of Reading*, 1, 161–195.

Tunmer, W. E. & Hoover, W. A. (1992) Cognitive and linguistic factors in learning to read. In P. B. Gough, L. C. Erhi & R. Treiman (Eds) *Reading Acquistion*. Hillsdale, NJ: Erlbaum, pp. 175–214.

Wagner, R. K. & Torgesen, J. K. (1987) The nature of phonological processing and its causal role in the acquisition of reading skills. *Psychological Bulletin*, 101, 192–212.

Wagner, R. K., Torgesen, J. K., Laughon, P., Simmons, K. & Rashotte, C. A. (1993) Development of young readers' phonological processing abilities. *Journal of Educational Psychology*, 85, 83–103.

Wagner, R. K., Torgesen, J. K., & Rashotte, C. A. (1994) Development of reading-related phonological processing abilities: Evidence of bi-directional causality from a latent variable longitudinal study. *Developmental Psychology*, 30, 73–87.

West, T. G. (1997) *In the Mind's Eye*. New York: Prometheus Books.

Chapter 8

LITERACY STANDARDS AND FACTORS AFFECTING LITERACY: WHAT NATIONAL AND INTERNATIONAL ASSESSMENTS TELL US

Gerry Shiel

Over the past decade, several international studies of reading and related skills have been carried out. These include the IEA (International Association for the Evaluation of Educational Achievement) Reading Literacy Study (IEA-RLS), the International Adult Literacy Study (IALS), the OECD (Organisation for Economic Co-operation and Development) Programme for International Student Assessment (PISA), and the IEA Progress in International Reading Literacy Study (PIRLS). In addition, several countries, including England and Ireland, have administered national surveys of reading literacy. As well as briefly summarising the outcomes of these assessments and their implications, this chapter considers the underlying definitions of reading literacy, the distribution of reading literacy within countries (including proportions of students or adults with serious reading difficulties), and variables associated with reading achievement, such as gender, socio-economic status, and school type. The outcomes of national, every-pupil assessments, such as National Curriculum Assessment in England and Wales and the Junior Certificate Examination in Ireland (administered to all students at the end of the Junior Cycle—age 15 years approximately), are not considered, as these assessments are designed to assess students' mastery of curricula, and are not suited to monitoring standards or providing answers to questions about variables associated with achievement in literacy.

Dyslexia and Literacy: Theory and Practice. Edited by Gavin Reid and Janice Wearmouth.
© 2002 John Wiley & Sons, Ltd.

International and national studies of reading literacy typically do not involve all the schools and students in a country/population. Instead, representative samples of schools and students (or communities and adults) are drawn, and levels of achievement in the population are estimated, based on the performance of persons in the sample.

It should be noted at the outset that most of the studies described in this chapter do not assess students' phonological knowledge or word-recognition skills. While these skills are very important, and some students, including those with dyslexia, continue to experience difficulties acquiring them well after the initial stages of learning to read, they explain relatively little of the variation in students' reading achievement from 9 years of age onwards, when the vast majority of students have acquired basic decoding skills, and concern shifts to their ability to understand and use information in texts.

INTERNATIONAL ASSESSMENTS OF READING LITERACY

In recent years, there has been increased interest in international assessments of reading literacy. There are several reasons why a country might wish to participate in such assessments. First, they allow a country to compare its achievement with that of other similar countries. Second, they allow for the study of variables associated with achievement, such as gender, socio-economic status, or levels of teacher education. Third, they provide policy-makers with information that can be used to monitor standards or implement reforms.

The IEA Reading Literacy Study (IEA/RLS)

The IEA/RLS assessed the achievement of 9- and 14-year olds in 32 countries (27 at the lower age level, and 31 at the higher age level) in 1991. Participating countries at both age levels included Finland, Canada, Ireland and the United States. Although England did not participate in the original study, the IEA test was administered by the National Foundation for Educational Research (NFER) in England and Wales to a representative sample of English and Welsh 9-year-olds in 1996, so the performance of English/Welsh students could be compared to that of 9-year-olds in other countries in 1991 (see Brooks et al., 1996).

In the IEA/RLS, reading literacy was defined as "the ability to understand and use those written language forms required by society and/or valued by the individual" (Elley, 1992, p. 3). The national samples of students who participated in the assessment were presented with three types of texts: narrative texts (continuous texts in which the writer's aim is to tell a story, whether fact or fiction); expository texts (continuous prose designed to describe, explain or convey factual information); and document texts (structured texts presented in the form of charts, tables, maps and sets of directions). The vast majority of comprehension questions based on these texts were of the multiple-choice variety; the remainder were of the short-answer type. Test questions tapped five levels of text processing that were assumed to be in roughly hierarchical order: literal response (verbatim match), paraphrase, main idea, inference, and locate and process information. As with other international studies, care was taken to ensure that both passages and questions represented the reading curricula in participating countries, and that strict guidelines were adhered to in translating test materials, to ensure comparability of outcomes across countries.

The outcomes of the IEA/RLS were reported in a variety of ways, including mean (average) overall reading literacy scores by country as well as mean country scores for understanding of narrative, expository and document texts. Finland achieved the highest mean score at 9 and 14 years of age. In a ranking of countries at age 9, Ireland and England/Wales were ranked 12th and 21st respectively out of 28 countries. However, because of measurement error, their respective mean scores were found not to be statistically significantly different from one another (Brooks et al., 1996). At age 14, Ireland was ranked 20th of 31 countries, suggesting a decline in achievement between 9 and 14 years. However, Ireland's mean score at age 14 was not significantly different from the mean scores of nine other countries, or from the international country average (Elley, 1992).

Differences were observed in the performance of students on the three text types used in the study. Nine-year olds in both Ireland and England/Wales did best on narrative texts, next best on expository texts, and poorest on documents. At age 14, students in Ireland performed at about the same level on the three text types.

An examination of the distribution of students' scores reveals that the performance of lower-achieving students in England/Wales and Ireland is lower relative to other countries with similar average achievement. At age 9, the score of students in England/Wales at the fifth percentile (a point near the bottom of the achievement distribution) was lower than that of all but three countries (Brooks et al., 1996). At age 14, Ireland had the second largest percentage of students (3.8) scoring two standard deviations or more below the overall country mean. England/Wales also had proportionately more students approaching the top end of the achievement distribution at age 9. Just four other countries had a higher score at the 75th percentile.

Relatively large gender differences in favour of girls were found in England and Wales at age 9, and in Ireland at ages 9 and 14. Indeed, Ireland had the sixth largest gender difference at age 9, and the third largest at age 14, suggesting that gender differences in Ireland may increase in size over time. Moreover, socio-economic status was also found to be related to the achievement of students. In England/Wales, 9-year-olds who were in receipt of free school meals achieved a mean score that was more than half of a standard deviation (57 score points) lower than that of their counterparts who were not in receipt of free meals. In Ireland, teachers were found not to participate in in-career development training as frequently as their colleagues in other countries, or to emphasise the teaching of higher-order comprehension processes such as diagramming story content, or eliciting generalisations and inferences during discussion.

In a review of the performance of English and Welsh students at age 9 on IEA/RLS, Brooks et al. (1996) noted three factors that may have negatively impacted on the performance of English/Welsh students—a possible ceiling effect on the documents component of the IEA/RLS test, lower representativeness of pupil samples in other participating countries, and a lower average age among students in England and Wales. They also noted that IEA/RLS did not measure students' ability to interpret texts by offering a personal response or taking a critical stance, and concluded, on the basis of this observation, that the IEA/RLS test was not very suitable for 9-year-olds in England and Wales.

The International Adult Literacy Study (IALS)

An international assessment of the literacy skills of adults aged 18 to 65 years was conducted in 24 countries, including Ireland and the United Kingdom, between 1994 and 1998, by Statistics Canada, the Educational Testing Service in the US and the Organisation for Economic Co-operation and Development (OECD) based in Paris. In IALS, reading literacy was defined as "the ability to understand and employ information in daily activities, at home, at work, and in the community—to achieve one's goals, and to develop one's knowledge and potential" (OECD/Statistics Canada, 2000). The definition implies a more functional view of literacy than IEA/RLS. Market survey techniques were implemented to assess adults in three domains:

- *Prose literacy:* the knowledge and skills needed to understand and use information from texts, including editorials, news stories, brochures and instruction manuals
- *Document literacy:* the knowledge and skills required to locate and use information contained in various formats, including job applications, payroll forms, transportation schedules, maps, tables and charts
- *Quantitative literacy:* the knowledge and skills required to apply arithmetic operations, either alone or sequentially, to numbers embedded in print materials, such as balancing a cheque book, figuring out a tip, completing an order form or determining the amount of interest due on a loan from an advertisement.

In addition to reporting mean achievement scores of participating countries, IALS reported the proportions of adults at five levels of proficiency in each of the three assessment domains. These levels were derived from a consideration of the technical properties of the underlying scales, and the skills and processes represented by items on the scales. Table 8.1 summarises the five levels of reading literacy, and indicates the proportions of adults in three countries—Ireland, Sweden (the highest-scoring country) and the United Kingdom. According to the authors of the final report, Level 3 is "considered by experts as a suitable minimum skill level for coping with the demands of modern life and work" (OECD/Statistics Canada, 2000).

Reaction to the IALS results was negative in some countries. In Ireland, newpapers informed readers that one-quarter of the adult population was "functionally illiterate", and considerable additional funding was allocated to the adult basic education. In the UK, researchers criticised the methodology underpinning the identification of reading proficiency levels (e.g. Goldstein, 2000). France decided to opt out of the reporting stages of IALS when 75% of adults were found to be at Levels

Table 8.1   Percentages of adults in Ireland, the UK and Sweden scoring at five proficiency levels on the IALS Prose scale (from OECD/Statistics Canada, 2000, Table 2.2)

			Percentage of Adults Achieving Specified Level		
Level	Points range	Short description	Ireland	UK	Sweden
5	376–500	Can search for information in dense text that contains a number of plausible distractors. If required, can make high-level inferences or use specialised knowledge.	13.5[a]	16.6	32.4
4	326–375	Can perform multiple-feature matching, or provide several responses where information must be identified through text-based inferences.			
3	276–325	Can locate information that requires low-level inferences or that meets specified criteria. Can integrate or compare and contrast information across parts of a text.	34.1	31.3	39.7
2	226–275	Can locate more than one piece of information in the text, in which several "distractors" may be present; can make low-level inferences if required.	29.8	30.3	20.3
1	0–225	Can locate one piece of information in the text that is identical to or synonymous with the information given in the directive.	22.6	21.8	7.5

[a] Refers to combined percentages for Levels 4 and 5. These two levels were combined as few adults in participating countries achieved Level 5.

1 and 2 of the Prose scale (compared with 52% in Ireland and the UK) (Blum & Guérin-Pace, 2000).

A number of observations can be made about the outcomes of IALS. First, Level 1, the lowest level of proficiency, included adults who could not read at all and adults who could perform Level 1 tasks only. Hence, it cannot justifiably be claimed, as journalists have, that all adults at Level 1 are illiterate. Second, the cut points used to establish IALS literacy levels were based on a response probability of 0.80 (the probability of answering the most difficult questions at a level correctly), so scores tended to cluster at the lower end of the distribution of proficiency levels. Kellaghan (2000) noted that, if one lowered the cut-off point for Level 1 from 225 to 200, the proportion of Irish adults at Level 1 would drop to 12%. Third, older adults, fewer of whom had access to upper secondary or tertiary education than younger adults, were more strongly represented at the lowest levels of reading proficiency. In Ireland, for example, 39% of adults in the 56–65 years age range, but just 15.9% in the 16–25 years range, were at the lowest Prose proficiency level (Morgan et al., 1997).

Performance on the Document and Quantitative literacy scales tended to be similar to performance on the Prose literacy scale. For example, 23.3% of adults in the UK achieved Level 1 on the Document scale, while 23.2% did so on the Quantitative scale.

Gender differences on IALS were smaller than those found in IEA/RLS, and varied across content domains. For example, males in Ireland were more strongly represented at the lowest level of proficiency on the Prose scale, and at the highest and lowest levels on the Document scale. Where differences were apparent, they tended to be small (Morgan et al., 1997). A relatively strong association was observed between the educational attainment of adults and their reading literacy skills. For example, in Ireland, just 1% of college graduates, but 23.6% of adults whose highest level of education was lower secondary, achieved Level 1 on the Prose scale. Literacy levels were also found to be associated with occupational status. Fewer managers, professionals and technicians were represented at the lowest levels on the Prose proficiency scale than skilled craft workers, machine operators and those involved in agriculture. However, those with low literacy skills (as measured by the IALS assessment) generally did not consider their lack of skills to present them with major difficulties, indicating instead that their literacy skills were sufficient to meet their everyday needs (OECD/Statistics Canada, 2000).

The OECD Programme of International Student Assessment (OECD-PISA)

The OECD-PISA assessment, which is targeted at 15-year-olds in OECD countries (including Ireland and the United Kingdom), involves three assessment domains: reading literacy, mathematical literacy, and scientific literacy. In the first cycle of PISA, which was administered in 28 OECD countries and four non-OECD countries in 2000, the main focus was on measuring students' proficiency in reading literacy, and on identifying policy-relevant factors associated with literacy proficiency at the levels of educational systems, schools and students. (PISA does not select intact classes of students, nor do teachers of participating students complete a questionnaire.) It is planned to focus on mathematical literacy in 2003 and on scientific literacy in 2006, though reading literacy will be assessed as a minor domain in those years, and trends in proficiency in reading literacy can be tracked over time. PISA differs from other international assessments of reading literacy in that it the national governments of participating countries (rather than research organisations) are involved in the design and implementation of the assessment, and the specific issues that are addressed relate directly to the policy concerns of participating countries. The focus on 15-year-olds represents an attempt to measure the cumulative yield of education at or near the end of compulsory schooling.

Reading literacy in PISA is defined as "the capacity to understand, use and reflect on written texts, in order to achieve one's goals, to develop one's knowledge and potential, and to participate in society" (OECD, 2000b, p. 10). This definition overlaps with the IALS definition, in that there is a focus on "using" written texts for functional purposes, and with that of IEA/PIRLS (see page 140) in that students' ability to reflect on text is of interest. The phrases, "to achieve one's goals" and "to develop one's knowledge and potential" focus on the role of literacy in enabling the fulfilment of individual aspirations, and engagement in lifelong learning. Reference to participation in society emphasises the role of reading literacy in economic, political, cultural and social life. The definition emphasises students' future use of reading ("preparedness for life") as opposed to what they have achieved in school. The PISA framework for assessing reading literacy includes the following elements:

- *Process—Reading Tasks:* various tasks required of readers including (i) retrieving information; (ii) developing an interpretation; (iii) reflecting on the content and form (structure) of texts
- *Content—Types of Texts:* the form in which written material is encountered. PISA includes two broad text types: Continuous texts (narrative, expository, descriptive, argumentative/persuasive and injunctive) and non-continuous texts (charts/graphs, tables, diagrams, maps, forms and advertisements)
- *Context—Purpose of Texts:* the situations in which reading takes place, defined in PISA as how the author intended the text to be used. These contexts include: (i) reading for private use; (ii) reading for public use; (iii) reading for work (occupational); and (iv) reading for education.

Using this framework, it was possible to construct an assessment compatible with the definition of reading literacy offered above. The assessment included equal numbers of multiple-choice and short-answer questions, representing a shift in emphasis from earlier assessments such as IEA/RLS where multiple-choice items predominated. To the extent that questions assessing students' ability to reflect on and evaluate the content and form of texts were included, one of the concerns raised by Brooks et al. in relation to the IEA/RLS appears to have been addressed.

Finland achieved a significantly higher mean score (546.5) than any other country in PISA (Table 8.2). Ireland, ranked fifth, and the United Kingdom, ranked seventh, were among a group of seven countries with mean scores that were significantly higher than the OECD country average. Countries with the lowest mean scores on combined reading literacy included Spain, Greece, Portugal and Mexico.

Even though the United States' mean score of 504.4 is lower than those of Austria, Belgium, Iceland, Norway and France, the relatively large standard error associated with the US mean score means that it was not significantly different from those of the UK or Ireland.

It is relevant to observe that countries tend to cluster together on the combined reading literacy scale. For example, just 6 score points separate New Zealand (ranked

Table 8.2   Mean achievement scores and standard deviations on combined reading literacy—Ireland and OECD countries (from Shiel et al., 2001, p. 35, reproduced with permission)

Country	Mean (SE)	SD (SE)	Country	Mean (SE)	SD (SE)
Finland	546.5 (2.58)	89.41 (2.57)	USA	504.4 (7.05)	104.78 (2.70)
Canada	534.3 (1.56)	94.63 (1.05)	Denmark	496.9 (2.35)	98.05 (1.77)
New Zealand	528.8 (2.78)	108.17 (1.97)	Switzerland	494.4 (4.25)	102.02 (2.02)
Australia	528.3 (3.52)	101.77 (1.55)	Spain	492.6 (2.71)	84.74 (1.24)
Ireland	526.7 (3.24)	93.57 (1.69)	Czech Rep.	491.6 (2.37)	96.32 (1.91)
Korea, Rep. of	524.8 (2.42)	69.52 (1.63)	Italy	487.5 (2.91)	91.41 (2.71)
UK	523.4 (2.56)	100.49 (1.47)	Germany	484.0 (2.47)	111.21 (1.88)
Japan	522.2 (5.21)	85.78 (3.04)	Hungary	480.0 (3.95)	93.86 (2.09)
Sweden	516.3 (2.20)	92.17 (1.16)	Poland	479.1 (4.46)	99.79 (3.08)
Austria	507.1 (2.40)	93.00 (1.60)	Greece	473.8 (4.97)	97.14 (2.67)
Belgium	507.1 (3.56)	107.03 (2.42)	Portugal	470.2 (4.52)	97.14 (1.80)
Iceland	506.9 (1.45)	92.35 (1.38)	Luxembourg	441.3 (1.59)	100.44 (1.46)
Norway	505.3 (2.80)	103.65 (1.65)	Mexico	422.0 (3.31)	85.85 (2.09)
France	504.7 (2.73)	91.74 (1.69)			
			OECD Country Avg.	**500.0** *(0.60)*	**100.0** *(0.40)*

☐ Mean achievement significantly higher than Ireland
☐ Mean achievement not significantly different from Ireland
☐ Mean achievement significantly lower than Ireland
SE = Standard error

third) from Japan (ranked eighth). Similarly, just 3 points separate Austria (ranked 10th) from the United States (ranked 15th). The large standard deviations associated with some countries suggest that differences were as great within those countries as between them.

Like IALS, PISA also reported performance on the combined reading literacy scale in terms of reading proficiency levels. However, there is an important method-ological difference. Whereas the probability of getting the more difficult items at a particular level correct in IALS was set at 0.80, the corresponding probability in PISA was 0.62. Hence, all other things being equal, fewer students achieved at the lowest levels of reading proficiency, and more achieved the highest levels. In Ireland, just 11.0% of students achieved Level 1 or below, while 14.2% achieved Level 5 (the highest level). "Below Level 1" describes those students who did not meet the minimum criteria to achieve Level 1. In the UK, the corresponding per-centages were 12.8% and 15.6%. One reason put forward for the relatively strong performance of Irish students on PISA combined reading literacy was that there was a strong match between PISA reading literacy and the syllabus for the Junior Cycle programme, which is completed by students in the 12–15 years age range. The positive performance was also attributed to the inclusion of several questions that involved reflection on and evaluation of the content and format of texts. Such questions are also included in the Junior Certificate English exam, which Irish students take at age 15.

PISA identified a range of variables associated with achievement in literacy. These can be divided into four broad categories:

Table 8.3   Brief descriptions of proficiency levels on combined reading literacy scale, and percentages of students achieving each level—Ireland and OECD area (from Shiel et al., 2001, p. 39, reproduced with permission)

Level	Brief Description	Percentage of Students (SE)		
		Ireland	UK	OECD Average
Level 5	Can complete the most complex PISA reading tasks, including managing information that is difficult to locate in complex texts, evaluating texts critically, and drawing on specialised information.	14.2 (0.8)	15.6 (1.0)	9.5 (0.1)
Level 4	Can complete difficult reading tasks, such as locating embedded information, constructing meaning from nuances of language, and critically evaluating a text.	27.1 (1.1)	24.4 (0.9)	22.3 (0.2)
Level 3	Can complete reading tasks of moderate complexity, including locating multiple pieces of information, drawing links between different parts of a text, and relating text information to familiar everyday knowledge.	29.7 (1.1)	27.5 (0.9)	28.7 (0.2)
Level 2	Can complete basic reading tasks, including locating one or more pieces of information which may require meeting multiple criteria, making low-level inferences of various types, and using some outside knowledge to understand text.	17.9 (0.9)	19.6 (0.7)	21.7 (0.2)
Level 1	Can complete the most basic PISA reading tasks, such as locating a single piece of information, identifying the main theme of a text, and making a simple connection with everyday knowledge.	7.9 (0.8)	9.2 (0.5)	11.9 (0.2)
Below Level 1	Has a less than 0.50 chance of responding correctly to Level 1 tasks. Reading abilities not assessed by PISA.	3.1 (0.5)	3.6 (0.4)	6.0 (0.1)

- *Student Background*, including student gender, parents' Socio-economic status (SES), parents' educational attainment, home educational climate (number of books in the home) and parent support for learning
- *Student Reading Habits and Attitudes*, including diversity of reading (the frequency with which a student read a range of different texts), frequency of borrowing library books, frequency of leisure reading, and attitude towards reading
- *Student As Learner*, including drop-out risk, attendance at learning support (remedial English) classes, and use of learning processes and strategies
- *School Characteristics*, including school management and funding, disadvantaged status, disciplinary climate, and school resources (student–teacher ratio, class size, student–computer ratio).

Female students achieved significantly higher mean scores on combined reading literacy than male students in all participating OECD countries. Differences ranged from 51 points (Finland) to 14 (Korea). The difference in Ireland was 29 points (nearly one-third of a standard deviation), while in the UK, it was 26 (one-quarter of a standard deviation).

In Ireland, the student background variables that were most strongly associated with achievement on the PISA combined reading literacy scale were parents' educational attainment ($r = 0.21$), parents' SES ($r = 0.31$), and home educational climate (books in the home) ($r = 0.33$). Students with 11–50 books at home (one-fifth of students) had a mean combined reading literacy score that was some two-thirds of a standard deviation lower than the mean score of students with more than 250 books (one-quarter of students). However, it is unlikely that simply having books at home accounts for such a large difference in achievement. Having a large number of books at home may mean that students live in a home climate in which there is a strong focus on reading, and on discussing what has been read in newspapers or texts. Such homes may be particularly conducive to facilitating the development of literacy skills.

The correlation between attitude to reading and achievement on the combined reading literacy was 0.43, indicating that students with the most positive attitudes to reading tended to have the highest reading scores. This relationship may be reciprocal, with a positive attitude enhancing the development of reading skills, and good reading skills contributing towards a positive attitude.

Among the learning processes and strategies that were related to reading literacy were academic self-concept ($r = 0.29$), academic self-efficacy ($r = 0.24$), control expectations ($r = 0.25$), use of control strategies ($r = 0.22$), and effort and persistence ($r = 0.12$).

Students in Irish schools designated as educationally disadvantaged had a mean score on the combined reading literacy scale that was some 49 points (one-half of a standard deviation) lower than the mean score of students not in designated schools. Students attending schools that were privately funded and privately managed had a mean score on combined reading literacy that was over two-thirds of a standard deviation higher than that of students in public, government-funded schools.

The IEA Progress in International Reading Literacy (IEA/PIRLS) Study

IEA/PIRLS focuses on the reading achievement of fourth-grade students (9- and 10-year-olds) and the experiences they have at home and at school in learning to read. According to Campbell et al. (2001), this age group represents the transition between "learning to read" and "reading to learn". Participating countries include England, Scotland, France, Germany, Australia and New Zealand. The first PIRLS assessment was administered in 2001. An initial international report is expected in 2003, while future assessments are planned for 2005 and 2009. It will be possible to compare the performance of countries who participated in the IEA/RLS study (see above) with their performance in PIRLS. However, PIRLS also reflects new thinking about the reading process, and approaches to measuring reading literacy that have emerged in recent years. For PIRLS, reading literacy is defined as:

> The ability to understand and use those written language forms required by society and/or valued by the individual. Young readers can construct meaning from a variety of texts. They read to learn, to participate in communities of readers, and for enjoyment.
> (Campbell et al., 2001, p. 3).

The IEA/PIRLS definition of reading is consistent with the view that reading is a constructive and interactive process. According to this view, meaning is constructed in the interaction between the reader and the text in the context of a particular reading experience. The PIRLS definition is similar to PISA's in that both reflect an interactive, constructivist view of reading, and both focus on the importance of a positive attitude towards reading. The PIRLS definition differs from PISA to the extent that it focuses on the typical environment or community in which students read (home and classroom) whereas PISA stresses students' readiness to participate in the larger society. PISA also reflects a more cross-curricular perspective than PIRLS. These differences might be due to the different developmental levels of students participating in the two assessments.

The PIRLS assessment framework focuses on three aspects of reading literacy: processes of comprehension, purposes for reading, and reading behaviours and attitudes. PIRLS identifies four comprehension processes that are broadly similar to those in the PISA reading literacy framework:

- Focus on and retrieve explicitly stated information (20% of items)
- Make straightforward inferences (30%)
- Interpret and integrate ideas and information (30%)
- Examine and evaluate content, language, and textual elements (20%).

Two purposes for reading are identified:

- Acquire and use information (50% of items)
- Literacy experience (50%).

A student questionnaire addresses students' attitudes towards reading and their reading habits, while a teacher questionnaire addresses the teaching of reading.

PIRLS consists of two item-types: multiple-choice (55%) and constructed response (45%). Data-gathering for PIRLS took place in 2001. Participating countries included England and Scotland. The results are expected to be available in Autumn 2002. PIRLS plans to provide scales for overall reading and for the two identified purposes of reading—acquiring and using information, and literacy experience.

NATIONAL ASSESSMENTS OF READING LITERACY

National assessments of reading literacy also provide information about standards in reading and variables associated with reading achievement. In the Republic of

Ireland, there is a national assessment programme in Fifth class (primary level). National assessments of reading have been conducted at regular intervals in Northern Ireland, and in England and Wales at a range of age levels.

National Assessments in Ireland

Since 1972, national assessments of reading literacy in the Republic of Ireland, involving representative samples of 11-year-olds, students in fifth class (primary level) (equivalent to Year 7 in England and Northern Ireland), or both have been conducted at regular intervals. Although standards improved significantly between 1972 and 1980, they have not changed significantly since then, despite improvements in the pupil–teacher ratio, access to remedial teaching (learning support) and in the provision of library services to schools (Cosgrove et al., 2000).

In its current form, the survey assesses understanding of narrative, expository and document texts, mainly using multiple-choice type items. In the 1998 survey, it was found that girls attained significantly higher mean achievement scores than boys on a range of text types, that boys were more strongly represented at the lowest levels of achievement, and that both boys and girls whose parents were in possession of medical cards (an indicator of social and economic status) had a mean score that was one standard deviation lower than that of students whose parents did not have a medical card. Students in schools in designated areas of educational disadvantage also did poorly as a group relative to their counterparts in schools not designated as disadvantaged. Whereas the proportion of students in receipt of remedial teaching in English at the time of the 1993 survey was 8.3%, it had risen to 12.2% by the 1998 survey.

Teachers of students in the 1999 survey rated the reading proficiency of about one in ten students as "weak/inadequate", and an equal number as reading at a third-grade level or lower (i.e. at least two years behind their class level). The students' teachers indicated that about 3.0% of students would not be able to cope with the reading tasks at post-primary level, while a further 17.9% would require assistance in coping with such tasks. Similarly, teachers judged that 1.9% of students would not be able to cope with the everyday demands in reading, while a further 12.4% would require support. These data suggest underlying concerns among teachers about students' literacy levels. While the proportions of students with very serious difficulties are judged to be relatively small (between 2% and 3%), the proportions with less serious difficulties are quite large.

National Assessments in the UK

Surveys of literacy attainment have been conducted in the UK since 1948. In a review of surveys between 1948 and 1996, Brooks (1998) noted that, in general, literacy standards had changed very little over time.

In a series of assessments involving students in Years 6 and 11 (ages 11 and 15/16, corresponding to the last year of primary education and the final year of compulsory schooling) in England and Wales between 1947 and 1979, conducted by the Inspectorate or by the NFER, it was found that average scores rose slightly between 1948 and 1952—an improvement that is widely attributed to a recovery in the education system after the war years—and remained essentially unchanged from 1952 to 1979.

In the years of the Assessment Performance Unit Language Monitor Project based at the NFER (1979–1988), assessments of reading and writing were carried out by the NFER in Northern Ireland, England and Wales on three occasions—1979, 1983 and 1988. The assessments featured the introduction of more authentic literacy tasks than in earlier surveys. Again, the target population was students in Years 6 and 11. Year 6 students experienced small increases in achievement between 1979 and 1983, and again between 1983 and 1988. Year 11 students experienced a slight rise between 1979 and 1983, and no change between 1983 and 1988.

Students in England and Wales in Year 3 were assessed in surveys conducted in 1991 and 1995, using NFER's *Reading Ability Series*. Taking the 1987 standardisation of the test as baseline, a significant drop in achievement (about 2.5 standardised score points) occurred between 1987 and 1991, while, between 1991 and 1995, the average score rose again by almost the same amount, so that the 1995 average was identical to that for 1987. The initial drop was attributed by Brooks et al. (1996) to the introduction of the National Curriculum (in which less time was available for literacy instruction as teachers sought to present a broader curriculum) and to a large proportion of primary school teachers leaving their jobs (14% in 1990). Between 1991 and 1995, teachers became more familiar with the National Curriculum (which itself was revised). Teacher turnover also fell. However, low achievement persisted among students in Year 3 who were assessed in 1991. In 1994, when the cohort entered secondary schools, their principal teachers observed that entry test scores had declined, and could cite test results to that effect.

Surveys of reading were mounted by NFER in Northern Ireland in 1993 and 1996, involving students aged 8, 11 and 14 years on both occasions, and students aged 15/16 years in 1995 only. The tests used at age 8, the *Reading Abilities Series* (RAS), allowed for comparisons over time as norms were available from the 1987 standard-isation, and from the use of level A of the series in a national assessment in England and Wales in 1991. Otherwise, tests developed for a 1988 survey in England by the Assessment Performance Unit at the NFER were used. Because of sampling diffi-culties in 1993, the results for age 14 did not provide reliable evidence on the trend at that age between then and 1996. The only significant increase in achievement that was observed among 11-year-olds between 1993 and 1996 (Brooks et al., 1995; Brooks, 1996).

In Scotland, national assessments were carried out in 1953 and 1963, involving stu-dents in Year 5 (10-year-olds). Substantial increases in achievement were observed on two measures—English Usage (prepositions, tense, spelling and punctuation) and Comprehension (reading). In the late 1970s, Scotland re-established a moni-toring programme involving students in Years 4 (9-year-olds) and 7 (12-year-olds), and conducted assessments in 1978 and 1981. In 1983, an Assessment of Achieve-ment Programme was established to carry out monitoring exercises. It carried out cross-sectional surveys of reading (and writing) in Years 4, 7 and 9 (P4, P7 and S2) in 1984, 1989, 1992 and 1995. Students in Year 4 experienced a slight but significant rise in achievement between 1978 and 1981, a slight but significant fall between 1981 and 1984, no change between 1984 and 1992, and a slight but significant fall between 1992 and 1995. Whereas students in Year 7 experienced no change between 1978 and 1992, they experienced a slight but significant fall in scores between 1992 and 1995. Finally, students in Year 9, who were first tested in 1984, experienced a slight but significant rise in achievement between 1984 and 1989, no change between 1989 and 1992, and a slight but significant fall between 1992 and 1995 (Scholastic Survey Committee, 1968; Neville, 1988; Scottish Office of Education (and Industry) Department Assessment of Achievement Programme, 1984, 1989, 1992, 1995).

CONCLUSIONS

Both national and international studies of reading literacy have provided useful information on standards in reading, and variables associated with achievement in reading. One of the most interesting findings is that reading standards do not change dramatically over time. For example, in Ireland, no differences in achievement were observed across national assessments involving fifth-class students that were conducted between 1980 and 1998. What is less clear is whether lack of change is due to inactivity in areas that might promote growth (for example, the provision of additional resources to schools, the development of teachers' knowledge and skills, the implementation of innovative curricula, the provision of programmes for at-risk students) or whether change at national level is simply very difficult to achieve.

National and international studies confirm the association between reader gender and reading achievement, and between socio-economic status and performance in reading. It is clear that gender differences in reading emerge at an early age, and persist, at least into second-level schooling. Moreover, boys and men are over-represented at the lowest levels of literacy in the general population—a finding that also emerges in research involving students with dyslexic difficulties. It is interesting to observe that in PISA, large gender differences in favour of girls are found in even the highest scoring countries. The challenge facing researchers is to identify more clearly those factors or combinations of factors that dispose boys to do less well in reading than girls.

The association between socio-economic status and reading literacy is not new. In Ireland, for example, large differences between students in schools designated as disadvantaged and in non-designated schools persist, despite the implementation of several programmes designed to narrow the gap. It remains to be seen whether the programmes that are being implemented to combat educational disadvantage in Ireland and elsewhere are sufficiently strong in their focus to raise literacy levels over time.

The finding in PISA that a number of learning strategies and processes are associated with achievement in reading is encouraging, and suggests that programmes designed to develop students' metacognitive skills are worthwhile.

The studies reviewed here provide relatively little information about the proportions of students with dyslexia in particular countries, or about variables associated with students' dyslexic learning difficulties. Indeed, in some studies, dyslexic students may be excluded from testing if they are in receipt of special education services, and/or their school principal believes that they are unable to attempt the test. However, the studies reviewed here point to a range of variables that need to be considered in addressing the needs of students with difficulties in reading. Further, it is clear that several of these variables can occur in combination, presenting educators with quite a challenge as they seek to address students' difficulties.

REFERENCES

Blum, A., & Guérin-Pace, F. (2000). Weaknesses and defects of the IALS. In S. Carey (Ed.), *Measuring Adult Literacy: The International Adult Literacy Survey in the European Context* (pp. 68–98). London: Office for National Statistics.

Brooks, G. (1998). Trends in standards in the United Kingdom, 1948–1996. *TOPIC*, 19, Item 1.

Brooks, G., Fernandes, C., Gorman, T., & Wells, I. (1995). *Reading Standards in Northern Ireland Revisited*. Slough, Berks: NFER.

Brooks, G., Pugh, A.K., & Schagen, I. (1996). *Reading Performance at 9*. Slough, Berks, UK: NFER and the Open University.

Campbell, J.R., Kelly, D.L., Mullis, I.V.S., Martin, M.O., & Sainsbury, M. (2001). *Framework and Specifications for PIRLS Assessment 2001* (2nd Edn.). Boston, US: PIRLS International Study Centre.

Cosgrove, J., Kellaghan, T., Forde, P., & Morgan, M. (2000). *The 1998 National Assessment of English Reading*. Dublin: Educational Research Centre.

Elley, W.B. (1992). *How in the World Do Students Read?* The Hague: International Association for the Evaluation of Educational Achievement.

Goldstein, H. (2000). IALS—A commentary on the scaling and data analysis. In S. Carey (Ed.), *Measuring Adult Literacy: The International Adult Literacy Survey in the European Context* (pp. 34–42). London: Office for National Statistics.

Kellaghan, T. (2000). 'Reading standards in Ireland'. Paper presented at the National Reading Initiative Conference, Malahide, Co. Dublin.

Morgan, M., Hickey, B., and Kellaghan, T. (1997). *International Adult Literacy Survey: Results for Ireland*. Dublin: Stationery Office.

Neville, M. (1988). *Assessing and Teaching Language: Literacy and Oracy in Schools*. Basingstoke, UK: Macmillan Education.

Organisation for Economic Co-operation and Development (OECD)/Statistics Canada. (2000). *Literacy in the Information Age. Final Report of the International Adult Literacy Survey*. Paris: OECD.

Organisation for Economic Co-operation and Development (OECD). (2000). *Measuring Students' Knowledge and Skills: The PISA 2000 Assessment of Reading, Mathematical and Scientific Literacy*. Paris: OECD.

Organisation for Economic Co-operation and Development (OECD). (2001). *Knowledge and Skills for Life. International Report on the PISA 2000 Assessment*. Paris: OECD.

Scottish Office of Education (and Industry) Department Assessment of Achievement Programme. (1984, 1989, 1992 & 1995). (Various authors). *Reports on English Language*. Edinburgh: Scottish Office.

Shiel, G., Cosgrove, J., Sofronion, N., and Kelly, A. (2001). *Ready for Life?: The Literacy Achievements of Irish 15-year-olds with Comparative International Data*. Dublin: Educational Research Centre.

Part II

PRACTICE

This section of the book on practice is not intended to be prescriptive; rather, we hope it will engage the reader in critical thinking as s/he considers the different approaches offered in this section. These approaches are closely linked to theory, and have an established theoretical framework which supports their use in dealing with difficulties in literacy and dyslexia.

Some of the key points are discussed below in this introduction to Part 2 of the book.

THE SHIFT TO A MODEL OF ASSESSMENT WHICH INCORPORATES AN INTERACTIVE MODE

Wearmouth and Reid, in discussing theoretical aspects of teaching and how these may relate in practice, discuss the shift from a medical/traditional model of assessment to a model which incorporates an interactive/dynamic mode. This perception of assessment has considerable implications for the class teacher, and in Chapter 11 Reason discusses the implications of this shift for educational psychologists. One implication is that the learning environment as well as the learner needs to be part of the assessment. It also paves the way for metacognitive assessment, which is discussed in a number of chapters in this section. Wearmouth and Reid indicate that this involves looking at the actual process of learning—how the student learns, not only the product of learning. An interactive model can also include the use of learning styles as a means of identifying the most appropriate teaching and learning approaches for individual children. In relation to this, Reason discusses the concept of "noticing and adjusting". The interplay between these aspects is central to identifying and adjusting to the individual needs of students.

This point is also emphasised in Burden's chapter, which discusses Vygotsky's socio-cultural framework and focuses on cognitive models as a means of acquiring and conceptualising meaning from text. In this context, Burden also discusses learning from the perspective of Feuerstein's theory of cognitive modifiability, which incorporates the input, elaboration and output phases of information processing. Essentially Burden is emphasising that thinking and learning are not static entities and that children do not learn in a vacuum. Thinking and learning, according to Burden, are not personal characteristics but socio-cultural processes.

A REAPPRAISAL OF THE PRACTICE OF TEACHING READING

Many chapters in this section suggest that it is now time to reappraise the practice of teaching reading. Ehri, in Chapter 10, focuses on the learner rather than on methods and materials. She analyses four reading processes—decoding, analogy, prediction and sight—and suggests that sight word reading may be the most efficient in terms of reading effort and fluency. However, some readers may not know all the words, so other strategies are also needed. Nevertheless, by studying the phases of acquiring sight words through the pre-alphabetic, partial alphabetic phase and full alphabetic phase, she shows how all of these stages are interrelated in the development of sight words. In essence, Ehri is indicating the importance of early reading, the need to acquire the alphabetic foundation to read words and the need to teach students strategies to read words by sight. Interestingly, she points out the high correlation between reading in first grade and in later grades.

Topping, in Chapter 18 on paired thinking, and Wray, in Chapter 19 on metacognition and literacy, tackle the reading process from a top-down perspective and relate this to the above notion of thinking and learning expressed by Burden, and the higher-order reading and metaliteracy skills also suggested by Wray. This implies that metacognitive strategies should be inclusive to any reading programme from the outset, and that children's literacy experience should always be meaningful and purposeful from their perspectives. Wray provides suggestions to achieve this through metacognitive strategies such as thinking aloud, teacher modelling and reciprocal teaching.

The meaningfulness of literacy as a basis for understanding and for motivation is also picked up by Hunt in Chapter 20 on critical literacy. Hunt suggests that a problem that can be encountered by programmes aimed at automatic word recognition is that of transferring the sub-lexical skills acquired through the programme into the real-life reading activity. Literacy, according to Hunt, is not necessarily empowering unless it is accompanied by critical awareness. This clearly has implications for dyslexic students, who may be able to grasp the critical awareness of the text but may need support in accessing the text itself. Yet accessing the text should not be the end product, rather the beginning, as the notion of critical awareness brings the text into the reader's own world.

Eames concludes Part 2, and indeed the book, by redefining definitions and concepts of literacy, which is a theme emerging from many of the chapters in this book. She suggests that, as definitions of literacy have changed, so have the curriculum, teaching and assessments associated with them. For that reason it is important to acknowledge the role of definitions in literacy, as definitions have the potential to drive the curriculum. Literacy is an important construct in the macro/context level and the micro/individual level, and is broader than reading alone. If literacy is therefore an agent of change, it is crucial that the broader definition and wider access to literacy suggested by contributors to this book should be acknowledged and incorporated in daily teaching, the curriculum and the assessment procedures for literacy. This concurs with the view, expressed by many of the authors in this section of the book, that there is a need to broaden the teaching of literacy but at the same time to be aware of the need to establish a literacy foundation based on alphabetic knowledge.

THE NEED TO ACKNOWLEDGE DIVERSITY

Diversity is a key theme in literacy learning, and this includes cultural and textual, as well as the diverse learning experiences and skills which children bring to the learning task. Crombie acknowledges the diversity in the needs, interests and skills which children bring to the classroom and the challenge that this presents for the class teacher. Teachers need to be prepared to adopt different strategies at different times to meet children's needs. Crombie emphasises the importance of the learning environment to be "dyslexia-friendly" in order to support the diverse strengths and needs of dyslexic children.

One way of meeting the diverse needs of children is through the development of Individual Education Plans (IEPs). Tod elaborates the rationale behind IEPs, as well as giving examples of principal aspects of them. She highlights the dilemma of meeting both individual needs and the needs of learning communities inherent in the inclusionary movement and shows how, through constructive and effective use of IEPs, the school can address "individual learner needs within a politically led educational agenda". Tod touches on the dilemmas facing teachers in the construction of IEPs and the notion of whether IEPs should "measure what is valuable or value what is easily measurable". This implies that IEPs should be proactive and not a response to a difficulty, and it is important that some targets build on strengths and self-esteem.

Cline continues the theme of meeting individual needs through focusing on children learning English as an additional language (EAL). He acknowledges that all readers require a range of language-related skills and knowledge, but that there are certain elements that present a particular challenge for those learning to read in their second or third language. For example, they need a full appreciation of the cultural background to the content of a text. Children reading in their second language tend to make less effective use of contextual cues. It is interesting to note in this regard that those children who are in the early stages of learning English as a second language benefit less from the regular Literacy Hour routines, in countries of the UK where these apply, than other pupils. It is important, according to Cline, to be aware of the wider aspects of literacy as these can help children engage with a range of texts and enhance both their understanding and enjoyment of the world and their cultural and intellectual heritage.

CHALLENGES FOR ALL

The theme of challenges is discernible throughout this book. In the first part contributors analyse and discuss research challenges. In this part they discuss the challenges implied in practice. Teaching is challenging; teaching of reading, with its diversities of models, methods and materials, in addition to the demands of the curriculum and the need to embrace all learners in the "literacy journey", represents further challenges to teachers. Eames points out two key aspects of that challenge: the need to cater for the diverse range of students with age-appropriate and reading level-appropriate materials and at the same time to engage students in critical thinking to enable them to be powerful communicators. This incorporates a perspective of literacy as central to the notion of citizenship. Literacy impacts on life experience and has considerable implications post-school, as well as for learning success in school. This is highlighted in Chapter 15 by Peer and Reid on the challenges in the secondary school. These challenges relate to demands stemming from the currently prevalent philosophy of inclusion, the increasing accountability of the teaching profession, demands stemming from government legislation and, particularly in secondary school, the need for planning and differentiation, to ensure that literacy difficulties should not deprive students of benefiting from a full curriculum. This point was emphasised by David Blunkett when, as Secretary of State, he suggested that many pupils are disadvantaged on reaching secondary school as a result of poor literacy skills generally, and dyslexia in particular. Part 2 of the book, therefore, has considerable implications not only for the literacy development of students but for the development of cognitive, intellectual and academic skills necessary for success in school and the workplace, and for the social and cultural enrichment of society.

Chapter 9

ISSUES FOR ASSESSMENT AND PLANNING OF TEACHING AND LEARNING

Janice Wearmouth and Gavin Reid

INTRODUCTION

Recent years have witnessed a number of developments in the area of assessment of "special" learning needs, including the needs of those who experience difficulties in literacy development. Firstly, there has been a growing awareness that the whole issue of assessment is highly political. Any kind of assessment rests on particular assumptions about the nature of human beings and the nature of human learning and achievement. Certain ways of assessing individual differences carry particular implications at a personal, school and also societal level. Secondly, there has been a move away from the solely "medical" model of difficulties in learning to one that recognises the interactive nature of these difficulties (Wedell, 2000) and a broader concept of what specially "needs" to be done to address such difficulties. In this "interactive model", the barriers to pupils' learning arise as a result of the interaction between the characteristics of the student and what is offered through the pedagogy and supporting resources. Thirdly, as a result of legal and moral considerations (Gersch, 2001) and, additionally, the implications of current models of learning which emphasise the agency of the learner (Vygotsky, 1987), the issue of pupil self-advocacy has assumed an increasing significance. Finally, the rights of parents and carers not just to be consulted over the formal process of educating young people, but also to be actively engaged in the decision-making processes, have been given explicit recognition in many countries, for example in England in the *Parents' Charter* (DfE, 1992). The complex challenges for those addressing assessment of difficulties in literacy development in order to plan programmes to address dyslexic pupils' learning needs are therefore:

Dyslexia and Literacy: Theory and Practice. Edited by Gavin Reid and Janice Wearmouth.
© 2002 John Wiley & Sons, Ltd.

- To be aware of some of the major issues and debates surrounding assessment of "special" learning needs of any kind, in particular those in the area of literacy
- To be aware of a broad range of assessment strategies in order to consider how most appropriately to assess the characteristics of the individual pupil within and outside the context of the classroom. This includes the assessment of pupils' metacognitive strategies and individual learning styles
- To be able to assess ways in which the learning environment potentially creates barriers to, or facilitates, literacy development
- To be aware of the issues raised by the growing expectation that the perspectives of the "users" of the system, that is both students and their parents or carers, will be taken into account in the assessment process, in addition to those of education professionals.

ISSUES AND DEBATES IN THE ASSESSMENT OF "SPECIAL" LEARNING NEEDS

There are a number of important issues about which professionals must be very clear in their assessment of dyslexic pupils. The first relates to the underlying assumptions of particular forms of assessment of pupils' "special" learning needs and the consequences of these assumptions. The second relates to what professionals are trying to achieve in the assessment process.

Underlying Assumptions and Their Consequences

With regard to the first, underlying the formulation of assessments for statutory purposes there are assumptions which intrinsically contradict notions of inclusion. In the first place, available resources have often dictated the provision made for individual pupils (Cline, 1992). In order to decide who is eligible for additional services, special educational provision depends on norm-referenced assessment designed solely to indicate a learner's achievement in comparison with others and, therefore, identify some students who are "different". Some writers, for example Booth and Goodey (1996), have criticised the dyslexia label on two counts. Firstly, they have criticised the way that the label enables some parents to claim for their own children an unjust proportion of the funds designated for all "special educational needs":

> The [dyslexia] lobby's new-found vigour diverts funds and attention from children who have genuine disabilities or difficulties worthy of being covered by a statement.... The tendency to look for the source of reading difficulties within individuals is financially driven. (Booth & Goodey, 1996)

Furthermore, it is obvious that norm-referenced tests of ability and attainment carry the power to "determine selectively the way in which issues are discussed and solutions proposed" (Broadfoot, 1996). The influence of psychometric thinking leads to deterministic views of ability and achievement which limit what we expect from certain students, and restrict developments in assessment. Those identifying and assessing pupils through standardised forms of assessment which appear to indicate the deficiency of some pupils in comparison with others must take some responsibility for the potential effect of this. For some students, for example those from the poor or lower class, lowered expectations can lead to a reproduction in society of underpriviledged groups. Tomlinson (1988) argues that from the perspective of critical theory (Habermas, 1974) the existence of special educational arrangements which appear to be the result of rational and pragmatic assessment of pupils should be questioned. In order to explain the existence of such arrangements we should look to the function that they serve in maintaining the power of the privileged and dominant groups in society:

> The ideas of critical theorists can suggest that the stupidity or dullness of some individuals or social groups is not necessarily self-evident or "true". Acquiring the label and being treated as "less-able" is likely to be the result of complex social, economic and political judgements and considerations. (Tomlinson, 1988, p. 45)

Bourdieu and Passeron (1973) examined how schools can assist the process of reproducing the pattern of control and subordination within society which is inextricably linked to the economic context. From this perspective, there is a contradiction between the rhetoric of humanitarian concern that education exists to promote equality and the reality that the system of education functions to reproduce the children of underprivileged groups, for example the working class and those who are physically disabled, into powerless positions in society. From this perspective also, "success" and "failure" are not objective "givens". They are social categories whose labels serve the vested interests of dominant, powerful groups in society. The reason why children fail in the education system can be given with reference to the social, economic and political status quo as much as to the existence of a deficit in the child. Tomlinson argues that, if this were not so:

> Why does being a poor reader and lower-class, seem to have much more serious and long-term consequences than being a poor reader and upper or middle class?
> (Tomlinson, 1988 p. 48)

There is a crisis for education in a post-industrial age where achievements assessed through reading and writing are the prerequisites to obtaining a job with a salary above subsistence level. The inability of illiterate citizens to find well paid employment is legitimised if they have been labelled in advance through special education:

> Special education reproduces and controls lower-status groups, and legitimates their life-long treatment, but is, in itself, an acceptable, legitimating, humane development.
> (Tomlinson, 1988, p. 49)

Low scores on IQ tests or standardised tests of reading and spelling allow schools to "blame" the child and also absolve themselves from taking responsibility for that child's progress in school.

> The way the black and working-class Johnnys with reading problems are dealt with will usually ensure that they are reproduced into the low-status sections of society.
> (Tomlinson, 1988, p. 55)

In the case of dyslexia, however, some groups of parents, as seen from this perspective, have found a way of removing the stigma of failure from their children and of normalising them:

The dyslexia label says to parents, "Your child has a problem, but your child is normal," and, by its nature, it discriminates against other disability labels. (Booth and Goodey, 1996)

The Purpose of Assessment

Whatever the ideological arguments, the fact remains that some pupils experience difficulties in literacy development. It is important to tease out factors contributing to this difficulty if those pupils are to acquire literacy, one of the fundamentals of a cultural toolkit (Bruner, 1986). Crucial to what professionals are trying to achieve in relation to the individual student, are the distinctions in kind and purpose of different types of assessment. In some countries in the UK, Individual Education Plans or Records or Individual Profiles have become major tools in planning programmes of study for individual students who experience difficulty in literacy acquisition. In drawing up these individual programmes, the assessment of students is both formative and summative. Formative and summative assessment are different in kind as well as purpose (Harlen & James, 1997). Ongoing formative assessment is carried out by teachers to collect information and evidence about a pupil's literacy development and to plan the next step in his/her learning. It combines the assessment of skills required for specific tasks, and pupil-referenced (ipsative) techniques where the same pupil's progress is tracked across time. Summative assessment takes place at certain intervals when achievement has to be recorded and is intended to provide a global picture of the learner's literacy development to date. It requires a high degree of reliability, and may involve a combination of different types of assessment, for example the measurement of individual pupil progression in learning against public criteria.

Range of Assessment Strategies

As we have noted above, if difficulties in literacy learning can be seen as a function of the interaction between within-child and environmental factors, then it follows that there must be an assessment of the student's characteristics and also of the learning environment. Identification of what needs to be measured in terms of literacy development at the level of the individual student is not simple (Beard, 1990). Some aspects of the process of literacy acquisition, for example awareness of sound–letter correspondence during the process of reading, can be broken down into measurable objectives. However, other aspects, for example assessment of enjoyment of reading or of the finer points of the comprehension and appreciation of text, are much more problematic.

Assessment of Within-Child Factors

One of the key issues in relation to assessment is the selection of assessment strategies. The types of strategies often used to assess within-child factors related to poor achievement in literacy include those discussed below.

Normative, psychometric tests. Norm-referenced tests imply measurement and the use of standardised instruments and typically produce measures in terms of ranks, for example standardised reading and spelling scores. Whilst this type of assessment has some uses, it must be treated with some caution as the results of such norm-based tests can be misinterpreted and misused. They cannot, for example, indicate appropriate intervention strategies because:

> ...the scores do not provide details of what the child knows or does not know, nor do they elucidate the processes that are involved in the child's difficulty. (Dockrell & McShane, 1993, p. 34)

We have noted above other problematic issues associated with the way in which the use of normative testing procedures may result in the marginalisation and exclusion of students who experience difficulty in learning. If assessment systems are to be inclusive then, as Dockrell and McShane (1993, p. 35) note, they need to be criterion-based, using task analysis, and result in such measures as developmental profiles and checklists to "help identify whether or not an individual possesses some particular skill or competence...allow for the analysis of error patterns...provide a clear indication of what a child can and [indicate] what skills should be taught next."

Dynamic and metacognitive. Whilst standardised assessment can provide information on the student's level of attainments in comparison with peers, it is static since it emphasises what the learner can do unaided and therefore does not provide information about the learner's thinking processes. Dynamic assessment, on the other hand, focuses on the process of learning, can identify the strategies being used by the learner and can also be a useful teaching tool through the development of concepts and ideas during teacher/student interaction. One such method, known as reciprocal teaching, can be particularly useful; this consists of a dialogue between teacher and student "for the purpose of jointly constructing the meaning of text" (Palincsar & Brown, 1984, p. 19) and therefore assessment and teaching can be combined.

The traditional view of teaching dyslexic individuals is based on a number of well-founded principles (Thomson, 1989; Pumfrey & Reason, 1991; Augur & Briggs, 1992; Reid, 1998; Ott, 1997; Peer, 1999). These principles tend to suggest that dyslexic students would benefit from a teaching programme which is characterised by its multi-sensory, sequential, cumulative and structured nature. Often this type of programme is implemented on a one-to-one basis with considerable over-learning. While this procedure may be effective for those with a low baseline in literacy, we suggest that it can perform a disservice to many dyslexic students by over-looking metacognitive aspects of learning, potential in thinking skills and learning styles.

It is argued that dyslexic students may have difficulty with the metacognitive aspects of learning (Tunmer & Chapman, 1996), that is, being consciously aware of, and being able to control and monitor, their own thinking processes. This implies that they need to be shown how to learn and that the connections and relationships between different learning tasks need to be highlighted. The emphasis should not necessarily be on the content or the product of learning but on the process, that is, how learning takes place. Metacognition has an important role in learning and can help to develop thinking skills, and enhances an awareness of the learning process and the utilisation of effective strategies when learning new material. The teacher then has an instrumental role to play in assessing metacognitive awareness and supporting its development (Peer & Reid, 2001). This can be done by asking the student some fundamental questions and also through observing the learning behaviour of students. For example, when tackling a new task does the student demonstrate self-assessment by asking questions such as:

- Have I done this before?
- How did I tackle it?
- What did I find easy?
- What was difficult?
- Why did I find it easy or difficult?
- What did I learn?
- What do I have to do to accomplish this task?
- How should I tackle it?
- Should I tackle it the same way as before?

The use of metacognitive strategies can help to develop reading comprehension and expressive writing skills.

Wray (1994) provides a description of some of the skills shown by good readers which can provide a good example of metacognitive awareness in reading. Good readers, according to Wray, usually:

- Generate questions while they read
- Monitor and resolve comprehension problems
- Utilise mental images as they read
- Re-read when necessary
- Self-correct if an error has been made when reading.

These factors can help to ensure that the reader has a clear picture of the purpose of reading and an understanding of the text about to be read. There is considerable evidence to suggest that pre-reading discussion can enhance reading fluency and understanding.

Assessing understanding through re-telling. Assessment instruments are often based on restrictive criteria, examining what the student may be expected to know, often at a textual level. However, they may ignore other rich sources of information which can inform about the student's thinking, both cognitive and affective, and provide suggestions for teaching. Ulmer and Timothy (2001) developed an alternative assessment framework based on re-telling as an instructional and assessment tool. This indicated that informative assessment of a student's comprehension could take place by using criteria relating to how the student re-tells a story. Ulmer and Timothy suggested the following criteria: textual—what the student remembered; cognitive—how the student processed the information; and affective—how the student felt about the text. Their two-year study indicated that 100% of the teachers in the study assessed for textual information, only 31% looked for cognitive indicators and 25% for affective indicators. However, the teachers who did go beyond the textual found rich information. Some examples of information provided by the teachers indicated that by assessing beyond the textual level in relation to the use of the re-telling method of assessment could provide evidence of the student's "creative side", and teachers discovered that students could go "beyond the expectations when given the opportunity". This is a good example of how looking for alternative means of assessing can link with the student's understandings of text and promote and develop thinking.

Assessing individual learning styles. Consideration of learning styles and metacognitive approaches can be useful for both assessment and teaching of dyslexic students and can provide them with an opportunity to focus on their own understandings of text and utilise their own strengths in learning to access text across the curriculum.

Learning is a process. It is important, therefore, to focus on the information-processing cycle involved in literacy learning and to consider potential metacognitive and learning styles aspects within the information-processing cycle. The stages of the information-processing cycle essentially relate to input, cognition and output. Some suggestions which highlight the importance of each of these stages are shown below. This is particularly important for dyslexic students as they can show difficulties at each of the stages of information processing.

At the input stage:

• Acknowledge the student's preferred learning style
• Present information in small units
• Ensure that over-learning is used; vary this, using a range of materials
• Present key points at the initial stage of learning new material.

At the cognition stage:

• Encourage organisational strategies; new material to be learned should be organised into meaningful chunks or categories at each of the stages of the information-processing cycle
• Relate information to previous knowledge to ensure that concepts are clear and the information can be placed into a learning framework or schema by the learner
• Use specific memory strategies such as mind mapping and mnemonics.

At the output stage:

• Use headings and subheadings in written work to help provide a structure
• Encourage the use of summaries in order to identify the key points.

The above points highlight the importance of learning styles as a crucial factor in all stages of the information-processing cycle. At present there are more than 100 instruments especially designed to identify individual learning styles. Most were developed to evaluate narrow aspects of learning, such as preference for visual, auditory, tactual or kinaesthetic input (Grinder, 1991). Others are far more elaborate and focus on factors primarily associated with personality issues, such as intuition, active experimentation and reflection (Gregorc, 1982; 1985; Kolb, 1984; Lawrence, 1993; McCarthy, 1987).

Many approaches attempt to identify how individuals process information in terms of its input, memory and expressive functions (Witkin & Goodenough, 1981). A few theorists emphasise the body's role in learning and promote cross-lateral movement in hopes of integrating the left- and right-brain hemispheric activity (Dennison & Dennison, 1989). Some perspectives to learning-style approaches are briefly described below.

- Riding and Rayner (1998) combine cognitive style with learning strategies. They describe cognitive style as a constraint which includes basic aspects of an individual's psychology such as feeling (affect), doing (behaviour) and knowing (cognition). The individual's cognitive style relates to how these factors are structured and organised.
- Kolb's (1984) Learning Style Inventory is a derivative of Jung's psychological types combined with Piaget's emphasis on assimilation and accommodation, Lewin's action research model and Dewey's purposeful, experiential learning. Kolb's 12-item inventory yields four types of learners: divergers, assimilators, convergers and accommodators.
- Dunn and Dunn's (Dunn et al., 1996) Learning Style Inventory contains 104 items that produce a profile of learning-style preferences in five domains (environmental, emotional, sociological, physiological and psychological) and 21 elements across those domains. These domains and elements include: environmental (sound, light, temperature, design); emotional (motivation, persistence, responsibility, structure); sociological (learning by self, pairs, peers, team, with an adult); physiological (perceptual preference, food and drink intake, time of day, mobility); and psychological (global or analytic preferences, impulsive and reflective).
- Given (1998) constructed a new model of learning styles derived from some key elements of other models. This model consists of emotional learning (the need to be motivated by one's own interests), social learning (the need to belong to a compatible group), cognitive learning (the need to know what age-mates know), physical learning (the need to do and be actively involved in learning), and reflective learning (the need to experiment and explore to find what circumstances work best for new learning).

Learning styles using observational criteria. In addition to using standardised instruments, learning styles may be identified through classroom observation. This form of assessment can yield informative data which can inform teaching. Observational assessment is contextualised and can be used flexibly to ensure that the data obtained is the type of information required. It is important, however, that the observer recognises the drawback of observational assessment, in that it often only provides a snapshot of the student unless it is implemented in different contexts over time. Nevertheless, this type of assessment can be particularly useful for students with dyslexic difficulties as some standardised tests may not provide the kind of diagnostic information which is needed in order to develop a teaching programme.

Whilst observation in itself may not be sufficient to identify learning styles fully, the use of a framework for collecting observational data can yield considerable information and can complement the results from more formal assessment. Observational assessment can be diagnostic, because it is flexible, adaptable and can be used in natural settings with interactive activities. Reid and Given (1999) have developed such a framework—the Interactive Observational Style Identification (IOSI). A summary of this is shown below.

Motivation
- What topics, tasks and activities interest the student?
- What kind of prompting and cueing is necessary to increase motivation?
- What kinds of incentives motivate the student—leadership opportunities, working with others, free time or physical activity?

Persistence
- Does the student stick to a task until completion without breaks?
- Are frequent breaks necessary when working on difficult tasks?

Responsibility
- To what extent does the student take responsibility for his/her own learning?
- Does the student attribute success or failure to self or to others?

Structure
- Are the student's personal effects (desk, clothing, materials) well organised or cluttered?
- How does the student respond to someone imposing organisational structure on him/her?

Social Interaction
- When is the student's best work accomplished—when working alone, with another student or in a small group?
- Does the student ask for approval or need to have work checked frequently?

Communication
- Does the student give the main events and gloss over the details?
- Does the student interrupt others when they are talking?

Modality preference
- What type of instructions does the student most easily understand—written, oral or visual?
- Does the student respond more quickly and easily to questions about stories when heard or read?

Sequential or simultaneous learning
- Does the student begin with one step and proceed in an orderly fashion or have difficulty following sequential information?
- Is there a logical sequence to the student's explanations or do her/his thoughts bounce around from one idea to another?

Impulsive/reflective
- Are the student's responses rapid and spontaneous or delayed and reflective?
- Does the student seem to consider past events before taking action?

Physical mobility
- Does the student move around the class frequently or fidget when seated?
- Does the student like to stand or walk while learning something new?

Food intake
- Does the student snack or chew on a pencil when studying?

Time of day
- During which time of day is the student most alert?
- Is there a noticeable difference between morning work and afternoon work?

Sound
- Does the student seek out places that are particularly quiet?

Light
- Does the student like to work in dimly lit areas or say that the light is too bright?

Temperature
- Does the student leave his/her coat on when others seem warm?

Furniture design
- When given a choice, does the student sit on the floor, lie down, or sit in a straight chair to read?

Metacognition
- Is the student aware of his/her learning style strengths?
- Does the student demonstrate self-assessment

Prediction
- Does the student make plans and work towards goals, or let things happen?

Feedback
- How does the student respond to different types of feedback?
- How much external prompting is needed before the student can access previous knowledge?

There are too many manifestations of style to observe all this at once. One way to begin the observation process is to select one of the learning systems and progress from there. The insights usually become greater as observation progresses.

Learning Environment

Understanding how the learning environment can contribute to barriers to pupils' learning is complex. There are a number of ways of conceptualising the interactional relationship between the learning environment and the learner. For example, from an ecosystemic perspective Bronfenbrenner (1979) identifies four levels that influence student outcomes:

- **Microsystem**: the immediate context of the student—school, classrooms, home, neighbourhood
- **Mesosystem**: the links between two microsystems, e.g. home–school relationships
- **Exosystem**: outside demands/influences in adults' lives that affect students
- **Macrosystem**: cultural beliefs/patterns or institutional policies that affect individuals' behaviour.

In a wide-ranging review of the literature on learning environments, Ysseldyke and Christenson (1987b) identified three categories of environmental factors influencing instructional outcomes. These are school district conditions, within-school conditions and general family characteristics.

Walberg's (1981; 1982) multi-factor psychological model of educational productivity holds that learning is a multiplicative, diminishing-returns function of student age, ability and motivation; of quality and quantity of instruction; and of the psychosocial environments of the home, the classroom, the peer group and the mass media. Any factor at zero-point will result in zero learning because the function is multiplicative. It will do more good to improve a factor that is currently the main constraint to learning than to raise a factor that is already high. Empirical probes of the educational productivity model (Walberg, 1984) showed that classroom environment is a strong predictor of both achievement and attitudes even when a comprehensive set of other factors was held constant.

Ysseldyke and Christenson (1987b) note that those who feel that classroom teaching is a potential source of barriers to pupil learning recommend that assessment of such teaching should begin by analysing instruction and assessing the extent to which teaching is matched to the developmental level of the pupil. They argue that it is potentially profitable to focus on features of classroom practice because these can be altered to facilitate learning more effectively, and go on to identify a number of instructional factors in the classroom that influence student outcomes:

• Planning procedures
• Management procedures
• Teaching procedures
• Monitoring and evaluation procedures.

Based on their analysis of these features in the learning environment, Ysseldyke and Christenson (1987b) designed "The Instructional Environment Scale" (TIES) in order to support the systematic collection of data to analyse contextual barriers to pupils' learning. The two major purposes for using TIES are stated as:

> • To describe systematically the extent to which a student's academic or behaviour problems are a function of factors in the instructional environment, and
> • To identify starting points in designing appropriate instructional interventions for individual students. (Ysseldyke & Christenson, 1987b, p. 22)

Data are gathered through classroom observation and interview with both pupil and teacher on twelve components of teaching:

> *Instructional Presentation:* Instruction is presented in a clear and effective manner; directions contain sufficient information for the student to understand what kinds of behaviours or skills are to be demonstrated; and the student's understanding is checked before independent practice.

> *Classroom Environment:* The classroom is controlled efficiently and effectively; there is a positive, supportive classroom atmosphere; time is used productively.

> *Teacher Expectations:* There are realistic yet high expectations for both the amount and accuracy of work to be completed, and these are communicated clearly to the student.

Cognitive Emphasis: Thinking skills needed to complete assignments are communicated explicitly to the student.

Motivational Strategies: The teacher has and uses effective strategies for heightening student interest and effort.

Relevant Practice: The student is given adequate opportunity to practise with appropriate materials. Classroom tasks are clearly important to achieving instructional goals.

Academic Engaged Time: The student is actively engaged in responding to academic content; the teacher monitors the extent to which the student is actively engaged and redirects the student when the student is not engaged.

Informed Feedback: The student receives relatively immediate and specific information on his or her performance or behaviour; when the student makes mistakes, correction is provided.

Adaptive Instruction: The curriculum is modified to accommodate the student's specific instructional needs.

Progress Evaluation: There is direct, frequent measurement of the student's progress toward completion of instructional objectives; data on pupil performance and progress are used to plan future instruction.

Instructional Planning: The student's needs have been assessed accurately and instruction is matched appropriately to the results of the instructional diagnosis.

Student Understanding: The student demonstrates an accurate understanding of what is to be done in the classroom. (Ysseldyke & Christenson, 1987, p. 22)

USERS' PERSPECTIVES

Over recent years in many countries there has been an increased emphasis on taking account of the perspectives of the "users" of the system, that is both students and their parents or carers, during the process of assessment and planning to meet special learning needs, for example in the area of literacy. This seems to have resulted from a growing interest in human rights issues as they apply to "special" forms of education (see, for example, UNESCO, 1994), and the "marketisation" of education, as in England and Wales subsequent to the 1988 Education Reform Act. Taking full account of perspectives beyond those of professionals raises a number of issues in educational institutions.

Students' Perspectives

In order to conform with national advisory documents (DfES, 2001; DENI, 1998) which apply to a number of UK countries, it is important that assessment at the level of the individual student takes into account his/her perspective on learning. One of the major challenges facing those responsible for the progress of dyslexic students is engaging with student perspectives in a positive and meaningful way. Garner and Sandow (1995) have identified philosophical and practical problems surrounding student self-advocacy. Among these are that the model of student as participant and self-directed learner rather than empty vessel to be filled implies that the traditional role of the teacher as purveyor of wisdom and transmitter of knowledge must change to that of facilitator. This development in the teacher's role may be uncomfortable. Self-advocacy may run contrary to the traditional behaviourist model of learning adopted in some schools, which relies on learning programmes designed to reinforce desired behaviour and inhibit undesired behaviour. Additionally, some pupils may be seen as undeserving of the right to self-advocacy; others, even at secondary level, may be perceived as incapable of contributing rationally to decisions about their own lives. Pupils, especially teenagers, may verbally challenge teachers' authority openly, as well as the structure and organisation of the school. Self-advocacy involves a transfer of power from teacher to pupil in the degree of legitimacy accorded to pupils' opinions.

Gersch (2001) notes that progress made in involving students more actively in their education over the past 20 years "has been patchy, unsystematic and slow". However, without exploring pupil perspectives it is impossible to understand anything of the "competing values and expectations stemming from internal idiosyncratic processes or from differing family and sub-cultural values" (Ravenette, 1984) that pupils may experience which lead them to rejection of everything associated with school.

Gersch (2001), reporting on a project which aimed to enhance pupils' active participation in school through encouraging self-evaluation and advocacy, encountered a number of dilemmas:

- How does one deal with other colleagues who might feel that students should be seen and not heard?
- Are some students not mature or capable enough to participate? . . .
- How does one deal with parent–child dislike?
- What about scope needed for students to negotiate, try things and change their minds?
- How do adults distinguish what a student needs from what he or she prefers or wants?
- What if the SENCO comes into conflict with the head teacher over ways of meeting a student's needs? What then happens to the student's views? (Gersch (2001) p. 241)

Clearly there are no easy solutions to these dilemmas which represent, essentially, conflict between the roles of the participants. The nearest Gersch himself comes to offering an answer is to point to the "the importance of a trusting, listening, open, non-judgmental relationship" between teacher and pupil.

Parents' and Carers' Perspectives

In the same documents referenced above (DfES, 2001; DENI, 1998) there is a requirement that education professionals must take parent or carer views into account in assessing the difficulties experienced by students with literacy difficulties. Parents or carers, of course, may have views about either or both within-child and environmental barriers to literacy acquisition.

There are a number of contentious issues that must be addressed if parents' and carers' perspectives on their children's learning are to be taken seriously. Firstly, there may be a big difference between what is perceived as fair and necessary by different groups of parents and between parents and the individual school. Competing or conflicting parents' voices may be irreconcilable within the walls of one school. For example, parental concern about replacing withdrawal from class and individual tuition in literacy with in-class support assumed great significance in a research project at "Downland", an urban comprehensive school attempting to move towards an inclusive approach (Clark et al., 1997). This particular school was finally forced to recreate special forms of provision for some pupils as a result of pressure from parents of those pupils with Statements who regarded generalised in-class support as insufficient to meet specific literacy needs.

Secondly, some parents are better able to exercise their rights than others as a result, sometimes, of access to financial resources and legal representation. The Audit Commission (1992) observed that factors other than the level of a student's need influenced the decision to issue a Statement of special educational needs in England and Wales. The most significant of these factors at that time were "the level of determination of the school or the parent and whether the parent was represented by a lawyer or voluntary organisation".

Clearly there needs to be a great deal of negotiation with parents and carers in the area of assessment and provision for students' difficulties in learning, for example, literacy. This is the reason why, in some countries, arrangements have been made at local education authority level to provide mediation services between home and school.

CONCLUSION

Many factors, singly and in complex interaction, influence pupil achievement. Some of these factors are intrinsic to the individual learner while others relate to the learning environment and methods of teaching. Others still are connected to the environment outside the control of the teacher. Those responsible for supporting the literacy development of those learners who experience difficulties must be familiar with the whole range of techniques appropriate to assessing the factors over which they have some control. Additionally, they should also be aware of the underlying assumptions of particular forms of assessment and potential effects of their use. It is crucial that responsibility for assessment should not rest with one individual but should be a whole-school responsibility. This means that school or education authority policy on assessment should inform the class or specialist teacher on the type of information required from the assessment, when to obtain the information and how it should be used. Assessment needs to have a purpose and a rationale and not merely be used as a means to a label.

REFERENCES

Audit Commission (1992). *Getting in on the Act: Provision for Pupils with Special Educational Needs.* London: HMSO.
Augur, J. & Briggs, S. (1992). *The Hickey Multisensory Language Course.* London, Whurr.
Badia, N. A. (1997). Dyslexia and the double deficit hypothesis.

Beard, R. (1990). *Developing Reading 3–13*. London: Hodder and Stoughton.

Booth, T. & Goodey, C. (1996). "Dyslexia: Playing for the sympathy vote", *The Guardian*, 21 May 1996, p. 5.

Bourdieu, P. & Passeron, J. C. (1973). *Reproduction in Education, Society and Culture*. London: Sage.

Broadfoot, P. (1996). *Education, Assessment and Society*. Buckingham: Open University Press.

Bronfenbrenner, U. (1979). *The Ecology of Human Development*. Cambridge, MA: Harvard.

Bruner, J. (1986). *Actual Minds, Possible Worlds*. Cambridge, MA: Harvard.

Clark, C., Dyson, A., Millward, A. & Skidmore, D. (1997). *New Directions in Special Needs*. London: Cassell.

Cline, T. (Ed.) (1992). *The Assessment of Special Educational Needs*. London: Routledge.

DENI (Department of Education, Northern Ireland) (1998). *Code of Practice for the Identification and Assessment of Special Educational Needs*. DENI: Bangor, N Ireland.

Dennison, P. E. & Dennison, G. E. (1989). *Brain Gym: Teacher's Edition, Revised*. Ventura, CA: Edu-Kinesthetics, Inc.

Department for Education (1992). *Children with Special Needs: A guide for Parents*. London: DfE.

DfES (Department for Education and Skills) (2001). *Special Educational Needs Code of Practice*. London: DfES.

Dockrell, J. & McShane, J. (1993). *Children's Learning Difficulties: A Cognitive Approach*. Oxford: Blackwell.

Dunn, R., Dunn, K. & Price, G. E. (1996). *Learning Style Inventory*. Lawrence, KS: Price Systems.

Garner, P. & Sandow, S. (1995). *Advocacy, Self Advocacy and Special Needs*. London: Fulton.

Gersch, I. (2001). Listening to Children. In J. Wearmouth, *Special Educational Provision in the Context of Inclusion*, ch 12, pp 228–244. London: Fulton.

Given, B. K. (1998). Psychological and neurobiological support for learning-style instruction: Why it works. *National Forum of Applied Educational Research Journal*, 11(1), 10–15.

Gregorc, A. F. (1982). *An Adult's Guide to Style*. Columbia, CT: Gregorc Associates, Inc.

Grinder, M. (1991). *Righting the Educational Conveyor Belt* (2nd edn.). Portland, OR: Metamorphous Press.

Habermas, J. (1974). *Theory and Practice*. Translated from the German by John Viertel. London: Heinemann.

Harlen, W. & James, M. (1997). Assessment and learning: differences and relationships between formative and summative assessment. *Assessment in Education*, 4(3), 365–379.

Kolb, D. (1984). *Experiential Learning: Experience as the Source of Learning and Development*. Englewood Cliffs, NJ: Prentice-Hall.

Lawrence, G. (1993). *People Types and Tiger Stripes* (3rd edn.). Gainsville, FL: Center for Applications of Psychological Type.

McCarthy, B. (1987). *The 4mat System: Teaching to Learning Styles with Right/Left Mode Techniques*. Barrington, IL: EXCEL Inc.

Ott, P. (1997). *How to Detect and Manage Dyslexia—A Reference and Resource Manual*. Oxford: Heinemann.

Palincsar, A. & Brown, A. (1984). Reciprocal teaching of comprehension fostering and comprehension monitoring activities. *Cognition and Instruction*, 1(2), 117–175.

Peer, L. (1999). What is dyslexia? In *British Dyslexia Association Handbook*. Reading: BDA.

Peer, L. & Reid, G. (Eds) (2001). *Dyslexia: Successful Inclusion in the Secondary School*. London: David Fulton Publishers.

Pumfrey, P. D. & Reason, R. (1991). *Specific Learning Difficulties (Dyslexia) Challenges and Responses*. Windsor: NFER Nelson.

Ravenette, T. (1984). The recycling of maladjustment. *AEP Journal*, 6(3), 18–27.

Reid, G. (1998). *Dyslexia: A Practitioners Handbook*. Chichester, UK: Wiley.

Reid, G. & Given, B. K. (1999). The interactive observation style identification. In B. K. Given, & G. Reid *Learning Styles—A Guide for Teachers and Parents*. Lancashire, UK: Red Rose Publications.

Riding, R. & Rayner, S. (1998). *Cognitive Styles and Learning Strategies, Understanding Style Differences in Learning and Behaviour*. London: David Fulton.

Stein, J. F. (2000). "Genetic studies in dyslexia". Paper presented at the BDA. Training for Trainers Conference, Manchester, May 2000.

Thomson, M. E. (1989). *Developmental Dyslexia* (3rd edn.) London: Whurr.

Tomlinson, S. (1988). Why Johnny can't read: critical theory and special education. *European Journal of Special Needs Education*, 3(1), 45–58.

Tunmer, W. E. & Chapman, J. (1996). A developmental model of dyslexia—can the construct be saved? *Dyslexia*, 2(3), 179–189.

Ulmer, C. & Timothy, M. (2001). How does alternative assessment affect teachers' practice? Two years later. Paper presented at the 12th European Conference on Reading, Dublin, Ireland, 1–4 July 2001.

UNESCO (1994). *Salamanca Statement and Framework for Action*, Publication of the World Conference on Special Needs Education. Paris: UNESCO.

Vygotsky, L. S. (1987). *The Collected Works, Vol 1. Problems of General Psychology*. New York: Plenum.

Walberg, H. J. (1981). A psychological theory of educational productivity. In F. Farley & N. Gordon (Eds) *Psychology and Education*. Berkeley, CA: McCutchan.

Walberg, H. J. (1982). Educational productivity: Theory, evidence and prospect, *Australian Journal of Education*, 26, 115–122.

Walberg, H. J. (1984). Improving the productivity of America's schools'. *Educational Leadership*, 41, 19–30.

Wearmouth, J. B. (ed.) (2001). *Special Educational Provision in the Context of Inclusion: Policy and Practice in Schools*. London: Fulton.

Wedell, K. (2000) Interview transcript in *E831 Professional Development for Special Educational Co-ordinators*. Milton Keynes, UK: Open University.

Witkin, H. & Goodenough, D. (1981). Cognitive styles: Essence and origins. *Psychological Issues Monograph 51*. New York: International Universities Press.

Wray, D. (1994). *Literacy and Awareness*. London: Hodder & Stoughton.

Ysseldyke, J. E. & Christenson, S. L. (1987a). *The Instructional Environment System*. Austin, TX: PRO-ED.

Ysseldyke, J. E. & Christenson, S. L. (1987b). Evaluating students' instructional environments. *Remedial and Special Education*, 8(3), p. 17–24.

Chapter 10

READING PROCESSES, ACQUISITION, AND INSTRUCTIONAL IMPLICATIONS[*]

Linnea C. Ehri

The question of how children learn to read can be answered in different ways. Answers might focus on methods of instruction or they might focus on the processes that children acquire to accomplish this feat (Adams, 1990). The purpose of my chapter is to focus on the learner rather than on teaching methods, to explain the word-reading processes that beginners acquire, the course of acquisition, and what creates difficulties for struggling readers as indicated by theory and evidence. The reason for examining processes separately from instruction is to clarify the target of instruction. Once the processes have been described, then implications for instruction will be considered.

It will become apparent that in order for students to become skilled at reading words, they must acquire knowledge of the alphabetic system and they must learn to use it to read and spell words. These are the processes that give struggling readers the most difficulty. Teachers need to understand these processes in order to implement instruction effectively for each student.

Learning to read involves two basic processes captured in the simple view of reading (Gough & Tunmer, 1986; Hoover & Gough, 1990). One process involves learning to decipher the print, that is, learning to transform letter sequences into familiar words. The other involves comprehending the meaning of the print. When children attain reading skill, they learn to perform both of these processes in a way that allows their attention to focus on the meaning of the text while the

[*] This chapter was adapted from a chapter by L. Ehri (1998), entitled "Grapheme–phoneme knowledge is essential for learning to read words in English" in J. Metsala and L. Ehri (Eds), *Word Recognition in Beginning Literacy* (pp. 3–40). Mahwah, NJ: Erlbaum. Parts are reprinted by permission from Erlbaum Associates.

Dyslexia and Literacy: Theory and Practice. Edited by Gavin Reid and Janice Wearmouth.
© 2002 John Wiley & Sons, Ltd.

mechanics of reading, including deciphering, operate unobtrusively and out of awareness.

Children acquire listening comprehension skill in the course of learning to speak, but they do not acquire deciphering skill. Learning to decipher print is not the "natural" process that learning to speak is. The brain is specialized for processing spoken language but not written language (Liberman, 1992). In order that reading and writing skills develop, written language must penetrate and gain a foothold in the mechanisms used by the brain to process speech. First we will consider the nature of word-reading skills and how they operate as part of the reading process. Then we will consider how learners acquire these skills.

READING WORDS IN TEXT

The interactive model of reading adapted from Rumelhart (1977) and displayed in Figure 10.1 portrays how words are processed during the act of reading text. The box in the center represents a central processor that receives information from the eyes and interprets it. The boxes around the center depict the various information sources that are stored in the reader's memory and used to recognize and interpret text. Readers' knowledge of language enables them to recognize sentences and their meanings. Readers have factual, experiential, and schematic knowledge about the world. This enables them to understand ideas and to fill in gaps in the text where meanings remain implicit. Readers' metacognitive knowledge consists of reading comprehension strategies that are used to monitor the quality of their comprehension, to ensure that the information makes sense and meets specific purposes, and to detect and make repairs when necessary. Memory for a text is constructed as readers use these knowledge sources to comprehend the sentences and paragraphs

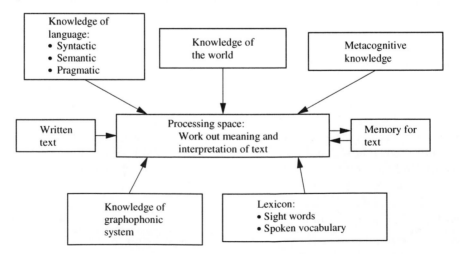

Figure 10.1   Interactive model depicting the sources of knowledge contributing to text reading

in that text. Readers' understanding of the text is stored in memory, accessed to understand subsequent text, and revised to accommodate new information.

At the bottom of Figure 10.1 are depicted two knowledge sources that enable readers to process letters and words in the text. Readers' knowledge of the alphabetic system enables them to convert letters into sounds in identifying unfamiliar words. Lexical knowledge refers to something like a dictionary of words that readers hold in memory, including the written forms of words that readers have read before and know by sight. All of the knowledge sources in Figure 10.1 operate together interactively to facilitate text comprehension.

Let us consider how readers read words as they process text. We can identify at least four different ways (Ehri, 1991, 1994). Readers might read words:

—by decoding
—by analogizing to known words
—by predicting words from graphophonemic and context cues
—by memory (by "sight").

The first three ways are strategies applied to read unfamiliar words. The final way is used to read words read before and retained in memory. In each case, the processes differ. As readers attain skill, they learn to read words in all four ways.

Decoding words involves transforming letters into sounds and blending the sounds to form recognizable words. Beginners learn to transform graphemes into phonemes, not only single letters but digraphs such as TH and OI. More advanced readers learn how common letter patterns are pronounced and how to assemble these into pronunciations as well. Table 10.1 displays common endings of single-syllable words (Stahl et al., 1990) and common affixes occurring in words (Becker et al., 1980). Studies show that words having common letter patterns are easier to decode by readers who are familiar with the patterns (Bowey & Hansen, 1994; Juel,

Table 10.1   Common spelling patterns in words

Common Spellings of Rimes in Single Syllable Words						
-ack	-all	-ain	-ack	-ale	-ame	-an
-ank	-ap	-ash	-at	-ate	-aw	-ay
-eat	-ell	-est				
-ice	-ick	-ide	-ight -ill		-in	-ine
-ing	-ink	-ip	-ir			
-ock	-oke	-op	-ore	-or		
-uck	-ug	-ump	-unk			

Common Affixes						
-al	-able	-ate	-ant			
-ed	-en	-er	-ent			
-ize	-ist	-ing	-ive	-ite	-ion	-ic
-ful	-ly	-less	-ment	-ness	-ous	
com-	con-	de-	dis-	ex-	im-	-in
or-	pre-	pro-	re-	un-		

1983; Laxon et al., 1988; Treiman et al., 1990). In reading English, decoding works sometimes but not always because many spellings have variable or irregular pronuncations.

A very different way to read words is from memory by sight. Consider how skilled readers read the following words (Adams & Huggins, 1985): *island, depot, yacht, guitar, rhythm*. They can read them quickly and accurately even though the spellings deviate from conventional grapheme–phoneme correspondences and hence thwart decoding efforts. Readers are able to read these words by accessing them in memory. Adams and Huggins' words are useful for showing that the process of reading words from memory is different from the process of decoding words. However, it is not the case that only irregularly spelled words are read from memory. Rather, all words may become sight words.

When readers read words by sight, they access information stored in memory from previous experiences reading the words (Ehri, 1992). Sight of the written word activates its spelling, pronunciation, and meaning immediately in memory without any decoding steps required. Reitsma's (1983) evidence suggests that even first-graders can retain sight words in memory after reading the words as few as four times. You can tell when readers are reading words by sight because they read the words as whole units, with no pauses between sounds, faster than it would be possible to decode the words (Ehri & Wilce, 1983; Perfetti & Hogaboam, 1975).

There is one property of sight word reading that makes it especially valuable for reading text. Sight words known well enough can be read automatically (LaBerge & Samuels, 1974). That is, readers can read these words without expending any atten- tion or effort. In Figure 10.2, try to name the rows of pictures quickly while ignoring the words. You will find it impossible to ignore the words. This is evidence that your mind is processing the words automatically. Studies using the picture–word interference task have shown that not only the pronunciations but also the mean- ings of words are recognized automatically (Ehri, 1977; Golinkoff & Rosinski, 1976; Rosinski et al., 1975) and that readers as young as the end of first grade can read familiar words automatically (Guttentag & Haith, 1978). Even poor readers can read words automatically.

Another way to read words is by analogy (Baron, 1977; Bowey & Hansen, 1994; Cunningham, 1976; Gaskins et al., 1988; Glushko, 1979, 1981; Goswami, 1986, 1988; Laxon et al., 1988; Marsh et al., 1981). Readers may read a new word by recognizing how its spelling is similar to a word they already know as a sight word, for example, reading *fountain* by analogy to *mountain*, or *beak* by analogy to *peak*. Goswami (1990) showed that beginning readers can use their knowledge of rhyming words to read words by analogy, especially if the rhyming clue words are in view. However, having some decoding skill appears to be required for beginners to analogize using sight words in memory (Ehri & Robbins, 1992).

One final way to read words is by prediction. Readers might predict the identity of an unfamiliar word by using context cues such as pictures or the preceding text (Goodman, 1976), or they might use beginning letters (Tunmer & Chapman, 1998). Alternatively, they might use their knowledge about language or their world

Figure 10.2   Picture-naming task to demonstrate that words are processed automatically despite the reader's intention to ignore them (From Ehri, L. (1987). Learning to read and spell words, *Journal of Reading Behavior, 19*, 5–11. Copyright 1987 by National Reading Conference. Reprinted by permission)

knowledge (see Figure 10.1). This way of reading words is evident in the miscues that readers produce when they read text aloud. Typically, when words are misread, readers substitute a word that fits the sentence structure and meaning, indicating that context influenced the choice of words (Biemiller, 1970; Clay, 1968; Goodman, 1976; Weber, 1970).

Predicting words based on context cues, however, does not account for the way that readers read most words in text (Stanovich, 1980). Studies show that only 25–30% of the words can be guessed correctly. The most important content words are the least predictable, with only 10% guessed correctly (Gough & Walsh, 1991). Thus, for readers to guess words effectively, they must know most of the surrounding words in a text. To read these accurately, readers must use processes other than contextual guessing.

Having identified the various ways to read words, let us consider how words are processed during text reading. Eye-movement studies reveal that the eyes fixate on practically every word in a text, sometimes more than once (McConkie & Zola, 1981; Rayner & Pollatsek, 1989). Even the most predictable words are not skipped. Text reading operates most efficiently when the words can be read accurately and automatically by sight with little attention or effort. This allows the reader's attention to focus on the meaning of the text. In contrast, each of the other ways of reading words requires that attention be shifted to the word itself to determine its identity. Although sight word reading is the most efficient way to read words in text, readers may not know all of the words by sight, so the other strategies are needed to identify unknown words.

Being able to read most of the words in text is required in order for the text to be read with ease and comprehension. The rule of thumb is that if students can read 98% of the words in a text, the text is considered easy. If students can read around 95% of the words, the text is at their instructional level. If students fall much below 90% accuracy, the text becomes frustrating (Johns, 1991). The need for high accuracy underscores the importance to readers of acquiring large sight vocabularies as well as strategies for attacking unfamiliar words. Findings of Juel (1988) raise doubts that poor readers ever read school texts this accurately. She analyzed poor readers' ability to read words they had already read in basal books in their classrooms at the second- and third-grade reading levels. She found that their average accuracy ranged from 70% to 83%, indicating frustration-level reading.

SIGHT WORD LEARNING

To explain sight word reading, we must specify how readers are able to look at printed words they have read before and recognize those specific words while bypassing in memory thousands of other words, including those with very similar spellings or meanings. Moreover, we must specify how readers are able to remember new words easily after reading them only a few times (Reitsma, 1983). The kind of process we have found to be at the heart of sight word learning is a *connection-forming* process. Connections are formed that link written words to their pronunciations and meanings in memory.

What kinds of connections are formed to store sight words in memory? One view holds that readers memorize associations between the visual shapes of words and their meanings. However, shape is not a sufficient cue to enable readers to distinguish among the many words they can read, for example, *stick, stink, slick,* and *slink,* words having very similar shapes. Sight word reading must involve remembering letters in the words. These are the distinctive cues that make one word different from all the others.

Another view holds that readers decode words by transforming letters into sounds and sounds into meanings. However, we have found that even beginning readers can read familiar words such as *book, man,* and *car* as rapidly as they can name single digits and much faster than they can decode simple pseudowords such as *jad, mig,* and *des* (Ehri & Wilce, 1983). This suggests that readers read sight words as single whole units, not as a sequence of letters transformed into sounds.

Findings of my research indicate that readers learn sight words by forming connections between graphemes in the spellings and phonemes in the pronunciations of individual words. The connections are formed out of readers' general knowledge of grapheme–phoneme correspondences. Graphemes are the functional letter

```
    S  T  O  P              CH  E  CK
    |  |  |  |               |   |  /
   /s/ /t/ /a/ /p/          /č/ /ɛ/ /k/


    G  I  GG  LE             B  IR  D
    |  |  |   /              |  |   |
   /g/ /I/ /g/ /L/          /b/ /r/ /d/


    N  E  V  ER              B  R  IGH  T
    |  |  |  /               |  |   |   |
   /n/ /ɛ/ /v/ /r/          /b/ /r/ /ay/ /t/


    S  I  G*  N              I   S*  L  A  N  D
    |   \   /                 \   /  /  |   \
   /s/ /ay/ /n/              /ay/ /L/ /ae/ /n/ /d/


    S  W*  O  R  D           L  I  S  T*  E  N
     \   /  /  /             |   \   \   /  /
    /s/ /o/ /r/ /d/         /L/ /I/ /s/ /ə/ /n/


   CH  E  S  T             CH   EST
    |  |  |  |              |    |
   /č/ /ɛ/ /s/ /t/         /č/  /ɛst/


   I  N  T  ER  E  S  T  I  NG     IN  TER  EST  ING
   |  |  |  |   |  |  |  |  |        |   |    |    \
  /I/ /n/ /t/ /r/ /ɛ/ /s/ /t/ /I/ /ŋ/   /In/ /tər/ /ɛst/ /Iŋ/
```

Figure 10.3 Illustration of the connections formed in memory between graphemes and phonemes, or between consolidated graphemes and syllabic units, to remember how to read specific words

units symbolizing phonemes. Phonemes are the smallest units of "sound" in words. Readers look at the spelling of a particular word, they pronounce the word, and they apply their graphophonemic knowledge to analyze correspondences within that word. Forming these connections secures the sight word in memory (Ehri, 1980, 1984, 1987, 1991, 1992, 1994; Ehri & Saltmarsh, 1995; Ehri & Wilce, 1979, 1980, 1983, 1986, 1987a).

Figure 10.3 reveals how beginning readers might analyze several different words to secure them as sight words in memory. In this figure, capital letters designate the spellings of words, lower-case letters between slashes indicate phonemes, and lines linking letters to phonemes indicate connections. Notice that although the grapheme G may symbolize either /j/ or /g/ in words, in the word "giggle," the letter G gets remembered as the phoneme /g/, not /j/, because the pronunciation of the word specifies /g/. In this way, the spelling is bonded to the word's pronunciation and meaning in memory. The next time readers see the word, they can retrieve it from memory to read it. Perfetti (1992) has described a similar process for representing words in memory.

To bond spellings to pronunciations, readers must know conventional grapheme–phoneme correspondences and they must have phonemic segmentation skill to distinguish and match up phonemes to graphemes. In analyzing words, readers attempt to achieve an optimum match by searching pronunciations for distinguishable phonemes symbolized by graphemes. For example, we observed fourth-graders segment words such as PITCH into four phonemes corresponding to the graphemes P-I-T-CH but they segmented RICH into three phonemes matched to the graphemes R-I-CH (Ehri & Wilce, 1980). A phoneme corresponding to T can be found in articulating these words, but it is not distinguished without a spelling to suggest it.

The process of forming connections allows readers to remember how to read not only words containing conventional grapheme–phoneme correspondences but also words that have less regular spellings. Connections that might be formed to remember irregular words are illustrated in Figure 10.3. Note that the same types of connections are evident. In fact, many letters in irregular words may conform to grapheme–phoneme conventions, for example, all but S in "island". In remembering letters that do not correspond to phonemes, readers may remember them as extra visual forms, or they may flag them as silent in memory, or they may remember a special spelling pronunciation that includes the silent letter, for example, remembering "listen" as "lis-ten" or "chocolate" as "choc-o-late" (Ehri, 1984; Ehri & Wilce, 1982; Drake & Ehri, 1984).

Spellings of words are like maps that lay out the phonological forms of words visually. Readers need to become skilled at computing these mapping relations very quickly when they read words. Knowledge of letter–sound relations provides a powerful mnemonic system that bonds the written forms of specific words to their pronunciations in memory. Once the graphophonemic spelling system is known, readers can learn to read words and build a lexicon of sight words easily.

Phases of Development

In studying the course of development of sight word learning, we have found that different types of connections predominate at different points in development (Ehri, 1991, 1994, 1995, 1999; Ehri & McCormick, 1998). Sight word learning begins as a non-alphabetic process involving memory for connections between selected visual cues and words. However, once learners acquire some knowledge about the alphabetic system, sight word learning changes into an alphabetic process. At first, connections are partial, linking only some letters to sounds. When readers acquire full knowledge of the alphabetic system, complete connections can be formed between graphemes in spellings and phonemes in the pronunciations of words. As sight words accumulate in memory in fully analyzed forms, letter sequences recurring in different words become consolidated into multi-letter patterns symbolizing syllabic units. Being able to retain fully analyzed connections of words in memory enables mature readers to recognize the pronunciations and meanings of thousands of words accurately and automatically upon seeing them in print (Ehri, 1980, 1984, 1987, 1992; Perfetti, 1992).

Four phases characterized by the involvement of the alphabetic system capture the changes that occur in the development of sight word reading: pre-alphabetic, partial alphabetic, full alphabetic, and consolidated alphabetic (Ehri, 1995, 1999; Ehri & McCormick, 1998). Each phase is labeled to reflect the predominant type of connection that links the written forms of sight words to their pronunciations and meanings in memory.

Pre-Alphabetic Phase

During the pre-alphabetic phase, beginners remember how to read sight words by forming connections between selected visual attributes of words and their pronunciations or meanings. Gough and Hillinger (1980) describe this as a process of paired associate learning. We have called this "visual cue reading" (Ehri & Wilce, 1985). Gough et al. (1992) showed that pre-alphabetic readers select single salient visual cues to remember words. In one case, a thumbprint appearing next to a word was the salient cue. When it accompanied the word, children could read the word. When it did not, the word was not recognized. Other examples of salient visual cues that readers might use to form connections are the two round eyes in *look*, the tail dangling at the end of *dog*, two humps in the middle of *camel* (Gough et al., 1983).

This phase is called pre-alphabetic because letter–sound relations are not involved in the connections. When pre-alphabetic readers read print in their environment, such as stop signs and fast food restaurant signs, they do this by remembering visual cues accompanying the print rather than the written words themselves, for example, the golden arches behind *McDonalds* rather than initial M in the name. Masonheimer et al. (1984) selected children who could read environmental print and presented the print with one letter altered, for example, *PEPSI* changed to *XEPSI*. Children failed to notice the change even when prompted to look for an error. Our explanation is that the children failed to use letters to form the connections in memory that enabled them to read the signs.

The pre-alphabetic phase is really a phase that occurs by default, as Byrne (1992) has pointed out. Young children may have a desire to remember how to read words, but they cannot take advantage of systematic relations between letters and sounds. By default, they resort to noticing and remembering visually salient cues. However, these cues are unreliable because they recur in several words. Also, they are hard to remember because most are arbitrary (Mason, 1980).

Partial Alphabetic Phase

During the next phase, beginners remember how to read sight words by forming partial alphabetic connections between only some of the letters in written words and sounds detected in their pronunciations. Because first and final letters are especially salient, these are often the cues that are remembered. We have called this "phonetic cue reading." To remember sight words in this way, partial alphabetic readers need to know some letter–sound correspondences and have some phonemic segmentation. For example, to remember how to read *spoon*, beginners might detect initial /s/ and final /n/ in the pronunciation of the word, and recognize that the letters they see, S and N, symbolize these sounds. Recognizing these connections is facilitated by the fact that the names of these letters contain the relevant sounds (i.e. "ess" and "en") (Templeton & Bear, 1992; Treiman, 1993). These connections are retained in memory and enable learners to read "spoon" the next time they see it. The reason why the connections are partial rather than complete is that readers lack full knowledge of the spelling system, particularly vowels, and they cannot segment speech into phonemes that match up with the array of graphemes.

Ehri and Wilce (1985) found that partial alphabetic readers differed from pre-alphabetic readers in their sight word learning. Both groups were taught to read two types of words, those whose letters were visually distinctive but bore no relationship to sounds (e.g. WcB as the spelling for "elephant"), and those whose letters could be linked to some sounds in the words (e.g. "LFT" for "elephant"). Partial alphabetic readers learned to read the sound-based spellings more easily than the visual spellings, indicating phonetic cue reading, whereas pre-alphabetic readers learned the visual spellings more easily, indicating visual cue reading.

Rack et al. (1994) confirmed the phenomenon of phonetic cue reading in children. They showed that beginners remembered how to read words better when the spellings provided connections that were phonetically close rather than distant. For example, beginners were taught to read two different spellings of "garden," either KDN or BDN. Both /k/ and /b/ differ from /g/, but /k/ is closer phonetically to /g/ in being articulated at the same place in the mouth. Results showed that students learned to read KDN more easily than BDN. Thus, even though both spellings contained incorrect letters, the letters that enabled the formation of plausible graphophonemic connections were the ones that facilitated sight word learning.

There is an advantage to forming connections out of partial phonetic cues rather than visual cues. Ehri and Wilce (1985), and also Mason (1980), found that phonetic cue readers retained the ability to read the words they learned much better than visual cue readers. This is because phonetic cue readers had a system available to support memory. Knowing the alphabetic system greatly facilitates the task of forming and remembering relevant connections between written words and their pronunciations. In contrast, visually based connections are idiosyncratic and often arbitrary, making them much harder to remember.

Ehri and Saltmarsh (1995) compared older disabled readers and first-grade normal readers in their ability to learn to read words. They were taught simplified phonetic spellings, for example, MESNGR for *messenger*. The disabled readers took more trials to learn to read the words than the first-graders. Also, reaction times to read original and altered spellings of the words suggested that disabled readers retained less complete memory for letters in the words than normal readers. These findings suggest that disabled readers operate at the partial alphabetic phase in learning to read words.

Full Alphabetic Phase

During the full alphabetic phase, beginners remember how to read sight words by forming complete graphophonemic connections. This is possible because readers know how the major graphemes symbolize phonemes in the conventional spelling system (Venezky, 1970, 1999). In applying this knowledge to form connections for sight words, spellings become fully bonded to pronunciations in memory (Ehri, 1992; Perfetti, 1992). For example, in learning to read *spoon*, full-phase readers recognize how the five letters correspond to four phonemes in the word, including how OO symbolizes /u/.

One advantage of representing sight words completely in memory is that word reading becomes much more accurate. Whereas phonetic cue readers' limited memory for letters may cause them to misread *soon* or *spin* as *spoon*, full alphabetic readers' representations are sufficiently complete to eliminate confusion. This difference in the tendency to confuse similarly spelled words was apparent in a study comparing readers in the partial phase with readers in the full alphabetic phase (Ehri & Wilce, 1987b).

To study the impact of analyzing words fully, Ehri and Wilce (1987a) selected children who were in the partial phase and assigned them to one of two treatments. The experimental group was taught to read words by fully connecting letters to sounds in the words. The control group practiced the letter–sound connections in isolation rather than in words. Following training, children received a sight word learning task. They were given several trials to learn to read 15 similarly spelled words. The full-phase readers mastered the list within three trials, whereas the partial-phase readers read only 40% of the words after seven learning trials. The difficulty exhibited by partial-phase readers was confusing words having similar letters, for example, BEND and BLOND, DRIP and DUMP, LAP and LAMP, STAB and STAMP. These results reveal the great advantage to word reading that occurs at the full alphabetic phase.

At this phase, readers acquire two other word-reading strategies. They become able to decode words. Also they become able to read words by analogy to known sight words. Ehri and Robbins (1992) found that full alphabetic readers analogized in reading new words whereas partial-phase readers did not. Rather they tended to mistake the new words for the known words because of shared letters, for example, misreading the new word SAVE as the word they had learned to read, CAVE. Our explanation is that partial-phase readers do not store sight words in memory in sufficient letter detail to recognize similarities and differences in the new and known words. In contrast, readers in the full phase possess full representations of sight words plus decoding skill, both of which support an analogy strategy.

Consolidated Alphabetic Phase

Full alphabetic readers are able to decode words by transforming graphemes into phonemes, and they are able to retain sight words in memory by connecting graphemes to phonemes. These processes acquaint them with the pronunciations of syllabic and subsyllabic spelling patterns that recur in different words. The letters in these patterns become consolidated into larger spelling–sound units which can be used to decode words and to retain sight words in memory. Consolidation allows readers to operate with multi-letter units that may be morphemes, syllables, or subsyllabic units such as onsets and rimes. These letter patterns become part of readers' generalized knowledge of the alphabetic system.

Larger letter units are valuable for sight word reading because they reduce the memory load involved in storing sight words in memory. For example, -EST might emerge as a consolidated unit in a reader's memory from its occurrence in several sight words known by the reader—*nest, pest, rest, test*. Knowing -EST eases the task of forming connections to learn the new word *chest* as a sight word. Whereas full-phase readers need to form four separate connections linking CH, E, S, T to the phonemes /c/, /e/, /s/, /t/, respectively, a consolidated-phase reader is able to form only two separate connections, CH, and EST, linked to /c/ and /est/, respectively. If a reader knows EST, TION, IN, and ING as consolidated units, the task of forming connections to retain longer sight words such as *question* and *interesting* in memory is much easier.

Studies have shown that students above first grade are more sensitive to letter co-occurrence patterns than beginning readers (Leslie & Thimke, 1986). Second grade appears to be when the use of consolidated units becomes more prevalent. Treiman et al. (1990) showed that students read words containing familiar letter patterns more accurately than words containing unfamiliar patterns, even when the words are constructed out of the same grapheme–phoneme correspondences. Such effects are more apparent in advanced beginning readers than in novice beginners, indicating that having a larger sight vocabulary contributes to knowledge of common spelling patterns (Bowey & Hansen, 1994). Juel (1983) showed that knowledge of letter patterns enabled children beyond second grade to read familiar words faster, indicating that consolidation of letters improves word-reading speed.

To summarize, the development of sight word learning occurs in several phases differing from each other in the involvement of alphabetic knowledge. The pre-alphabetic phase occurs by default because preschoolers lack much knowledge or ability to use letters in their sight word reading, so this phase makes little contribution to subsequent phases of development. In contrast, the three alphabetic phases—partial, full, and consolidated—are closely related and extend development from immature to mature forms of sight word learning. The partial phase characterizes novice beginners, typically kindergartners, who know the names or sounds of many letters but have not learned conventional grapheme–phoneme correspondences, especially vowels. The full phase characterizes first-graders who have acquired graphophonemic knowledge and can use it to read words. The consolidated phase characterizes second-graders who have learned to use larger units to read words.

Strategies for reading unfamiliar words emerge as well during these phases. A decoding strategy becomes available during the full phase. Analogizing to read unfamiliar words becomes possible during the full phase and increasingly prevalent during the consolidated phase as readers' sight vocabularies grow.

Disabled readers beyond first grade who lag behind their peers in learning to read typically have difficulty remembering the full spellings of words they can read by sight (Ehri & Saltmarsh, 1995), they have difficulty decoding unfamiliar words (Rack et al., 1992), and they are less skilled at analogizing than normally developing readers (DiBenedetto, 1995).

READING–SPELLING RELATIONSHIPS

The term *spelling* refers not only to the act of writing a word but also to the product that is written. People not only write spellings but also read spellings, so it is not surprising that reading words and spelling words are very closely related (Ehri, 1997).

There is evidence from eye-movement research that when readers read text, they automatically notice when words are misspelled (McConkie & Zola, 1981). Correlational findings reveal that reading and spelling words are highly related (Ehri, 1997; Morris & Perney, 1984). In several studies, students were asked to read a list of words, or to write words to dictation, or to distinguish correct from incorrect spellings of words. Most correlations were above $r = 0.70$. The high values are not explained by more general factors such as intelligence (Greenberg et al., 1997).

Such high correlations indicate that similar if not identical processes are involved. Both reading and spelling rely on two types of knowledge. One type consists of the spellings of specific words held in memory and secured by graphophonemic connections. In English, specific words must be remembered because variable spellings are possible. For example, "telephone" might be spelled in several ways, as TELIPHONE, TELLAFOAN, or TELUFOWN. When learners see one spelling and process its grapheme–phoneme connections, they remember this spelling and not the alternatives. The second type consists of knowledge about the general alphabetic system, including phonemic segmentation, graphophonemic correspondences, and syllabic patterns. General alphabetic knowledge is used to invent spellings of unfamiliar words and to detect the regularities in correct spellings of words.

Examining the quality of spellings that beginners invent to write unfamiliar words provides valuable diagnostic evidence regarding beginners' knowledge of the alphabetic system and hence their phase of development. During the pre-alphabetic phase, children may produce scribbles that superficially resemble features of the writing system. They may write some letters but these are not selected because they do not correspond to any sounds in the words being written. Often children draw letters from their personal names (Bloodgood, 1999).

During the partial phase, children write letters for sounds in words, but only some sounds are represented. Letter names provide the basis for their selection. For example, *peeked* might be written PT, *buzz* BZ, *jail* JL, *wife* YF. Their spellings are partial rather than complete representations of the sounds in words because they have difficulty segmenting words fully into phonemes and because they do not know how to represent all the sounds with letters, particularly vowel sounds.

During the full phase, children invent spellings by detecting the full array of phonemes in words and selecting conventional graphemes to represent those phonemes. For example, *peeked* might be spelled PEKT, *buzz* BUZ, *jail* JAL, *wife* WIF. In stretching out the sounds in words to spell them, children may find extra sounds, for example, spelling *blouses* as BALAOSIS (Ehri, 1986). Children understand the alphabetic system that underlies and accounts for the presence of many letters in conventional spellings. As a result, they are much more skilled at remembering the correct spellings of words than partial-phase readers.

During the consolidated phase, children utilize spelling patterns along with phoneme–grapheme units to invent plausible spellings. For example, *picking* might be spelled PIK<u>ING</u> (consolidated unit underlined), *peeked* as PEAK<u>ED</u>, *operation* as OPURA<u>TION</u>.

Whereas reading and spelling are highly related in normally developing readers, they are less closely related in children beyond first grade who are struggling to learn to read. Guthrie (1973) examined normal second-grade readers and older disabled readers matched to normals in reading age. On word reading and spelling recognition tasks, correlations were all positive and strong, but those among normal readers were substantially higher ($r = 0.84, 0.91$) than those among disabled readers ($r = 0.68, 0.60$). Greenberg et al. (1997) obtained the same results: $r = 0.86$ for normal readers vs. $r = 0.57$ for disabled readers.

My interpretation is that the lower correlations among disabled readers reflect the reason for their difficulty learning to read and spell. Their progress is impaired because their word-reading and word-spelling processes have not become sufficiently integrated. This arises from inadequate detection of phonemes in words and deficient knowledge of the alphabetic system. Both of these deficiencies impair the process of establishing sight words in memory, by limiting the strength of the bonds formed between spellings and pronunciations and the attachment of spellings to phonemes.

IMPLICATIONS FOR READING INSTRUCTION

My focus has been on word-reading processes and their course of acquisition in normally developing and disabled readers. Understanding these processes is part of effective teaching. Several implications for instruction deserve special attention.

At the outset, beginners need to learn all their letters and learn how to apply their letter knowledge to represent speech. Letters need to be mastered so that names can be produced quickly and shapes can be written from memory. The major grapheme–phoneme correspondences need to be learned. Facility with letters is essential for learners to operate alphabetically with words.

Beginners also need to break the sound barrier and become aware that words contain phonemes with acoustic and articulatory properties (Liberman et al., 1974). As this awareness is cultivated, it needs to dovetail with knowledge about sounds in letter names and sounds depicted in the spellings of words. Mastery is evidenced when children can generate phonetically complete and graphemically plausible spellings of words they have never seen written.

Teachers need to monitor beginners' progress in acquiring letter knowledge and phonemic awareness to make sure that it is occurring for each student. In kindergarten and first-grade classrooms there is tremendous variability among students in this respect. Extra instructional time will be required for students who enter school without this knowledge or who find it more difficult to acquire.

First-grade teachers need to adopt as a primary goal that of helping students operate at the full alphabetic phase in their sight word reading. This means teaching the major grapheme–phoneme correspondences, especially vowel correspondences. This means teaching students how to segment pronunciations into the full array of phonemes and how to match these up to graphemes in the spellings of words to analyze words fully.

It may be important to enhance children's interest in the spellings of new words and in discovering how letters connect to sounds systematically. This element has been incorporated into Benchmark's word detectives program to teach word identification skills (Gaskins et al., 1996). Students are taught to count the phonemes in words, then to look at spellings and match up graphemes to phonemes by placing letters in Elkonin boxes which provide one space for each letter that symbolizes a separate sound. Also, teaching students to spell words by analyzing and remembering how letters represent sounds in the words helps them fully analyze the graphophonemic relations needed to store words in memory.

Very often the first step in adding a new sight word to memory is successfully decoding the word (Share, 1995) or reading it by analogy to a known word. Students need to be taught these two strategies for reading unfamiliar words. The strategies are easier to acquire once students reach the full alphabetic phase and once they begin accumulating a growing number of sight words whose spellings have been fully connected to pronunciations and meanings in memory.

Explicit instruction in spelling is also important. As soon as children begin learning letters, they can be taught to use the letters to invent partial sound spellings of words as part of phonemic awareness instruction. As the major grapheme–phoneme relations are learned, spelling instruction should focus on helping students generate phonetically complete, graphemically plausible spellings. Learning the spellings of specific words by memorizing word lists should not begin until students understand how the conventional system works graphophonemically. Once this point is reached, remembering the spellings of specific words will be much easier, so spelling instruction can shift to this learning activity.

In addition to learning the spellings of specific words, another goal of spelling instruction should be to cultivate more advanced knowledge of the alphabetic system that extends to consolidated units, including root words, affixes, and families of related words. The more that students understand about the alphabetic system, the easier time they should have retaining information about individual words in memory for reading as well as for spelling.

In one study, Bhattacharya (2001) worked with adolescent disabled readers reading at the third- to fifth-grade-equivalent levels. She taught them to count syllables in the pronunciations of words and to match up these sounds to syllable spellings in 100 multisyllabic words. One control group practiced reading the same words as wholes, while another group received no instruction. On post-tests, the syllable analysis group read and spelled words much better than the other two groups, who did not differ. This suggests the value of teaching students to analyze words fully to improve their word-reading and spelling skills.

SUMMARY

It is during the primary grades that teachers make their greatest contribution to students' ultimate reading success, by helping them acquire the alphabetic foundation necessary for learning to read words and by teaching students the word-reading strategies they need to build their memory for sight words. The correlation between reading in first grade and reading in later grades is very high (Juel, 1988). Early on, instruction needs to be aimed at teaching phonemic awareness, letter knowledge, the strategy of decoding words, sight word reading by fully analyzing graphophonemic connections in words, and spelling. Later milestones include learning spelling patterns in words and achieving automaticity and speed in reading sight words during text reading.

REFERENCES

Adams, M. (1990). *Beginning to Read: Thinking and Learning About Print*. Cambridge, MA: MIT Press.

Adams, M., & Huggins, A. (1985). The growth of children's sight vocabulary: A quick test with educational and theoretical implications. *Reading Research Quarterly, 20*, 262–281.

Baron, J. (1977). Mechanisms for pronouncing printed words: Use and acquisition. In D. LaBerge, & S. Samuels (Eds), *Basic Processes in Reading: Perception and Comprehension* (pp. 175–216). Hillsdale, NJ: Erlbaum.

Becker, W., Dixon, R., & Anderson-Inman, L. (1980). *Morphographic and Root Word Analysis of 26,000 High Frequency Words*. Eugene, OR: University of Oregon College of Education.

Bhattacharya, A. (2001). The benefits of syllable segmentation and word reading practice for adolescents with reading and spelling difficulties. Unpublished doctoral dissertation, Graduate Center of the City University of New York.

Biemiller, A. (1970). The development of the use of graphic and contextual information as children learn to read. *Reading Research Quarterly, 6*, 75–96.

Bloodgood, J. (1999). What's in a name? Children's name writing and name acquisition. *Reading Research Quarterly, 34*, 342–367.

Bowey, J., & Hansen, J. (1994). The development of orthographic rimes as units of word recognition. *Journal of Experimental Child Psychology, 58*, 465–488.

Byrne, B. (1992). Studies in the acquisition procedure for reading: Rationale, hypotheses and data. In P. Gough, L. Ehri, & R. Treiman (Eds), *Reading Acquisition*. (pp. 1–34). Hillsdale, NJ: Erlbaum.

Clay, M. (1968). A syntactic analysis of reading errors. *Journal of Verbal Learning and Verbal Behavior, 7*, 434–438.

Cunningham, P. (1976). Investigating a synthesized theory of mediated word identification. *Reading Research Quarterly, 11*, 127–143.

DiBenedetto, B. (1995). Analogous nonword reading in normal and poor decodings at a variety of word recognition levels: Comparisons before and after remedial intervention. Unpublished doctoral dissertation, Graduate Center of the City University of New York.

Drake, D., & Ehri, L. (1984). Spelling acquisition: Effects of pronouncing words on memory for their spellings. *Cognition and Instruction, 1,* 297–320.

Ehri, L. (1977). Do adjectives and functors interfere as much as nouns in naming pictures? *Child Development, 48,* 697–701.

Ehri, L. (1980). The development of orthographic images. In U. Frith (Ed.), *Cognitive Processes in Spelling* (pp. 311–338). London: Academic Press.

Ehri, L. (1984). How orthography alters spoken language competencies in children learning to read and spell. In J. Downing, & R. Valtin (Eds), *Language Awareness and Learning to Read* (pp. 119–147). New York: Springer Verlag.

Ehri, L. (1986). Sources of difficulty in learning to spell and read. In M. Wolraich, & D. Routh (Eds), *Advances in Developmental and Behavioral Pediatrics* (pp. 121–195). Greenwich, CT: Jai Press.

Ehri, L. (1987). Learning to read and spell words. *Journal of Reading Behavior, 19,* 5–31.

Ehri, L. (1991). Development of the ability to read words. In R. Barr, M. Kamil, P. Mosenthal, & P. Pearson (Eds), *Handbook of Reading Research Volume II* (pp. 383–417). New York: Longman.

Ehri, L. (1992). Reconceptualizing the development of sight word reading and its relationship to recoding. In P. Gough, L. Ehri, & R. Treiman (Eds), *Reading Acquisition* (pp. 107–143). Hillsdale, NJ: Erlbaum.

Ehri, L. (1994). Development of the ability to read words: Update. In R. Ruddell, M. Ruddell, & H. Singer (Eds), *Theoretical Models and Processes of Reading* (4th edition, pp. 323–358). Newark, DE: International Reading Association.

Ehri, L. (1995). Phases of development in learning to read words by sight. *Journal of Research in Reading, 18,* 116–125.

Ehri, L. (1997). Learning to read and learning to spell are one and the same, almost. In C. Perfetti, L. Rieben, & Fayol, M. (Eds), *Learning to Spell: Research, Theory and Practice Across Languages* (pp. 237–269). Mahwah, NJ: Erlbaum.

Ehri, L. (1999). Phases of development in learning to read words. In J. Oakhill, & R. Beard (Eds.), *Reading Development and the Teaching of Reading: A Psychological Perspective* (pp. 79–108). Oxford, UK: Blackwell Publishers.

Ehri, L., & McCormick, S. (1998). Phases of word learning: Implications for instruction with delayed and disabled readers. *Reading and Writing Quarterly, 14,* 135–163.

Ehri, L., & Robbins, C. (1992). Beginners need some decoding skill to read words by analogy. *Reading Research Quarterly, 27,* 12–26.

Ehri, L., & Saltmarsh, J. (1995). Beginning readers outperform older disabled readers in learning to read words by sight. *Reading and Writing: An Interdisciplinary Journal, 7,* 295–326.

Ehri, L., & Wilce, L. (1979). The mnemonic value of orthography among beginning readers. *Journal of Educational Psychology, 71,* 26–40.

Ehri, L., & Wilce, L. (1980). The influence of orthography on readers' conceptualization of the phonemic structure of words. *Applied Psycholinguistics, 1,* 371–385.

Ehri, L., & Wilce, L. (1982). The salience of silent letters in children's memory for word spellings. *Memory and Cognition, 10,* 155–166.

Ehri, L. C., & Wilce, L. S. (1983). Development of word identification speed in skilled and less skilled beginning readers. *Journal of Educational Psychology, 75,* 3–18.

Ehri, L., & Wilce, L. (1985). Movement into reading: Is the first stage of printed word learning visual or phonetic? *Reading Research Quarterly, 20,* 163–179.

Ehri, L., & Wilce, L. (1986). The influence of spellings on speech: Are alveolar flaps /d/ or /t/? In D. Yaden & S. Templeton (Eds) *Metalinguistic Awareness and Beginning Literacy* (pp. 101–114). Portsmouth, NH: Heinemann.

Ehri, L., & Wilce, L. (1987a). Cipher versus cue reading: An experiment in decoding acquisition. *Journal of Educational Psychology, 79,* 3–13.

Ehri, L., & Wilce, L. (1987b). Does learning to spell help beginners learn to read words? *Reading Research Quarterly, 22*, 47–65.

Gaskins, I., Downer, M., Anderson, R., Cunningham, P., Gaskins, R., Schommer, M., & The Teachers of Benchmark School. (1988). A metacognitive approach to phonics: Using what you know to decode what you don't know. *Remedial and Special Education, 9*, 36–41.

Gaskins, I., Ehri, L., Cress, C., O'Hara, C., & Donnelly, K. (1996). Procedures for word learning: Making discoveries about words. *The Reading Teacher, 50*, 312–327.

Glushko, R. J. (1979). The organization and activation of orthographic knowledge in reading aloud. *Journal of Experimental Psychology: Human Perception and Performance, 5*, 674–691.

Glushko, R. J. (1981). Principles for pronouncing print: The psychology of phonography. In A. M. Lesgold, & C. A. Perfetti (Eds), *Interactive Processes in Reading* (pp. 61–84). Hillsdale, NJ: Erlbaum.

Golinkoff, R., & Rosinski, R. (1976). Decoding, semantic processing and reading comprehension skill. *Child Development, 47*, 252–258.

Goodman, K. (1976). Reading: A psycholinguistic guessing game. In H. Singer, & R. Ruddell (Eds), *Theoretical Models and Processes of Reading* (2nd ed., pp. 497–508). Newark, DE: International Reading Association.

Goswami, U. (1986). Children's use of analogy in learning to read: A developmental study. *Journal of Experimental Child Psychology, 42*, 73–83.

Goswami, U. (1988). Orthographic analogies and reading development. *Quarterly Journal of Experimental Psychology, 40*, 239–268.

Goswami, U. (1990). A special link between rhyming skill and the use of orthographic analogies by beginning readers. *Journal of Child Psychology and Psychiatry, 31*, 301–311.

Gough, P., & Hillinger, M. (1980). Learning to read: An unnatural act. *Bulletin of the Orton Society, 30*, 180–196.

Gough, P., & Tunmer, W. (1986). Decoding, reading, and reading disability. *Remedial and Special Education, 7*, 6–10.

Gough, P., & Walsh, S. (1991). Chinese, Phoenicians, and the orthographic cipher of English. In S. Brady, & D. Shankweiler, (1991). *Phonological Processes in Literacy: A Tribute to Isabelle Y. Liberman.* Hillsdale, NJ: Erlbaum.

Gough, P., Juel, C., & Roper/Schneider, D. (1983). Code and cipher: A two-stage conception of initial reading acquisition. In J. A. Niles & L. A. Harris (Eds), *Searches for Meaning in Reading/Language Processing and Instruction* (32nd Yearbook of the National Reading Conference, pp. 207–211). Rochester, NY: National Reading Conference.

Gough, P., Juel, C., & Griffith, P. (1992). Reading, spelling and the orthographic cipher. In P. Gough, L. Ehri, & R. Treiman (Eds), *Reading Acquisition* (pp. 35–48). Hillsdale, NJ: Erlbaum.

Greenberg, D., Ehri, L., & Perin, D. (1997). Are word reading processes the same or different in adult literacy students and 3rd–5th graders matched for reading level? *Journal of Educational Psychology, 89*, 262–288.

Guthrie, J. (1973). Models of reading and reading disability. *Journal of Educational Psychology, 65*, 9–18.

Guttentag, R., & Haith, M. (1978). Automatic processing as a function of age and reading ability. *Child Development, 49*, 707–716.

Hoover, W., & Gough, P. (1990). The simple view of reading. *Reading and Writing: An Interdisciplinary Journal, 2*, 127–160.

Johns, J. (1991). *Basic Reading Inventory* (5th edition). Dubuque, Iowa: Kendall/Hunt.

Juel, C. (1983). The development and use of mediated word identification. *Reading Research Quarterly, 18*, 306–327.

Juel, C. (1988). Learning to read and write: A longitudinal study of fifty-four children from first through fourth grade. *Journal of Educational Psychology, 80*, 437–447.

LaBerge, D., & Samuels, J. (1974). Toward a theory of automatic information processing in reading. *Cognitive Psychology, 6*, 293–323.

Laxon, V., Coltheart, V., & Keating, C. (1988). Children find friendly words friendly too: Words with many orthographic neighbours are easier to read and spell. *British Journal of Educational Psychology, 58*, 103–119.

Leslie, L., & Thimke, B. (1986). The use of orthographic knowledge in beginning reading. *Journal of Reading Behavior, 18*, 229–241.

Liberman, A. (1992). The relation of speech to reading and writing. In R. Frost, & L. Katz (Eds), *Orthography, Phonology, Morphology, and Meaning* (pp. 167–177). North Holland: Elsevier.

Liberman, I., Shankweiler, D., Fischer, F., & Carter, B. (1974). Reading and the awareness of linguistic segments. *Journal of Experimental Child Psychology, 18*, 201–212.

Marsh, G., Freidman, M., Welch, V., & Desberg, P. (1981). A cognitive-developmental theory of reading acquisition. In G. Mackinnon, & T. G. Waller (Eds), *Reading Research: Advances in Theory and Practice* (Vol. 3, pp. 199–221). New York: Academic Press.

Mason, J. (1980). When do children begin to read: An exploration of four-year-old children's letter and word reading competencies. *Reading Research Quarterly, 15*, 203–227.

Masonheimer, P., Drum, P., & Ehri, L. (1984). Does environmental print identification lead children into word reading? *Journal of Reading Behavior, 16*, 257–272.

McConkie, G., & Zola, D. (1981). Language constraints and the functional stimulus in reading. In A. Lesgold, & C. Perfetti (Eds), *Interactive Processes in Reading* (pp. 155–175). Hillsdale, NJ: Erlbaum.

Morris, D., & Perney, J. (1984). Developmental spelling as a predictor of first grade reading achievement. *Elementary School Journal, 84*, 441–457.

Perfetti, C. (1992). The representation problem in reading acquisition. In P. Gough, L. Ehri, & R. Treiman (Eds), *Reading Acquisition* (pp. 107–143). Hillsdale, NJ: Erlbaum.

Perfetti, C., & Hogaboam, T. (1975). The relationship between single word decoding and reading comprehension skill. *Journal of Educational Psychology, 67*, 461–469.

Rack, J., Snowling, M., & Olson, R. (1992). The nonword reading deficit in developmental dyslexia: A review. *Reading Research Quarterly, 27*, 29–53.

Rack, J., Hulme, C., Snowling, M., & Wightman, J. (1994). The role of phonology in young children learning to read words: The direct-mapping hypothesis. *Journal of Experimental Child Psychology, 57*, 42–71.

Rayner, K., & Pollatsek, A. (1989). *The Psychology of Reading*. Englewood Cliffs, NJ: Prentice Hall.

Reitsma, P. (1983). Printed word learning in beginning readers. *Journal of Experimental Child Psychology, 75*, 321–339.

Rosinski, R., Golinkoff, R., & Kukish, K. (1975). Automatic semantic processing in a picture–word interference task. *Child Development, 46*, 243–253.

Rumelhart, D. (1977). Toward an interactive model of reading. In S. Dornic (Ed.), *Attention and Performance VI*. Hillsdale, NJ: Erlbaum.

Share, D. (1995). Phonological recoding and self-teaching: sine qua non of reading acquisition. *Cognition, 55*, 151–218.

Stahl, S., Osborn, J., & Lehr, F. (1990). *Beginning to Read: Thinking and Learning about Print by Marilyn Jager Adams: A Summary*. Urbana-Champaign, IL: Center for the Study of Reading.

Stanovich, K. (1980). Toward an interactive-compensatory model of individual differences in the development of reading fluency. *Reading Research Quarterly, 16*, 32–71.

Templeton, S., & Bear, D. (Eds) (1992). *Development of Orthographic Knowledge and the Foundations of Literacy: A Memorial Festschrift for Edmund H. Henderson*. Hillsdale, NJ: Erlbaum.

Treiman, R. (1993). *Beginning to Spell*. New York: Oxford University Press.

Treiman, R., Goswami, U., & Bruck, M. (1990). Not all nonwords are alike: Implications for reading development and theory. *Memory and Cognition, 18*, 559–567.

Tunmer, W., & Chapman, J. (1998). Language, prediction skill, phonological recording ability, and beginning reading. In C. Hulme, & R. Joshi (Eds), *Reading and Spelling: Development and Disorders* (pp. 33–68). Mahwah, NJ: Erlbaum.

Venezky, R. (1970). *The Structure of English Orthography*. The Hague: Mouton.

Venezky, R. (1999). *The American Way of Spelling: The Structure and Origins of American English Orthography*. New York: Guilford Press.

Weber, R. (1970). A linguistic analysis of first grade reading errors. *Reading Research Quarterly, 5*, 427–451.

Chapter 11

FROM ASSESSMENT TO INTERVENTION: THE EDUCATIONAL PSYCHOLOGY PERSPECTIVE[*]

Rea Reason

The concept of dyslexia is relevant not only to educational practice but to several areas of psychological research. In cognitive psychology it has for many years been a shorthand for marked difficulties with the alphabetic script. In neuropsychology a distinction has been made between acquired and developmental dyslexia, where the former examines adult patients who, because of known neurological damage, have lost their ability to read and write, and the latter refers to learning difficulties starting in childhood when there is no known relevant damage. From the angle of social psychology, we may consider the effects of public understanding and policies if perceived links between reading ability, privilege and intelligence have their roots in educational and social history. As practitioners, whether clinical, occupational, counselling or educational psychologists, we will meet individuals who are struggling with print and may have other difficulties associated with that struggle.

In 1998 the Division of Educational and Child Psychology (DECP) of the British Psychological Society convened a working party to consider relevant research and to survey current practice in order to publish a report that made recommendations about the concept of dyslexia and the principles of educational psychology assessment related to it. The focus was primarily on younger school-aged children. Following wide-ranging consultation on the basis of a draft, the revised report, entitled *Dyslexia, Literacy and Psychological Assessment*, was published in November 1999 (BPS, 1999a). In order to investigate the impact of the report on the practices

[*]This chapter is an expanded and updated version of an article entitled Educational Practice and Dyslexia (Reason, R. (2001) Educational practice and dyslexia. *The Psychologist*, 14(6), 298–301.)

Dyslexia and Literacy: Theory and Practice. Edited by Gavin Reid and Janice Wearmouth.
© 2002 John Wiley & Sons, Ltd.

of educational psychologists, a further survey was undertaken in summer 2001 and the results have been discussed in Reason and Woods (2002). As chair of the working party that published the report[1], this chapter gives me a chance to:

- explain the rationale of the report
- consider further developments since its publication
- stress the importance of learning opportunities.

TERMINOLOGICAL DEBATES

Educational psychologists have always been actively involved in helping teachers and parents assist those children and young people who have reading, spelling and related difficulties. The term "dyslexia" has often been avoided because its predominant focus on within-child causative factors has tended to detract attention away from instructional circumstances. Following considerable debate in the 1970s and 1980s (for a review see Pumfrey & Reason, 1991), when practitioners expressed reservations about the term, education in the UK opted for "specific learning difficulties" while similar developments in the USA resulted in the terms "learning disabilities" or "specific learning disabilities". With the continued use of "dyslexia" in cognitive and psycho-medical research and by the public at large, subsequent national policy documents have introduced compromise phrases such as "specific learning difficulties (for example dyslexia)". As dyslexia is now well embedded in popular language, a key purpose of the DECP report was to clarify the concept within an educational context.

A WORKING DEFINITION

Debates about causes, definitions and terminology made it particularly important to define dyslexia in a descriptive way without explanatory elements (Tonnessen, 1997). Different theoretical rationales and research initiatives would then be considered in the third section of the report as alternative or complementary hypotheses that had the working definition as their common starting point. This could be done in relation to the causal modelling framework, introduced by Morton and Frith (1995), with its three levels of observation and explanation: the biological, the cognitive and the behavioural (see below).

The draft report circulated for consultation in 1999 proposed a working definition in the form of a single stark sentence:

> Dyslexia is evident when accurate and fluent word reading and/or spelling develops very incompletely or with great difficulty.

An example of a similar working definition was already available to us in a report published in the Netherlands (Gersons-Wolfensberger & Ruijssenaars, 1997). While

---

[1] Co-authors of the report were Norah Frederickson, Maria Heffernan, Conrad Martin and Kevin Woods. The full report, entitled *Dyslexia, Literacy and Psychological Assessment*, is available from the British Psychological Society.

a very substantial majority of respondents found this acceptable, comments showed that many wished to delimit the working definition further by including more reference to learning opportunities. The following addition was made in the final report:

> This focuses on literacy learning at the "word level" and implies that the problem is severe and persistent despite appropriate learning opportunities. It provides the basis of a staged process of assessment through teaching.

Since publication, we have needed to remind readers that the term "working" was used to show that developments in research and practice were ongoing, while we needed a starting point for the report. It was something to work with and not necessarily the final word, and it was particularly important to recognise that the descriptive *working* definition was not an *operational* definition. We could not resolve issues of deciding how long to wait before considering that accurate/fluent word reading and/or spelling were developing "very incompletely" and "with great difficulty". Nor was there a simple way of quantifying "severe and persistent". This depended on the age and developmental stage of the learner and the amount of instructional effort involved. Furthermore, with difficulties of a dyslexic nature ranging from mild to severe, cut-off points within a continuum of special educational needs and provision remained a thorny issue related to social policy.

A further misconception could arise if it was assumed that the concept of dyslexia existed in a vacuum unrelated to what was known about children's literacy development in general and the methods of teaching and learning involved. For this reason, the reference to appropriate learning opportunities and the staged process of assessment through teaching was essential in educational practice. In terms of the National Literacy Strategy (DfEE, 1998), dyslexia could be defined as marked and persistent problems at the word level of the NLS curricular framework and so link with the evaluation of learning opportunities and teaching methods as mainstream educational issues. In terms of the *Code of Practice on the Identification and Assessment of Pupils with Special Educational Needs*, and its revision still under consultation at the time of writing, the working definition accorded with the staged process of assessment through teaching central to the Code (DfEE, 1994, 2000).

The survey of educational psychology practice in summer 2001 (see Reason & Woods, 2002) showed that the vast majority of respondents regarded the approach adopted in the report as very useful. Below are some illustrative quotes:

- I am comfortable with a very broad conceptualisation of dyslexia . . . I have found the working definition very useful in clarifying for parents, teachers and young people themselves what we mean when we use the term dyslexia.
- . . . it was a breath of fresh air . . . . We have amended our service assessment guidelines in line with the definition although not espousing it verbatim.
- It is a functional and descriptive definition . . .
- It avoids some of the unhelpful aspects of a discrepancy model, e.g. unfulfilled potential . . .
- It provides a more equitable way of looking at literacy difficulties.
- The phrase "severe and persistent despite appropriate learning opportunities" is very useful.
- Focusing on the "word level" is useful as it separates out decoding and comprehension difficulties.

While most welcomed the broad and inclusive approach, a small minority found it over-inclusive: "The definition encompasses a huge population of children—almost every pupil who has literacy difficulties. It will mean that, for example, most of the pupils with moderate learning difficulties will now be dyslexic". This quote illustrates a discomfort with the lack of reference to general ability in the working definition. While it must be taken for granted that a certain level of cognitive ability is necessary for the learning involved, it is debatable what that level needs to be. There is now convincing evidence that general ability or IQ are not, as such, determinants of basic reading skills (see sections 4.10, 6.3 and 6.4 of the report). A number of studies have investigated differences between children with IQ–achievement discrepancies and those with poor reading skills but no discrepancy on reading and spelling skills and on cognitive skills related to reading. The research has resulted in a considerable body of evidence, from many countries and with children of different ages, which supports the conclusion that children of different IQ levels with reading difficulties perform similarly on a variety of reading and spelling measures and, in particular, those reflecting phonological processing and memory.

The working definition has no exclusionary criteria. Pupils from all social and cultural backgrounds can have learning difficulties of a dyslexic nature, and pupils with moderate learning difficulties or sensory impairments can also, in addition, have such difficulties if they struggle with basic reading or writing (Greaney & Reason, 1999). However, their special educational needs will vary, as will their "appropriate learning opportunities", because, in the individual case, we need to consider all aspects of the child's learning and the educational and curricular priorities of that child.

The broad and inclusive starting point of the DECP report accords well with current trends such as those illustrated in the British Dyslexia Association booklet entitled *Achieving Dyslexia Friendly Schools* (BDA, 2000). Dyslexia is now firmly regarded as a mainstream educational issue where a continuum of special educational needs is met by a continuum of educational approaches and resources. Foremost among these are the resources represented by knowledgeable and sympathetic mainstream teachers.

Another concern expressed about the working definition relates to early identification: "... it waits for failure rather than looking at early uneven development...". We recognise indeed that speech and language abilities and phonological competencies of young pre-reading children can predict their subsequent reading development. There are pitfalls, however, in identifying "false positives" and the consequent labelling of children as having special needs or a disability. It is more helpful to include, in the early curriculum, activities that develop literacy skills such as phonological awareness and letter knowledge. Given the tools for interactive assessment and teaching that can be included in the Early Years Curriculum and the Reception Year of the National Literacy Strategy, teachers can monitor progress and notice the children that continue to need help. Consequently, as a mainstream educational issue, early identification is built into the educational process and children's needs responded to at an early age without waiting for "failure" or formal labels of disability. In a later section of this chapter, I shall link this approach with the concept of "noticing and adjusting" researched by a group of psychologists at Manchester University (Barrett et al., submitted).

RESEARCH AND THEORY

With the working definition as a starting point, an important section of the report was devoted to outlining research into literacy learning and included extensive referencing to enable those interested in the field to undertake further reading. According to this research, phonological coding currently provided a central unifying thread in the word-reading process. However, the role, amount and relative weight of phonological processes, and how complete they had to be, were not yet clear and could alter in the course of reading development. Indeed, since the publication of the report, there has been a focus on research that has demonstrated the role of rapid processing rate in the components necessary for fluent reading (Wolf & O'Brien, 2001). This research has provided further support for the word "fluent" in the working definition discussed above.

The next substantial section of the report considered 10 possible theoretical explanations, and their research bases, as represented within the causal modelling framework introduced by Morton and Frith (1995). The basic framework, shown in Figure 11.1, involves three levels of description: the biological, the cognitive and the behavioural. In addition, the framework recognises the operation of environmental factors at all three levels of explanation.

The Biological Level

Observations and facts about the brain are placed at the biological level. Brain functioning can be influenced both by internal genetic factors and external environmental factors, such as quality of nutrition or levels of toxins. While educational psychologists are not in a position to carry out any formal neuro-diagnostic procedures or genetic analyses, they may hypothesise about factors within these domains. They may also observe signs, such as hereditary patterns, which they suspect may be indicative of hypothesised neurological or genetic factors.

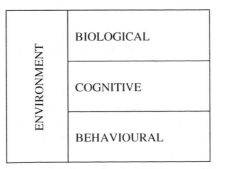

Figure 11.1   Causal modelling framework (from Morton & Frith, 1995)

Table 11.1   Alternative or complementary theoretical hypotheses

- Phonological delay or deficit
- Temporal processing
- Skill automatisation
- Working memory
- Visual processing
- Syndrome
- Intelligence and cognitive profiles
- Subtypes
- Learning opportunities and social context
- Emotional factors

The Cognitive Level

Hypothesised within-child causes are situated at the cognitive level. Cognitive skills or deficits/delays must be separated from observed behavioural data because they can only be inferred. The inferred and hypothetical underlying cognitive processes are different in different theories. This is clearly illustrated by the different types of hypotheses that are discussed in the report and modelled using the causal modelling framework.

The Behavioural Level

Observations and facts about performance in reading and spelling activities and/or tests are situated at the behavioural level. We can directly observe behaviour, such as words spelt incorrectly or words read inaccurately. Any observations and data collected will be subject to the effects of a range of environmental factors (such as social and physical conditions) and within-child factors other than those directly related to literacy difficulties (such as motivation) which are themselves open to environmental influences.

Using the causal modelling framework, the report presented 10 different theoretical accounts of dyslexia as alternative or complementary hypotheses to explain learning difficulties of a dyslexic nature. These are listed in Table 11.1. Although information is provided elsewhere in this volume about many of these theoretical explanations, I would strongly recommend that those interested in their evaluation through the causal modelling framework obtain the report from the British Psychological Society (BPSa, 1999).

Some of the theoretical accounts of dyslexia included comprehensive descriptions at each level in the framework and, in addition, modelled causal links between the features included at different levels. It was important, therefore, to consider the extent to which available empirical evidence suggested that these should be regarded as alternative accounts of a unitary construct of "dyslexia", as opposed to being regarded as accounts of different types of dyslexia. However, the phonological deficit/delay hypothesis provided the main focus, both because of the broad empirical support that it commanded and because of the role phonology was accorded in many of the other explanations, such as those examining temporal order, skill automatisation and working memory hypotheses.

It is important to point out that the use of the term "hypothesis" in this section of the report related to different theoretical approaches rather than the hypotheses formulated by practitioners, because practitioners do not only look for single causative factors but also for multivariate explanations that take account of instructional, interpersonal and emotional factors in the individual case. Central to educational psychology practice is an understanding of the reciprocal effects of cognitive processes, instructional circumstances and the learner's perceptions and experiences.

THE ROLE OF COGNITIVE ASSESSMENT

It seemed to us that the syndrome hypothesis, i.e. dyslexia as a constellation of difficulties also affecting areas other than reading and spelling, and the core phonological deficit/delay hypothesis had more in common than may have been recognised. Both rejected exclusionary criteria and looked for positive indicators, including phonological processing and memory. Both could examine associated difficulties, whether cognitive, emotional or physical, in order to specify individual educational needs. Both acknowledged that literacy problems of a dyslexic nature could occur in children representing a wide range of cognitive ability.

In reviewing current research, it seemed that dimensions of individual differences in dyslexia were more important than discrete subtypes. Test scores obtained from batteries designed to assess overall cognitive performance might aid understanding of the learner's particular strengths and weaknesses, bearing in mind that the use of such tests was not a requirement as there were also other paradigms of assessment. No particular pattern of scores could be regarded as necessary or sufficient in deciding whether, and to what extent, learning difficulties could be described as dyslexic. It was also important to consider the validity and reliability of test results in relation to children's cultural experiences and life events, such as recent trauma.

An appendix in the report evaluated a selection of commercially available tests designed to examine cognitive processes, including phonological competencies, associated with dyslexia. The evaluations showed that some of the tests were better supported by current research than others and that information about their standardisation was also very variable. The evaluations demonstrated that no one test could be considered obligatory in educational psychology assessments.

Assessment in Practice

Within a comprehensive framework for psychological assessment and intervention (BPS, 1999b), we focused primarily on word reading and spelling. The working definition of dyslexia then required that three aspects be evaluated through the assessment process:

- that the pupil was learning/had learned accurate and fluent word reading and/or spelling very incompletely
- that appropriate learning opportunities had been provided
- that progress had been made only as a result of much additional effort/instruction and that difficulties had, nevertheless, persisted.

We assumed that, with increased knowledge and awareness of literacy learning and literacy difficulties in the primary school, monitored intervention could take place early enough to ensure that the process did not result in any unnecessary delay for those learners with severe and persistent difficulties. Nevertheless, we recognised that there could be instances where the persistence of difficulties was inferred in more indirect ways because of personal and educational circumstances, such as illness or school absences.

The accuracy and fluency of word reading and spelling could be assessed normatively through standardised tests and/or curriculum-referenced assessments, using a series of literacy-related tasks that reflected teaching content and approaches. Such measures would then trigger an investigation of factors that would be important in understanding the nature of the difficulties being experienced and in identifying ways of overcoming or alleviating them.

EFFECTIVE INSTRUCTION

Some reviewers of the report suggested that it should have given more attention to evaluating the effectiveness of intervention programmes (Gredler, 2000). While such research was beyond the brief of the working party, we did agree, and further work is being planned. Nevertheless, we must not assume that, as soon as the word "dyslexia" is mentioned, something very separate and different to what is available in mainstream education must happen. As already mentioned above, it is significant that charitable organisations such as the British Dyslexia Association have recently published a document emphasising the importance of "dyslexia-friendly schools" while a publication by the Irish Dyslexia Association stresses that "all children learn differently". There is thus a shift of emphasis away from targeted intervention focusing only on the individual to approaches aimed at developing appropriate educational strategies for a wide range of learners with different aptitudes and achievements.

Established learning theory has stressed the importance of repetitive and cumulative practice to the point of "mastery" (Linsley, 1992; Reason & Morfidi, 2001). Evidence also demonstrates the effectiveness of teaching approaches that introduce code instruction in the context of reading and writing meaningful text (Adams, 1993; Hatcher et al., 1994; Wasik & Slavin, 1994). Furthermore, motivation is developed through ensuring that the learner has a sense of competence and control when undertaking the learning (Sansone & Harackiewicz, 2000). Drawing on these considerations, Pietrowski and Reason (2000) compared three kinds of commercially published materials with a strong emphasis on the teaching of phonics: first, those developed for all children as meeting the requirements of the NLS at the word level; second, those intended for learners making slower progress in literacy; and, third, those targeted at learners regarded as having difficulties of a dyslexic nature. The materials were audited in terms of the following eight questions:

1. *A comprehensive model*: With their focus on phonics, do the materials reflect a comprehensive model of reading and/or spelling development, i.e. NLS search-lights that include comprehension of the text as a whole and the anticipation of words and letter sequences?
2. *Progression*: Do the materials show a clear progression of phonological targets, starting from phonological awareness and moving gradually to more advanced phonic structures?
3. *Speaking and listening*: Are children exploring and reinforcing the learning of phonological regularities through both speaking and listening?
4. *Reading and writing*: Are children exploring and reinforcing the learning of phonological regularities through both reading and writing?
5. *Assessing to teach*: Do the materials provide guidance on "assessing to teach", i.e. on assessing what the children know in order to plan, in appropriately small steps, what should be learnt next?
6. *Mastery learning*: Are the materials based on "mastery learning", i.e. on planned repetition and revision that ensures the retention of what has been learnt?
7. *Role of the learner*: In terms of motivational influences, is there explicit guidance on the involvement of the children themselves in setting their own targets and monitoring progress?
8. *Home–school links*: Is there clear guidance on how parents and carers can help their children at home?

The comparisons showed that materials developed for all children were more likely to have a comprehensive model of literacy as their major emphasis. Most of the special programmes, in contrast, may contain an implicit assumption that the learning of phonics is but one element of literacy but explicit links between text, sentence and word levels are not made. The headings "assessing to teach" and "mastery learning" brought out the differences between the publications. It seemed that those materials intended for learners making slower progress placed an even greater emphasis on "assessing to teach" than did the programmes developed under the heading of dyslexia. Both kinds of special programmes had, as their major emphasis, "mastery learning", which remained implicit but not explained in the general programmes.

The eight questions highlighted the similarities and differences between the approaches included in the comparison. Of particular note was the issue of reciprocal assessment and teaching, i.e. "assessing to teach". If those following the materials developed under the heading of "dyslexia" assumed that the learner inevitably needs to start from the beginning of the programme and plough through every aspect of it, then this may result in frustration and boredom. Conversely, the general programmes, and the NLS itself, did not seem to provide enough guidance or detail on how to establish what each child had learnt and how to plan and teach following the principles of "mastery learning" (Palmer & Reason, 2001). If these aspects were addressed more explicitly, the teaching materials would be suitable for all children, including those with learning difficulties of a dyslexic nature, and would provide the basis for the kind of inclusive practices in schools advocated by the charitable organisations mentioned above and by educational researchers in the field of inclusion.

Examining the Persistence of Difficulties

It seemed that the framework of the National Literacy Strategy could provide a pathway for the cumulative, hierarchical and incremental presentation of word-level targets recommended in approaches addressing dyslexic difficulties. Problems have been identified, however, in Year 1 (children aged 5 to 6 years) where the ambitious learning targets may result in some children being considered to have special needs or dyslexic difficulties simply because the pace is too fast and the coverage too superficial. In recognition of these problems and on the basis of pilot studies currently in progress, The National Literacy Strategy has introduced resources to all schools involving additional help to children in Year 1 (Early Literacy Support). It has previously introduced Additional Literacy Support to children in Year 3 (aged 7 to 8 years). While we do not yet have systematic evaluations of these initiatives, there can be debates as to their rationales, methods and staffing. Nevertheless, the initiatives can provide the opportunities we need for introducing more deliberate monitoring of progress to determine the persistence of literacy difficulties in line with the practices recommended in the DECP report. This can involve a set of strategies for carrying out focused assessments over time and for recording progress in a way that facilitates judgements about the accuracy and fluency of performance.

The Concept of "Noticing and Adjusting"

One aspect of the report that was particularly welcomed, and subsequently incorporated in the revised DfEE *Code of Practice on the Identification and Assessment of Pupils with Special Educational Needs* currently under consultation (DfEE, 2000), was the introduction of the concept of "noticing and adjusting". When considering early identification, we wrote that the term "identification" may imply too narrow a focus on within-child determinants of learning. An alternative, broader formulation would describe teachers and carers as *noticing* children's individual needs and then adjusting their responses accordingly. This interplay between "noticing" and "adjusting" seemed the most appropriate basis for monitoring the progress of young children at risk of reading failure. Furthermore, the framework of the National Literacy Strategy provided a common approach and an agreed terminology for baseline assessments and observations that linked curriculum-related assessments with teaching plans.

With the report on dyslexia as their starting point, a group of educational psychologists, representing four LEAs in the North West of England, have undertaken work

1. **Nature of noticing that leads to adjustments:** What kinds of observations and adjustments take place in the classroom? What is the range of school-based approaches, both formal and informal, for monitoring the progress of individual children?

2. **Teacher confidence and perception:** How are teachers incorporating their observations on how children are learning in order to make adaptations accordingly?

3. **Inclusive teaching methods:** How is teaching being tailored to individual needs within "inclusive" group and class settings?

4. **Mastery learning principles in teacher adjustments:** How are teachers providing opportunities for each child to consolidate their learning at word level? How does assessment continuity and progression work?

5. **Monitoring and motivation:** How are the children themselves involved in the monitoring of their own word-level progress?

6. **Working together:** How is information about teaching and progress communicated between all those involved for the benefit of the pupil? How is progress defined?

Figure 11.2   Framework of enquiry for monitoring literacy learning

to clarify and apply the concept of noticing and adjusting in practice (Barrett et al, submitted). More specifically, the purpose has been to develop approaches for joint monitoring of literacy progress and to make explicit teacher skills in fine tuning their responses to children's learning needs. In describing adjustments in relation to what has been observed, the focus has moved away from isolated assessments to developing and evaluating the teaching and the interactions that have been planned.

On the basis of initial pilot work and discussion, the group formulated a "framework for enquiry" as a draft protocol for work in schools on literacy learning at different levels, i.e. discussion of individual children and initiatives involving whole-school development. It was hoped that the framework, shown in Figure 11.2 and discussed in Barrett et al. (submitted), would be flexible enough to be applied as a realistic and useful tool of investigation across a variety of school and class settings, yet still furnish accurate monitoring of literacy word-level progress and effective learning opportunities. As such it could be useful not only for educational psychologists working with schools but also for schools developing their own practices.

The pilot projects reported in Barrett et al. (submitted) focused on teaching literacy for the whole class within Literacy Hour, literacy programme planning for individual children and teacher development/training. A key feature of the framework of enquiry, across the different projects, was that the teacher/psychologist relationship felt considerably different. Embarking together on collaborative projects

rather than dealing with a problem "case" provided fruitful, solution-oriented discussions focusing on teachers' practice and innovative thinking rather than child,
teacher or resource/environmental deficits. It enabled the psychologists to keep
separate the special needs policy aspects of their work and to join with teachers in
collaborative reflection on teaching and learning.

CONCLUSION

The phrase "from assessment to intervention" in the title of this chapter has been
chosen to emphasise two key aspects. First, educational psychology assessments
are only as useful as the interventions that result from them. While terminology,
such as dyslexia, phonological delay or temporal processing, can aid our understanding of the learner's difficulties, it is the "So what?" question that matters in
both educational practice in general and educational psychology practice in particular. How useful is the information obtained? What instructional plans result
from the assessments? It is not enough to make blanket statements such as "this
child needs more one-to-one teaching" without clarifying the content in terms of
literacy learning and access to the overall curriculum. As discussed earlier, the
term "dyslexia" by itself does not imply that learners need something separate
and different from that provided in mainstream education. The audit of materials undertaken by Pietrowski and Reason (2000) has demonstrated the need for
more deliberate planning that takes account of individual rates of progress and the
principles of consolidated learning.

A second important point is to do with the nature of educational psychology assessments. There is sometimes a misconception that such as assessment consists
of a set of tests administered in relative isolation from the teaching and learning
that has taken place. As demonstrated by the research on "noticing and adjusting",
described above, the most fruitful and constructive contributions of educational
psychologists take place when all those involved work together, over time, to examine, plan and monitor teaching and learning, whether for the individual or for
a group of children.

There is a difference between cognitive psychological research and educational
psychology practice in the scope of information to be included in explanations.
While theoretical stances seek to control for variables in order to focus on particular
processes, practitioners base their understandings on information from as many
sources as possible. Their role is then to combine that which they see as useful
into workable plans of action that promote both literacy learning and curriculum
access. Inevitably, this leads to the consideration of instructional, interpersonal and
environmental factors in dyslexia.

This chapter has focused mainly on the issues in the report on dyslexia published
by the Division of Educational and Child Psychology of the British Psychological
Society. My purpose has been to explain its rationale, to clarify some misconcep-
tions, particularly in relation to the working definition introduced in the report, and
to consider developments since its publication. I hope that my chapter has done jus-
tice to the densely written report containing extensive referencing and also covering

other aspects not selected for mention here. What I have wished to emphasise is the logic of the report, where a descriptive working definition, within a comprehensive model of literacy learning, can link with both theoretical and practical issues. Key implications for practice are summarised in the following points:

1. Identification/explanation of dyslexia is conceptually separate from the assessment/determination of special educational needs. While the former draws on cognitive research and theory, the latter depends on issues relating to social policy concerned with the effects of learning difficulties. In considering severity and persistence of learning difficulties, both can start from the working definition in the report.
2. Educational psychologists have always been actively involved in helping teachers and parents help those children and young people who have reading, spelling and associated difficulties. It is not constructive, therefore, to focus debate on whether the word "dyslexia" is used or not.
3. Within the educational context, dyslexia involves a continuum of assistance as determined, in the first instance, by the severity and persistence of word-reading and spelling difficulties. It is not a medical condition requiring diagnosis and treatment but a shorthand for a range of learning difficulties needing to be noticed and acknowledged so that suitable educational actions can take place.
4. While the processes involved in literacy development provide the starting point, comprehensive assessment and planning also take account of associated special educational needs, whether cognitive, emotional or physical.
5. Assessment is usually undertaken over time in response to teaching. Educational psychologists work with schools to develop effective school-based assessment, intervention and monitoring, and, within that context, also carry out individual psychological assessment and programme planning to promote the progress of those children whose difficulties are most severe and persistent.
6. Together with pupils, parents/carers, teachers and other relevant professionals, educational psychologists evaluate the reciprocal effects of educational achievements, cognitive processes, instructional circumstances and the learner's perceptions, strategies and experiences.

REFERENCES

Adams, M.J. (1993) Beginning to read: An overview. In R. Beard (Ed.) *Teaching Literacy: Balancing Perspectives*. London: Hodder and Stoughton.

Barrett, M., Reason, R., Regan, T., Rooney, S., Stothard, J., Williams, C. & Woods, K. (submitted) Co-researching the concept of 'noticing and adjusting' in monitoring literacy learning. *Educational Psychology in Practice*.

British Dyslexia Association (2000) *Achieving Dyslexia Friendly Schools*. Reading, UK: BDA.

British Psychological Society Division of Educational and Child Psychology (BPS) (1999a) *Dyslexia, Literacy and Psychological Assessment*. Leicester: The BPS.

British Psychological Society Division of Educational and Child Psychology (BPS) (1999b) *A Framework for Psychological Assessment and Intervention*. Leicester: The BPS.

Department for Education and Employment (DfEE) (1994) *Code of Practice on the Identification and Assessment of Special Educational Needs*. London: HMSO.

Department for Education and Employment (DfEE) (1998) *The National Literacy Strategy Framework for Teaching*. London: HMSO.

Department for Education and Employment (DfEE) (2000) *Draft SEN Code of Practice on the Identification and Assessment of Pupils with Special Educational Needs*. London: DfEE.

Gersons-Wolfensberger D.C.M. & Ruijssenaars, W.A.J.J.M. (1997) Definition and treatment of dyslexia: A report by the Committee on Dyslexia of the Health Council of the Netherlands. *Journal of Learning Disabilities, 30(2)*, 209–213.

Greaney, J. & Reason, R. (1999) Phonological processing in Braille. *Dyslexia: An International Journal of Research and Practice, 5(4)*, 8–20.

Gredler, G.R. (2000) Book review special feature: Dyslexia, literacy and psychological assessment. *The Psychology of Education Review, 24(2)*, 33–36.

Hatcher, P., Hulme, C. & Ellis, A. (1994) Ameliorating early reading failure by integrating the teaching of reading with phonological skills. *Child Development, 65*, 41–57.

Linsley, O.R. (1992) Precision teaching: Discoveries and effects. *Journal of Applied Behaviour Analysis, 25(1)*, 51–57.

Morton, J. & Frith, U. (1995) Causal modelling: A structural approach to developmental psychopathology. In D. Cicchetti & D.J. Cohen (Eds) *Manual of Developmental Psychopathology* (pp. 357–390). New York: Wiley.

Palmer, S. & Reason, R. (2001) *Checking Individual Progress in Phonics (ChIPPs)*. Windsor: NFER-Nelson.

Pietrowski, J. & Reason, R. (2000) The National Literacy Strategy and dyslexia: A comparison of teaching methods and materials. *Support for Learning, 15(2)*, 51–57.

Pumfrey, P. & Reason, R. (1991) *Specific Learning Difficulties (Dyslexia): Challenges and Responses*. London: Routledge.

Reason, R. & Morfidi, E. (2001) Literacy difficulties and single case experimental design. *Educational Psychology in Practice, 17(3)*, 227–244.

Reason, R. & Woods, K. (2000) Dyslexia, literacy and psychological assessment: What is the evidence base? *Educational and Child Psychology, 19(3)*.

Sansone, C. & Harackiewicz, J.M. (2000) *Intrinsic and Extrinsic Motivation*. London: Academic Press.

Tonnessen, F.E. (1997) How can we best define dyslexia? *Dyslexia: An International Journal of Research and Practice, 3*, 78–92.

Wasik, B.A. & Slavin, R.E. (1994) Preventing reading failure with one-to-one tutoring: A review of five programmes. *Reading Research Quarterly, 28*, 178–200.

Wolf, M. & O'Brien, B. (2001) On issues of time, fluency and intervention. In A. Fawcett (Ed.) *Dyslexia Theory and Good Practice*. London: Whurr.

Chapter 12

ISSUES IN THE ASSESSMENT OF CHILDREN LEARNING ENGLISH AS AN ADDITIONAL LANGUAGE

Tony Cline

INTRODUCTION

In 1996–1997 over 10% of pupils attending schools in England were from an ethnic minority background, and just over half a million pupils were learning English as an additional language (EAL), about 7.5% of all pupils. (DfEE, 1999). Most of these children lived in urban areas, but even in shire counties one in seven primary schools and almost one in five secondary schools had more than 5% ethnic minority pupils (figures derived from DfEE, 1999, Table E). In a more recent survey of nine Scottish counties, pupils learning EAL comprised 4% of the school population, and 26% of schools had at least one such pupil on roll (Deponio et al., 2000).

The main focus of this chapter is on children who are learning to read in English at school although a different language is spoken in their home. Much of what is said here applies equally to other bilingual children (e.g. those attending International Schools where they are taught in more than one language and those learning to read in a second or third language other than English). But the main focus is on children learning EAL in English schools from linguistic minority communities.

If we are to develop effective strategies for the identification and assessment of learning difficulties, we need to take account of what is known about how literacy skills in English develop normally in most children learning EAL. It is beyond the scope of this chapter to provide a full analysis of the subject (see Baker, 2001, chapters 15 & 16; Cline & Shamsi, 2000, chapter 3; Hudelson, 1994). The following list of general findings will indicate some key underlying issues:

Dyslexia and Literacy: Theory and Practice. Edited by Gavin Reid and Janice Wearmouth.
© 2002 John Wiley & Sons, Ltd.

- All readers, whether monolingual or bilingual, require a range of language-related skills and knowledge (e.g. phonological awareness and knowledge of syntax and morphology in the target language). But there are certain elements of necessary knowledge that present a particular challenge for those learning to read in their second or third language. These include aspects of knowledge that are often implicit rather than explicit for most readers, e.g. an appreciation of how texts in different genres are organised or a full understanding of the cultural background to the content of a text.
- There is a crucial phase in the development of fluent reading skills when learners automatise the process of word recognition for most of the words that they encounter in print. This change means that readers can give more of their attention to understanding the text rather than concentrating on decoding individual words and searching for them in memory. That shift seems likely to present a greater challenge to children learning in their second language (L2) than it normally does to L1 learners. A key factor may be that they will take longer to access the L2 words in their lexical memory, and the vocabulary store will in any case be more limited. Geva and Clifton (1994) have suggested that this problem is exacerbated when they are reading text at the "frustration" level.
- When children have established reading skills beyond a basic level in L1 and subsequently start learning to read in L2, they transfer some of their literacy knowledge to the new task. There is some evidence that they then make quicker progress in L2 reading than would otherwise have been the case (see review in Baker (2001) pp. 351–354). It should be noted, however, that we do not yet have a full understanding of the process of transfer. There appears to have been little research on the issue among emerging biliterate learners in the United Kingdom. As the language landscape here is very different from that in North America and other countries where much of the work on transfer has been carried out, there is a need for more detailed research in this field here (Cline & Shamsi, 2000).
- How a person approaches literacy will depend, in part, on what books and print and writing mean to them. In the case of bilingual people, an important factor will be the use they normally make of the language in which they encounter print and how it relates to their sense of cultural affiliation and their identification with a particular group (Leung et al., 1997).
- Observational studies of children and young people from a range of linguistic minority communities have indicated that literacy in L1 and literacy in English serve different functions for them and are learned in different ways (Gregory, 1993, 1998; Martin-Jones & Bhatt, 1998; Kenner, 1999; Blackledge, 1999). It seems clear that for some children literacy practices in their LEA school may be out of line with expectations they bring from their experiences elsewhere, whether at home or in a community school.
- Studies of the phonological processing skills of children learning EAL have indicated a similar pattern of development to L1 learners. For example, children who obtain low scores on a phonological test battery in L2 tend to do less well in L2 reading generally, as is the case with monolingual learners (Frederickson & Frith, 1998). In fact, Geva (2001) has reviewed evidence that there is cross-language transfer from phonological skills in L1 to accuracy in word reading in L2—a more surprising finding.

- Successful reading involves moving between the different levels of a text and putting together what it says and what it means from all the clues available. Children reading in their second language may make less effective use of contextual cues than L1 readers (e.g. Rodriguez-Brown & Yirchott, 1983). Their levels of achievement in reading aloud are often more advanced than their ability to understand what they are reading, and the gap between their performance and that of L1 readers is often greater in comprehension than in accuracy (Frederickson & Frith, 1998; Landon, 1999). The comprehension task requires resources that are more developed for most people in their first language—a broad and well-catalogued vocabulary, a clear understanding of syntactic structures, an appreciation of the expectations linked to the genre of the passage, and access to the full variety of cultural reference that the author takes for granted in the reader.

In a recent review of the literature (to which you are referred if you require a more detailed account of the evidence than is possible in this chapter) Cline and Shamsi (2000) wrote: "It is important to keep in mind a crucial distinction. On the one hand, there is likely to be a substantial number of children learning EAL who experience reading difficulties in the early stages because of linguistic and cultural obstacles which they are not always given sufficient help to negotiate. On the other hand, there is a much smaller number who will experience severe and continuing difficulties at the word level that may go undiagnosed. We will move between these two groups in our discussion, and much of our analysis will apply to both groups equally. But a central aim of this report is to identify how the distinction between them can be made more confidently and accurately in assessment and teaching." (pp. 4–5)

Overview of Reading Difficulties Among Children Learning EAL

Recent reviews of the educational achievements of black and ethnic minority pupils have focused on performance across core subjects at the end of a key stage and on overall GCSE results (Demie, 2001; Gillborn & Mirza, 2000). The development of literacy skills has not been charted recently in the same detail. But there are good reasons to assume that significant numbers of children learning EAL underperform in literacy. Yet case studies of individual schools have indicated that pupils learning EAL who have learning difficulties may not receive the specialist teaching that they need, even though they are overrepresented in low English sets (e.g. Troyna & Siraj-Blatchford, 1993; Scarr et al., 1983). HMI observed that, even where multiethnic schools use tight setting in their efforts to raise achievement, few monitor ability sets by ethnic group (Ofsted, 1999). This is particularly unfortunate because of the uncertainty in individual cases as to whether slow progress towards literacy is caused by serious and abiding learning difficulties or is simply the result of limited knowledge of the language in which teaching is offered. It seems quite possible that this uncertainty causes delays in arranging appropriate provision for those children learning EAL who do have underlying learning difficulties in literacy over and above any difficulties related to their language status.

Table 12.1   Pupils learning EAL as a percentage of the total school population and of the population of SpLD units in Glasgow, 1984/85–1988/89. (Curnyn et al., 1991)

Year	Total school	%EAL/Total	Total SpLD	%EAL/SpLD
1984	106 413	3.83	87	1.15
1985	102 726	4.37	87	2.30
1986	99 014	4.38	94	1.06
1987	94 810	5.01	95	1.05
1988	92 012	5.09	93	1.08

Evidence that there is a problem comes from data suggesting that children learning EAL are underrepresented in such provision. The authorities in the United Kingdom have not in the past kept national statistics on the take-up of SEN support by ethnic or language group. But the representation of children learning EAL in specialist provision for children with specific learning difficulties (SpLD) or dyslexia has been investigated in a small number of regional and local studies. Cline and Shamsi (2000) summarised findings from surveys in three urban LEAs over a period of 15 years. They concluded that there was a clear and consistent picture of very low representation of children learning EAL in this provision. For example, Curnyn et al. (1991) reported on the representation of children learning EAL in SEN provision in Glasgow over the five-year period 1984/85 to 1988/89 (Table 12.1). As in most local surveys on this topic, the data relating to specific learning difficulties in literacy need to be treated with some caution because of the relatively small numbers involved. But the pattern it reveals is in line with other findings reviewed by Cline and Shamsi, and a follow-up survey of Scottish schools across a much wider area confirmed a pattern of low identification of "suspected dyslexia" in bilingual pupils (Deponio et al., 2000).

The questions about access to specialist provision need to be seen in the context of a history of serious concern about the assessment of ethnic minority pupils for SEN provision in Western countries. Many commentators have identified evidence of the operation of institutional racism in the delivery of SEN services. Institutional racism has been defined as "the collective failure of an organisation to provide an appropriate and professional service to people because of their colour, culture or ethnic origin. It can be seen or detected in processes, attitudes and behaviour which amount to discrimination through unwitting prejudice, ignorance, thoughtlessness, and racist stereotyping which disadvantage minority ethnic people" (Macpherson Committee of Enquiry, 1999, para. 6.34)

When ethnically based statistics were collected on SEN provision after the post-war expansion of these services in the UK and the USA, it emerged that there were higher than expected numbers of children from some minority communities in some forms of special provision (Franks, 1971; Tucker, 1980; Tomlinson, 1984). One example of this phenomenon concerned the West Indian communities that were then becoming established in many cities in England and Wales. In 1972 children from these communities constituted only 1.1% of all children in maintained primary and secondary schools, yet 4.9% of all children in schools for the educationally subnormal came from the West Indian communities (Tomlinson, 1984, pp. 21–22).

There was a very vigorous public debate on the issue, and slowly the most dramatic forms of overrepresentation of black pupils in SEN provision were reduced. But there still remain important areas where anomalies persist. For example, African-Caribbean pupils have continued to be overrepresented in schools for pupils with emotional and behavioural difficulties (ILEA, 1985: 15) and among the increasing numbers of pupils who are excluded from school (Bourne et al, 1995).

These concerns focus on *overrepresentation*. Why should we be concerned when there is *underrepresentation* of children learning EAL in specialist provision for specific learning difficulties? Three main reasons have been given in the literature for deploring this outcome too. Firstly, accepted procedures for identification and assessment may not be valid when applied to bilingual and multilingual pupils. Secondly, children with learning difficulties who are overlooked may miss out on specialist help that they need while continuing to make poor progress with normal teaching instruction. Thirdly, scarce resources will be wasted if they are not allocated to those who most need them. So the aim must be "to develop approaches to work with children learning EAL that are valid, fair and efficient" (Cline & Shamsi, 2000, p. 11).

The Impact of Definitions of Dyslexia on Work with Children Learning EAL

Other chapters in this book, notably Chapter 1, have discussed the evolution of theories of dyslexia. Some early definitions relied on exclusionary criteria, e.g. including a requirement that a child has "adequate intelligence" and excluding those whose intelligence fell below an apparently arbitrary point on the normal curve. On this basis it became common to restrict the term "dyslexia" to situations where a discrepancy was found between measured IQ and reading achievement. There are strong reasons for doubting the validity and utility of diagnosing dyslexia in this way. (For a fuller discussion see, for example, Chapter 1 in this book and Frederickson & Cline (2002, Chapter 11).) In addition, there are specific problems in employing this approach for children who are learning EAL. IQ tests administered in English tend to underestimate the potential of children for whom English is an additional language (Cummins, 1984). As a result these children may fail to meet criteria for access to additional resources where these are based on IQ–achievement criteria (Cline & Frederickson, 1999). Definitions that make no reference to IQ, such as that proposed in BPS (1999), avoid this problem.

IDENTIFICATION AND ASSESSMENT OF LEARNING DIFFICULTIES

When and By Whom?

It is generally recognised that the early identification of learning difficulties in literacy enables educators to provide appropriate help before problems of understanding and motivation become acute and before a child's overall education has suffered because of obstacles to their access to classroom texts. Unfortunately, effective early identification appears to be particularly difficult when working with children who are learning English as an additional language (EAL). Interestingly, similar conclusions have been drawn in a study of the identification of specific language impairment among children learning EAL (Crutchley et al., 1997). The greatest challenge is to distinguish between literacy problems which are due to EAL and those which are due to SEN, such as specific learning difficulties. Is a child struggling with text simply because the language is unfamiliar, or do they have a more deep-seated learning difficulty?

Who shall be involved in answering this question? Clearly the task of assessment "requires a highly sensitive and sympathetic understanding of a child's community, culture, family life and individual characteristics" (Baker, 2001, p. 310). Specialist EAL teachers, bilingual support staff and interpreters may have an important role to play in identification and assessment for many children learning EAL, but there is little guidance, or even agreement, on what their contribution can best be and how their collaboration with class teachers and SEN specialists should be managed (Cline & Shamsi, 2000, p. 23). Some commentators have advocated an extended "pre-referral" stage during which minority community professionals are consulted (Barona & Barona, 1987; Graf, 1992). A more radical view of the process requires that professionals such as psychologists should act as advocates for the children and subject what society and the school offers them to critical scrutiny (Cummins, 2000).

With What Basic Information?

Certain basic factors need to be taken into account in the assessment of any child with learning difficulties—their position in society, their situation in their family, their educational history and the current educational provision, including language provision. In the case of a child learning EAL each of these issues requires more careful consideration. This is made explicit in the revised Code of Practice issued by the DfEE (DfEE, 2000). The need for basic background information may appear obvious, but the little published evidence that is available suggests that such information is often not collected or fully considered or recorded. For example, Desforges (1995) examined SEN statements for 300 children learning EAL written during 1989–1991 in an urban area of northern England. The first language was not identified at all in the papers in 34% of cases and had been assessed in only 36% of cases. Similar evidence from surveys in other areas was reported by Curnyn et al. (1991) and Cline (1991).

Cline and Shamsi (2000) reviewed checklists of basic information that various writers have suggested should be collected and recorded whenever a child learning EAL shows difficulties in the classroom or is formally assessed in relation to SEN. They argued that this information is needed if a teacher or psychologist is to determine, for example, whether any reading problems they identify are attributable to limited knowledge of L1 or lack of educational opportunity rather than to an underlying learning difficulty that is likely to persist. Their list had five key headings:

- *Cultural and religious background*, e.g. religion, dietary requirements, festivals and customs observed by the family
- *Family details and history*, e.g. details of family composition, recent or past separations from family
- *Language history*, including current usage of L1 and L2, e.g. language(s) spoken at home, reading/writing skills in home language(s), experience and competence in English
- *School history*, including past and current EAL and SEN support and attendance at community/religious classes, e.g. previous schooling in the UK and abroad, attendance at community or religious school, extended visits abroad
- *Medical history*.

Teachers of children learning EAL who may have learning difficulties in literacy will find it helpful to develop a list for their own use that highlights background information that is relevant to the communities with which they work.

The most important and complex information in this list for our purposes concerns language proficiency. Literacy is a language-based skill, and children's difficulties with literacy learning can only be understood if their experience, proficiency and use of the languages in their repertoire are fully appreciated. The draft revised DfEE Code of Practice for SEN assessment highlights this point: "At an early stage a full assessment should be made of the exposure they have had in the past to each of the languages they speak, the use they make of them currently and their proficiency in them. The information about their language skills obtained in this way will form the basis of all further work with them both in assessing their learning difficulties and in planning any learning support for them" (DfEE, 2001). Accounts of how language may be assessed in this context may be found in Baker (2001, Chapter 2) and Frederickson and Cline (2002, Chapter 10).

The second crucial piece of background information concerns the child's educational history. For example, if fundamental language-learning needs have not been adequately addressed, one cannot know whether or not they have enduring learning difficulties of a serious kind. First, it will be necessary to discover how they respond if they have appropriate language learning provision at school. "The minimum aim must be that problems that really arise from the setting are not defined as being located within the child." (Cline & Shamsi, 2000, p. 31)

In the UK the National Literacy Strategy now effectively sets the classroom context for literacy learning. There is some evidence that pupils who are struggling with the reading process and those at the very early stages of learning English as a second language benefit less from the regular Literacy Hour routines than other pupils (Sainsbury et al., 1998). However, these routines may be used to observe and evaluate such pupils' strengths and difficulties in detail. It has been suggested that important features of good practice include:

- exploration of the use of dual language texts and texts in languages other than English (White, 1998)
- the deployment of additional staff in the most effective way (OFSTED, 1998; NALDIC, 1998)

- fine-tuning of differentiation within the Hour for those children who are only just becoming familiar with English as well as for those with SEN (Sainsbury et al., 1998).

Through What Strategies?

Children who are learning EAL will be likely to vary in their intellectual performance over time and across settings more than monolingual pupils. This has led writers working in this field to argue against relying on a single, comprehensive test for assessment purposes. Instead, they emphasise the advantages of drawing upon multiple sources of evidence. On the basis of our review of the literature, Cline and Shamsi (2000, p. 34) suggested that this might involve one or more of the following:

- sampling the child's performance and behaviour in different roles and in different situations
- using multiple indicators to assess progress over time
- sampling a child's reading across a range of texts and genres
- comparing performance in settings where L1 is the main medium of communication with performance in the mainstream classroom
- consulting any religious or community school that children attend.

In any work with children from minority communities it is essential to reduce to a minimum any possible sources of bias affecting observation, assessment and judgement. When test materials are employed, it is good practice for a test developer to have a code of practice that covers the issue of content bias. For example, the National Foundation for Educational Research has a section on Fair Assessment in its Code of Practice for the Development of Assessment Instruments, Methods and Systems. This states that in order to produce fair assessments, NFER developers will:

- Review and revise questions, items or tasks and related materials to avoid potentially insensitive content or language.
- Enact procedures that help to ensure that differences in performance are related primarily to the knowledge, skills, aptitudes or attitudes being assessed rather than to irrelevant factors.
- Investigate the performance of people of different ethnic, gender and socio-economic backgrounds when institutions helping with trials are willing to provide this information and when samples of sufficient size are available.
- The investigation of performance of different groups will be carried out using data provided on the first actual administration of the assessment.
- Where feasible, provide appropriately modified forms of the assessment procedures for people with disabilities.

For fuller accounts of test bias and strategies for reducing it, see Cline and Shamsi (2000, pp. 34–37) and Frederickson and Cline (2002, Chapter 6).

One way of thinking about the process of assessment is as a hypothesis-testing process. Wright (1991) and her colleagues regarded assessment as being like a piece of detective work. There was a situation to be explained. They thought of various hypotheses that might provide a satisfactory explanation in the case of a child who is learning to speak English as an additional language:

- The child is learning more slowly than others because the ethos and curriculum of the school are experienced as challenging and alien, rather than welcoming and accommodating.
- The child is not learning because the child's good level of conversational English has misled the teacher into setting tasks that are too abstract for the child's current language level.
- The child is learning at an appropriate rate, and just needs more time to get used to the demands of working in their second language.
- The child has not attained a basic language proficiency in any language, because neither language has been given adequate opportunities to develop.
- The child is failing because of a preoccupation with stress that is affecting their family or their community.
- The child has a general difficulty in learning compared to other children of the same age.
- The child is failing because of a specific language disorder.

An advantage of this approach is that the list of possible hypotheses may be varied to fit the situation with which a teacher is dealing. The approach also emphasises that there are a variety of explanations to be explored before one assumes the existence of a specific learning difficulty in the target area of performance.

ISSUES IN THE ASSESSMENT OF READING ABILITIES

The evaluation of pupils' progress in literacy development may be based on regular testing or observation that is systematically recorded on successive occasions. An analysis of cumulative records makes it possible to identify changes in the rate of progress over time. When children start school at an early stage in learning EAL, it can be expected that their progress in literacy, particularly in reading comprehension, will speed up as their oral use of English improves and their vocabulary increases. It is a reasonable working hypothesis that, if the pace of progress does not pick up in this way, the original obstacle to reading progress is more likely to have arisen from learning difficulties relating to literacy and not simply from a lack of knowledge of English.

When a child has been identified as "at risk", teachers will wish to assess their reading and reading-related skills in more detail. Our recent review showed that the manuals of published individual diagnostic tests have rarely reported data on the performance of children learning EAL. Fawcett and Nicolson (2000) have described two case studies employing the Dyslexia Screening Test. Frederickson and Frith (1998) presented fuller data on the performance of a sample of London children whose first language was Sylheti on the Phonological Assessment Battery (see Chapter 4, this volume). We concluded our review of the available information on reading assessment with a general observation that applies to all forms of assessment of EAL learners: "A simple guideline for interpreting the significance of scores on such batteries would be impossible. The specific experience and language proficiency of each individual L2 learner would need to be considered in order to draw safe conclusions from the results" (Cline & Shamsi, 2000, p. 52).

CONCLUDING COMMENTS

It should be noted that research and pedagogy relating to children learning EAL who have learning difficulties have tended to focus on the development of reading skills and to ignore wider aspects of literacy. That emphasis is reflected in this chapter. Readers may wish to correct that bias in their own teaching observations of pupils learning EAL. The ultimate aim must be that children have the skills of reading *and* writing and also that they will be motivated to engage with a wide range of texts. Their literacy skills have the potential to enhance their understanding and enjoyment of the world and their capacity for action (Hudelson, 1994). The literacy curriculum must be designed to empower them not only with the skills required for that, but with a strong sense of what those skills can be used for. There is an additional potential dimension for children learning EAL: biliteracy may offer direct access to a further cultural and intellectual heritage (Baker, 2001). They will not experience those benefits if the educators working with them fail to identify specific learning difficulties that inhibit their progress.

REFERENCES

Baker, C. (2001). *Foundations of Bilingual Education and Bilingualism*, (Third edn). Clevedon, Avon, UK: Multilingual Matters.

Barona, A., & Barona, M. S. (1987). A model for the assessment of limited English proficient students referred for special education services. In S. H. Fradd & W. J. Tikunoff (Eds), *Bilingual Education and Bilingual Special Education: A Guide for Administrators* (pp. 183–210). Boston, MA: College-Hill Press.

Blackledge, A. (1999). Reading interactions at the threshold of power: home and school strategies in hearing young Bangladeshi children read. In H. South (Ed.), *Literacies in Community and School* (pp. 30–50). Watford, UK: NALDIC.

Bourne, J., Bridges, L., & Searle, C. (1995). *Outcast England: How Schools Exclude Black Children*. London: Institute of Race Relations.

BPS (1999). *Dyslexia, Literacy and Psychological Assessment*. Leicester, UK: British Psychological Society.

Cline, T. (1991). Professional constructions of the concept of moderate learning difficulties. In P. L. C. Evans & A. D. B. Clarke (Eds), *Combatting Mental Handicap: A Multidisciplinary Approach* (pp. 86–100). Bicester, UK: AB Academic.

Cline, T., & Frederickson, N. (1999). Identification and assessment of dyslexia in bi/multilingual children. *International Journal of Bilingual Education and Bilingualism, 2*(2), 81–93.

Cline, T., & Shamsi, T. (2000). *Language Needs or Special Needs? The Assessment of Learning Difficulties in Literacy Among Children Learning English as an Additional Language: A Literature Review*. London: DfEE. (The research brief and the full report can be accessed at http://www.dfee.gov.uk/research/re_paper/RR184.doc.)

Crutchley, A., Botting, N., & Conti-Ramsden, G. (1997). Bilingualism and specific language impairment in children attending language units. *European Journal of Disorders of Communication, 32,* 267–276.

Cummins, J. (1984). *Bilingualism and Special Education: Issues in Assessment and Pedagogy.* Clevedon, UK: Multilingual Matters.

Cummins, J. (2000). *Language, Power and Pedagogy: Bilingual Children in the Crossfire.* Clevedon, UK: Multilingual Matters.

Curnyn, J. C., Wallace, I., Kistan, S., & McLaren, M. (1991). Special educational need and ethnic minority pupils. In Scottish Education Department/Regional Psychological Services (Ed.), *Professional Development Initiatives 1989–1990* (pp. 271–300). Edinburgh: Scottish Education Department.

Demie, F. (2001). Ethnic and gender differences in educational achievement and implications for school improvement strategies. *Educational Research, 43*(1), 91–106.

Deponio, P., Landon, J., Mullin, K., & Reid, G. (2000). An audit of the processes involved in identifying and assessing bilingual learners suspected of being dyslexic: a Scottish study. *Dyslexia, 6*(1), 29–41.

Desforges, M. (1995). Assessment of special educational needs in bilingual pupils: changing practice? *Schools Psychology International, 16,* 5–17.

DfEE (1999). *Ethnic Minority Pupils and Pupils for whom English is an Additional Language: England 1996/97. Statistical Bulletin No. 3/99.* London: HMSO.

DfEE (2000). *SEN Code of Practice on the Identification and Assessment of Pupils with Special Educational Needs and SEN Thresholds: Good Practice Guidelines or Identification and Provision for Pupils with Special Educational Needs.* London: DfEE.

Fawcett, A., & Nicolson, R. (2000). Systematic identification and intervention for reading difficulty: case studies of children with EAL. *Dyslexia, 6*(1), 57–71.

Franks, D. J. (1971). Ethnic and social status characteristics of children in EMR and LD classes. *Exceptional Children, 37,* 537–538.

Frederickson, N., & Cline, T. (2002). *Special Educational Needs, Inclusion and Diversity: A Textbook.* Buckingham, UK: Open University Press.

Frederickson, N. L., & Frith, U. (1998). Identifying dyslexia in bilingual children: A phonological approach with Inner London Sylheti speakers. *Dyslexia, 4,* 119–131.

Geva, E. (2000). 'Issues in the asssessment of reading disabilities in 12 children—Beliefs and research evidence.' *Dyslexia, 6*(1), 13–28.

Geva, E. (2000). Issues in the assessment of reading disabilities in children who are working in their second language—Beliefs and research evidence. *Dyslexia, 6*(1), 13–28.

Geva, E., & Clifton, S. (1994). The development of first and second language reading skills in early French immersion. *The Canadian Modern Language Review, 50*(4), 646–667.

Gillborn, D., & Mirza, H.S. (2000). *Educational Inequality: Mapping Race, Class and Gender.* London: HMSO.

Graf, V. L. (1992). Minimizing the inappropriate referral and placement of ethnic minority Students in special education. In T. Cline (Ed.), *The Assessment of Special Educational Needs: International Perspectives* (pp. 186–198). London: Routledge.

Gregory, E. (1993). Sweet and sour: Learning to read in a British and Chinese school. *English in Education, 27*(3), 54–59.

Gregory, E. (1998). Siblings as mediators of literacy in linguistic minority communities. *Language and Education, 12*(1), 33–54.

Hudelson, S. (1994). Literacy development of second language children. In F. Genesee (Ed.), *Educating Second Language Children: The Whole Child, The Whole Curriculum, The Whole Community* (pp. 129–158). Cambridge: Cambridge University Press.

ILEA (1985). *Educational Opportunities for Au? Research Studies: Fish Report* (vol. 2). London: Inner London Education Authority.

Kenner, C. (1999). What meanings does Gujerati literacy hold for Meera, age seven? In H. South (Ed.), *Literacies in Community and School* (pp. 51–61). Watford, UK: NALDIC.

Landon, J. (1999). Early intervention with bilingual learners: towards a research agenda. In H. South (Ed.), *Literacies in Community and School* (pp. 84–96). Watford, UK: NALDIC.

Leung, C., Harris, R., & Rampton, B. (1997). The idealised native speaker, reified ethnicities and classroom realities. *TESOL Quarterly, 31*(3), 543–560.

Macpherson Committee of Enquiry (1999). *Report of the Stephen Lawrence Enquiry*. London: Stationery Office.

Martin-Jones, M., & Bhatt, A. (1999). Literacies in the lives of bilingual learners in local communities in Britain. In H. South (Ed.), *Literacies in Community and School* (pp. 1–20). Watford, UK: NALDIC.

NALDIC (1998). *NALDIC Response to the Draft Proposals for Baseline Assessment*. Watford, UK: National Association for Language Development in the Curriculum.

Ofsted (1998). *The National Literacy Project: An HMI Evaluation*. London: Office for Standards in Education.

Ofsted (1999). *Raising the Attainment of Minority Ethnic Pupils: School and LEA Responses*. London: HMSO.

Rodriguez-Brown, F. V., & Yirchott, L. S. (1983). *A Comparative Analysis of Oral Reading Miscues made by Monolingual versus Bilingual Students*. Los Angeles, CA: Evaluation, Dissemination and Assessment Center, California State University.

Sainsbury, M., Schagen, I., & Whetton, C. (1998). *Evaluation of the National Literacy Project: Cohort 1, 1996–1998*. Slough, UK: National Foundation for Educational Research.

Scarr, S., Caparulo, B. K., Ferdman, M., Tower, R. B., & Caplan, J. (1983). Developmental status and school achievements of minority and non-minority children from birth to 18 years in a British Midlands town. *British Journal of Developmental Psychology, 1*, 31–48.

Shorrocks, D., Daniels, S., Frobisher, L., Nelson, N., Waterson, A., & Bell, J. (1992). *ENCA 1 Project Report: The Evaluation of National Curriculum Assessment at Key Stage 1*. London: Schools Examinations and Assessment Council.

Tomlinson, S. (1984). Minority groups in English conurbations. In P. Williams (Ed.), *Special Education in Minority Communities* (pp. 18–32). Milton Keynes, UK: Open University Press.

Troyna, B., & Siraj-Blatchford, I. (1993). Providing support or denying access? The experiences of students designated as 'ESL' and 'SN' in a multiethnic secondary school. *Educational Review, 45*(1), 3–11.

Tucker, J. A. (1980). Ethnic proportions in classes for the learning disabled: issues in non-biased assessment. *Journal of Special Education, 14*, 93–105.

Verhoeven, L. T. (1990). Acquisition of reading in a second language. *Reading Research Quarterly, 25*, 90–114.

White, J. (1998). The National Literacy Strategy and provision for children who are learning English as an additional language. *NALDIC News, 15*, 11–12.

Wright, A. (1991). The assessment of bilingual pupils with reported learning difficulties: a hypothesis-testing approach. In T. Cline & N. Frederickson (Eds), *Bilingual Pupils and the National Curriculum: Overcoming Difficulties in Teaching and Learning* (pp. 185–192). London: University College London Department of Psychology.

Chapter 13

THE ROLE OF THE LEARNING SUPPORT CO-ORDINATOR: ADDRESSING THE CHALLENGES

Janice Wearmouth

INTRODUCTION

On the face of it, the role of a learning support co-ordinator in the UK with re-sponsibility for students "with special educational needs" in the area of literacy development is straightforward. In law, in England, Scotland, Wales and Northern Ireland, a student has a special educational need in the area of literacy development only if the difficulties s/he is experiencing require "special" provision to be made. A student has a special educational need if s/he has:

> a learning difficulty which calls for special educational provision to be made for him or her. (DfE, 1994, para. 2:1; DENI, 1998, para. 1.4; Education Act (Scotland) 1980, section 1(5)(d))

From this definition, the role of an individual designated as having a responsibility for co-ordinating the provision for these students should be clear: to oversee the implementation of whatever might be deemed necessary to address the difficulty. However, educational institutions are complex. The agendas of those associated with them, students, teachers, parents, other professionals, are diverse. To assume that appropriate provision to meet students' literacy difficulties can be drawn up and put into operation in an objective, "scientific" manner, that co-ordination is a question of "the application of scientific theory and technique to the instrumental problems of practice" (Schön, 1983, p 30) is to adopt a "technical rational" view of the special educational needs co-ordinator's role of a kind critiqued by Schön (1983) as denying the "messiness" of the real-life role of the teacher in the context of the educational institution. One "major contributing factor to the 'messiness'

Dyslexia and Literacy: Theory and Practice. Edited by Gavin Reid and Janice Wearmouth.
© 2002 John Wiley & Sons, Ltd.

of many problematic situations and issues in education" is the "perceptions" and "intentions" of educators themselves (Frederickson, 1993). This chapter addresses the "messinesss" evident in the diversity of perspectives on provision for students who experience difficulties in literacy amongst school professionals and the consequences of this for the learning support co-ordinator. It discusses issues ranging from the national through to the school system and individual literacy programmes. These issues are associated with:

- the national curricular context within which students with literacy difficulties are educated
- interpretations and implications of "special" educational needs
- the impact of school ethos on literacy learning
- the relationship between the social and cultural background of students and literacy learning in educational institutions
- decisions about which model of the reading process it is most appropriate to rely on to conceptualise approaches to overcome difficulties.

It will conclude by briefly outlining possible approaches to conceptualising improved provision for students with literacy difficulties in ways which take account of this "messiness".

SIGNIFICANCE OF NATIONAL CURRICULAR CONTEXTS

Since the 1981 Education Act reaffirmed the principle of integration, the law has made provision for all students to be educated in mainstream schools. However, establishing "child-centred" practices which cater for individual differences and diversity in schools that are more accustomed to catering for majority interests is not straightforward. School practices in relation to pupils who experience difficulties are heavily constrained by national and local authority policies. For example, in England and Wales, since the 1988 Education Act national education policies have attempted to promote the majority interest through setting normative targets to be achieved within the lifetime of one parliament, and through establishing league tables of academic achievement. Much of the assessment on which these achievement tables rest is carried out through the medium of literacy. The problems created for many pupils with difficulties in literacy acquisition are therefore very hard to resolve. Walford (1996) notes, for example, that the effect of imposing additional pressure on schools to improve their overall literacy standards has resulted in making some lower-achieving pupils unpopular to schools.

Tensions and contradictions permeate the whole UK education system in its attempts to reconcile principles of individuality, distinctiveness and diversity with inclusion and equal opportunities (Norwich, 1996). In England, for example, in the area of literacy learning, the drive to raise standards of the learning of all students through whole-class and whole-group teaching, standardised forms of assessment (Broadfoot, 1996) and the encouragement of competition between schools, stands in stark contrast to the statutory requirement to pay due regard to the principle of inclusion of students, and, within this, to address the identified learning needs of individuals who experience difficulties in literacy. What may appear as somewhat fragmented and contradictory government policies create dilemmas for schools which may be addressed in some cases by actions which themselves stand the criticism of offering an unfair advantage to some students and discriminating against others. One clear example of a situation where individuals have been driven to seek redress against perceived injustice in the formal curriculum is the system for seeking special dispensation for formal examinations for individual students who experience certain types of difficulties in learning, including literacy difficulties. The learning support co-ordinator may be in an unenviable position of contributing to decision-making about which should be the students for whom special dispensation cases should be prepared, and which should be omitted.

Where students experience difficulty in the acquisition of literacy, schools' and teachers' autonomy over curricular decision-making is a particularly important issue. Across the world teachers have varying degrees of opportunity to make their own decisions about what should comprise the literacy curriculum. Countries which have legally required national literacy curricula which prescribe content, modes of teaching and forms of assessment may offer learning support co-ordinators less room for manoeuvre in making decisions about how to organise special literacy programmes compared with the greater freedom elsewhere. The national literacy curricula frameworks of the different countries of the UK, for example, vary in their flexibility and prescription of both content and teaching approach. It is crucial that learning support co-ordinators are fully conversant with the detail of requirements of their own national curriculum context, and the room for manoeuvre they have within it, to respond appropriately to individual students' learning needs. As Wragg (1997) notes:

> One important element of the craft skills of teaching...is the ability to pick ways through a curriculum, even a prescribed one, via as imaginative and challenging routes as possible. (Wragg, 1997, p 23)

INTERPRETATIONS AND IMPLICATIONS OF "SPECIAL" EDUCATIONAL NEEDS

A number of commentators have noted the "messiness" that surrounds the interpretation of the relativist notion of what, in law, constitutes a "special educational need" in general, and, therefore, special needs in the area of literacy in particular. In principle, the law is based on individually defined need. However, in practice resource limitations have meant that only a proportion of individuals have been covered by the legislation. In Britain, since the Rutter et al. (1970) study showed that teachers' perceptions are that, on average, 20% of their students were experiencing difficulty of some kind, the figure of 20% has been used to estimate the number of students nationally who might experience difficulties. Of that 20%, an arbitrary figure of approximately 2%, drawn from a count of students in special schools in 1944, are seen by policy-makers as likely to have difficulties which require additional or extra resources to be provided for them.

Implicit in any discussions of the law in relation to individually defined provision for students who experience difficulties in literacy development are issues of equality of opportunity in education, fairness in allocation of resources and the question of whether individual learning programmes for students or a whole-school approach to learning support is more likely to encourage all learners to reach their potential. Different beliefs about the root causes of literacy difficulties and different beliefs about equity issues can imply conflicting curricular responses. Translating the law into the context of the educational institution may not be easy in situations where sets of beliefs held by those associated with that institution are in tension and fundamentally irreconcilable. A proposal to implement the same solution to overcoming barriers to students' learning may be received very differently in different institutions, and also by different teachers in the same institution, where underlying beliefs and viewpoints are in conflict. Frederickson (1993, p 4) follows Kauffman (1989) in distinguishing between the issues involved in organising appropriate provision for those students identified as experiencing difficulties in learning. On the one hand, students may be seen as more similar than different. From this perspective, no "special" teaching is necessary to address literacy difficulties, although some "adjustments" might be made to accommodate individual differences. There is no need to identify individuals as "different" or to target funds separately to pay, for example, for specialist teaching of dyslexic students. Furthermore, segregation away from the mainstream classroom for any students is unethical. On the other hand, some students may be viewed as "very different" from peers in the extent and degree of the difficulties they experience in learning. The implication for those with difficulties in literacy is that these difficulties must be assessed and appropriate provision clearly specified and quantified so that special expertise can be deployed. Alternative locations outside the mainstream classroom must sometimes be used to provide "more intensive individualised instruction" and ensure that other students' education is not prejudiced.

These contrasts are illustrated in the way in which the duties of the co-ordinator have been described in the national advisory documents of some countries in the UK. In England and Wales the Code of Practice for the assessment and identification of special educational needs (DfE, 1994; DENI, 1998) sets out the duties as follows:

- the day-to-day operation of the school's SEN policy
- liaising with and advising fellow teachers
- co-ordinating provision for students with special educational needs
- maintaining the school's SEN register and overseeing the records on all students with special educational needs
- liaising with parents of students with special educational needs
- contributing to the in-service training of staff
- liaising with external agencies, including the educational psychology service and other support agencies, medical and social services and voluntary bodies

One way of looking at the way in which this role has been outlined is that it represents an attempt to mediate the tensions and dilemmas inherent in an approach to special provision in school which adopts a whole-school view of curriculum support at the same time as meeting individual needs. As I have noted elsewhere

(Wearmouth, 2000, p 48), on the one hand the co-ordinator must be proactive in identifying, assessing and organising provision appropriate to meeting individual needs. On the other hand, s/he must support curriculum differentiation in order to meet a diversity of need in every classroom.

Inherent in the above guidelines is a clear tension for the co-ordinator attempting to meet students' special literacy needs between:

- fulfilling the law to uphold the entitlement of individual students to special literacy programmes versus supporting common entitlement to accessing the mainstream literacy curriculum
- sustaining a system for identifying, assessing and meeting the "special" literacy needs of individual students versus liaising with other staff to identify curriculum areas which could be made more inclusive of all students' literacy learning
- liaising with staff, parents and outside agencies with regard to individual students' difficulties versus differentiated classroom approaches to teaching and assessment for all students
- negotiating, reviewing and evaluating Individual Education Plans versus team and support teaching in-class to benefit all students
- advocacy for individual students with difficulties in literacy versus advocacy of curricular improvements in the literacy curriculum for all.

Whatever the individual co-ordinator may feel about issues of equity and of curriculum organisation, s/he cannot afford to neglect statutory obligations. A special educational needs tribunal operates in some countries of the UK. It is one arena where differences in opinion, for example, between parents on the one hand and the local authority and/or the school on the other are likely to become apparent, and it relies heavily on the evidence available from LEA personnel, including special educational needs or learning support co-ordinators. Additionally, the House of Lords' recent judgment in a number of cases concerning allegations of negligence against local education authorities (LEAs) heightens the need for all those associated with the education of students with "special" literacy difficulties to be aware of their statutory obligations. One of these, Phelps v London Borough of Hillingdon, is particularly pertinent to this book because it concerns the issue of dyslexia. Ruebain (2001) notes its implications:

> The House of Lords decision of 27 July, 2000, has made it more possible for individuals to bring claims for compensation.
>
> ... Local authorities and schools can be held vicariously liable for the negligent actions of staff members, including educational psychologists, teachers, education officers, etc.
>
> ... Claims in education negligence are likely to be considered as personal injury claims.

SCHOOL ETHOS

As Soler et al. (2002) note, there is considerable evidence that programmes designed to address literacy difficulties also need to take account of the fact that literacy is grounded in wider cultural and social contexts. Literacy can be seen as forming part of the semiotic (symbol) system of the environment in which it is used. It is therefore important for the co-ordinator to consider the relationship between the learning environment and the cognitive processes of the individual learner who experiences difficulties in literacy. A useful model of literacy learning which examines the dynamic of learning at the interface between the individual and the environment is that afforded by Vygotsky (1987). In his theory of social constructivism, the cultural and social context within which learning takes place is crucial in mediating how a learner gains access to the signs and symbols in the environment. Vygotsky emphasises the child's active role in his/her own learning through meaningful interactions with others. Children first develop literacy within a social setting in which cultural interpretations are communicated by more experienced members of society. They acquire the meanings attached to the signs and symbols of a culture, for example literacy skills and knowledge, first in interaction with more experienced others (adults or peers) in a social context. Later they internalise both the skills and knowledge and also the culturally accepted values of these for personal use in the mental context.

From a Vygotskian perspective, it is important for the co-ordinator to consider the relationship between the learner's cognitive processes and the immediate environment of the school. From that standpoint, the need to pay due regard to the model of the student as an *active* participant in his or her own learning goes beyond the advice to take the student's views seriously given in the Code of Practice (DfE, 1994; DENI, 1998) and should pervade learning support co-ordinators' thinking about practice for those who experience difficulties. If students need to engage positively with their literacy learning, it follows that the issue of student motivation is a crucial consideration. Particular areas in the school literacy curriculum are bound to impinge on the motivation of students with difficulties in literacy motivation. One example is that of marking and spelling policies. Bentley (1990) argues that, on the one hand, for some students, repeatedly receiving back scripts covered with marks indicating errors is very demoralising. On the other, there has to be a rational, structured approach to ensuring that students make progress in recognising mistakes and learning how to correct them. With regard to spelling, tests may be a required part of a school's approach to supporting students' literacy development. On the other hand, there may be a general consensus that the value of spelling tests closely reflects the way in which spellings are chosen for students to learn, and how far they are tailored to the needs of the individual student. Whichever strategy is chosen will have both advantages and disadvantages and should be supported by reasoned argument.

Demotivation of students is one issue often associated with the consequences of difficulties in literacy (Riddick, 1996). A number of motivational theories within a cognitive psychology perspective have proposed that the beliefs students develop about their abilities and efforts influence how hard they try and, consequently, influence their efforts. Various studies have shown that, when students find a task difficult, those who attribute their difficulties to controllable factors, such as insufficient effort, are more likely to persist than are students who attribute their difficulties to uncontrollable factors, such as insufficient ability (Butkowsky & Willows, 1980; Diener & Dweck, 1978: Dweck & Reppucci, 1973; Licht et al., 1985).

One important factor that contributes to the development of poor self-efficacy is the visibility of information relating to how a student performs relative to his or her peers. Where competition between and within schools is actively encouraged, the extent to which both success and failure should be visible, for example through the public display of some pupils' work and the neglect of others', may be a contentious area. Research conducted in mainstream classrooms suggests that students who experience difficulty in learning are more likely to evaluate their abilities as poor when information of this sort is made obvious (Ames & Archer, 1988).

The issue of the particular forms of support offered in mainstream classrooms is an important factor in determining the visibility of particular students and, therefore, in maintaining, or undermining, their motivation. Practice of support in class appears to vary enormously from one school to another. A recent University of Manchester research report on learning support assistants (LSAs) (Farrell, 1999) confirms the key role that many LSAs play in acting as the main source of support for students with exceptional needs in mainstream schools and, therefore, the role of the learning support co-ordinator in managing this resource. Although teachers were often responsible for planning schemes of work that were then implemented by LSAs, in many cases, especially when LSAs were working in non-resourced schools or employed by LEAs, "they took the lead in adapting programmes of work and in planning new programmes" (Farrell, 1999: 17, reported in Mittler, 2000). Farrell's (1999) report reflects a strong consensus among teachers and LSAs on how effective in-class support *should* be organised. One of the findings of this report was that everyone involved—students, teachers and LSAs—all agreed that support in class should be offered at a distance but should be immediately available when needed. Where special resourcing has been allocated to address individual students' learning needs, this finding may be seen as conflicting with the requirement to show how the resource is targeted at that individual, however. This is a further example of a real-life potentially "messy" situation.

One of the problems associated with the continuation of an individualised notion of "special educational need" is that provision which is targeted at the individual student tends to remain on the periphery of the school curriculum rather than becoming an integral part of it. As Dyson (1997) has argued, an "army" of special educators has "colonised" rather than transformed mainstream schools. The full inclusion of students identified as experiencing particular difficulties in learning in the area of literacy, therefore, presents a number of challenges to mainstream schools:

> The challenge confronting the inclusive school is that of developing a student-centred pedagogy capable of successfully educating all students, including those who have serious disadvantages and disabilities. . . . Special needs education incorporates the proven principles of sound pedagogy from which all students may benefit. It assumes that human differences are normal and that learning must accordingly be adapted to the needs of the student rather than the student fitted to pre-ordained assumptions regarding the pace and nature of the learning process. (UNESCO, 1994, p 7)

Many researchers in the area of inclusion and special educational needs are agreed on the kind of changes that will have to occur in schools for pupils who experience difficulties in learning, for example difficulties in literacy acquisition, to be included. Mittler (2000), for example, considers that the inclusion in schools of such pupils requires:

> ...a process of reform and restructuring of the school as a whole, with the aim of ensuring that all pupils can have access to the whole range of educational and social opportunities offered by the school. This includes the curriculum on offer, the assessment, recording and reporting of pupils' achievements, the decisions that are taken on the grouping of pupils within schools or classrooms, pedagogy and classroom practice, ... (Mittler, 2000, p 2)

IMPACT OF SOCIAL AND CULTURAL CONTEXTS

The social and cultural context within which the student is being educated may itself support or militate against literacy learning. The learning support co-ordinator's perspective on the barriers to literacy learning within this context obviously will impact upon literacy teaching and interpretations of how to interpret and implement best research-based practice. Clearly, the attitude of any educational institution to the role of families as prime educators of children and to families' social and cultural backgrounds is of significance in this regard. Different approaches and strategies have, embedded within them, different underlying assumptions, not only about the reading process, but also about the ability and right of families and/or carers from a diversity of backgrounds and cultures to support the literacy development of their students. It is fundamentally important for the co-ordinator to recognise these assumptions in order to plan programmes that will address difficulties in literacy development within the context of respect for the students' family and cultural background.

The assumption that the homes of poor working-class and ethnic minority-culture families are less good literacy-learning environments than those of dominant culture, middle-class families was common until comparatively recently. In the 1970s and 1980s a number of studies, for example the National Child Development Study (Davie et al., 1972) which followed all the children born in one week in 1958 through from birth, suggested that achievement on standardised tests of reading is strongly related to social class. Children whose fathers were semi-skilled manual workers were more than twice as likely to be poor readers as those students whose fathers held professional or technical posts. The work on "family literacy" in recent years has represented an interesting diversity of views on the ability of some families to support their children's literacy development where those families have little tradition of literacy. Hannon (1999) discusses the rhetoric surrounding "restricted" family literacy programmes, which he defines as programmes which insist that parents or carers must participate in initiatives designed to raise the level of their literacy level simultaneously with that of their children. These "restricted" family literacy programmes are premised on the notion of some families as "literacy-deficient". Hannon sums up his views on the difficulties inherent in this deficit perspective on some students' families for those conceptualising appropriate ways in which to support the improvement of students' literacy:

- the school is absolved from responsibility for addressing the literacy difficulties of those students from "literacy-deficient" families
- the families themselves cannot be viewed as a source of positive support for the student's developing literacy until and unless their deficiency in literacy in addressed.

Soler et al. (2002) notes Martin's (1999) arguments that, in relation to immigrant families for whom English is an additional language, a deficit view forms part of a "widely held ... thesis" where "becoming bilingual is perceived as a problem and a disadvantage to learning". However, as Martin points out, some other cultures and languages have an implicitly different relationship between the spoken and written language. Bilingual and multilingual students draw upon multiple meanings across a wide range of cultural and social events through their knowledge of different languages. Viewing bilingualism as a deficit can therefore cut off valuable resources and contexts for developing literacy with these students.

There is a further reason for considering that the deficit view of learners' families is unhelpful in conceptualising ways to address students' difficulties in literacy. The assumption of a necessarily reciprocal relationship between low levels of parental literacy and the poor literacy development of their offspring is not fully supported by research findings. Hannon argues that, rather than targeting a few families for restricted literacy programmes, it may be more profitable to provide universal, literacy-rich, early-childhood education which should seek to involve parents in their children's literacy development and offer opportunities for parents and carers to enhance their own literacy if they wish to.

Learning support co-ordinators therefore need to focus on how families and schools can work together to support the learning of students who experience difficulties in literacy development in ways which take account of a diversity of family and cultural backgrounds. Part of carrying out that role is to be aware of the power relationship between schools and the families of students experiencing literacy difficulties which is inherent in many current home-based strategies and programmes designed to support literacy development. In a wide-ranging review of the literature on parent–professional partnerships, Dale (1996, chapter 1) identified a number of common partnership arrangements between schools and parents/carers which are reflected in some of these programmes. Among them are:

- The traditional "Expert Model", where the parent is expected to rely on the expertise of the professional in making judgements and taking control of what needs to be done.
- The "Transplant Model", where the role of professionals is to transplant skills to the parents to help the parents to become teachers. The professional still has the ultimate responsibility for decision-making.
- The Empowerment Model, where the right of the parent to choose as a consumer is combined with a professional recognition of the family as a social system. Here the job of the professional is to help empower the family to meet its own needs rather than to make judgements and decisions about those needs.

In the past, studies have shown that parents from every social class are often very keen and able to help their students with reading at home (Newson & Newson, 1977). The Haringey project (Hewison & Tizard, 1980) is an example of such an initiative. It might be interpreted as reflecting the "empowerment model" in its recognition of the social system of the family with a right to make choices. Hewison (1988) speculates that the crucial factor in its success may have been the motivational context of the home itself in which the opportunity for extra reading practice occurred. A further example is the New Zealand-based "Pause, Prompt and Praise" (PPP) procedures which were developed, initially, in South Auckland in 1977 to raise the poor reading achievement of older (10–12-year-old) pupils in schools by training parents to tutor their children in oral reading. Amongst the considerations set out by McNaughton et al. (1981) in their rationale for involving parents were:

- "a growing concern for parental involvement in the education of their children ... parents, while still feeling and being held responsible for their children, are becoming more and more powerless to influence their own children's development. ... The parents in our research certainly felt keenly the segregation of home and school. ... We felt that parents, as well as being willing and able to help their low progress children, have a right to take part in their children's schooling" (McNaughton et al., 1981, p 4)
- the existence of research to suggest that early educational initiatives that produced lasting effects were those where parents were trained to teach children who had fallen behind, despite the apparent growing sense of powerlessness over children's education among parents (Bronfenbrenner, 1974; Chilman, 1976; Donachy, 1979). Parents appeared to have the potential for assuming a direct teaching role with older, lower-achieving children.

In recent years, the introduction of PPP into different settings, for example, the "Rotorua Home and School Project" (Glynn et al., 2000) has led to a greater awareness of the importance of the cultural context of the family and community for children's learning:

> While it is clear that home and school exercise joint influences on children's literacy, facilitating learning across the two contexts depends on home and school knowing and understanding what literacy values and reading and writing practices are operating in the other. (Glynn et al., 2000, p 9)

Involving families in ways that respect cultural background entails the sharing of understandings and actions that are reciprocal, not unidirectional from school to home. PPP may therefore be seen as developing from a "transplant model" with the transfer of skills to parents by teachers into an "empowerment model", with much greater emphasis placed on the family and community system.

There are many other examples of successful initiatives involving parents in the reading development of their students where the emphasis is much more upon the teacher as expert and the parent as needing control from external experts. Topping (1992, 1996), for example, has set out a number of steps for the generic "training" of parents in programmes to support students' literacy development. His (1992) "Paired Reading" technique is an example of an approach with strong directives from teachers to parents about how the technique should operate. Topping (1996, p 46) warns against assuming that "any old thing that two people do with a book" constitutes "Paired Reading". The choice of home-based programme may be pragmatic as well as philosophical. Undoubtedly some parents prefer and, for various reasons, "need" expert direction from teachers. Others do not. There is no one "right" approach, and this is part of the "messiness" with which the co-ordinator is confronted and must deal.

MODELS OF THE READING PROCESS

At the level of the individual student with literacy difficulties, the choice of literacy intervention programme is crucial. There are many different literacy approaches and strategies designed to address barriers to literacy development, but there appears to be no one programme that can overcome all of them:

> Within every instructional method studies, there were students who learned to read with thorough success and others who experienced difficulty. Furthermore, students in some school systems markedly outperformed those in others for no traceable reason. This was true regardless of instructional approach. (Bond & Dykstra, 1967, reported in Adams, 1994)

There are a number of different views on how children learn to read, the component skills of the reading process and the way in which the process operates. Different models of the reading process underpin the different programmes and interventions designed to address difficulties students may have with literacy. Before the learning support co-ordinator can make any decisions about which programme or intervention to implement, it is essential for him/her to understand what these models are.

Goodman (1976) advocated the "top-down", concept-driven model which assumes that fluent readers first anticipate the meaning of text before checking the available syntactic and graphic cues, the "psycholinguistic guessing game". The implication of this, according to Goodman, is that good readers will have less need to rely on graphic cues and therefore do not have to process every characteristic of the word and letter. The top-down, whole-book/whole-language approach implies that students learn to read through reading, being read to and being immersed in a literacy-rich environment. From this perspective, techniques appropriate for students with literacy difficulties include, for example, paired and shared reading. Adams (1994, p 422), in contrast, whilst acknowledging the importance of semantic cues in reading and other "critical sources of information", notes the place of phonics in competent reading (Adams, 1994, p 131). Beginning readers should first learn to recognise individual letters quickly in order to optimise their ability to recognise whole words. They also need to pay attention to the sequence of letters in a word, not simply the whole word. This is the "bottom-up", data-driven model that suggests fluent readers look first at the stimulus, that is the component features of the letters in the words, before they move on to consider the meaning of the print. The implication of this view is that "synthetic" phonics, writing and spelling of whole words, "exercise with frequent blends and digraphs, and practice with word families" and attention to attend to every letter of the word, in left-to-right order, are useful for this purpose. One way to reinforce the links between sounds and symbols in order to develop skills in phonics is to take a multisensory approach to teaching focusing on all modalities, auditory, visual, kinaesthetic and tactile. This is particularly important when considering the learning needs of students for whom the acquisition of phonics skills is problematic. Cumulative, structured, multisensory programmes tackle reading from a bottom-up perspective to ensure a basic grasp of the subskills of reading.

Stanovich (1988) suggests that both top-down and bottom-up methods have limitations, and that readers use information simultaneously from different levels. During the development of reading skills, some readers may rely more heavily on some levels than others. Readers' weaknesses are compensated by her/his strengths, the Interactive Compensatory model. Poor readers rely on context to compensate for their difficulties in processing the individual sounds of words. In the area of dyslexia, there are many examples of individuals who have learned to read through predominantly top-down approaches. However, despite being able to read through using problem-solving, meaning-based approaches, some may still experience particular difficulties at the level of word accuracy and spelling (Stanovich, 1988). For these students it may be appropriate also to introduce programmes with a more rigorous, focused approach to the subskills of reading, but the balance between top-down and bottom-up approaches for individual students may be a matter for the professional judgement of the teacher.

ADDRESSING "MESSINESS"

Fischer (1990) suggests that expert knowledge in finding the solutions to problems in real-life situations, in this case knowledge about how best to make provision for difficulties in literacy, cannot be assumed to be the preserve of any one professional who, in schools, might be the learning support co-ordinator. It is much more productive to assume a collaborative, participatory approach which seeks to engage all those involved in genuine, authentic dialogue about their own concerns. For the learning support co-ordinator seeking to implement teaching programmes and initiatives for students with difficulties in literacy which may imply considerable change to various aspects of the whole-school curriculum, it is essential to take account of potentially conflicting philosophies and personal agendas.

In the area of special provision for literacy difficulties, when there are so many clear differences in the perspectives of those involved, there is often no consensus on how a problem is constituted, or what the objectives of change might be. The situation is often clouded by "messiness", therefore. The learning support co-ordinator may well be in conflict with a colleague over provision for pupils with difficulties in literacy acquisition or, alternatively, have to behave as the mediator between other parties who are in disagreement with each other. Change which cuts across what teachers feel is in the best interests of those they teach or which appears impractical is likely to be resisted and/or resented. For example, in the area of raising literacy achievement, Wragg et al. (1998) concluded that teachers' personal philosophy, awareness and understanding of literacy are the factors which guide pedagogy and predispose to effective teaching.

A number of researchers have proposed slightly different models of conflict resolution and problem-solving within institutions (Friend & Cook, 1996; Heitler, 1990). One model potentially of use to the learning support co-ordinator is to frame the problem as a conflict between different agendas. Heitler (1990), for example, suggests that one approach is to adopt a three-phase process of negotiation which aims to address the concerns of all participants:

- the expression of initial position, stating everyone's wishes
- the exploration of underlying personal concerns about the situation
- the selection of mutually satisfying solutions for addressing these concerns.

An alternative approach which learning support co-ordinators might feel is useful in accommodating conflicting views is that of "Soft Systems Methodology" (SSM) (Frederickson, 1993). The SSM approach focuses on designing initiatives from an understanding of the context in which a problem is seen to be located. Like Heitler's model, it takes into account the varying perceptions of those involved and is a sequential, staged, process which consists of:

- investigating the "problem situation" and drawing up a representation of "reality", for example in diagrams or drawings
- using aspects of systems theory for analysing the problem situation and developing a conceptual model of what a system relevant to improving matters might look like
- comparing the model against the representation of reality and analysis of the problem situation to enable clarity of thinking about where action for improvement might be taken which is appropriate to the context and implementing changes.

Frederickson (1993, p 8) follows Checkland and Scholes (1990) in offering specific guidelines for the initial stages. Teachers are encouraged to find out about:

- "the context of the analysis itself" by asking questions about the roles of those involved in the problem situation: the "client", the "problem solvers" and the "problem owners"
- "the social aspects of the situation" by investigating the "norms, roles and values which exist in the situation"
- "the political aspects of the situation" through investigating the sources of power and how such power is gained and passed on to others.

These two suggested approaches are not the only ways to conceptualise how to bring about change in educational institutions in a flexible but structured way, but they may be seen as useful in offering a very clear adaptable framework for the change process.

CONCLUSION

For any learning support co-ordinator, there is a challenge in keeping abreast of ways to conceptualise the barriers facing students with difficulties in literacy and the interventions which are the corollary of these conceptualisations, as well as the micro and macro political contexts and the changes in funding arrangements which facilitate the implementation of some interventions rather than others. There is also a challenge in thinking through the way in which change to bring about improved provision for students with difficulties in literacy might be developed and implemented, whilst simultaneously harnessing sufficient support throughout the school for it to be sustained. There is considerable difference of opinion surrounding issues core to particular students' education in literacy and the difficulties that they experience, and there is no single view on what constitutes the "problem". Therefore it is clear that identifying and assessing literacy needs and organising and implementing appropriate provision cannot be a matter of the application of simple protocols or formulae by one person. Having a responsibility for bringing about change in these circumstances is stressful. Learning support co-ordinators would do well to consider how to base their work on a systematic yet flexible and adaptable approach, such as those outlined above, which sets out to take clear account of these differences and the "messiness" of the real-life situation.

REFERENCES

Adams, M.J. (1994) *Beginning to Read: Thinking and Learning about Print*. London: MIT Press.

Ames, G., & Archer, J. (1988) Achievement goals in the classroom: Students' learning strategies and motivation processes. *Journal of Educational Psychology*, 80, 260–267.

Bentley, D. (1990) *Teaching Spelling: Some Questions Answered*. Reading, UK: University of Reading.

Bond, G.L., & Dykstra, R. (1967) The co-operative research program in first-grade reading instruction. *Reading Research Quarterly*, 2, 5–142.

Broadfoot, P. (1996) *Education, Assessment and Society*. Buckingham, UK: Open University Press.

Bronfenbrenner, U. (1974) *Is Early Intervention Effective? A Report on Longitudinal Evaluations of Pre-School Programs: Vol 2*. Washington, DC: Department of Health, Education and Welfare, Office of Child Development.

Butkowsky, I.S., & Willows, D.M. (1980) Cognitive-motivational characteristics of children varying in reading ability: Evidence for learned helplessness in poor readers. *Journal of Educational Psychology*, 72, 408–422.

Checkland, P.B. & scholes, J. (1990) *Soft Systems Methodology in Action*. London Wiley.

Chilman, C.S. (1976) Programs for disadvantaged parents: Some major trends and related research. In H Leitenberg (Ed.) *Handbook of Behavior Modification and Behavior Therapy*. New Jersey: Englewood Cliffs.

Dale, N. (1996) *Working with Families of Children with Special Needs: Partnership and Practice*, London: Routledge.

Davie, C.E., Butler, N., & Goldstein, H. (1972) *From Birth to Seven: A Report of the National Child Development Study*. London: Longman/National Children's Bureau.

DENI (1998) *Code of Practice for the Assessment and Identification of Special Educational Needs*. Bangor, UK: DENI.

DfE (1994) *Code of Practice for the Assessment and Identification of Special Educational Needs.* London: HMSO.

Diener, C.I., & Dweck, C.S. (1978) An analysis of learned helplessness: Continuous changes in performance, strategy and achievement cognitions following failure. *Journal of Personality and Social Psychology*, (36), 451–462.

Donachy, W. (1979) Parent participation in pre-school education. In M.M. Clark & W.M. Cheyne (Eds) *Studies in Pre-School Education.* London: Hodder & Stoughton.

Dweck, C.S., & Reppucci, N.D. (1973) Learned helplessness and reinforcement responsibility in children. *Journal of Personality and Social Psychology,* 25, 109–116.

Dyson, A. (1997) Social and educational disadvantage: reconnecting special needs education. *British Journal of Special Education,* 24(4), 152–157.

Farrell, P. (1999) *The Management, Role and Training of Learning Support Assistants, RR 161.* London: DfEE.

Frederickson, N. (1993) Using soft systems methodology to re-think special needs. In A. Dyson & C. Gains (1993) *Re-thinking Special Needs in Mainstream Schools.* London: Fulton.

Fischer, F. (1990) *Technocracy and the Politics of Expertise.* London: Sage.

Friend, M., & Cook, L. (1996) *Interactions: Collaboration Skills for School Professionals.* White Plains, NY: Longman.

Glynn, T., Berryman, M., & Glynn, V. (2000) "Reading and writing gains for Maori students in mainstream schools: Effective partnerships in the Rotorua Home and School Literacy Project." Paper presented at the 18th World Congress on Reading, Auckland, New Zealand.

Goodman, K. (1976) Reading, a psycholinguistic guessing game. In H. Singer & R. Ruddell (Eds), *Theoretical Models and Processes of Reading* (2nd edn). Newark, DE: International Reading Association, pp 497–508.

Hannon, P. (1999) Rhetoric and research in family literacy. *British Educational Research Journal,* 26(1), 122–137.

Heitler, S.M. (1990) *From Conflict to Resolution: Skills and Strategies for Individual, Couple and Family Therapy.* New York: W.W. Norton.

Hewison, J. (1988) The long-term effectiveness of parental involvement in reading: a follow-up to the Haringey Reading Project. *British Journal of Educational Psychology,* 58, 184–190.

Hewison, J., & Tizard, J. (1980) Parental involvement and reading attainment. *British Journal of Educational Psychology,* 50, 209–215.

Kauffman, J.M. (1989) The regular education initiative as Reagan–Bush education policy: a trickle-down theory of education of the hard to teach. *The Journal of Special Education,* 23(3), 319–325.

Licht, B.G., Kistner, J.A., Ozkaragoz, T., Shapiro, S., & Clausen, L. (1985) Causal attributions of learning disabled children: Individual differences and their implications for persistence. *Journal of Educational Psychology,* 77, 208–216.

McNaughton, S. Glynn, T. & Robinson, V. (1981) *Pause, Prompt and Praise: Effective Remedial Reading Tutoring.* Birmingham, UK: Positive Products.

Mittler, P. (2000) *Working Towards Inclusive Education: Social Contexts.* London: Fulton.

Newson, J., & Newson, E. (1977) *Perspectives on School at Seven Years Old.* London: Allen & Unwin.

Norwich, B. (1996) *Special Needs Education, Inclusive Education or Just Education for All?* London: University of London Institute of Education.

Riddick, B. (1996) *Living with Dyslexia.* London: Routledge.

Ruebain, D. (2001) Education negligence cases. On Independent Panel for Special Education Advice (IPSEA) web site at http://www.ipsea.org.uk/phelps.htm.

Rutter, M., Tizard, J., & Whitmore, K. (1970) *Education, Health and Behaviour.* London: Longman.

Schön, D.A. (1983) *The Reflective Practitioner: How Professionals Think in Action.* London: Temple Smith.

Soler, J., Wearmouth, J., & Reid, G. (2002) Study Guide Part 1. In *E801 Difficulties in Literacy Development.* Milton Keynes, UK: The Open University.

Stanovich, K. (1988) Explaining the difference between the dyslexic and the garden-variety poor readers: the phonological core model. *Journal of Learning Disabilities*, 21(10), 590–604.

Topping, K. (1992) Short and long term follow-up of parental involvement in reading projects. *British Educational Research Journal*, 18(4), 369–379.

Topping, K. (1996) Tutoring systems for family literacy. In S. Wolfendale & K. Topping, *Family Involvement in Literacy*. London: Cassell.

UNESCO (1994) Salamanca Declaration and Framework for Action. In *World Conference on Special Needs Education: Accesss and Quality*. Paris: UNESCO.

Vygotsky, L.S. (1987) *The Collected Works, Vol 1. Problems of General Psychology*. New York: Plenum.

Walford, G. (1996) School choice and the quasi-market in England and Wales. *Oxford Studies in Comparative Education*, 6(1), 49–62.

Wearmouth, J. (2000) *Special Educational provision: Meeting the Challenges in Schools*. London: Hodder.

Wragg. E.C. (1997) *The Cubic Curriculum*. London: Routledge.

Wragg, E.C., Wragg, C.N., Haynes, G.S., & Chamberlain, R.P. (1998) *Improving Literacy in the Primary School*. London: Routledge.

Chapter 14

DEALING WITH DIVERSITY IN THE PRIMARY CLASSROOM—A CHALLENGE FOR THE CLASS TEACHER

Margaret Crombie

INTRODUCTION

Class teachers have a responsibility for recognising the signs of a whole range of different needs as well as ensuring that more able children have their needs met. From the perspective of local education authorities, it would not be politically or ethically correct to recognise only the difficulties of one group of children. In an inclusive school, appropriate intervention must be put in place for all who require it. While class teachers cannot be "expert" on every area of need, they must be able to recognise typical profiles for autistic spectrum disorders, ADHD and all other areas which will require specific strategies for intervention and support. Dealing with diversity in any classroom is a challenge which today's teachers must acknowledge. Dyslexia is just one of a large family of needs which teachers must support if they are to succeed in the task they have set themselves.

Over recent years definitions of dyslexia have changed. However, in spite of a new definition of dyslexia produced by the British Psychological Society in 1999 (DECP, 1999) which relates dyslexia to persistent difficulties with word-reading and spelling, the most common perception still seems to be that of the underachieving child who presents as an anomaly to teachers because of a range of discrepancies, difficulties and differences (DfEE, 1998; Pumfrey, 2001; Reid, 1997; Walker, 1997). While definitions may change over time, there is little doubt that children with specific literacy difficulties remain a challenge to their teachers wherever and whenever these difficulties occur. There is little doubt, too, that the vast majority of teachers in the course of their career will encounter a significant number of dyslexic

Dyslexia and Literacy: Theory and Practice. Edited by Gavin Reid and Janice Wearmouth.
© 2002 John Wiley & Sons, Ltd.

pupils. It is important, therefore, that every teacher should know how to recognise a dyslexic pupil, and know what can be done to enable full access to the curriculum. It is the class teacher who can facilitate curricular access through ensuring appropriate and timely support for pupils who seem to be at risk of failure to learn to read and write adequately.

THE EARLY YEARS

In order to minimise the damage which can be done by late recognition of dyslexia, it is important for all teachers and nursery nurses to be aware of the signs even before a child goes into formal schooling. Traditionally, dyslexia was not recognised until a child had been in school for long enough to have mastered reading and then be seen to fail in a standardised test. While the definition of dyslexia still suggests that dyslexic children are only dyslexic if they fail to learn to read, we now know that dyslexia is often inherited, and is therefore often genetic in origin (Grigorenko, 2001). If some children are born with a predisposition to dyslexia, then ignoring this fact until failure takes place is inexcusable.

Early Recognition

Early recognition of the precursors of dyslexia (Elbro et al., 1998; Fawcett & Nicolson, 1996), can be facilitated by a screening process before entry to primary school. Indicators of dyslexia such as problems with phonological awareness, balance and automaticity may be apparent very early and can indicate the child who will require close observation when reading is being taught (Crombie, 1997b; Crombie, 2001). The significance of hereditary factors should not be ignored, and it is easy for education authorities to check if parents are aware of any family history of difficulties by asking parents when they enrol their child for school or nursery. A positive response to this question should not result in presupposition of dyslexia, but in close observation of the child, so that at the first sign of difficulty, appropriate intervention is put in place. The use of early palliative measures in terms of teaching early phonological awareness, motor skills, memory strategies and visualisation techniques through a games approach, can be of considerable benefit. Even if dyslexia cannot actually be prevented, its effects can be minimised with subsequent positive effects on self-esteem and motivation. At this stage, as indeed later, learning should be fun, and children must not feel they are being forced into doing things they cannot do. For this reason, it is important to find the child's strengths and give constant praise and encouragement for positive efforts or success.

Not all children, however, have a nursery education. To ensure that those who have not had the opportunity to benefit are not lost in the system, screening during the first year of primary education can ensure that no child is allowed to struggle for any length of time without their problems being recognised. The school management team can greatly facilitate a screening process by giving their time and skills in a collaborative approach. Self-esteem and confidence can then be maintained, and acknowledgements made of how hard the children are working. The challenge for the early years teacher is to ensure that underachieving children are recognised and appropriate intervention takes place. Staff development is therefore vital if class teachers are to be aware of all the different factors which might affect young children.

While much can be achieved by the class teacher alone, much more can be gained when the local authority, school management, teaching and ancillary staff are working with parents to meet the needs of all children. In this way, the isolation which a class teacher can feel in dealing with a whole range of children with a variety of differing needs can be minimised.

LABELLING

Labelling children too early in their school career can be just as damaging as labelling too late. What may appear to be a learning difficulty may turn out to be a slight developmental delay which will respond to appropriate and timely intervention. Not labelling once it is clear that the child's problems are persistent can cause considerable distress to both children and their parents, as they struggle to make sense of a seemingly unknown problem (Crombie, 2001). What is required for the dyslexic child is good communication with parents and an understanding of dyslexia which enables teachers to discuss with parents the reasons for their seeming reticence to label before the child has had the chance to make a real effort to learn to read. Appropriate intervention strategies for struggling readers are then vital if children are to have an effective opportunity of success in spite of a slow start. For those at the early stages, who have only very mild difficulties, even though these may initially appear dyslexic in nature, no label may be required, as timely intervention may produce a rapid acceleration in reading and spelling results.

INTERVENTION AND SUPPORT

There is a considerable body of evidence that intervention strategies for teaching reading and spelling skills to dyslexic children should be both multisensory and phonic. This type of teaching, however, benefits the majority of children in any class to a greater or lesser extent at the early stages so there should be no deterrent to appropriate effective intervention. Dyslexic children, however, require considerable overlearning to reach automaticity, a skill which releases processing capacity to concentrate on understanding the material being read rather than dwelling on decoding. In addition, learning experiences should be structured to meet the needs of the individuals within the classroom (Hunter-Carsch, 2001). Structuring learning, however, is considerably more than knowing the teaching order of the points which children must learn. It is knowing the aspects and techniques to apply to teaching which will make the learning experiences worthwhile. Children who are being taught to spell, for example, require to "tune in" to words and sounds. If they do not, and are not aware of the sounds they are hearing, then spelling will be affected. For example, if a child needs to spell a word but is unaware of the order of the sounds being heard, jumbling of letters will be likely to occur unless visual memory can compensate for this weakness. Time spent training the child to repeat words to himself, while listening to the order of the sounds, is therefore worthwhile. Not all children pick this up as part of the learning process, so some will need to be taught. Making this type of activity fun can present a challenge, but it can be turned into a sorting activity, classifying picture cards showing pictures of things ending or beginning with a specific sound. Games where children have to find picture cards beginning or ending with specific sounds or think of the most words ending in that particular letter sound can be fun if children are matched according to their ability in such tasks.

These are all areas where the specialist teacher and the generalist can work together to benefit the children. In today's inclusive classrooms, there simply are not enough specialists to ensure all children with their differing needs will have these needs met. Specialists must pass on their skills to class teachers and thus ensure that the skills and expertise are not lost. Class teachers, however, feel the pressures of time. For children who require individual support, there simply are not enough hours in the working day. This is where teachers must maximise their use not only of their own skills but also of those around. A sound working knowledge of technology, support materials and how these can be used will be of enormous benefit when it comes to utilising all the support available. In most classrooms today, teaching assistants can be accessed. Parent helpers too can be used to support the teaching which is taking place. Senior pupils can sometimes be "paired" appropriately with younger students (Topping, 1996),

While children who have mild dyslexic difficulties may respond to timely intervention, those with more severe difficulties are likely to require continuing support and additional work. The class teacher who does not experience complete success after considerable effort should not feel a failure, as there are some children whose difficulties are considerable and will persist in spite of appropriate help and support. For these children, sustained support and encouragement are vital. While sustained support may indicate the need for more of the same, it does not mean that learning must become tedious and boring. The main challenge which the teacher faces is to find varied approaches to learning which will continue to motivate while at the same time providing the key elements which the child requires. The use of technology is just one method of allowing children to work at their own pace while providing opportunities for overlearning without constant close supervision.

Class teachers therefore need to have, or be able to access, a range of knowledge about the hardware and software which is available to support individual needs, as well as having a knowledge of how the appropriate materials can be accessed. Some of the voluntary organisations, for example, have libraries of resources which can be borrowed for an appropriate annual fee. These resources can be tried out and evaluated before spending precious budgets on materials which may or may not be useful. Resources such as taped books may be available from local libraries, and parents too can learn what they themselves can access to help at home. In this way home and school can form a partnership which can extend into all learning.

While early structured, multisensory, phonic work will benefit many children at the early stages, the provision of support within the classroom becomes more difficult for the class teacher as the child becomes older, and the type of work appears to the other children to be beneath their level. In today's classrooms, however, it will not just be the dyslexic children who require additional support. There will be many who from time to time will require extra help. An understanding teacher can elicit from the children the best way of undertaking this, as what works for one child is not necessarily the same as what works for another.

LEARNING STYLES

The notion of adapting teaching to the learning style of the child is a relatively new model. While dyslexia teaching programmes have existed for most of the last century, it is only during the latter part of that century that teachers started to take a learning styles model of teaching seriously. Given (1998) developed a model which considers emotional, cognitive, social, physical and reflective elements of learning. While this type of model is not entirely new, it none the less gives a structure to help teachers focus on what might be important to the individual. In such a way, children themselves can focus on what seems important for their own learning, and begin to adopt a metacognitive approach. Knowing whether they learn best in certain environments or at certain times of the day, with or without background noise or music, and how often they need to take a break for refreshments may or may not be helpful in the classroom, depending on whether their teacher acknowledges the importance of learning style or not. It will, however, be important for their learning at home where they are likely to be more free to adapt. For teachers who recognise the benefits of teaching children according to their learning styles, there are adaptations which can be made within the classroom. Some children may require to move around the classroom more while learning, while others will need more light than their peers, so will require to sit in good lighting conditions. Teachers already alter their seating arrangements for children with a hearing or visual impairment, so it is possible to allow for various modifications at certain times. Seating arrangements require to be flexible to suit individual needs. To accommodate the whole range of learning styles within one classroom, however, is not easy, and most teachers may wish to start by taking only a few steps at a time, and evaluating the differences observed by teaching this way. For some children, the approach may not make an observable difference, but for children who are dyslexic, the differences are likely to be more apparent and accommodating them will equip them with tools for "life-long learning" (Given & Reid, 2001, p.143).

METACOGNITION

As dyslexic children get older they can more readily adopt a metacognitive approach. Metacognition is here taken to be the conscious control which is taken over the thought processes which lead to an understanding of how learning is taking place. Metacognition, however, may require to be taught, as very few children will pick it up without help. Thus strategies which promote active learning can be tailored *by* the individual *for* the individual while being guided by the teacher. Often children, dyslexic or not, are unaware of their thought processes and how they think, and therefore are unable to maximise their potential. With help, children can learn to use visual strategies such as mind mapping. They need to know when this might help them—perhaps when planning essays, devising plans for a talk, memorising for exams or making notes. Bright colours, too, can add to the effectiveness and be an aid to memory if this is what is desired. Many, though not all, dyslexic people are artistic (West, 1997) and can adopt visual strategies with greater ease than verbal ones. They may have sequencing difficulties, so they can plan from a central idea, and then put their ideas into sequence later. Then when undertaking their talk or writing their essays, they can follow the order they have decided on, which may differ from the order in which they initially thought it up.

There is no reason why these skills cannot begin at an elementary stage, early in primary school, then be extended later as the child begins to draw on their own knowledge of learning and how this matches what they are being taught and the way in which they are taught. When there is a mismatch between the child's learning style and the teacher's teaching style, young people can learn how to tackle this to their own advantage. Some teachers may be prepared to adopt different strategies at different times, and this will help young people to try out different strategies themselves to determine the best fit to their own needs. Matching teaching style to suit a range of needs in an inclusive classroom situation can for many represent a major paradigm shift, but will pay dividends not only in terms of achievement but also in affective terms, with consequent results on motivation and self-esteem.

While early and appropriate intervention will alleviate the worst effects of dyslexia and retain self-esteem and motivation, later a counselling and study skills approach can help further enable young people to cope with the curriculum (Ostler, 2001). Organisation difficulties can be a hurdle to achieving success, particularly in exams. Provided the young people have ability, then help in how to plan and organise will enable them to achieve their desired aims. This, combined with a knowledge of how memory works and in particular how their own memory works, will enable them to tailor a study plan to allow for the revision they need and make best use of the most appropriate mnemonic strategies as an aid to memory. Many of the suggestions of Buzan (1982, 1986) can be useful and can be taught to a whole class. The more possibilities that are discussed, the more options the pupils will have and better will be their chances of selecting the best fits for themselves. In this manner the diversity of the children's needs can be taken into account.

If difficulties are persistent and severe, then reading and scribing may be required to help students demonstrate their abilities. If these are to be successful, practice of these skills will be needed to ensure that they gain maximum advantage from these special arrangements. Making the best use of a reader and scribe is not automatic for many, and so familiarity with the reader and/or scribe can make a difference. Building up trust and having the confidence to ask for parts to be reread when necessary will facilitate positive outcomes. While circumvention strategies in the

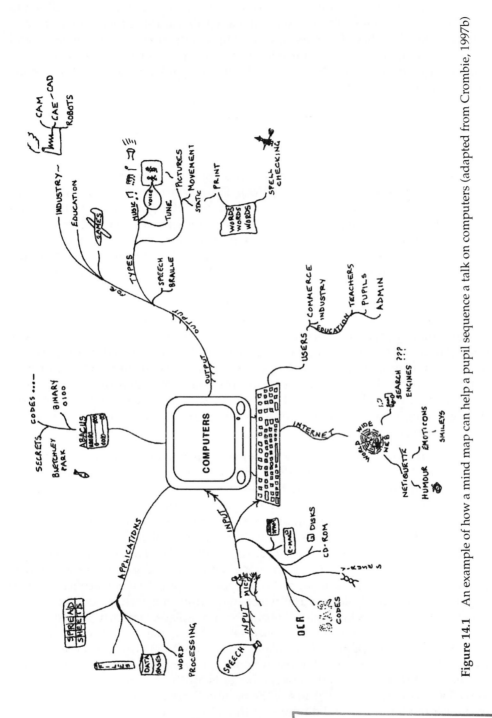

Figure 14.1 An example of how a mind map can help a pupil sequence a talk on computers (adapted from Crombie, 1997b)

Learning Resources Centre
Middlesbrough College
Dock Street
Middlesbrough
TS2 1AD

form of a reader or scribe are best for some, there are others for whom a different mode of presentation will enable them to have full control of their own output of information. There have been many technological advances over recent years, and dyslexic young people should be able to gain considerably from a knowledge of what is available and how these new technologies can help empower them while working alongside their non-dyslexic peers.

TECHNOLOGY

The impact of modern technology on today's children must surely have had both negative and positive effects (Healey, 1990). From very early in life, television and computers are a pervading influence on most children. The early joy of listening to a story and visualising its content has to some extent been replaced by the immediate picture which comes ready-generated to be imposed on the young mind. No longer is there a necessity for imagination to aid understanding. Understanding, and therefore comprehension of stories, is a skill that for many of our children requires to be taught (Bell, 1991). It can, however, be taught, and programmes such as Nanci Bell's "Visualising and Verbalising" suggest what can be done to take children through a sequence of imagery stimulations to enable them to visualise images and comprehend information. While this type of programme is in no way limited to dyslexic individuals, the sequencing and organisation difficulties which often accompany dyslexia can be improved by the "visualising and verbalising" which is advocated. The programme works through from visualising a single word to visualising a complex passage. The positive results and greater detail of imagery through using a teaching programme such as this overlap into more creative areas such as writing.

While we may need to compensate for some of the negative effects of technology, there is another side to the technology coin, for it is the same coin we can use to motivate and stimulate those who find learning by other means difficult. Literacy skills, while valued by today's society, were less essential in previous generations, and will again be less essential in future generations as technology takes over the tedium of producing written text by handwriting or typing (Crombie & Crombie, 2001). Speech-to-text software is improving rapidly and will undoubtedly take over much of the tedium and trauma of dyslexic attempts to produce recognisable script. While the need for long hours of practising touch-typing to reach proficiency will be gone for all, the dyslexic pupil will benefit from not feeling different as the benefits of the "new technologies" become commonplace. Similarly, text-to-speech software will allow any computer-based text, such as that from the World Wide Web, to be spoken. Optical character recognition (OCR) will give access to the world of printed matter for all those who find reading problematic, as the text is scanned and reproduced verbally, with benefits for those with visual impairment as well as dyslexic people. The use of the basic skills of reading and writing which we have grown to value will diminish in time. Measuring ability in terms of these skills has become the dyslexic nightmare. Few dyslexic people will mourn their passing!

However, in the meantime there is still a demand for literacy through reading and writing, and technology has a part to play in improving these skills, which the current generation must still attempt to master. The principle of overlearning which is vital for dyslexic learning can be assimilated through allowing the computer a place in the teaching programme of children at all stages. The computer has infinite patience and can be used to practise tasks which would frustrate the teacher. A good range of software is available to allow practice of routine skills in a fun and rewarding way. The class teacher, however, may need to take advice on the best materials available. Where a specialist is available, a collaborative approach will again pay dividends for both teacher and child. Appropriate hardware and software can greatly facilitate the learning process.

ICT can be used across the curriculum. It can support and increase learning in a non-directive and non-critical way. Individuals can select from what is available to suit their needs and learning styles. Importantly, it benefits all and does not make the dyslexic young person feel different, yet the greatest benefits would be to the dyslexic pupils as they select tools which make learning suit their own styles.

Video can add greatly to the role of ICT in the curriculum. The toil of having to read to study a play, for example, can be made much less arduous through watching it on video. If the young person is allowed to take the tape or DVD home, they can watch as often as they wish without self-esteem being affected adversely. Interactive video can add another dimension, and make the learning even more multisensory as the young person responds actively to the material being presented. Working with parents makes this type of learning more beneficial; if parents too can become involved and take an active partcipatory interest in what the young person is doing, it has great effects when the young person goes back into the classroom.

SUBJECT CHOICES

Questions are often asked by parents about which subjects would be best for dyslexic pupils to select when it comes to subject choices. Dyslexic learners are often global and visual learners (West, 1997), but this will not necessarily be the case, and all must be treated as individuals with their own styles and motivating factors. For this reason it is impossible to delineate exactly what subjects the dyslexic person will benefit from. Future career options and expectations for lifestyle should be taken into account in the pupils' choices. It is true that many dyslexic students find modern languages difficult, because of a combination of factors such as phonological awareness, speed of processing, working and short-term memory, auditory discrimination and perception, sequencing, automaticity and low self-esteem (Crombie, 1997a, 2000; Sparks et al., 1989). If, however, motivation can be established and maintained, there is no reason why most young people will not meet with some degree of success, providing appropriate teaching is in place. Appropriate teaching, however, does not mean restricting the student to speaking and listening. This will actually deprive them of two channels of learning. Seeing the words and writing them will help establish connections in memory and give the student further opportunities to overlearn and reach automaticity. As in every other area, innovative methods of teaching to give repeated presentations of what we want the student to know will give much greater likelihood of success. The use of gesture, movement, mime, games, etc. can add greatly to enjoyment and can make learning much more interesting.

Even with appropriate teaching in place, there may be a few dyslexic pupils for whom the learning of a foreign language will still present enormous barriers. For these few, it may be necessary to decide if the outcome is going to be worth the effort, particularly if modern-language learning is affecting the pupil's attitude to other subject areas and to school in general. It may not always be easy to adapt a pupil's timetable to accommodate a major change such as this, but in a truly inclusive school curricular exemptions should be possible where, for reasons of special educational needs, the pupil is gaining no benefit. However, this can only be established after full consultation with all concerned: pupil, parents, teachers, educational psychologist and school management. If it is decided to discontinue a particular subject for educational reasons, then a suitable alternative must be discussed and arrangements put in place to ensure that the student gains from being included in alternative subjects. This is not generally a problem in the primary school, but could potentially cause one for severely dyslexic children if foreign-language learning is introduced at an early stage.

EMOTIONAL FACTORS

While the priorities of the class teacher are often seen as teaching and learning, there is none the less a need to consider emotional factors. The young person who has very low self-esteem is likely to progress only very slowly. Attitude and emotional intelligence are being increasingly recognised as important to pupils' futures (Goleman, 1995). These can make the difference between success and failure for the student. Early failure to thrive can result in a lasting feeling of low self-esteem, with accompanying poor motivation which can persist into adulthood. Teaching respect for others, self-awareness, persistence and self-belief through activities such as Circle Time (Curry & Bromfield, 1988; Mosly, 1997) and the provision of rewarding experiences which result in success can build self-belief. The difference this can make to the learning outcomes will not be insignificant.

Study support outside normal school hours can be of benefit if students are motivated to attend. While all students can benefit, for children with difficulties these classes can add to confidence in the period before formal examinations (MacBeath et al., 2001). If staff are aware of pupils' specific difficulties, then strategies aimed at providing additional overlearning, planning strategies and study skills will be likely to give added value to the provision. The benefits of this are likely to extend well beyond primary school education.

DYSLEXIA-FRIENDLY SCHOOLS

The model of good practice which is imbued in the concept of "dyslexia-friendly schools" (Peer, 2001) seems likely to improve attainment and achievement for all.

Being dyslexia-friendly and effective are closely linked. Leadership, staff development and quality teaching and learning, together with respect for the abilities and difficulties of all, are essential ingredients of the effective school. The notion of chartering schools which are dyslexia-friendly needs to be developed more widely, with an acceptance of the message that "it is 'okay to be dyslexic'" (MacKay, 2001) and that dyslexic children can learn and thrive in a supportive environment which will support all children with diverse needs and strengths.

CHALLENGES

The challenge for class teachers in today's primary classrooms is changing rapidly. The demands made are quite different now than a decade ago. In that time a major shift has occurred towards the inclusion of all children in mainstream classrooms, whatever the needs of these children may be. There is now an acceptance that with the appropriate support and strategies in place, all children can cope and thrive. For dyslexic children, however, the problems they face are still as real. Research has thrown considerable light on dyslexia in different cultures and languages. We now know much more about the effect of genes, environments and brains on development (Grigorenko, 2001). For the class teacher, however, the challenge is no less than it has always been. Finding the most appropriate means of support for individual children under the constraints of the time available in the working day and the limited personnel available to help presents the teacher with strategic and planning dilemmas. Budgets and resources are always limited, and this is likely to remain so. Within these constraints, it is for the teacher to find the means to motivate and generate appropriate learning. While this presents a complex and difficult challenge, it also presents the teacher with an opportunity for great reward—to see young people achieve, through appropriate methodology, a successful path through the education system, and to effect the removal of unnecessary hurdles along the way.

REFERENCES

Bell, N. (1991). *Visualising and Verbalising for Language Comprehension and Thinking.* Paso Robles, CA: Academy of Reading Publications.

Buzan, T. (1982). *Use Your Head.* London: BBC Publications.

Buzan, T. (1986). *Use Your Memory.* London: BBC Publications.

Crombie, M. A. (1997a). The effects of specific learning difficulties (dyslexia) on the learning of a foreign language in school. *Dyslexia*, 3, 27–47.

Crombie, M. (1997b). *Specific Learning Difficulties (Dyslexia): A Teachers' Guide.* Belford, Northumberland, UK: Ann Arbor.

Crombie, M. A. (2000). Specific learning difficulties (dyslexia) and the learning of a foreign language in school: Where are we going? *Dyslexia*, 6, 112–123.

Crombie, M. (2001). 'Early identification of dyslexia.' Paper presented at the Fifth International Conference of the British Dyslexia Association, York.

Crombie, A. & Crombie, M. (2001). ICT-based interactive learning. In M. Hunter-Carsch (Ed.), *Dyslexia: A Psychosocial Perspective*, pp. 219–231. London: Whurr.

Curry, M. & Bromfield, C. (1988). *Personal and Social Education for Schools through Circle Time.* Stafford, UK: NASEN.

Department for Education and the Environment (DfEE) (1998). *How Can I Tell if My Child May Be Dyslexic? Handy Hints for Primary School Teachers.* London: DfEE.

Division of Educational and Child Psychology of the British Psychological Society (DECP) (1999). *Dyslexia, Literacy and Psychological Assessment.* Leicester, UK: DECP.

Elbro, C., Borstrom, I. & Petersen, D. K. (1998). Predicting dyslexia from kindergarten: The importance of distinctness of phonological representations of lexical items. *Reading Research Quarterly*, 33(1), 33–60.

Fawcett, A. & Nicolson, R. (1996). *Dyslexia Early Screening Test.* London: The Psychological Corporation, Harcourt Brace & Company.

Given, B. (1998). Psychological and neurobiological support for learning-style instruction.: Why it works. *National Forum of Applied Educational Research Journal*, 11(1), 10–15.

Given, B. & Reid, G. (2001). Assessing learning styles. In I. Smythe (Ed.), *The Dyslexia Handbook 2001*, pp. 135–145. Reading, UK: The British Dyslexia Association.

Goleman, D. (1995). *Emotional Intelligence.* London: Bloomsbury.

Grigorenko, E. L. (2001). Developmental dyslexia: An update of genes, brains and environments. *Journal of Child Psychology and Psychiatry*, 42(1), 91–125.

Healey, J. M. (1990). *Endangered Minds: Why Children Don't Think and What We Can Do About It.* New York: Simon & Schuster.

Hunter-Carsch, M. (2001). Restructuring the structured approach. In M. Hunter-Carsch (Ed.), *Dyslexia: A Psychosocial Perspective*, pp. 49–84. London: Whurr.

MacBeath, J., Myers, K. & Kirwan, T. (2001). Switched on after hours. *Times Educational Supplement*, 1805 (34), 15 June.

MacKay, N. (2001). Dyslexia friendly schools. In L. Peer & G. Reid (Eds), *Dyslexia—Successful Inclusion in Secondary School*, pp. 166–173, London: David Fulton.

Mosly, J. (1997). *Quality Circle Time.* Wisbech, UK: LDA.

Ostler, C. (2001). Study skills: using strengths and weaknesses. In I. Smythe (Ed.), *The Dyslexia Handbook 2001*, pp. 268–273. Reading, UK: The British Dyslexia Association.

Peer, L. (2001). Dyslexia and its manifestations in the secondary school. In L. Peer & G. Reid (Eds), *Dyslexia—Successful Inclusion in Secondary School*, pp. 1–9. London: David Fulton.

Pumfrey, P. (2001). Specific developmental dyslexia (SDD): 'Basics to back' in 2000 and beyond? In M. Hunter-Carsch (Ed.) *Dyslexia: A Psychosocial Perspective*, pp. 137–159. London: Whurr.

Reid, G. (1997). *Dyslexia: A Practitioner's Handbook.* Chichester: John Wiley.

Sparks, R., Ganschow, L. & Pohlman, J. (1989). Linguistic coding deficits in foreign language learners. *Annals of Dyslexia*, 39, 179–195.

Topping, K. (1996). Parents and peers as tutors for dyslexic children. In G. Reid (Ed.), *Dimensions of Dyslexia*, Volume 2, pp. 63–75. Edinburgh: Moray House.

Walker, J. (1997). Introduction. In M. Crombie, *Specific Learning Difficulties (Dyslexia): A Teachers' Guide*, p. i Belford, Northumberland, UK: Ann Arbor.

West, T. G. (1997). *In the Mind's Eye* Buffalo, NY: Prometheus Books.

Chapter 15

DYSLEXIA AND LITERACY: CHALLENGES IN THE SECONDARY SCHOOL

Lindsay Peer and Gavin Reid

INTRODUCTION

David Blunkett, then Secretary of State for Education, in a foreword to a book on inclusion and dyslexia in the secondary school (Peer & Reid, 2001) suggested that "too many of our pupils are disadvantaged when they reach secondary school due to their dyslexia and poor literacy skills generally. This means they are unable to exercise their right to access a curriculum which is as broad and balanced as it should be" (p. v). This statement is an accurate reflection of the current situation and describes the inequities faced by young people with dyslexia and literacy difficulties. Furthermore, because they have often been in a situation of failure at primary school, particularly in relation to literacy, they are frequently demotivated and switched off from learning altogether. The purpose of this chapter, therefore, is not only to highlight the difficulties experienced by the dyslexic student but also to show how these can be addressed through a curriculum focused approach and whole-school responsibility. Too often the ready answer to dyslexic difficulties is a short–term reactive solution to the problems presented by one individual—yet the dyslexic student is not responsible for the curriculum nor the examination system which places him/her at a disadvantage. It is essential to take a proactive long-term approach through curriculum and task analysis and planned staff development involving teachers in all subject areas.

Dyslexia and Literacy: Theory and Practice. Edited by Gavin Reid and Janice Wearmouth.
© 2002 John Wiley & Sons, Ltd.

DEMANDS

This government has strongly promoted a philosophy of inclusion, placing many new challenges in the hands of those working within the secondary school system. Governors, head teachers, heads of department and mainstream teachers are all having to consider how to work most effectively with many children who hitherto may not have been placed in their schools.

New demands are being made by the National Literacy Strategy (NLS). For the first time there is a welcome requirement on Key Stage 3 and 4 teachers across the curriculum to take responsibility for the developing literacy skills of all learners. This new demand will have particular implications for teachers' work with the literacy development of their special needs children, as identified on the various stages of the Code of Practice. However, it has to be said that in order for such a requirement to work satisfactorily, training and resources will have to be put into place. Without such provision, inclusion would by definition mean exclusion (Peer, 2001).

The teaching profession is a hard-working and caring one, but teachers have to work continually under constraints of time and resources. Increasingly they are subject to accountability from various sources and often feel as though they are under a public microscope. The resulting pressure is often passed on inadvertently to the learners in their classrooms. For the majority of secondary school pupils, it is something with which they learn to deal. For the learner with special needs, the pressure is immense and often affects their daily functioning, which can in fact be quite stressful. The National Literacy Strategy demand is a challenging one. It is not a simple matter to expect subject teachers to know how to take responsibility for the full range of literacy needs of their students. Teachers are expected to be able to identify those learners with particular needs, then decide which aspects of literacy and accompanying methodologies are the most appropriate for supporting and stretching them. A range of teachers is being required to action the entire programme. This, of course, also implies that subject teachers will need to work together under the guidance of those that understand the requirements of special needs children. This will mean that SENCOs and a range of other SEN staff will have to be skilled in the identification, assessment and support of dyslexic and other SEN children. If this does not happen, each subject teacher will make varying demands upon their students and cause more confusion in the learners' minds than ever before.

There is good evidence that success motivates and can result in further success. Failure acts similarly, and the condition of learned helplessness can be evident in many dyslexic students by the time they reach secondary school. A student with un-acknowledged or badly handled specific learning difficulties will not be successful, and the most vulnerable period is often within the adolescent age group—the secondary school sector. Educational factors, such as the demands of the curriculum, complexities of the timetable and the internal and external pressures put on teachers and their pupils to reach agreed national targets within a publicly monitored system, exacerbate the situation.

SELF-ESTEEM

Experience shows us that demotivation and low self-esteem very often go hand in hand for many learners with language and/or literacy weaknesses. Equally, we know that the sooner any difficulties are pinpointed and addressed, the sooner success becomes a self-fulfilling prophecy. This results in progress across the curriculum and into the public examination arena. In place of diminished self-esteem, often with associated behavioural difficulties, there is a complete turnaround and motivation begins to underpin rising levels of achievement. Therefore time spent initially solving those difficulties by supporting learners in an appropriate manner will undoubtedly lead to less disruptive behaviour and greater success for all pupils learning in the same classroom. This means fewer long-term problems for the student and a significant improvement in the daily life of the teacher and other children.

It is important to consider that the principle of inclusion will be more successful when issues have been recognised, systems, training and resources have been put in place, and each student is given the special support that they need.

PLANNING

When planning for a "dyslexia-friendly" school, which will give the necessary support to those in need, there are a set of questions which must be asked by those involved with the reorganisation. These include the following:

- Are the needs of dyslexic students recognised across the curriculum and within the social structure?
- Who is responsible for provision?
- Who monitors and measures progress?
- Who liaises with parents, examination boards, careers services and further education institutions?

Without such questioning, provision cannot be fully and effectively met.

Furthermore, provision is needed for those who fall outside the categories which have traditionally been placed within the dyslexic group. They include students who:

- are hyperactive or hyper-reactive (Peer, 2001)
- are multilingual
- have overlapping specific learning difficulties.

In addition to these groupings, training is needed in the identification and provision for those exhibiting signs of stress, unacceptable and/or deviant behaviour, demotivation and low self-esteem.

Secondary schools successful in supporting dyslexic learners will ensure that the situation will be win–win for teachers, pupils and parents alike, and that every subject teacher should be geared up to the needs of dyslexic children. By taking responsibility and working within the framework, success will be a more likely outcome.

Where schools have implemented the dyslexia friendly schools charter on a planned basis it has quickly become clear that there are wider benefits, including improvements in literacy across the curriculum, better teaching of literacy for all pupils, greater awareness of individual learning needs and the use of more varied teaching strategies.

(Warwick, 1999)

PROVISION AND PRACTICE

A key issue in relation to successful outcomes in secondary school concerns the notion of responsibility. It is important to ensure that provision is firmly in place and that all members of staff become fully involved. Head teachers, for example, need to ensure that:

- The ethos of the school is supportive. The philosophy of the school, together with attitudes and actions, must be upheld by teachers, support staff and midday supervisors.
- All staff need to be made aware that, although children might have weaknesses with specific parts of curriculum access, they are likely to be at least of average ability, if not a great deal higher. They must always work to the highest expectations and encourage the children to believe in themselves.
- All curriculum staff should be encouraged to explore the range of access routes via differentiation. They must be shown that even though written literacy may be poor, dyslexic children need to have information given to them at the appropriate intellectual level. It is the disparity of abilities that in fact so often identifies dyslexic children from other groups.
- All teaching staff need to be supported in order to adapt their subjects and encourage dyslexic learners to succeed.
- Parents need to be involved in the changing set-up. They will often be sceptical about statements that their children will be understood and supported appropriately, based on their past experience. When their concerns are heard and they experience empathy, co-operation and support given to their children on the part of all staff members, they will generally work well with the school and support the measures being taken.

Awareness

Dyslexia needs to be seen to have status within the school. This can be achieved by ensuring that the governors and senior managers are firmly committed to supporting dyslexic children across the curriculum. Whole-school approaches to issues such as marking should be put in place—ensuring that children can receive a high mark for understanding and knowledge rather than always being marked down because of poor presentation skills, spelling, punctuation and grammar. Alongside this, literacy development needs to be highlighted to teach dyslexic children the skills that they need in order to succeed. All teachers need to be aware of the current area of learning and mark only that which has been taught, in order to boost motivation and encourage success. Learners need to see that, even though their literacy skills may be weak, their thoughts, ideas and knowledge are valued at the same level as those of their peers.

Training Needs

A range of training must be carried out with relevant staff. It is recognised that differing roles have varying needs. The requirements of mainstream teachers will be different from those of special needs staff. Subject teachers will need something different from Learning Support Assistants. It would be very useful for head teachers and governors to attend awareness-raising sessions on the needs of the dyslexic child and the benefits to the school of dyslexia provision.

Currently, in Swansea LEA, there is a dyslexia-trained specialist in every school, both primary and secondary. They have been given no extra funding, yet standards are rising and children are reaching targets that were hitherto considered unreachable (MacKay, 2001). Parents are working well with schools, and dyslexia provision is considered a national success.

It has also been recognised is that dyslexia-type methodology is good for a range of learning needs in the secondary school; as MacKay points out, "making the changes necessary to become dyslexia friendly will, without doubt, enhance the effectiveness of instruction and the learning of all, whether dyslexic or not" (p. 172).

The cost of not providing appropriately for dyslexic students, to society and to teachers' health, is very high indeed, and this provides added value to the expenditure and effort involved in supporting dyslexic students.

THE WAY FORWARD

Some of the key issues relating to dyslexia in the secondary school therefore include:

- the subject content
- subject delivery
- assessment
- crosscurricular aspects
- metacognitive factors
- learning styles
- training.

It is important that these issues are fully addressed so that the student with dyslexic difficulties can achieve some success in different subject areas.

Subject Content

It can be suggested that if the subject materials and teaching are developed and implemented in a manner which is compatible with the dyslexic student, the student should be able to perform on the same terms as his/her peers. Although much of the subject content is determined by examination considerations and the National Curriculum, much can still be done to identify those areas of the curriculum which may present difficulties for dyslexic students. An example of this is highlighted by Holmes (2001) in relation to physics. Physics is a subject which can present some difficulties to dyslexic students, but it is also one in which they can do well because it involves less reading and a high degree of scientific understanding. Holmes suggests a top-down approach, first providing a whole-school awareness of dyslexia and allowing subject teachers to reflect on the implications of providing for dyslexic students in their own subjects. Other factors which Holmes considers include: building a bank of support materials which can become a whole-school resource, and recognising the implications of secondary difficulties which can affect a student's performance in a particular subject. For example the relationship between maths and physics could mean that the students difficulties in physics are a consequence of difficulties in maths. This emphasises the need for a whole-school approach on dealing with dyslexia.

Essentially, the differentiation required for dyslexic students is not a special case but an essential component of preparation which would be carried out for all pupils— differentiation is described as "the action necessary to respond to the individual's requirements for curriculum access" (DfEE and QCA 1999). Williams and Lewis (2001), in relation to geography, show how differentiation can take place by task, by outcome and by support. They suggest that differentiation by resource does not mean writing worksheets with reduced content. Factors such as readability levels, the design of resources, with diagrams clearly labelled, provision of printed materials such as maps and notes to prevent tracing and copious note-taking, the provision of key words and specialised vocabulary spelling lists, and tape-recordings of key passages can all be useful. Williams and Lewis also suggest that differentiation by task, such as providing the student with a range of tasks from which to select, and by outcome, which means using a range of assessment strategies so that the dyslexic student can demonstrate their knowledge and understanding of the subject, also needs to be considered.

Staff need to be made aware of the general types of difficulties displayed by dyslexic students, which can affect sequencing, organisation, visual—spatial areas, retention and recall of information, structuring of information, and confusion of similar sounding and visually similar terms.

Teaching

As most teachers are aware, teaching involves more than just providing the student with knowledge. It requires a skilful combination of knowledge of the student, varied mode of presentation, and awareness of environmental factors which can influence the outcome of the teaching and learning process. Teaching and learning therefore should be planned together. Hunter (2001), in referring to the layout of the science classroom, highlights potential pitfalls, particularly relating to organisation of group work. This can result in the dyslexic student missing vital information if, for example, seated out of view of demonstrations or even the board. There are organisational implications here, particularly if there are booklets and materials to refer to which need to be readily accessible and readily identifiable. The laboratory setting can, however, be very compatible with the learning style of a dyslexic student, as it provides scope and space for group work, and flexibility in approaches to learning.

Other subjects, such as modern foreign languages, English, art and drama, can prove challenging in terms of amount of reading but can lend themselves quite easily to kinaesthetic approaches by focusing on experiential learning activities.

In modern languages, for example, often seen to be a source of considerable difficulty for the dyslexic student and consequently frustration for the teacher, Crombie and McColl (2001) show how use of appropriate strategies and consideration of the mode of presentation can help dyslexic students to achieve success. For example they suggest:

- the use of charts and diagrams to highlight the bigger picture
- adding mime and gesture to words
- adding pictures to text
- using colour to highlight gender and accents
- labeling diagrams and charts
- using games to consolidate vocabulary
- making packs of pocket-sized cards
- using different colours for different purposes
- combining listening and reading by providing text and tape
- using mind maps and spidergrams
- allowing the students to produce their own tapes
- presenting information in small amounts, using a variety of means, and providing frequent opportunities for repetition and revision
- providing an interest in the country, through showing films, and highlighting literature and culture.

Generally it is important in most subjects for instructions to be short and clear, preferably using bullet points. It is also worth considering the use of labels and key terms to highlight various points—the dyslexic student often has a word-finding difficulty and may need to be overexposed in relation to some of the terms used.

Assessment

Traditional forms of assessment can disadvantage the dyslexic student, because there is usually a discrepancy between their understanding of a topic and how they are able to display that understanding in written form. This can be overcome through continuous and portfolio assessment in most subject areas, but we still need to consider the importance of public examinations—many of which are set without any awareness of the needs of dyslexic students. As Dodds and Lumsden (2001) point out, as well as making special arrangements for dyslexic students, there are other forms of preparation which subject teachers can implement. They mention, for example, aspects such as course choice and the need for management to monitor option groupings. Strategies include the use of writing frames to help the student develop a full written response, the use of headings and sub-headings to prompt responses, the teaching of subject-specific words and "direct activities related to texts" (DART) (Dodds & Lumsden, 2001). These can help with labelling and understanding graphs and models, and include pupil-devised questions, prediction and sequencing activities.

It may be argued that many internal school exams are in fact no more than preparation for major public examinations. If this is the case, then they will probably follow the same style and format as public exams. This means we are prompted to think of compensatory strategies for dyslexic students—the word "compensation" here implies that a deficit exists and the dyslexic student requires supports to deal with that deficit. Yet is this really the case? Is the deficit not with an assessment process which is unable to accommodate to the diversity of learners? We argue strongly that teaching should be differentiated and diversified—then surely the same should apply to assessment!

Teaching processes which focus on metacognitive learning, looking at the process rather than the product, are commendable, as is the notion of "multiple intelligences" (Gardner, 1983) and the development of approaches consistent with this philosophy. For example, Lazear (1991), using Gardner's model of multiple intelligences, shows how the seven areas of intelligence (verbal/linguistic, logical mathematical, visual/spatial, body/kinaesthetic, musical/rhythmic, interpersonal and intrapersonal) can be used within an assessment paradigm. For example, Lazear suggests the following can be assessed under verbal/linguistic: reading, vocabulary, formal speech, journal-keeping, creative writing, poetry, verbal debate and storytelling. He also shows how kinaesthetic activities can be assessed using drama, role play and games. One particularly interesting aspect of Lazear's model is the development of "giving feedback" under the interpersonal section. It is good practice to encourage students to give feedback as this requires a sense of self-reflection which has important metacognitive elements. It also encourages students to summarise their views and report on these aspects that can sometimes prove challenging for dyslexic students.

While we still are a long way from a dynamic assessment paradigm that focuses on metacognitive strategies and views assessment as a teaching rather than a testing tool, such assessment is being used in some classroom contexts (Ayers, 1996). Campione and Brown (1989) suggest that in many education systems the link between assessment and teaching is weak, due to the shortcomings of traditional tests. They suggest that these tests are static and provide little or no information about the processes involved in the acquisition of the responses. Indeed, some children may get the right answer for the wrong reason! Additionally, in traditional assessment one does not know how close the student is to actually acquiring the right response. Metacognitve assessment holds considerable promise, as it can provide information about children's true potential and can be used to develop teaching approaches, thereby strengthening the link between assessment and teaching.

Crosscurricular Factors

It is important to view dyslexia, not as the responsibility of one teacher, or even one specialist teacher, but from a whole school perspective. Todd and Fairman (2001) suggest that this can be achieved through skilful use of Individual Education Programmes (IEPs) which need to be contextualised to identify the nature of the differentiation required. These authors also identify the need for flexible arrangements that would support individual provision for all students, including dyslexic students. The essence of the philosophy expounded by Todd and Fairman is the dominance of the positive aspects rather than the compensatory ones. They use terms such as *enabling, empowering, purposeful* and *motivating* to describe the key factors that should be associated with IEPs, therefore highlighting the whole-school emphasis on supporting dyslexic students through the use of IEPs, and the shift from a deficit to a positive model of support.

Staff Development

If supporting dyslexic students is to be a whole-school responsibility, then staff development involving all staff is essential. Such staff development should first focus on identifying staff needs in relation to dyslexia, both as a whole and through individual subjects. The curriculum, however, should be the vehicle for such staff development and not the difficulties exhibited by the student; such curriculum-focused in-service training places the responsibility of supporting dyslexic students— through curriculum planning, including teaching and learning styles—on the subject teachers and the staff as a whole. The process of learning needs to be highlighted, with some criteria to evaluate learning and teaching styles put in place. The two aspects—supporting the student in the subject areas through additional considerations such as examination and material support, and longer-term planning, curriculum differentiation and staff development—both need to be valued if dyslexic students are to achieve their true potential in all subjects within the secondary school curriculum.

CONCLUSION

There is no easy answer to helping students with dyslexia overcome their difficulties in secondary school. Peacey (2001), in discussing the general Inclusion Statement in the National Curriculum, highlights the first sentence that "teachers should aim to give every pupil the opportunity to experience success in learning and to achieve as high a standard as possible"; further, he cites a subsequent sentence which indicates that "teachers should take specific action to respond to pupils' diverse needs by creating effective learning environments" (p. 21). In both these statements it is clear that the responsibility lies squarely on the teacher and the curriculum. In a subject-oriented, perhaps even examination-driven, secondary education system, it is difficult for teachers to manage the juggling act between meeting the needs of all and of each individual, and particularly those with special needs. Yet the message and the spirit of inclusion mean that teachers have to do just that—and at the same time ensure that no student is disadvantaged. This highlights the key message of this chapter—dealing with dyslexia in the secondary school is the responsibility of the whole school, and not of an individual specialist or subject teacher. School management must recognise these responsibilities and ensure that all staff are equipped to deal with them and with the challenges presented by dyslexia and literacy difficulties in the secondary school. Only then will the real force of inclusion, and the equality inherent in it, be realised.

REFERENCES

Ayers, D. (1996) Assessment of intelligence, cognition and metacognition: Reflections, issues and recommendations. In G. Reid (Ed.) *Dimensions of Dyslexia, Vol.1: Assessment, Teaching and the Curriculum*. Edinburgh: Moray House.

Campione, J.C. & Brown, A.L. (1989) Assisted assessment: a taxonomy of approaches and an outline of strengths and weaknesses. *Journal of Learning Disabilities*, 22(3), 151–165.

Crombie, M. & McColl, H. (2001) Dyslexia and the teaching of modern foreign Languages. In L. Peer & G. Reid (Eds), *Dyslexia—Successful Inclusion in the Secondary School*. London: Fulton.

Dodds, D. & Lumsden, D. (2001) Examining the challenge: Preparing for examinations. In L. Peer & G. Reid (Eds), *Dyslexia—Successful Inclusion in the Secondary School*. London: Fulton.

Gardner, H. (1983) *Frames of Mind: The Theory of Multiple Intelligences*. New York: Harper & Row.

Holmes, P. (2001) Dyslexia and physics. In L. Peer & G. Reid (Eds), *Dyslexia—Successful Inclusion in the Secondary School*. London: Fulton.

Hunter, V. (2001) Dyslexia and general science. In L. Peer & G. Reid (Eds) *Dyslexia—Successful Inclusion in the Secondary School*. London: Fulton.

Lazear, D. (1991) *Seven Ways of Teaching: The Artistry of Teaching with Multiple Intelligences*. Tucson, Az.: Zephyr Press.

MacKay, N. (2001) Dyslexia friendly schools. In L. Peer & G. Reid (Eds), *Dyslexia—Successful Inclusion in the Secondary School*. London: Fulton.

Peer, L. (2001) Dyslexia and its manifestations in the secondary school. In L. Peer & G. Reid (Eds), *Dyslexia—Successful Inclusion in the Secondary School*. London: Fulton.

Peer, L. & Reid, G. (Eds), (2001) *Dyslexia—Successful Inclusion in the Secondary School*. London: Fulton.

Todd, J. & Fairman, A. (2001) Individualised learning in a group setting. In L. Peer & G. Reid (Eds) *Dyslexia—Successful Inclusion in the Secondary School*. London: Fulton.

Williams, F & Lewis, J. (2001) Dyslexia and geography. In L. Peer & G. Reid (Eds), *Dyslexia—Successful Inclusion in the Secondary School*. London: Fulton.

Warwick, C. (1999) *Dyslexia Friendly Schools Pack*. Reading: British Dyslexia Association.

Chapter 16

INDIVIDUAL EDUCATION PLANS AND DYSLEXIA: SOME PRINCIPLES

Janet Tod

INTRODUCTION

This chapter seeks to examine Individual Education Plans (IEPs) from a range of perspectives in order to address questions pertinent to the development of effective IEPs for dyslexic pupils in contemporary educational contexts. The questions posed relate to:

- Policy for IEPs: What are the policy requirements for IEPs and consequent expectations on schools and teachers?
- Practice in relation to IEPs: How have practitioners responded to policy initiatives for IEPs and how can they continue to develop effective IEPs?
- Research and theoretical perspectives: Why are IEPs considered to be necessary for some pupils who experience difficulty and difference in literacy learning?

Following a consideration of responses to these questions, some principles for IEPs and dyslexia will be extrapolated which will enable those involved to evaluate critically and improve their policies and practices for IEPs within their own settings.

WHAT IS AN IEP?

The term "Individual Education Plan" (IEP) refers to both a process and a document. An example of an IEP can be seen in Appendix I. Within the framework of the Code of Practice (DfE, 1994; DfEE, 2000) an IEP describes "the provision which is *additional to* or *different from* the differentiated curriculum plan that is part of normal provision".

Dyslexia and Literacy: Theory and Practice. Edited by Gavin Reid and Janice Wearmouth.
© 2002 John Wiley & Sons, Ltd.

The IEP should be crisply written and communicate:

> the short-term targets to be met, the teaching strategies and provision to be put in place, when the plan is to be reviewed, and the outcome of the action taken and anticipated learning outcomes (DfEE 2000 page 23 Section 1).

The IEP should focus on three or four key targets. The IEP should be discussed with the parents and reflect that the pupil's views have been sought and recorded. The Office for Standards in Education (OfSTED) express the view that "IEPs are considered to be of considerable significance and anticipates that they will play a strategic role in schools... The IEP is probably seen as the most important and viable component of a school's SEN (Special Educational Needs) policy by many inspectors." (OfSTED 1999b)

POLICY DEVELOPMENTS AND IEPs

> A debate which has not taken place in the inclusive education movement is that around the balance between individual responsive pedagogy and the systematic deployment of evidence based strategies. (Dyson & Millward (2000))

This statement, although referenced to "inclusive" education, illustrates an enduring dilemma for educational policy-makers. Individuals in compulsory education are traditionally educated in group settings, which begs the question of how differences, difficulties and delay in individual learners can be effectively addressed. In seeking to be responsive to these individual differences, educational trends have been characterised historically by policies for segregation, integration and inclusion. Individual planning, although not necessarily via a document labelled an "IEP", has been a feature of special-school planning and provision for at least 20 years. During the era of segregation "IEPs" were traditionally framed within a model in which learning difficulties were characteristically attributed to "deficits or delays" within the individual learner. Individual plans were designed to target and address individual "weaknesses", either via over-learning and specific skill training or by the use of small steps programmes guided by the influence of behavioural psychology. Individual Education Plans (IEPs) were introduced to mainstream settings via the 1994 Code of Practice (DfE 1994). This Code attempted to balance whole-school and individual specialist provision by introducing a five-staged model of identification and assessment with provision being enhanced by Individual Education Plans at Stage 2 and beyond. During this period IEP policy was influenced by two requirements:

- The need to translate some aspects of special school /"specialist" provision into the mainstream setting as part of government planning for the increased integration of SEN pupils.
- The need to be responsive to the Audit Commission's report (Audit Commission & HMI, 1992) which noted that: "the delegation (of the SEN budget) should go hand in hand with accountability" (p. 57).

These two factors influenced prescription and practice in relation to IEP developments. IEPs became a required source of evidence at review meetings to inform requests for additional resourcing or action via the five-stage model of the Code. Additionally, many LEAs and advisors instructed schools that IEPs or IEP's targets should be SMART (SMART: Specific, Measurable, Achievable, Relevant and Timely (Lloyd & Berthelot, 1992)), reflecting an emphasis that IEPs should provide a mechanism for "measuring" the outcomes of "additional and extra" provision.

Global initiatives for increased social inclusion were transposed onto national educational policy in the late 1990s, and inclusive education became the educational thrust for the new millennium (DfEE, 1998a; DfEE/QCA, 1999; DfEE, 2000; DRC, 2001) The revised draft Code of Practice, designed to update the 1994 Code in the light of recent legislation, including the National Curriculum 2000 (DfEE/QCA 1999) has retained IEPs as a means of "recording strategies employed to enable the child to make progress" (DfEE 2000). The revised Code will provide additional guidance on IEPs, including sample formats and short-term targets. The School Stage model has been reduced from three to two—School Action and School Action Plus.

For many, the retention of IEPs within inclusive settings is paradoxical:

> The principle of individual and alternative pathways through the curriculum for all pupils would set IEPs for a minority of students in a broader and less exclusionary context. (Mittler, 2000, p. 93)

The notion that all children would benefit from individualised learning plans has been given ministerial support and taken on board by some schools (Kirkman, 1999). Individual planning via IEPs is designed to address the needs of those pupils who are identified as having "special educational needs" (SEN). However, many dyslexic students may not be designated "SEN" by the Code of Practice criteria (DfE, 1994; DfEE, 2000) but still experience difficulties in learning which may be transient or subject-specific. While it is clear that the debate about the role and realisation of individual planning within the context of inclusion continues, it is necessary for the time being for teachers to work within existing constraints and perceived paradoxes. Paperwork remains "the biggest single problem" in relation to the implementation of the Code of Practice (OfSTED, 1999b), and schools will be guided to reduce gradually their total number of IEPs by improving whole-school provision to cater for individual difference, diversity and difficulty. National Curriculum 2000 (DfEE/QCA 1999) gives guidance on this to schools via its statement on inclusion (pp. 30–37). Schools and LEAs will be motivated by inspection criteria to monitor the impact of their strategies for addressing inclusion (OfSTED, 1999a). Schools will also be required to improve the quality of IEPs so that they become more action-based, and impact as much on pupil progress as they have on planning and review procedures.

Mittler (2000) states that:

> IEPs have quickly acquired an aura of orthodoxy and have come to be regarded as a hallmark of good practice and therefore a target for OfSTED inspection.

Policy developments in relation to IEPs reflect the need for schools to address individual learner needs within a politically led educational agenda which seeks to prepare individuals to become participating and productive members of a "knowledge society". Basic skills, high expectations, inclusive practices and lifelong learning are key themes in the current educational climate. It is likely that within this context there will be a reduction in curriculum prescription and an increased focus on developing styles of teaching which ensure the "access, engagement and participation" central to the social and academic aims of inclusive education. Six key principles, expressed in Table 16.1 below, logically follow from IEP policy developments and reflect likely expectations placed upon schools in terms of continued developments in IEP practices.

In addition to the key principles outlined in Table 16.1, schools will be advised to take note of the following OfSTED reporting concerning IEPs:

> The proposed revision of the Code of Practice should address the question of *purpose and function* of IEPs, including the link between the plan and the SEN register. Basic clarification is needed on what should be the basic content of the IEP, pinpointing what staff need to know about each pupil with SEN and what needs to be done to help the pupil to make progress towards stated education goals. Guidance is also needed on the relationship of the IEP to the overall plan for the pupil's curriculum. (OfSTED, 1999b)

> IEPs are most likely to be effective when they operate within a culture of effective and detailed educational planning. (OfSTED, 1999b)

> While inclusion of IEPs in a school portfolio of evidence at Stage 4 formal assessment is appropriate, it is important that this *does not become their main justification* at Stage 3 (author's emphasis).

From the above OfSTED quotes it follows that schools are expected to be clear about the content, purpose and function of IEPs. The purpose of IEPs should not mainly be that of providing evidence for formal assessment/Statementing, and IEPs should be contextualised within a culture of effective and detailed educational planning. In essence, OfSTED are asking schools to implement "effective" and detailed IEPs without creating a paper overload. This is no easy task. Certainly it will be of benefit for schools to agree on what they see is "effective" from the perspective of pupils and their parents. The implementation of provision that is *"additional to or different from"* without undue paperwork remains a significant challenge for schools.

The next section examines how far schools have progressed towards developing IEPs—or perhaps *Inclusive Extra Provision?*

PRACTICE IN RELATION TO IEPs

The pattern of development of IEPs in Britain followed that observed in the States (Rodger, 1995), with initial efforts being directed towards the development of an IEP format, which could evidence compliance to the prescriptions of the Code of Practice. Subsequent developments sought to reduce the burden on Special Educational Needs Co-ordinators (SENCOs) by delegation of the task of target-setting to class and subject teachers, increased use of ICT and "off the shelf" targets in the hope of reducing the repetitive writing needed for IEP updating. (Tod et al., 1998).

Table 16.1   Key principles for IEP policy development

Focus	Principle	Possible action
Diversity/ Inclusion	IEP planning should be contexturalised within whole-school planning for diversity. IEPs should ONLY be initiated for those individuals who need "*additional to or different from* provision from that normally given to their mainstream pupils. Ideally, as planning for inclusion becomes more effective IEPs should decrease, although some schools may retain individual planning for *all* pupils.	Schools need to audit their "collective IEPs" in order to landscape their SEN provision and identify if some targets and strategies are repeated across pupils IEPs (e.g. behaviour and literacy). If this is the case then this would suggest that these "repeated" targets could be addressed by whole-school/class responses to diversity, such as curriculum differentiation or change in teaching strategies. As provision that is "*additional to or different from*" is *relative*, schools should seek to reduce the total number of IEPs (Tod, 2000 p. 99).
Reduce paperwork	"The DfEE has a commitment to reducing the bureaucratic burden on teachers (Circular 2/98) the evidence from OfSTED is that the format of the IEP is only part of what teachers describe as burdensome; the number of IEPs that need to be produced and reviewed constitutes a very significant burden for many teachers." (OfSTED, 1999)	This is a difficult area to address for schools as IEPs have to contain certain minimum information and are likely to continue to be used for monitoring and review of schools' SEN provision. However, use of ICT for commercial or school-developed IEPs can speed up procedures and reduce time for multi-agency planning—assuming that issues of confidentiality can be resolved.
Action Based	IEPs need to be implemented so that they trigger effective action. OfSTED will track action that is effected from IEP planning, i.e. they expect to see IEP strategies in teacher planners, targets in pupil workbooks etc. . . . "in looking to see whether assessments inform teaching particular attention should be paid to how assessment of the work of pupils with SEN relates to targets set in IEPs" (OfSTED, 1995, p. 71)	Suggest that schools perceive IEPs as the briefest form of documentation needed to inform appropriate action, e.g. an IEP for an individual dyslexic pupil could trigger action from the parent which would be recorded in a diary, from the class teacher and be in his/her planner, from peers in their timetable, from the LSA in her monitoring sheet, etc. This system of MAPs (Monitored Action Plans) serves to activate the IEP and monitor pupil response (Tod, 2000, p. 80)

continues overleaf

Table 16.1   *(continued)*

Focus	Principle	Possible action
High Expectations/ Standards Raising	IEPs should impact upon pupil progress and retain their links to standards raising initiatives—Literacy and Numeracy targets are likely to predominate. "when examining whether the curriculum requirements are met for pupils with SEN, inspectors need to look at 'the learning objectives in IEPs (OfSTED, 1995, p. 77) "in primary and special schools the planning of the Literacy Hour (and numeracy equivalent) for pupils with SEN will be dovetailed with any remedial strategies being used to ensure consistency and continuity of approaches" (OfSTED, 1999b, p. 21)	Difficult to predict school response to continued pressure on literacy attainment. Schools could concentrate on earlier intervention and extend Additional Literacy Support (DfEE, 1999c) to include a wider range of pupils including those who may be at risk for developing dyslexia. Additionally, as schools become more adept at delivering National Literacy initiatives they could become increasingly more able to deliver "additional and extra" provision as part of whole-class/school planning. These two strategies of early identification and action, plus increased flexibility of planning for diversity within the NLS could serve to reduce the pressure to prescribe IEPs containing additional literacy targets for pupils with dyslexia.
Monitoring of Effectiveness of Schools Response to SEN pupils	IEPs will continue to be used to monitor the effectiveness of provision that is *additional to* or *different from* normal provision and as part of increased inclusion to monitor admissions and outcomes of SEN pupils. "inspectors are required to judge levels of attainment and progress for pupils with SEN (OfSTED, 1999b) . "detailed information on prior attainment, targets for improvement and progress made can be gained from IEPs, statements and annual reviews (OfSTED, 1995, p. 71).	In addition to monitoring IEP outcomes, schools will need to develop effective strategies for monitoring the progress of pupils with SEN and as part of their response to Curriculum 2000 develop procedures which improve access and participation for SEN pupils—if SEN budgets are increasingly devolved to schools.
Pupil involvement	From OfSTED report on IEPs (1999b) plus new Code "pupils with SEN should become progressively more involved in setting and evaluating targets within the IEP process". . . . will contribute to improved confidence and self image (DFEE, 2000)	Most schools have responded to OfSTED guidelines to improve pupil participation in their IEPs, and pupils are informed of the targets that have been set in their IEPs. However, further developments will be expected in relation to pupil involvement in evaluation of IEP outcomes.

Table 16.2 Teacher response to IEP procedures

Positive features of IEPs	Areas of concern
• The provision of a vehicle for the development of collaboration and involvement with parents, and a mechanism for enabling pupils to become more involved in their own learning plans.	• The written IEP is not always translated into practice—it thus becomes a cumbersome paperwork exercise which results in little educational benefit for the pupil.
• Directing teacher attention towards the setting and resetting of clear educationally relevant targets.	• If the SENCO takes on a major administrative role then his/her expertise in SEN teaching and co-ordination is not being effectively used.
• Involving staff in the development and implementation of strategies to meet those targets, thereby improving and sharing classroom practice.	• The IEP procedure is at risk of being used as an instrument for securing increased resources via "evident failure"—this has been termed "perverse incentive" by those critical of a sequential staged approach to SEN provision.
• Establishing a mechanism for providing clearer evidence as to the effectiveness of additional SEN provision.	• An adherence to an objectives model of teaching via the writing of clear (SMART) targets may lead to a narrowing of learning opportunities for SEN pupils.
• Harnessing available resources to meet IEP strategies.	• By having to link targets to provision on the IEP, it may be that SEN will become resource-led rather than needs-led.
• Can be a vehicle for establishing procedures and systems for raising attainment for *all* pupils.	• The use of checklists and commercial IEP schemes and strategies to assist the IEP process could lead back to a "remediation of deficit" model for SEN provision.
• Increasing the emphasis on the monitoring of pupil response to teaching.	• Difficulties with the maintenance and monitoring of IEPs are such that there is a risk that IEPs will either remain static documents or become so simplified that their educational benefit is questionable.

Reproduced by permission of David Fulton Publisher, from Tod et al. (1998)

In reviewing IEPs it is clear that there have been both positive developments and remaining areas of concern, as described in Table 16.2.

OfSTED have published three reports on the implementation of the 1994 Code of Practice in schools (OfSTED, 1996; 1997; 1999b) in which they track progress made and concerns identified: "schools have responded in different ways to both the developments and use of IEPs". OfSTED report that schools have been more concerned about how the IEP is written and presented than with its purpose and function. For example, OfSTED state that the placement of the pupil on the SEN register at Stage 2 has been the trigger to start an IEP—not whether an IEP will be useful or particularly relevant to any particular child. Pupil and parent involvement is reported to be very variable—a concern that needs to be addressed.

Table 16.3   OfSTED findings regarding IEPs

Findings from 1996/7 HMI survey	Findings from 1997/8 survey
• Schools had appropriate procedures for preparing and reviewing IEPs. • Individual planning and provision for pupils with SEN often do not link to a schools literacy policy. • The writing and reviewing of IEPs is giving the greatest cause for concern to SENCOs. • The views of pupils themselves are rarely sought in the preparation of IEPs or in the review process.	• Improved liaison between primary and secondary schools . . . but the associated documentation has not always been linked to National Curriculum assessments. • Increased evidence that many pupils had achieved their targets and, following a review, had had new targets set, which provided greater challenges. • An increased understanding by all staff of their responsibility for all pupils, including pupils with SEN. There was a notable improvement in most schools' attitudes towards these pupils.

OfSTED also noted that "the schools in the 1997/8 survey, many identified for their effective practice in using IEPs, continued to have difficulties in meeting every child's special needs." Does this comment hint that IEPs are a necessary but not sufficient mechanism for meeting individual SEN? Was the report paving the way for additional policies—e.g. inclusion via the SEN Action Plan (DfEE, 1998a)? Or is there a suggestion that IEPs are limited in meeting every child's individual needs because they are triggered by Stage 2 and beyond of the Code, rather than by their perceived usefulness to individual pupils? This would be a pertinent issue for some individual dyslexic pupils who may benefit from an "early intervention" IEP but not by being on the SEN register.

Another interesting quote from OfSTED (1999b):

> However, many schools had become more effective in managing their paperwork, with the consequential benefit that they had a small amount of additional time to give to parents and pupils.

In essence this comment reflects the central critique of IEP procedures: Has the paper planning and recording of IEPs reduced contact time with SEN pupils, and if so are these procedures educationally justifiable?

In so far as developments in IEP practices for dyslexic pupils are concerned, there is little doubt that the introduction of the National Literacy Strategy (NLS) Framework for Teaching (DfEE, 1998c) and the Literacy Hour format has been influential. IEPs continue to remain the focus for additional literacy planning for dyslexic pupils, with provision that is *"additional to* or *different from"*, being mainly directed towards meeting targets which reflect the need to impact upon individual pupil's phonological development. Questions that have been raised in relation to IEPs for dyslexic pupils are similar to those raised for IEPs generally.

Table 16.4 Different and extra support

Different	Extra
A reduction in "whole class" time to give more group time;	An increase in group time—keeping class time same
Using objectives from earlier terms where appropriate; *"phonics and spelling in KS1 are ordered in tighter progression than other objectives. It is vital that every child makes this progression. Work for pupils with SEN may be developed using objectives drawn from earlier terms . . . the aim should be to teach to the year and term designed for pupil's chronological age."*	Allowing longer time for teaching some objectives.
Grouping pupils who may share IEP objectives—this may not be the same as ability grouping—*"pupils who have specific difficulties in literacy may have the same or better conceptual understanding as the pupils in the highest ability group"*	Time planning within the group and independent work to allow the class teacher some time during the week for intensive work with individual pupils.
Setting across a number of classes: *"it is important that setting does not lower expectation of what SEN pupils can achieve".*	Additional resources: e.g. more than one copy of "Big Book" so that LSA can assist, etc.; ICT, "speaking books", tape recorders, spelling games, big books, tactile cues, etc.
Taken out of the hour to work in parallel, e.g. to give access to talking books . . . *(only when extra support within the literacy hour is not enough). . . . pupils returning to the main group for the final part of the hour.*	Additional adult support within the literacy hour, plus parents, volunteers, older pupils possibly providing support for additional reading practice.
Differentiated delivery style to secure access for pupils with SEN, e.g. adapt questions, give additional visual/tactile cues, etc.	Explicit linking of literacy to other curriculum subjects to offer extra opportunities for pupils to extend and practise their literacy skills.

Do IEPs Describe Provision That is "Additional To or Different From" That Normally Given?

For example, is IEP guidance *additional* to the extra or different provision suggested as options for SEN pupils within the Framework for Teaching guidelines. The National Literacy Strategy guidance allows for different and extra provision as shown in Table 16.4.

Do IEPs Link to Medium- and Longer-term Aims and Impact Upon Progress?

IEP guidance in the *Framework for teaching: additional guidance* (DfEE 1998d) suggests the key requirements for IEP planning shown in Table 16.5.

Table 16.5   Key requirements for IEP Planning

Targets	Strategies/Resource	Monitoring and Evaluation
• Targets reflect high expectations • Objectives in the NLS *Framework for teaching* can be used to draw up the IEP with targets framed as small steps towards those objectives • Pupils with same objectives on their IEPs can work together • IEPs may include behavioural targets relating to different aspects of the literacy hour, e.g. sharing, participating, working independently, etc.	• Human—the IEP should make clear when and how any adult support should be used to achieve the objectives described on the IEP; SENCO to advise other teachers how best to support pupils with varying needs in the literacy hour. • Physical: need to decide what resources are needed in order to enable the pupil to take part in the literacy hour as independently as possible.	• In evaluating whether IEP objectives have been achieved it is important to take account of what the pupil has done in the literacy hour as well as other parts of the day. This is an important point as it stresses the need to assess the transfer of skills from IEP to class/group work and independent study.

There are some relevant points made in this guidance for dyslexic pupils—the need for targets to reflect high expectations, to consider the benefits of pupils working collaboratively to improve literacy attainment, clear descriptions of the use of adult support and, most importantly of all, examining the transfer of target achievement across other curriculum areas.

Should IEPs Target "Skills" or "Strategies"?

OfSTED (1999b) report that "in best practice primary schools identified specific areas of need within IEPs such as poor pencil skills, a difficulty in learning letter sounds and related these to planned outcomes". The emphasis for OfSTED appears to be on "skill" development, and indeed this may well be justified for younger dyslexic pupils. However, dyslexic pupils' are likely to experience a long-term difficulty with automatisation of literacy, and many pupils will need to develop strategies for coping with their literacy and organisational difficulties, particularly as they prepare for secondary school. Additional ICT provision prescribed on IEPs for dyslexic learners needs also to be critically examined in relation to whether it is "compensatory" or "enabling" (Blamires, 1999).

Are IEPs Concerned with Proactive or Reactive Planning?

IEPs have tended to be triggered by Code of Practice Stage rather than based on individual need (OfSTED, 1999b). This is not surprising, given the guidance within the 1994 Code of Practice. As an example, pupils who do not respond as expected to NLS teaching are offered Additional Literacy Support (ALS) (DfEE, 1999). This takes the form of additional phonics teaching, which is delivered by Learning Support Assistants (LSAs) and reportedly based on Reading Reflex approaches (McGuiness, 1998) and "synthetic" phonics (Watson & Johnson, 1998). Phonics teaching is ingrained within the Literacy Hour, but schools more often employ "analytic" phonics. It could be argued that ALS is a reactive approach to those pupils who experience literacy difficulties and can result in dyslexic pupils being exposed to two different types of phonics teaching within the framework of the NLS. Given that synthetic phonics is considered to be particularly successful with dyslexic pupils (Hepplewhite, 2001), it may be useful for schools to consider whether their IEP planning could adopt a more proactive approach to provision for dyslexic pupils.

Do IEPs Just Support SMART Targets?

IEPs have a role in monitoring the effectiveness of SEN provision that is "*additional to* or *different from*", and as a consequence emphasis has been placed on setting "measurable" targets. While this emphasis clearly has a place in monitoring individual pupil progress, it could lead to dyslexic pupils having a "diet" of narrow targets based on measurable outcomes. In seeking to set targets that impact upon pupil progress, it may be that schools need to re-examine whether IEPs "measure what is valuable or value what is easily measurable" (Muncey & McGinty, 1998).

For example, targets linked to psychological state (e.g. self-esteem) could have a powerful effect on improving learning (Pollard & Filer, 1996), particularly in the collaborative, interactive, creative environments that characterise effective literacy teaching (Grainger & Tod, 2000). It is also important for IEPs to build on pupil strengths—many targets for dyslexic pupils are designed to address weaknesses. If pupils are to be involved in their IEPs, it could have a negative effect on their learning if their weaknesses are always targeted for action, e.g. phonological skills, spelling accuracy and writing fluency. It may prove helpful for schools to consider "positive" IEP target-setting by ensuring that some targets build on strengths, e.g. "will use good speaking and listening skills to plan a range of written work with peers" . . . "will use good problem-solving skills to increase range of strategies to tackle new words".

Do IEPs Provide a Focus for Co-ordinated Educational Effort?

For IEPs to be effective they need to provide a vehicle for communicating the targets to be met to all those involved. Dyslexic pupils require this coordination if they are to receive effective additional focused support. Those involved in the IEP may include the pupil, their parents, peers, LSA, SENCO, class and subject teacher, specialist support teacher, etc. OfSTED (1999b) note that "Learning support assistants (LSAs) need to be suitably trained, supported and monitored if they are to be used increasingly to deliver IEPs". Certainly there is a trend for additional literacy support (DfEE, 1999) to be delivered by LSAs. Schools may need to examine if their IEP provision does indeed "harness" available human resources effectively or whether much of individual support is left to the LSA—a feature that may encourage dependency, undermine the importance of IEP provision for individual learners, limit transfer to other curriculum areas and jeopardise the development of inclusive practices (Ainscow, 2000).

These areas of emergent concern need to be contextualised within whole-school planning for meeting diverse learning needs: "The IEPs did not work in isolation ... they were supported by a holiday reading programme ... " (OfSTED, 1999b). Schools have worked hard to develop their IEP procedures and should be encouraged to continue to improve both their IEPs and constituent literacy provision in order to raise achievement for their individual dyslexic learners.

THEORY AND RESEARCH

In looking at the limited research evidence relating to the procedural and educational aspects of IEP development in the States and the UK (Rodger, 1995), there is as yet no evidence which supports that the written IEP is being systematically integrated into teacher planning, or translated into classroom practice (Lynch & Beare, 1990; Sigafoos et al., 1991; OfSTED, 1999b). This is a serious concern, given that IEPs have been a feature of SEN policy since 1994 in the UK and for over 20 years in the US.

It seems reasonable to conclude that the translation of IEP policy from the United States and Australia onto a UK education system was not based on research evidence or informed from any particular theoretical perspective, but was simply reactionary to the process of increased integration of SEN pupils in the UK. It could similarly be concluded that any underpinning theory to IEP design and implementation has been based on what Thomas and Loxley (2001, p. 24) refer to as a "what's wrong and cure it" paradigm. In deconstructing special education, they comment that the theory of special education is "an agglomeration of bits and pieces from Piagetian, psychoanalytic, psychometric, and behavioural theoretical models".

In following this train of thought, the 'what's wrong' with dyslexic learners: "dyslexia is present when fluent and accurate word identification (reading) and/or spelling does not develop or does so very incompletely or with great difficulty" (Reason et al., 1999); "the cure" in IEP terms is to offer individualised provision that is *additional to* or *different from*" that offered normally. Policy requires that this IEP provision should have clear pre-set short-term targets designed to support medium- and longer-term objectives. Strategies should be described prior to learning and targets should ideally be SMART. If this "cure" was based on theory, it would be expected that research into pedagogy would support the notion that teaching is more effective if directed towards the achievement of pre-set targets with pre-prescribed learning outcomes. While accepting the limitation that reviews of research which seek to extract generic principles may be flawed when applied to the individual with SEN, it is pertinent to note that although "clear goals" (targets) are considered to be an important component of effective pedagogy (Ireson *et al.*, 1999) the emphasis on predetermined measurable outcomes linked to pre-decided given strategies is not supported by research (Deforges, 2001). Research into literacy learning suggests that pupil involvement in learning, active experimentation with a range of strategies and the opportunity for learning to "occur" are crucial (Grainger & Tod, 2000), and that these components of effective literacy teaching may have been sacrificed to the precise written planning and the accountability function of the IEP. It is also important to note that "a learner brings to the learning experience a theory about themselves as a learner and this identity mediates personal commitment and motivation" (Deforges, 2001). If IEPs consistently target learner difficulties or delays (e.g. phonological processing), then they could affect how pupils feel about their ability in literacy and adversely affect how they approach the learning task.

The thinking behind IEPs also suggests, by offering provision that is *'additional to or different from,'* that learners with dyslexia either learn the same way as non-dyslexic learners but more slowly and therefore need "more of the same," *or* that dyslexic pupils require different provision that is "specialist" in some way. While the controversy about whether learners with dyslexia are distinctly different from other individuals who exhibit difficulties or delay in literacy attainment has yet to be resolved, there appears to be some consensus about the efficacy of teaching approaches. In the context of IEP developments these are:

- *Strategies*: there is a need to emphasise a range of approaches which combine phonic and whole language teaching (Snowling, 1966) and the links between them. Reason *et al.* (1988) concluded that there was nothing specific about teaching pupils with dyslexia—all pupils required suitable "cocktails" that reflected individual strengths, weakness and needs. Given this evidence, The National Literary Strategy (NLS) combines word, sentence and text level work for all, but offers opportunities for targeted word-level work via focused group work and IEPs.
- *"Extra" teaching*: for dyslexic pupils, this tended to concentrate more on skills (phonological interventions) than on meaningful reading and writing (Connor, 1994). Although there is evidence that with this approach dyslexic pupils become better at the targeted skills, there is only limited reporting concerning the impact of this skills-based teaching on other aspects of literacy development (i.e. spelling: Brooks, 1995).
- *"Different/special" teaching*: Most intervention studies involved individual teaching outside the mainstream. "Individual" teaching allows greater opportunity for continuous assessment, detailed record-keeping, immediate feedback and overlearning which, according to Veluntino (1987), discriminates "specialist" dyslexia teaching from classroom-based literacy teaching. However, two studies reported by Lewis and Norwich (2000) found that a cooperative integrated reading and comprehension programme delivered by special and mainstream class teachers produced greater gains than teaching that involved specialist daily withdrawal (Stevens & Slavin, 1995; replicated by Jenkins et al., 1994). In contrast Fuchs and Fuchs (1995, 1998), although supporting the enhancement

of mainstream teacher skills through training, retain the view that "specifically individualised instruction, small sized instructional groups, and the more highly trained teachers available through special education" (1998, p. 31) will be required for those pupils who remain unresponsive to adapted classroom practices.

There is growing consensus for the view that there are common approaches to teaching literacy for the diversity of pupils, including those with specific learning difficulties. However, the focus on more explicit and intense interventions (Torgeson et al., 1997) for those at risk with literacy difficulties can mean differences in actual programmes and something additional that is not needed by most pupils. This is consistent with the notion of "IEP" provision. It is important in this context to have regard to the term "additional to". This should mean what it says, and not mean "instead of".

> Targeting specific support through IEPs should not involve a narrowing of the curriculum, a reduction in the range of opportunities experienced or a diet of impoverished text ... readers need to use a range of different skills and strategies as they read in order to make meaning from the text (Grainger & Tod, 2000). In broad terms there are three general categories of such strategies that interrelate: strategies for problem-solving new words, strategies that maintain fluency and strategies that self-correct. (Clay, 1991)

It follows that an IEP cannot be evaluated out of the context in which it is delivered. Targeted, focused, additional, phonological support offered via the IEP needs to be housed within a rich interactive, effective and affective literary curriculum.

Ireson et al. (1999) additionally note that an effective pedagogy should be "theoretically sophisticated". In considering the design of IEPs, the "small steps" approaches and emphasis on SMART targets suggest a link to behavioural techniques. OfSTED (1999b) reported that:

> ... in best practice, primary schools identified specific areas of need within IEPs such as poor pencil skills, a difficulty in learning letter sounds ... and related these to particularly planned outcomes'.

This suggests that deficit-led remedial approaches within IEP planning are "best practice". Indeed, if IEP pedagogy is "theoretically sophisticated", it could be considered paradoxical that it is now accepted practice that LSAs are "used" to deliver IEPs to those individuals with significant learning difficulties (OfSTED, 1999b, p. 21). While there is no doubt that behavioural techniques have provided assistance in thinking about pedagogy for some children, there can be equal certainty that they have oversimplified the nature of learning. Sensible cautious thinking about educational aims has been replaced by the certainties of behavioural analysis (Hargreaves, 1978).

It is cautionary to note that, in attempting to explain reading difficulties and delays, researchers and theorists have developed a range of explanatory mechanisms, models and constructs. As a simplistic example it has been consistently observed that dyslexic pupils exhibit a difficulty with word segmentation and synthesis.

In order to "explain" this difficulty, theorists refer to models of hypothetical cognitive functioning which have been developed to represent human information-processing—characteristically, models which refer to input, processing and output activities. The "faulty" mechanism for dyslexic individuals is assumed to be in relation to phonological processing and thus subsequent descriptors, explanations and interventions refer to, and target, this difficulty. Thomas and Loxley (2001) point out that a causal explanation has, in this case, been simplistically applied to correlational evidence. Attempts to use a sub-skill explanation for reading difficulty—for example, the Illinois Test of Psycholinguistic Abilities (McCarthy & Kirk, 1963) in the hope of identifying specific cognitive weaknesses in, for example, memory and sequencing, with the view to strengthening these via remediation, have been dashed by reviews of outcomes-based evidence (e.g. Arter & Jenkins, 1979). It is important for those reviewing IEPs for dyslexic pupils to be aware that cognitive modelling and explanatory constructs used to inform IEP target-setting and strategy development are what they are, i.e. models and explanations. Their survival, particularly in special education, does not give them automatic credence. They are "thinking tools" (Bourdieu, 1989), not established facts. It is interesting to note in this context that it is generally considered that specialist teaching for dyslexic pupils should involve structured, multisensory, cumulative teaching of phonics—and that learning should be aimed towards mastery/automaticity. Such strategies are frequently recorded on IEPs for learners with dyslexia. However, as Piotrowski and Reason (2000) observe, this "prescription" has been based on "the charismatic work of Orten (1937), Fernauld (1943) and Gillingham and Stillman (1946) and Norrie (1960) and is not based on a body of systematic research".

It seems logical to conclude from this section that if IEPs are to become more effective, their theoretical underpinnings need to be kept under review and evaluated in the light of outcome-based evidence. In looking briefly at "research and theory" in relation to IEP development for dyslexic pupils, there is some cause for concern. To date the evidence suggests that schools have focused their efforts into the procedural aspects of IEP development and evaluated their IEPs against compliance to the Code of Practice guidance and the extent to which pupils have achieved the set targets. Although the theoretical underpinnings of IEPs have not been made explicit by policy-makers, notions of SMART short-term targets, pre-determined strategies, pre-set learning outcomes, and provision that is "additional to or otherwise different from" are reminiscent of the behavioural approaches, simplistic cognitive modelling and individual deficit remedial teaching which characterised much of special education in the 1970s.

Pupils can achieve pre-set targets, and IEP paperwork can evidence extra planning for SEN pupils. However, the question remains as to whether the time spent on IEP activity is justified in terms of the impact it is having on teacher planning and pupil learning and progress. It could be that, in addition to examining how IEP procedures might be improved, there is a case for schools and their teacher researchers to evaluate critically the theoretical underpinnings and evidence base of their existing IEPs.

PRINCIPLES FOR EFFECTIVE PRACTICE

Findings from the previous sections suggest that although schools have complied with policy directives for IEPs, there remains an imbalance between the amount of paperwork and planning and the observable educational benefits to individual pupils. In essence, those involved in IEP development have become entrenched in "doing IEPs" without sufficient questioning about the principles, purpose and practices behind such activity. IEPs are currently contextualised within an educational philosophy that supports increasing inclusion. It is essential that schools adopt a critical stance when re-examining their IEPs. Hopefully it will be helpful for schools to use the following principles extrapolated from a review of policy, practice and research in Sections 1–3 of this chapter to evaluate their IEPs critically, including those for dyslexic pupils.

- There is a need for those involved in IEPs to be clear about the educational purpose of an IEP, both for individual pupils and as part of whole-school planning and provision. Evaluation of IEPs should be undertaken in relation to the identified and agreed purpose. Clearly it is not enough to say that "the purpose of an IEP is to show inspectors and parents that we have additional planning in place for SEN pupils".
- IEPs for literacy should be contextualised within the NLS and whole-school planning for literacy in order to identify additional to or different provision to that given for all pupils; IEP provision should not be compensatory or reduce entitlement to a rich, interactive literacy curriculum.
- IEPs should impact upon curriculum development and delivery, and upon pupil learning and progress.
- IEPs need to be managed at whole-school level, with identified roles and responsibilities to ensure that outcomes are monitored and responsive adjustments made.
- Targets set should reflect high expectations, the need to develop social and academic aspects of learning, address skills and strategies, and build on pupil strengths.
- IEPs should be capable of supporting early identification of literacy difficulties and trigger proactive planning.
- IEPs should support learning that is purposeful and motivating and reflect pupil involvement in the planning and assessment of their learning and progress.
- IEPs should be both enabling and empowering—possibly by linking literacy, PSHE and Citizenship targets (Grainger & Tod, 2000).
- Schools should encourage staff to adopt a critical distance towards IEPs in terms of policy, practice and theory/research so that their impact on pupils' progress and whole-school response to diversity can be evaluated and improved.
- IEPs should harness and support efficient use of resources and reflect collaborative educational effort.

Considerable groundwork has been undertaken by schools in order to develop outcomes-monitored individual planning to support both excellence and equity in educational settings. If individual pupils and schools are to be beneficiaries of these IEP initiatives for literacy, then schools need to ensure that sound principles for individualised provision are embedded within planning for an accessible, proactive, interactive, evidence-based literacy curriculum.

APPENDIX 1

Example of an IEP used in School (Tod, 2000)

Name: Dominic

Date of Birth:

Current NCY: 5

Stage of Code:

Statement of Special Educational Needs: Yes

Staff involved: Class teacher, LEA learning support teacher, CA, parents.

Key Concerns: Failure to retain multiplication tables, malformation of letters in handwriting, all aspects of spelling, written work of every type, disorganised.

Reading is at chronological age and receiving support so is not a concern here. No behavioural concerns.

Agreed Target	Strategies	Resources	Home/ School	Method of Assessment	Outcome achieved and next action
Maths: improve fluency in multiplication tables	Provide easy access to the information he needs Support his learning of 3x and 6x	"turn and learn" table tubes; Computer games and chanting	School Home and School	Is his work more accurate and speedy? Can he chant unaided? (automatise)	Yes—much happier— suggest "turn and learn" replaced by charts— 2x,5x,10x as he is becoming too dependent. Still problems; try musical cassette and video
Handwriting: correct malformation of f, h, n, u, s, j	Individual work programme in hand-writing lessons— support at other times	Pattern practice sheets, wipe clean cards	Home and School	Observe letter formation in free writing and copying	Much improved, still needs reminding to write "u" not u—keep an eye out in case old habits return—no further special action now.

continues overleaf

(*continued*)

Agreed Target	Strategies	Resources	Home/ School	Method of Assessment	Outcome achieved and next action
Spelling: work on irregular words: come, have, said, were, are, could, should, would, does, goes.	Odd word list to take home—10 words per weekly list		Home and School	Are those words being spelt correctly for 90% of time?	Correctly spelt in tests but not in free writing. Press on with lists of 10 words and slip in some of previously learnt odd words.
Written work: better copying	Introduce chunking	Classroom assistant (CA)	School	Does his copying improve?	Slowly improving, keep this target until CA not needed as support
Organisational skills: improve planning	Planning next school day the night before	White Board felt tip	Home	Does he bring kit, books etc.?	Improving. Discuss with parents easing off their support.

Date of Review : 03.03.97

Summary of Outcomes and Proposed Further Actions: Scheme is helping Dominic—he is keen and very involved. Next update of IEP should include other spelling targets (regular words?). CA to help introduce use of tape recorder. Can class teacher use more varied methods of recording children's work e.g. 'fill in the blanks, worksheets instead of copying from the board?

REFERENCES

Ainscow M. (2000) The next step in special education: supporting the development of inclusive practices. *British Journal of Special Education*, 27(2); 76–80

Arter J.A. & Jenkins J.R. (1979) Differential diagnosis—prescriptive teaching: a critical appraisal. *Review of Educational Research*, 49(4): 517–555

Audit Commission & HMI (1992) *Getting in on the Act*. London: HMSO

Blamires M. (ed) (1999) *Enabling Technology for Inclusion*. London: Paul Chapman

Bourdieu P. (1989) cited in Wacquant L.D. (1989) Towards a reflexive sociology: a workshop with Pierre Bordieu. *Sociological Theory*, 7: 50

Brooks P. (1995) A comparison of the effectiveness of different teaching strategies in teaching spelling to a student with severe specific learning difficulties/dyslexia. *Educational and Child Psychology*, 12(1): 80–88

Clay M. (1991) *Becoming Literate: The Construction of Inner Control*. Portsmouth, NH: Heinemann

Connor M. (1994) Specific learning difficulties (dyslexia) and interventions. *Support for Learning*, 9(3): 114–119

Deforges C. (2001) Learning, thinking and classroom work. Paper presented at United Kingdom Reading Association (UKRA) conference 6–8 July 2001, Canterbury Christ Church University College, Kent

Department for Education (DfE) (1994) *Code of Practice on the Identification and Assessment of Special Educational Needs*. London: DfE

Department for Education and Employment (DfEE) (1998a) *Meeting Special Educational Needs—A Programme of Action*. London: DfEE

Department for Education and Employment (DfEE) (1998b) *Reducing the Bureaucratic Burden on Teachers*. Circular 1/6/98. London: DfEE

Department for Education and Employment (DfEE) (1998c) *The National Literacy Strategy Framework for Teaching*. London: DfEE

Department for Education and Employment (DfEE) (1998d) *The National Literacy Strategy Framework for Teaching (Additional Guidance) Children with Special Educational Needs*. London: DfEE

Department for Education and Employment (1999) *National Literacy Strategy Additional Literacy Support*. London: DfEE

Department for Education and Employment (DfEE) (2000) *Draft revised SEN Code of Practice*. www.dfee.gov.uk/sen/standard.htm

Department for Education and Employment and Qualifications and Curriculum Authority (DfEE & QCA) (1999) *The National Curriculum: Handbook for Primary and Secondary Teachers*. London: DfEE

Disability Rights Commission (DRC) (2001) *The Draft Code of Practice (Schools)—The Disability Discrimination Act 1995 (As Amended by the SEN and Disability Act 2001)* www.drc.gb.org

Dyson A. & Millward A. (2000) SENCOs as decision makers. Presented at ISEC International Special Education Congress 2000. http://www.isec2000.org.uk/abstracts/papers_d/dyson_1.htm

Fernauld J. (1943) *Remedial Techniques in Basic School Subjects*. New York: McGraw-Hill

Fuchs D. & Fuchs L. (1995) What's 'Special' about Special Education? *Phi Delta Kappa*, March: 522–530

Fuchs L.S. & Fuchs D. (1998) 'General educators': instructional adaptations for students with learning disabilities. *Learning Disability Quarterly*, 21, Winter: 23–33

Gillingham A. & Stillman B.U. (1946) *Remedial Training for Children with Specific Difficulty in Reading, Spelling and Penmanship*. Cambridge, MA: Educators Publishing Service

Grainger T. & Tod J. (2000) *Inclusive Educational Practice: Literacy*. London: David Fulton Publishers

Hargreaves D.H. (1978) The proper study of educational psychology. *Association of Educational Psychologists' Journal*, 4(9): 3–8

Hepplewhite D. (2001) cited in "Synthetic' phonics seen as real reading McCoy". Article in *Times Educational Supplement (TES)* 27 July: 7

Ireson J., Mortimore P. & Hallum S. (1999) The common strands of pedagogy and their implications. In Mortimore P. (ed) *Understanding Pedagogy and Its Impact on Learning*. London: Paul Chapman

Jenkins J., Jewell M., Leicester N., O'Connor R., Jenkins L. & Troutner N. (1994) Accommodations for individual differences without classroom ability groups: An experiment in school restructuring. *Exceptional Children*, 60(4): 344–358

Kirkman S. (1999) "Under the same roof" *TES "Special" Times Educational Supplement*, Summer, 7

Lewis A. & Norwich B. (2000) Is there a distinctive SEN pedagogy? In Norwich B (ed) *Specialist Teaching for Special Educational Need and Inclusion*, Policy Paper 4 (third series) Tamworth, UK: NASEN publications

Lloyd S.R. & Berthelot C. (1992) *Self Empowerment: How to Get What You Want From Life*. London: Kogan Page

Lynch E.C. & Beare P.L. (1990) The quality of IEP objectives and their relevance to instruction for students with mental retardation and behavioural disorders, *Remedial and Special Education*, 11, 48–55

McCarthy J.J. & Kirk S.A. (1963) *The Construction, Standardisation and Statistical Characteristics of the Illinois Test of Psycholinguistic Abilities.* Illinois: University of Illinois

McGuiness D. (1998) *Why Children Can't Read and What We Can Do About It.* London: Penguin

Mittler P. (2000) *Working Towards Inclusive Education: Social Contexts.* London: David Fulton Publishers

Muncey J. & McGinty J. (1998) Target Setting and Special Schools. *British Journal of Special Education*, 25(4): 173–178

Norrie E. (1960) *The Edith Norrie Letter Case.* London: Helen Arkell Word Blind Centre

Office for Standards in Education (1995) *The OFSTED Handbook—Guidance on the Inspection of Nursery and Primary Schools.* London: HMSO

Office for Standards in Education (1996) *The Implementation of the Code of Practice for Pupils with Special Educational Needs.* London: OFSTED /HMSO

Office for Standards in Education (1997) *The SEN Code of Practice: Two Years On.* London: OFSTED

Office for Standards in Education (1999a) *Evaluating Educational Inclusion—Guidance for Inspectors and Schools* (HMI 235) London: OFSTED http://ofsted.gov.uk

Office for Standards in Education (1999b) *The SEN Code of Practice Three Years On: The Contribution of Individual Education Plans to the Raising of Standards of Pupils with Special Educational Needs* (HM221) London: OFSTED

Orten S.T. (1937) *Reading, Writing and Speech Problems in Children.* New York: Norton

Piotrowski J. & Reason R. (2000) The National Literacy Strategy and dyslexia: a comparison of teaching methods and materials. *Support for Learning*, 15(2)

Pollard A. & Filer A. (1996) *The Social World of Children's Learning.* London: Cassell

Reason R. Brown B. Cole M. & Gregory M. (1988) Does the specific in specific learning difficulties make a difference to the way we teach? *Support for Learning*, 3(4): 230–236

Reason R., Frederickson N., Hefferenan M., Martin C. & Woods K. (1999) "Dyslexia, Literacy and Psychological Assessment". Draft Report of Working Party of the Division of Educational and Child Psychology. Leicester: The British Psychological Society

Rodger S. (1995) Individual Education Plans revisited: a review of the literature. *International Journal of Disability, Development and Education*, 42(3): 221–239

Sigafoos J., Kigner J., Holt K., Doss S. & Mustonen T. (1991) Improving the quality of written development policies for adults with intellectual disabilities. *British Journal of Mental Subnormality*, 37: 35–46

Snowling M. (1966) Contemporary approaches to the teaching of reading. *Journal of Child Psychology and Psychiatry*, 37(2): 139–148

Stevens R.J. & Slavin R.E. (1995) Effects of co-operative learning approaches in reading and writing on academically handicapped and non-handicapped students. *Elementary School Journal*, 95(3): 241–262

Thomas G. & Loxley A. (2001) *Deconstructing Special Education and Constructing Inclusion.* Milton Keynes: Open University Press

Tod J. (2000) *Individual Education Plans (IEPs): Dyslexia.* London: David Fulton Publishers

Tod J., Castle F. & Blamires M. (1998) *Individual Education Plans (IEPs): Implementing Effective Practice.* London: David Fulton Publishers

Torgeson J.K., Wagner R.K. & Rashotte C.A. (1997) Longitudinal studies of phonological processing and reading. *Journal of Learning Disabilities*, 27(5): 276–286

Veluntino F. (1987) Dyslexia. *Scientific American*, 256(3): 34–41

Watson J. & Johnson R. (1998) Accelerating Reading Attainment: The Effectiveness of Synthetic Phonics. *Interchange 57*. Edinburgh: The Scottish Office

Chapter 17

A COGNITIVE APPROACH TO DYSLEXIA: LEARNING STYLES AND THINKING SKILLS

Bob Burden

For anyone working within the complex field of dyslexia, it goes without saying that it is a difficult concept to understand. One reason for such confusion is that a large number of definitions of dyslexia exist, many of which are mutually contradictory. This is not an issue which can be readily ignored, as some practitioners would prefer to do, because the action taken to intervene on behalf of those identified as dyslexic will always reflect one's implicit acceptance of how dyslexia can best be understood.

Thus, the attempt by the British Psychological Society's Working Party on Dyslexia to circumvent the issue of definition by suggesting that *"dyslexia is evident when accurate and fluent word reading and/or spelling develops very incompletely or with great difficulty"* (BPS, 1999) is both naïve and unhelpful. By focusing in a superficial manner on the manifestation of decoding difficulties at the level of single words, such a description provides neither an explanation of cause nor an indication for appropriate action. It is little more than tautology.

It is the underlying premise of this chapter that the term *dyslexia* is at best a shorthand form of convenience which makes possible rational discourse and promotes positive intervention, but at worst a barrier to helpful communication and appropriate action. The way in which concepts are defined and used in everyday speech will inevitably shape our thoughts and action. Thus, the difference between describing someone as "having dyslexia", "being dyslexic" or "displaying learning difficulties of a dyslexic nature" becomes highly significant. In the first instance, "dyslexia" is used as a noun and is thereby implicitly defined as a "thing" or analogous to a medical condition that one can develop or suffer from. One set of action implications that naturally follows from such a definition is likely to be the search

Dyslexia and Literacy: Theory and Practice. Edited by Gavin Reid and Janice Wearmouth.
© 2002 John Wiley & Sons, Ltd.

for a "cure" which will magically serve to remove the condition. In the second example, the adjectival use of the term "dyslexic" defines the whole person in a particular way. A dyslexic person may thereby come to be seen as "handicapped" and likely to be treated as different in most respects from other people. The third example, by contrast, has descriptive and action implications with regard to the nature of the learning difficulties exhibited at a particular moment in time.

From this third perspective it can be seen that dyslexia, like intelligence, is a hypothetical construct, a term of convenience to enable us to make sense of otherwise incomprehensible but apparently related aspects of learning behaviour. With this in mind, the approach taken here is that dyslexia is conceived as a descriptive term encompassing a loosely knit subset of people who manifest unexpected and long-lasting difficulties in learning to read, write or spell, and who can be distinguished from those displaying more general or "moderate learning difficulties" (MLD) in that they do not display similar difficulties in most other areas of learning, except as a result of their literacy difficulties. Dyslexia is thus used as a comparative term, not an all-or-none phenomenon. Rather than stating that a person "has dyslexia" or even "is dyslexic", it is considered more helpful to indicate that that person displays specific learning difficulties of a dyslexic nature, and then to identify exactly how and in what specific areas those difficulties are occurring.

Such an approach continues to avoid the issue of causation, but enables us to focus explicitly upon the action implications. One of the advantages of characterising dyslexia in this way is that children and adults manifesting unexpected ongoing difficulties in developing competence and/or fluency in literacy can, nevertheless, be viewed as active meaning-makers and participants in shaping their own destiny. They are not viewed from this perspective as innocent victims of some as yet undiagnosed brain dysfunction, helplessly waiting for a long-sought cure, nor as permanently handicapped in any general sense, nor as passive subjects differentially responsive to one or another intervention technique. It is an approach which is both holistic and humanistic rather than fragmented and mechanistic.

This preferred model is educational rather than medical, and embedded within the socio-cultural framework formulated by Vygotsky and his followers (Kozulin, 1999), in sharp contrast to more traditional medical, psychometric or behaviourist perspectives. This leads most naturally into a discussion of the kinds of social interactions and cultural contexts which might be most likely to generate and/or exacerbate difficulties of a dyslexic nature. Nevertheless, for the purpose of the present chapter, the major emphasis of what follows will be upon the ways in which individual learners make sense of and respond to their growing awareness of their specific learning difficulties, and some of the possible implications for intervention which follow from this. It will first be necessary, however, to examine some ways in which different cognitive psychologists have contributed to our understanding of the learning process.

COGNITIVE THEORIES OF LEARNING

Contrary to popular belief, there is no single cognitive theory of learning. In the US context the term has been most commonly employed to refer to the *information processing* approach advocated by Herbert Simon and his followers (Simon, 1979; Langley et al., 1987) and to models of brain functioning in such areas as memory (Phye, 1993). In recent years this kind of approach has been applied with particular success to analysing the reading process (Royer, 1993) and as is demonstrated elsewhere in this volume (Chapters 3, 4 and 7).

Two key points arise from such an approach. The first is that a more sophisticated analysis is made possible of how the brain functions in the process of learning to read, write, spell, etc. than has traditionally been applied by discrepancy theorists. Thus, each aspect of an assumed developmental progression, through recognising letters and graphemes, assigning sounds to these letters (phonemes) and then blending them into words which are subsequently transformed into a phonological code and held in various parts of the memory store, can be analysed in terms of the efficiency of a developing reader's functioning (Aarnoutse et al., 2001).

This, in turn, has led to a focus upon phonological awareness and processing (Goswami, 1999) and the development of tests such as the PhAB (Frederickson et al., 1997) to identify where problems within this aspect of processing may be occurring. Thus, the finding that more than 80% of people with dyslexia have difficulty with phonological processing has led to the currently popular theory that this is where the root of dyslexia lies (Snowling, 1998; Palmer, 2000). At the same time, other identified aspects of the process of becoming literate have included the importance of working memory (Palmer, 2000), the skill of serialisation (Das & Kendrick, 1997) and the development of meta-linguistic ability (Byrne & Liberman, 1999).

The second major point to emerge from the information-processing approach to becoming literate has been the need to develop adequate models to describe how different aspects of the process connect up (Snowling, 1998). Thus, Frith (1985) proposed an early three-stage model of reading development, moving from the logographic, through the alphabetic to the orthographic stage. An alternative model proposed by Stanovich (1986) combined "bottom up" (decoding) and "top down" (comprehension) approaches as integrative and interactive processes. It is to this "top down" issue of comprehension that I will turn next.

Reading Comprehension

When we begin to consider comprehension as the second major aspect of the reading process, we move also to a different conceptualisation of cognition, namely, the search for and construction of meaning. Here too there are different but complementary and interactive issues to consider with regard to the ways in which people make sense of learning tasks, both general and specific, perceive themselves as learners, and conceptualise the whole learning process. Allied to this are the cognitive and metacognitive strategies they employ in their attempts to solve the tasks with which they are presented, or even to avoid doing so in order to maintain their feelings of self-worth (Covington, 1992).

In this area also the development of mental models has been found to be helpful in analysing what happens in the minds of those who are grappling with learning to read. The interested reader is referred to Underwood and Batt (1996) and

Oakhill and Garnham (1988) for fuller explications of this approach. Within the so-called "situational" model of text comprehension, it is assumed that three types of mental representations are made: a surface representation formed from the words on the page, a prepositional representation inferred from the connection between the words in the text, and a situational representation which draws upon prior knowledge and the ability to construct new knowledge. A central aspect of these representations is the ability to draw inferences and the willingness to do so, together with the ability to discriminate between relevant and irrelevant information. A distinction has been drawn between causal inferences, which draw upon working memory and are used to build relationships between various aspects or events within the text, and elaborative inferences, which draw upon information in long-term memory to build upon what is given (Byrne & Liberman, 1999).

ALTERNATIVE COGNITIVE MODELS

Within cognitive psychology the whole process of thinking and learning has been subject to a similar process of construction of information-processing models. An early pioneer in this field was the now little-used Illinois Test of Psycholinguistic Abilities (ITPA) of Kirk and Kirk (1971), which was constructed in accordance with a tripartite *decoding, association, encoding* model allied to levels of automatic and representational processing. The demise of the ITPA was most probably related to the weaknesses of the test materials and the lack of evidence for the efficacy of the accompanying remediation activities (Hammill & Larsen, 1974), but the model itself had much to commend it as a simple means of making sense of the communication process and difficulties that can arise within it.

A similar model has been applied more recently to the identification of cognitive difficulties by Feuerstein and his associates (Feuerstein et al., 1979). Part of Feuerstein's theory of structural cognitive modifiability is the notion of learning *phase*. This is based upon a model of learning which incorporates the *input, elaboration* and *output* of information. Table 17.1 provides a description of the *deficient cognitive functions* (DCF) which Feuerstein considers can occur at each phase of the learning process.

Thus it is suggested that learning difficulties may arise at the *input* phase of information processing, for example, because the learner has an impulsive learning style or may suffer from blurred or sweeping perception of incoming stimuli. During the *elaboration* phase, it may well be that the learner is unable to discriminate between relevant and irrelevant cues in defining a problem or is lacking in spontaneous comparative behaviour. At the *output* phase an egocentric method of communication which draws no awareness of the needs of the recipient audience may be in evidence.

Such cognitive deficiencies are neither mutually exclusive nor necessarily sequential. Any one learner may manifest several cognitive deficiencies at any one time. However, they are not considered to be permanent traits but aspects of current retarded performance which can be improved by means of mediated learning experiences (Kozulin & Rand, 2000).

Table 17.1 Description of the deficient cognitive functions in Feuerstein's model

The key cognitive functions are usually described in negative terms, i.e. where they are deficient or missing, and are categorised under three headings: INPUT, ELABORATION and OUTPUT. Although there is necessarily a sequential aspect to these categories, they can also be seen as overlapping and contiguous.

- The INPUT level refers to those cognitive functions involved in gathering data when faced with a given problem, object or experience. The kinds of cognitive impairment that can hinder learning at this level are:
  1. Blurred and sweeping perception.
  2. Unplanned, impulsive and unsystematic exploratory behaviour.
  3. Inadequate receptive verbal tools necessary for understanding the task.
  4. Underdeveloped need for precision and accuracy in data-gathering.
  5. Inability to cope with more than one source of information at a time, thereby leading to piecemeal data-gathering.
  6. Impaired spatial orientation.
  7. Underdeveloped time concepts.
  8. Inability to conserve the constancy of size, shape, quantity, orientation when these are varied.
- The ELABORATION level refers to those cognitive functions involved in making efficient use of available data and existing cues. The kinds of cognitive impairment that can hinder learning at this level are:
  1. Lack of awareness that a problem even exists.
  2. Inability to define the nature of the problem.
  3. Inability to select relevant rather than irrelevant cues.
  4. Lack of spontaneous comparative behaviour.
  5. Inability to draw upon information already stored in one's brain.
  6. Lack of recognition of the need to pursue logical evidence.
  7. Inability to constantly "stay with" a problem in the real world rather than "drifting off" into fantasy or onto a totally irrelevant tack.
  8. Inability to internalise a problem rather than deal only with its external features.
  9. Inability to make hypotheses and draw inferences.
  10. Inadequate strategies for testing one's hypotheses.
  11. Lack of framework for problem-solving behaviour.
  12. Inability to automatically summarise information at one's disposal.
  13. Restricted use of concepts due to inadequate or underdeveloped verbal tools (language).
  14. Impaired ability to plan ahead.
- The OUTPUT level refers to those cognitive functions required to effectively communicate to others the outcome of one's elaborative processes. Here cognitive impairment may take the form of
  1. an egocentric form of communication that does not take into account the needs of the recipient (s).
  2. Impulsive expression of thoughts and actions.
  3. Underdeveloped verbal tools to communicate adequately elaborated responses.
  4. Lack of recognition of the need for precision and accuracy in use of words and concepts in communicating clearly to others.
  5. Emotional or physiological blocking of responses.

The application of Feuerstein's DCF model to the assessment of dyslexic-type difficulties offers interesting possibilities for differential diagnosis, particularly if carried out as a process of dynamic assessment (Feuerstein et al., 1979; Lidz, 1987). If those manifesting learning difficulties of a dyslexic nature do differ in their general and specific cognitive processing from those exhibiting literacy difficulties for other reasons, what we might expect to find is a differential pattern of cognitive strengths and weaknesses with specific action implications. It has been commonly assumed, for example, that one distinguishing feature of dyslexic individuals compared to those with more general learning difficulties is the specific cognitive strengths of the former group. If this is the case, then we might hypothesise that dyslexic difficulties are more likely to be related to cognitive deficiencies at the input phase of learning than at the elaboration phase, and that the application of metacognitive strategies is likely to offer a profitable means of remedial intervention (see Wray's chapter in this volume, Chapter 19). Those manifesting difficulties of a dyspraxic nature, on the other hand, might be expected to display their main weaknesses at the output level. Evidence in support of the first hypothesis could be inferred from studies which have found the listening comprehension of people diagnosed with dyslexica to be significantly in advance of their measured reading comprehension (Bedford-Feuell et al., 1995).

The DCF model provides us, moreover, with the opportunity of breaking away from more global approaches to the assessment process within the cognitive domain. Just as no literacy expert would accept a simple word recognition test as a true or, in itself, an even particularly helpful measure of reading ability, cognitive psychologists have come to reject the single IQ figure as anything more than limited information gathered from a specific test at a specific time under specific circumstances. Applying the DCF model as a means of understanding learning difficulties is analogous to applying error analysis to making sense of reading or spelling difficulties. The main difference here, however, is the effort to go beyond the learner's manifest performance to gain deeper insights into underlying cognitive structures.

Feuerstein first drew the distinction between manifest performance and underlying potential in his seminal work, *The Dynamic Assessment of Retarded Performers* (Feuerstein et al., 1979) in which he introduced the notion of "dynamic", as opposed to "static", assessment by means of the *Learning Potential Assessment Device*. Here he argues for a total rethinking of the way in which assessment is carried out, based not only on the DCF model but also upon an interactive style which made it possible for the person being assessed to contribute meaningfully in a series of "mini-learning situations" similar in kind to Miller et al.'s (1961) test-operate-test-exit (TOTE) model.

Thus, when faced with a person displaying severe, ongoing literacy difficulties, an assessor taking a dynamic approach would provide the learner with a variety of learning tasks within the literacy domain, then seek to discover what sense was being made of the tasks and how they were being approached (Clay, 1993). Analysing these aspects of the learner's actions might well reveal that there were problems at the *input* level, because the nature of the literacy task wasn't properly understood or was being tackled in an impulsive manner. Alternatively (or even at the same time), problems might be occurring at the *elaboration* level because of an inability to draw comparisons between meaningful letter groupings, use analogies or develop appropriate strategies, or at the *output* level due to expressive language or motor difficulties, or egocentric communication patterns. We might find, therefore, that, at the level of the individual, some patterns of dyslexic difficulties are related to problems at the initial information-input phase, whilst others related more to how individual learners' thoughts about reading or spelling were being organised at the elaboration phase, or to some aspect of output performance such as letter formation or serialisation.

The next step in the dynamic assessment process is to work out with the learner an appropriate set of strategies to apply to future learning tasks and mediate how and when these might be used. Further tasks of a similar nature to those previously causing difficulty are then provided, and the learner's performance carefully monitored. Once success has been achieved at this level, then application of the new strategies to future learning tasks is encouraged and, later, evaluated.

It can be seen that such an approach, whilst accepting that some common patterns are likely to emerge, assumes that each individual displaying difficulties of a dyslexic nature is likely to do so for a wide range of different reasons and therefore likely to be unique in his or her learning style. At one level there is confirmation for such conceptions as impulsive vs reflective learning styles (Kagan, 1966), deep vs surface learning (Biggs, 1987), and possibly even field dependence vs field independence (Witkin et al., 1962). At another level, however, it is the unique way in which each individual makes sense of their world and deals cognitively with the learning tasks with which they are faced that the dynamic approach to assessment seeks to identify and build upon.

For some, such as Sternberg (1997), this might involve reconceptualising learning styles as learning *preferences* and seeking to build on these, but for Feuerstein and others the challenge is literally to change learners' minds (Sharron, 1987). The approach taken by Feuerstein and his co-workers in Israel has been to construct a thinking skills development programme known as *Instrumental Enrichment* (IE) (Feuerstein et al., 1980). This programme, which consists of 14 sets of cognitive activities, each of which is aimed at the development of one or another aspect of efficient and effective cognitive functioning, can be employed as part of the normal school curriculum or as the basis for an individualised intervention process.

As yet, little systematic research employing IE as part of a literacy intervention programme has been recorded (but see Brainin's fascinating doctoral thesis (1982) as an excellent example of how this can be done). However, it would not be difficult to construct a literacy programme which builds upon and runs parallel to many of the 14 "instruments" of IE. *Organisation of Dots*, for example, presents a series of problems in the form of an amorphous mass, as, surely, does much printed material to those with severe literacy difficulties. Here the learner has to work out how to identify and supply appropriate strategies for shaping the dots into meaningful figures of a required nature. *Analytic Perception* is mainly concerned with learning to apply systematic search strategies in analysing complex visual problems and establishing figure–ground relationships. *Comparisons* deals with the fundamental skill of identifying similarities and differences at both a global and a fine-detailed level. This is later built upon in *Categorisations*, which demonstrates the importance of classification as a cognitive skill. Following dynamic assessment, identified areas of cognitive deficiency or weakness can be strengthened by the application of relevant aspects of programme and related literacy activities.

The suggestion by Stanovich (1988a) that dyslexia may be the result of core phonological deficits in conjunction with other information-processing deficiencies fits well with such an approach. There are other researchers, moreover, who claim that, however helpful phonological training may be, it is unlikely to be in itself the full or only answer for those with persisting literacy difficulties (Torgesen, 1995; Bus & Van Ijzendoorn, 1999). Thus, phonological difficulties may be considered a necessary but insufficient condition for a diagnosis of dyslexia.

Another cognitive approach to the assessment and remediation of dyslexic difficulties that appears particularly promising is the Das–Naglieri Cognitive Assessment System, usually referred to as *PASS* because it focuses on *planning, attention, simultaneous processing and successive processing* (Das & Naglieri, 1993; Das et al., 2000). This in turn has given rise to the *PASS Reading Enhancement Program* (PREP) which aims to improve simultaneous and successive processing in particular. An impressive and increasing body of research data is beginning to appear in support of the efficacy of this approach (Boden & Kirby, 1995; Carlson & Das, 1997; Parrila et al., 1999).

LEARNER SELF-PERCEPTION

The information-processing approach to cognition and learning has tended to focus exclusively upon constructing models to describe and explain how these processes function. Helpful though this is proving to be, it is only part of the story. An alternative or, more pertinently, a complementary cognitive approach is one in which the focus is directed on individual meaning-making. This constructivist perspective is exemplified by Kelly's Personal Construct theory (Salmon, 1995; Denicolo & Pope, 2001), within which every individual is considered to be a scientist in her or his own right, constantly seeking to make sense of the world by imposing a personal template on it.

The assumption here is that even more important than what happens to an individual learner is the sense that the learner makes of what happens and the subsequent action that he or she takes to adjust to this. Relating this to the Stanovich (1988b) phonological core variable difference model leads me to suggest that some of the distal variables referred to might include the view that a person with dyslexic difficulties has of her/himself as a learner, the attributions that they make for their successes and failures in learning, the level of importance that becoming literate has for them, the perceived level of importance that it has for their parents, the assumed consequences of refusal to try, and so on.

One consequence of developing a negative attitude set towards any educational activity as a result of initial learning difficulties is likely to be avoidance of that activity wherever or however possible. Motivation theorists such as Covington (1992) would account for this in terms of *self-worth concern*, where a failure to try can be ascribed to the individual's efforts to maintain feelings of self-worth by refusing to attempt activities in which s/he feels likely to fail. Others, such as Seligman (1975), on the other hand, refer to the consequences of repeated early failure in terms of feelings of *learned helplessness* accumulating as a result of those failures (see also Smiley & Dweck, 1994).

A related area of potentially great significance, which has been relatively unexplored in relation to dyslexia, has been that of learning self-concept. There has tended to be an assumption that all aspects of an individual's self-esteem are likely to be affected by being faced with learning difficulties of a dyslexic nature (Edwards, 1994). It may well be, however, that such an assumption is far too simplistic. Some will undoubtedly demonstrate overall depression or emotional disturbance, but others are likely to display extraordinary determination and application to overcome their difficulties and will refuse to be beaten by them.

It is important under such circumstances to discriminate between *global self-esteem*, which might be high or low for a variety of reasons, and *learning self-concept* which focuses in a non-evaluative way on the individual's perception of her/himself as a learner. In the latter case we might reasonably expect a person with specific learning difficulties to present a differential pattern of perceptions of his/her learning strengths and weaknesses.

The *Myself-As-Learner Scale (MALS)* (Burden, 2000) was developed with the express purpose of providing a simple, valid and reliable means of assessing only those aspects of a person's self-concept that are related to the learning process. A growing body of research is revealing this approach to be of potentially great value in identifying surprising differences between children in this respect, independent of IQ and achievement. Although significant correlations have been found between the MALS and measured cognitive abilities, there is an even closer relationship between learning self-concept and achievement in various educational areas than between IQ and achievement (Burden, 1998).

Of even greater interest to us in the present context is that clinical work with individuals suffering from dyslexic difficulties reveals a differential pattern of responses to the MALS in accordance with a wide range of associated factors. There are undoubtedly those whose overall learning self-concept is seriously affected by their history of repeated learning failure, particularly if this all-embracing view has been reinforced by significant others such as teachers and family members. In this respect self-concept and self-esteem are seen to merge, and a considerable amount of counselling or therapeutic work will need to be carried out before the individual can acquire the confidence to place her/himself at risk again with regard to learning in general.

In other instances, however, although an individual may declare strongly that s/he finds learning difficult, does not perform well in tests, needs lots of help with her/his work, and gets anxious when faced with new work, there may also be an acknowledgement that thinking carefully about one's work helps one to do it better, that problem-solving can be fun, that one might be good at discussing things, and even that in certain circumstances one might be clever. Here the counselling approach would be different, focusing more upon an exploration of the individual's perceived strengths as a means of understanding and coming to terms with his/her dyslexic difficulties.

A third, less common group are those demonstrating significant dyslexic difficulties who appear to have unrealistically positive learning self-concepts. Such individuals can reasonably be assumed to be heavily defended against facing up to the actuality of their learning difficulties by presenting an untroubled front to others and even themselves. The appropriate counselling approach here would be to work on getting the individual to develop a more realistic perspective without allowing this to damage their self-esteem.

The issue with which we are dealing here is that of *locus of control*, which is itself an aspect of *attribution theory* (Weiner, 1985; Williams & Burden, 1999). The key question asked here is "To what do I attribute the successes and failures in my life?" Attribution theory proposes that the reasons people give may be ones which they see as *internal* to themselves or as *externally* caused by powerful others. Furthermore, such attributions may be seen as *changeable* or *unchangeable*, and *controllable* or *uncontrollable*.

A person with dyslexic difficulties might attribute those difficulties to lack of ability on their part, which they might also see as unchangeable and outside their control. On the other hand, they might equally well interpret their difficulties as due to lack of effort or appropriate strategy use, which they might see as changeable and within their control. The first explanation would be more likely to lead to a sense of learned helplessness than the second (Hiebert et al., 1984). The purpose of remedial counselling here, therefore, will be to focus on some form of attribution retraining whereby the learner is helped to acknowledge that the locus of responsibility for overcoming his/her difficulties must be internalised, viewed as changeable, and accepted as being within her/his control. An attributional style which interprets failure in terms of inappropriate learning strategies accompanied by determined effort is much more likely to be helpful to the dyslexic individual than one which falls back on a perception of low ability or insurmountable task difficulty.

As yet, the possible application of attribution theory to exploring the self-concepts of those with dyslexic difficulties has received little attention, but would appear to offer considerable scope for worthwhile research and practical intervention.

BROADENING THE PERSPECTIVE

It is now generally accepted that individuals do not exist or learn in a vacuum. Learning difficulties of a dyslexic nature can no longer reasonably be seen as genetically imposed, lifelong characteristics of individual learners which arise in some decontextualised manner. Thinking and learning are not personal characteristics but socio-cultural processes. In this respect dyslexia must be seen as one aspect of a discursive process within which the dynamic interaction of learners, their teachers, the valued learning activities and the learning contexts shapes the meaning of the term.

This chapter has focused mainly upon the ways in which individual learners manifesting literacy difficulties of a dyslexic nature make sense of the learning tasks with which they are faced and of their own perceived failure to accomplish those tasks. What should not be overlooked, however, is the important role of parents and teachers as providers of mediated learning experiences (Kozulin & Rand, 2000), the specific nature of reading, writing and spelling as cultural artefacts, and the need for understanding and supportive environments at every level (classroom, school, regional, national). Only when all of these factors are functioning together in a holistic manner will the problems faced by those manifesting learning difficulties of a dyslexic nature be overcome.

REFERENCES

Aarnoutse, C., van Leeuwe, J., Voeten, M. & Oud, H. (2001) Development of decoding, reading comprehension, vocabulary and spelling during the elementary school years. *Reading and Writing: An Interdisciplinary Journal*, 14, 61–89.

Bedford-Feuell, C., Geiger, S., Moyse, S. & Turner, M. (1995) Use of listening comprehension in the identification and assessment of specific learning difficulties. *Educational Psychology in Practice*, 10(4), 207–214.

Biggs, J. B. (1987) *Student Approaches to Learning and Studying*. Camberwell, Australia: Australian Council for Educational Research.

Boden, C. & Kirby, J. R. (1995) Successive processing, phonological coding and the remediation of reading. *Journal of Cognitive Education*, 4(2+3), 19–32.

Brainin, S. S. (1982) The effects of Instrumental Enrichment on the reasoning abilities, reading achievement and task orientation of sixth grade underachievers. EdD Thesis, Columbia University Teachers' College.

British Psychological Society (BPS) (1999) *Dyslexia, Literacy and Psychological Assessment*. Report by a working party of the Division of Educational and Child Psychology (DECP). Leicester: British Psychological Society.

Burden, R. L. (1998) Assessing children's perceptions of themselves as learners and problem solvers: the construction of the Myself-As-Learner Scale (MALS). *School Psychology International*, 19(4), 291–305.

Burden, R. L. (2000) *The Myself-As-Learner Scale (MALS)*. Windsor: NFER-Nelson.

Bus, A. G. & Van Ijzendoorn, M. H. (1999) Phonological awareness and early reading: A metaanalysis of experimental training studies. *Journal of Educational Psychology*, 91, 403–414.

Byrne, B. & Liberman, A. M. (1999) Meaninglessness, productivity and reading. Some observations about the relation between alphabet and speech. In J. Oakhill & R. Beard (eds) *Reading Development and the Teaching of Reading*. Oxford: Blackwell.

Carlson, J. & Das, J. P. (1997) A process approach to remediating word-decoding deficiencies in chapter 1 children. *Learning Disabilities Quarterly*, 20, 93–102.

Clay, M. M. (1993) *An Observation Survey of Early Literacy Achievement*. Auckland: Heinemann.

Covington, M. E. (1992) *Making the Grade*. Cambridge: CUP.

Das, J. P. & Kendrick, M. (1997) PASS Reading Enhancement Program: A short manual for teachers. *Journal of Cognitive Education*, 5, 193–208.

Das, J. P. & Naglieri, J. A. (1993) *Das-Naglieri: Cognitive Assessment System (DN-CAS)*. Chicago: Riverside Publishing Co.

Das, J. P., Parrila, R. K. & Papadopoulos, T. C. (2000) Cognitive education and reading disability. In A. Kozulin & Y. Rand (eds) *Experience of Mediated Learning: An Impact of Feuerstein's Theory in Education and Psychology*. Oxford: Pergamon.

Denicolo, P. & Pope, M. (2001) *Transformational Professional Practice: Personal Construct Approaches to Education and Research*. London: Whur.

Edwards, J. (1994) *The Scars of Dyslexia*. London: Cassell.

Feuerstein, R., Rand, Y. & Hoffman, M. (1979) *The Dynamic Assessment of Retarded Performers*. Baltimore: University Park Press.

Feuerstein, R., Rand, Y., Hoffman, M. & Miller, R. (1980) *Instrumental Enrichment: An Intervention Programme for Cognitive Modifiability*. Baltimore: University Park Press.

Frederickson, N., Frith, U. & Reason, R. (1997) *Phonological Assessment Battery (PhAB)*. Windsor: NFER-Nelson.

Frith, U. (1985) Beneath the surface of developmental dyslexia. In K. E. Patterson, J. C. Marshall & E. Coltheart (eds) *Surface Dyslexia: Neuropsychological and Cognitive Studies of Phonological Reading*. London: Erlbaum.

Goswami, U. (1999), Phonological development and reading by analogy: Epilinguistic and metalinguistic issues. In J. Oakhill & R. Beard (eds) *Reading Development and the Teaching of Reading*. Oxford: Blackwell.

Hammill, D. D. & Larsen, J. C. (1974) The effectiveness of psycholinguistic training. *Exceptional Children*, 41(1), 5–14.

Hiebert, E. H., Winograd, P. N. & Danner, F. W. (1984) Children's attributions for failure and success in different aspects of reading. *Journal of Educational Psychology*, 76, 1139–1148.

Kagan, J. (1966) Reflection-impulsivity: The generality and dynamics of conceptual tempo. *Journal of Abnormal Psychology*, 71, 17–27.

Kirk, S. A. & Kirk, W. D. (1971) *Psycholinguistic Learning Disabilities: Diagnosis and Remediation*. Urbana, IL: University of Illinois Press.

Kozulin, A. & Rand, Y. (eds) (2000) *Experience of Mediated Learning: An Impact of Feuerstein's Theory in Education and Psychology*. London: Pergamon.

Kozulin, A. (1999) *Psychological Tools*. Cambridge, MA: Harvard University Press.

Langley, P., Simon, H. A., Bradshaw, G. L. & Zytkow, J. M. (1987) *Scientific Discovery: Computational Explorations of the Creative Process*. Cambridge, MA: MIT Press.

Lidz, C. S. (ed) (1987) *Dynamic Assessment*. New York: Guilford.

Miller, G. A., Galanter, E. & Pribram, K. H. (1961) *Plans and the Structure of Behaviour*. New York: Holt, Rinehart & Winston.

Oakhill, J. & Garnham, A. (1988) *Becoming a Skilled Reader*. Oxford: Blackwell.

Palmer, S. (2000) Development of phonological recoding and literacy acquisition: A four year cross-sequential study. *British Journal of Developmental Psychology*, 18, 533–555.

Parrila, R. K., Das, J. P., Kendrick, M. E., Papadopoulos, T. C. & Kirby, J. R. (1999) Efficacy of a cognitive reading remediation program for at-risk children in grade 1. *Developmental Disabilities Bulletin*, 27(2), 1–31.

Phye, G. D. (1993) Learning and remembering the basis for personal knowledge construction. In G. D. Phye (ed) *Handbook of Academic Learning*. San Diego: Academic Press.

Royer, J. M. (1993) A cognitive perspective on the assessment, diagnosis and remediation of reading skills. In G. D. Phye (ed) *Handbook of Academic Learning*. San Diego: Academic Press.

Salmon, P. (1995) *Psychology in the Classroom*. London: Cassell.

Seligman, M. (1975) *Helplessness: On Depression, Development and Death*. San Francisco: Freeman.

Sharron, H. (1987) *Changing Children's Minds*. London: Souvenir Press.

Simon, H. A. (1979) *Models of Thought*. New Haven: Yale University Press.

Smiley, P. A. & Dweck, C. S. (1994) Individual differences in achievement goals among young children. *Child Development*, 65, 1723–1743.

Snowling, M. (1998) Reading development and its difficulties. *Educational and Child Psychology*, 15(2), 44–58.

Stanovich, K. E. (1986) Matthew effects in reading: Some consequences of individual differences in the acquisition of literacy. *Reading Research Quarterly*, 21, 73–113.

Stanovich, K. E. (1988a) The right and wrong places to look for the cognitive locus of reading disability. *Annals of Dyslexia*, 38, 154–177.

Stanovich, K. E. (1988b) Explaining the differencess between dyslexic and the garden-variety poor reader: The phonological-core variable-difference model. *Journal of Learning Disabilities*, 21, 590–604, 612.

Sternberg, R. (1997) *Thinking Styles*. New York: CUP.

Torgesen, J. K. (1995) Instruction for reading disabled children: Questions about knowledge into practice. *Issues in Education*, 1.1, 91–95.

Underwood, G. & Batt, V. (1996) *Reading and Understanding*. Oxford: Blackwell.

Weiner, B. (1985) An attributional theory of achievement motivation and emotion. *Psychological Review*, 92, 548–573.

Williams, M. D. & Burden, R. L. (1999) Students' developing conceptions of themselves as language learners. *The Modern Language Journal*, 83(ii), 193–201.

Witkin, H. A., Dyk. R. B., Faterson, H. F., Goodenough, D. R. & Karp, S. A. (1962) *Psychological Differentiation*. New York: Wiley.

Chapter 18

PAIRED THINKING: DEVELOPING THINKING SKILLS THROUGH STRUCTURED INTERACTION WITH PEERS, PARENTS AND VOLUNTEERS

Keith Topping

"Readers are plentiful: thinkers are rare". (Harriet Martineau)

INTRODUCTION

"Thinking Skills" currently have a high profile. Everyone (including the government) is talking about the need to develop higher-order thinking. For the busy teacher overloaded with the National Literacy Hour, Numeracy Hour, national assessments and school inspections, how on earth to achieve this in practice is a problem. How to achieve it when there are one or more children in the class struggling with specific learning difficulties is an even bigger problem. This chapter describes how that problem might be turned into an opportunity.

WAYS OF DEVELOPING THINKING SKILLS

Past approaches to thinking skills were arguably of three types:

1. Teaching thinking skills embedded in a traditional curriculum subject (e.g. science).
2. Teaching thinking skills "across the curriculum"—infused into all curriculum subjects.
3. Teaching thinking skills as an abstract, free-standing activity, using special activities, tasks or games.

Dyslexia and Literacy: Theory and Practice. Edited by Gavin Reid and Janice Wearmouth.
© 2002 John Wiley & Sons, Ltd.

There has been considerable debate about the relative merits of these different approaches (Powell, 1987; Nickerson, 1988; Nisbet & Davies, 1990).

There are some very successful and well researched examples of the "embedded" type 1. A good example of this approach is the CASE (Cognitive Acceleration through Science Education) program of Adey and Shayer (1994). Perkins and Grotzer (1997) reviewed studies designed to teach students to be more able thinkers in particular subject areas. History, Social Studies, Psychology, and many other subjects feature. But do the gains transfer to other subject areas?

The problem with the "infusion" type 2 is that it requires very gifted, well organised and hard-working teachers in every subject area. The early work of Louis Raths and his colleagues (1967) offered an elaborated typology of questioning, which could be used by teachers in virtually any subject, as well as a typology of "thinking styles". A review of 26 studies of teaching students to generate questions as a means of improving their comprehension and thinking skills was conducted by Rosenshine et al. (1996). Overall, modest effect sizes in terms of outcomes on standardised tests were balanced by substantial effect sizes on criterion-referenced assessments.

In the UK, Coles and Robinson conducted a survey of a great many programmes for teaching thinking in 1991, summarising the "explosion" in the field in recent years. McGuinness (1999) reviewed the effectiveness of approaches for developing the thinking of school students, concluding that the teaching of thinking skills as a scheduled activity was less effective than the creation of the "thinking classroom". However, McGuiness acknowledges difficulties with implementing the "infusion" approach systematically on a whole-school basis, and provides no data on longer term maintenance of gains.

The problem with type 3 (the "bolt-on" approach) is that it tends to gobble up even more timetable space, and there are even bigger doubts about transfer of skills to other situations. Students who have learned to do "intelligence games" very competently, but still act stupidly in other aspects of their lives, have gained rather little.

Philosophy for Children (Lipman, 1984) aims to strengthen children's powers of reasoning and moral judgement through Socratic dialogue and other forms of discussion, intended to sharpen conceptual definition and analysis. Students bring any issues of interest to them into the dialogue. In addition to studies conducted by Lipman, there is some independent evidence of increased achievement in traditional subjects as well as reasoning, and of improvement in personal and interpersonal skills (Lim, 1995; Niklasson et al., 1996; Garcia-Moriyon et al., 2000). In the UK, the related work of Fisher (1990) is popular.

DeBono's work on "lateral thinking" is well known (e.g. DeBono, 1990). His CoRT programme of 60 thinking skills lessons for students aged 12 years or more is also long-established, but there is limited evidence of consistent gains, particularly of transfer to curriculum subjects.

Reuven Feuerstein's Instrumental Enrichment (IE) programme consists of 13 sections, each containing between one and 24 activities, to be taught for five hours each week for two years. It involves a general problem-solving model, including the stages of input, elaboration and output. An evaluation study indicated modest effect sizes on a type of intelligence test, with little significant transfer to performance in school subjects. However, there was evidence of greater differences at long-term follow-up (Rand et al., 1981). The empirical research on IE was reviewed by Savell et al. (1986), and by Shayer and Beasley (1987), suggesting that the evidence for generalised effects was tentative, and questioning cost-effectiveness. Blagg (1991) evaluated the impact of IE in the one large education authority in the UK using multiple outcome measures, but found no differences between experimental and control students on any measure, although there were questions about implementation integrity.

In a meta-analysis of 20 controlled studies of instruction for critical thinking, Bangert-Drowns and Bankert (1990) found that methods involving explicit instruction that addressed generalisation issues yielded the highest effect sizes.

However, virtually all the research literature is concerned with teacher-directed instruction in thinking skills. Much of it relates to higher education rather than schools. Very little focuses on developing thinking skills in pupils with specific learning difficulties. Very little is concerned with peer tutoring of thinking skills (with a few notable exceptions, discussed below). There is practically no literature on parent or volunteer tutoring of thinking skills. Thus the Paired Thinking method makes a significant original contribution to research and practice.

PEER TUTORING OF THINKING SKILLS

Over the years, many methods have included different constellations of a similar or common core of strategies. Prediction, Questioning and Summarising are particularly common features. However, even methods involving peer interaction have often involved a high degree of direct instruction and intervention by the professional teacher, rather than developing true learner-managed learning.

The Reciprocal Teaching method emerged from Annemarie Palincsar and Ann Brown (1988), with Prediction, Questioning, Summarising and Clarifying as the key strategies. Rosenshine and Meister (1994) published an excellent review of 16 quantitative studies of reciprocal teaching, which generally supported the efficacy of this method.

Yuill and Oakhill (1988) developed Inference Awareness Training, requiring children to make inferences, generate questions and check comprehension. Outcomes were positive with small numbers of lower-ability children, but no better than from more traditional comprehension exercises.

Transactional Strategies Instruction (Brown et al., 1996) is a year-long programme that instructs students in specific strategies to guide problem-solving when experiencing a failure of comprehension. (The programme thus seems to require high levels of 'meta-ignorance' in the students—the ability to know that they do not know.) TSI has proved effective in raising scores on standardised measures of reading comprehension with low-achieving children in second grade, in comparison to distal control groups.

Reading Comprehension strategy instruction and co-operative small-group learning were blended in Collaborative Strategic Reading (Klingner & Vaughn, 1999), which has demonstrated effectiveness in at least one controlled study. However, extending this into paired peer tutoring, with more precise specification of interactive behaviour, is relatively rare.

Bowers (1991) described the use of peer tutoring in second and third grade with at-risk students, who applied critical thinking skills to reading activities, 30 minutes each day for 12 weeks. The tutees improved from scores at the 35th percentile (on average) to post-test scores of 95%, but no control group was assessed.

The PALS (Peer Assisted Learning Strategies) programme integrates comprehension strategies (including re-telling, summarising, predicting and elaborated help-giving) within classwide peer tutoring. In a series of studies by Lynn and Doug Fuchs and their colleagues, PALS students were found to make greater gains in reading comprehension than controls, although elaborated help-giving proved more effective with older students (Simmons et al., 1994; Fuchs et al., 1999).

Mastropieri and Scruggs (2000) deployed reciprocal peer tutoring in comprehension strategies with middle-school students with learning disabilities. There was a strong emphasis on summarisation activity. Performance on reading comprehension tests showed significant performance advantages for students involved in tutoring, compared to a traditional reading instruction condition.

Alison King's (1999) approach essentially involves scaffolding "discourse patterns" through "guided peer questioning". Structured question stems are used to promote analytic and critical discourse in dyads and in small groups, at three levels of complexity. The programme has been shown to improve the solving of novel problems, in a controlled study. King (1997) developed the "Ask To Think—Tel Why" (*sic*) peer tutoring model, involving five types of questions (to review, elaborate, build, probe, hint, solicit meta-cognition, and so on). King et al. (1998) involved 58 seventh-graders in peer tutoring. The same-age, same-ability, same-gender dyads successfully reciprocally scaffolded higher-order thinking and learning. The trained discourse pattern was quite different from naturalistic untrained tutorial dialogue patterns.

The relatively few studies of peer tutoring in thinking skills have thus generally found encouraging results. This is in contrast to the teacher-directed methods that hitherto have been much more widely used, but generally poorly evaluated (with some notable exceptions).

Paired Thinking has strong links with King's work, in that it provides questions as cues to scaffold analytic and critical discourse between pairs. It differs from King's work in that it specifically builds that discourse on an individualised and differentiated reading experience chosen and shared by the pair.

PAIRED THINKING: WHAT IS IT?

Embedding the teaching of thinking skills in the transferable skill of reading has the advantage that reading is probably the most used means of obtaining information that requires deep processing, despite the competing claims of listening comprehension and visual comprehension. It is unclear quite where the borderline might be between thinking skills and "higher order reading skills" that focus on deep comprehension, but maybe this does not matter in practice.

Paired Thinking (PT) is a framework for pairs working together. Some difference in reading ability is needed in each pair. The pairs can be:

- peers of the same or different ages
- parents working with children at home
- teaching assistants working with children in school
- volunteer adults (such as senior citizens) working with children in school.

PT is:

- very active and interactive—both the helper and the helped child are busy thinking all the time
- low-cost to implement (in teacher time and other resources)
- socially inclusive (all children have an opportunity to participate)
- flexible (adaptive to a great variety of different neighbourhood, school and classroom contexts, and pupils of a wide range of ability)
- durable (remaining to some extent effective when less than perfectly implemented or disrupted by pupil and teacher absence or other factors).

PT "piggy-backs" thinking skills upon reading skills, particularly upon the specific structured method of "Paired Reading" (PR). It takes PR into higher-order reading skills and beyond.

PAIRED READING: WHAT IS IT?

The PR method has long been well known. PR is a kind of supported or assisted reading. It is intended only for use with individually chosen, highly motivating non-fiction or fiction books which are *above* the independent readability level of the tutee (but of course within the independent readability level of the tutor).

However, the name has been a problem—the phrase "Paired Reading" has such a warm, comfortable feel to it that some people have loosely applied it to almost anything that two people do together with a book. Of course, the effectiveness research only applies to "proper" Paired Reading—the specific and structured technique (described in Topping, 1995, 2001a).

In a recent review of the effectiveness of 20 interventions in reading, PR ranked as one of the most effective (Brooks et al., 1998, second edition in print at time of writing). The PR method has now been very widely disseminated all over the world, and has been demonstrated to be effective with thousands of children in hundreds of schools. It has been the subject of many research reviews (e.g. Topping & Whiteley, 1990; Topping & Lindsay, 1992; Topping, 1995, 2001a). There are many controlled studies demonstrating effectiveness. Follow-up studies indicate that gains are sustained and do not "wash out" over time.

A recent large-scale project involved cross-age peer tutoring using PR in many primary schools (the "Read On" project in Scotland—not the same as Read On in England). Pairings were typically between whole classes of 6–7-year-old and 10–11-year-old pupils. Pre–post reading test gains for *both tutors and tutees* were substantially larger than normally expected, and larger in experimental groups than control groups. Overall, the least able tutees gained the most on test, and the least able tutors gained the most. Low-ability tutors produced tutee gains at least equivalent to those produced by high-ability tutors, and low-ability tutors themselves gained more than high-ability tutors. Overall, male tutors did better than female tutors in terms of their own test gains, so perhaps boys learn better by being tutors than by being tutored.

Social gains were also widely reported. Each participating teacher recorded their observations of child behaviour in the classroom during PR. Very few teachers did not observe a positive shift in the majority of their children. For generalisation of positive effects to other subject areas and outside the classroom, the effects were not quite as strong, but still very positive, especially in motivation. Particularly striking were the improvements in pupil self-esteem and social competence (ability to relate to each other).

PT usually involves starting with PR, then moving the pairs on to "Reading And Thinking", expanding and developing the discussion inherent within PR. PT involves training tutors and tutees to ask increasingly "intelligent questions" about what they have read together. It thus develops Socratic questioning—a thinking skills method about 2500 years old.

HOW DOES PAIRED THINKING WORK?

"There is more to be learned from the unexpected questions of children than the discourses of men." (John Locke)

Paired Thinking provides:

* modelling of intelligent questioning for the tutee
* interactive cognitive challenge for both partners
* practice in critical and analytic thinking
* scaffolding
* feedback
* praise and other social reinforcement.

Paired Thinking also:

* flexibly applies to any reading experience shared by the pair
* enables the pair to pursue their own interests and motivations
* is highly adapted to the individual learner's needs of the moment
* is democratic and encourages learner-managed learning
* encourages critical and analytic discussion in the pair's vernacular vocabulary
* encourages self-disclosure of faulty or deficient thinking.

Paired Thinking thus includes Reading, Listening, Thinking, Feeling and Communicating. It also aims to help pupils to identify, review and evaluate the values they and others hold, and recognise how these affect thoughts and actions.

The PT structure of the 13 Activities in the three Stages is outlined in Box 18.1, together with some example (model or prompt) questions for each activity. The 13 Activities are supported by prompt sheets of questions, available in four differentiated Levels of complexity and difficulty, to suit different pairs and provide developmental progression. However, tutors are very much encouraged to view the prompt sheet only as a training and fallback resource, and to generate their own questions of high relevance to the text and their partner.

Box 18.1   Stages and activities in PT

BEFORE READING

(Priming)

Structure	"What do the parts of the book tell us?"
Type	"What kind of book is it?"
Difficulty	"How hard is it?"
Reader Aims	"What do you want from the book?"

DURING READING

(Formative)

Author Aims	"What does the writer want?"
Meaning	"What does it mean?"
Truth	"Is it true?"
Prediction	"What might happen next?"
Links	"What does it remind us of?"

AFTER READING

(Formative and Summative)

Summarise	"What are the main ideas?"
Evaluate	"How do you feel about it?"
Revisit	"What did you remember about it?"
Extend	"Have you questioned anything else?"

The interactive behaviour required is outlined in the Tips For Tutors handout, main points from which are summarised in Box 18.2. These are abbreviated for everyday use in the Tips For Tutors Reminder sheet. When initially presenting them to pairs, teachers often present just a few at a time, and not necessarily in this order.

Box 18.2   Interactive behaviour: tips for tutors

- Your *aim* is to *improve* the tutee's *quality of thinking* by asking helpful and *intelligent questions* which give clues. This is not as easy as you might think!
- Tutors have to think hard, too—they do not just work through a list of given questions. Good thinking is not easy—for either of you.

- You need to put tutees at their ease, boost their confidence, and *encourage* them to trust you—or they will be afraid to let you know what they are thinking.
- During reading, pause quite often at any *natural break* in the reading to think and talk about what you have read. This is especially difficult DURING reading—easier Before and After.
- Remember tutees don't know as much as you do, so *don't expect too much* or push them too hard.
- The questions listed are only examples to get you started—please do *think up your own questions* as well. Your own questions should encourage the tutee to say whatever they really think, not push them towards one "right answer".
- Some of the listed questions apply only to story books, some apply only to information books. Just *leave out the questions which don't apply* to the book you are reading.
- In the "During Reading" Stage, the five Activities (Author Aims, Meaning, Truth, Prediction, Links) can be worked through in *any order*. Choose any relevant questions from any Activity at any time.
- *It's OK* for *both* tutors and tutees *to say* they *"don't know"*—but be clear about what you need to know and think about how you might find out.
- *Never* say *"No"* or *"That's wrong"*—always ask another question to give a clue.
- Although there are many questions, *it is not a "test"* for the tutee. Indeed, often *there is no one "right" answer*, only many "better" or "worse" answers. Work toward getting more "better" answers. But even the tutor need not know the answer to the question at the beginning—you can work it out together.
- *Give* the tutees some *time to think*—they will not usually be able to answer straight away. But if they think for more than half a minute without success, maybe they need a clue in another question.
- *Praise* the tutee for all thoughtful responses—for example: "Good, I can tell you thought hard about that".
- Encourage tutees to *"think aloud"*, so you can hear HOW they are thinking and really understand them—if they think alone then just give you their final answer, you will not understand how they got there.
- You might "think aloud" yourself sometimes, to show them how to do it.
- Sometimes you can also try to *"brainstorm"* answers—this is where both of you say every possible answer that comes into your head, even if it seems silly or weird. Then choose the best.
- *Tutees can ask* tutors *questions*, too! Keep each other thinking!
- Tutors can say what they think, too—but be careful not to let tutees assume that must be the "right answer"—ask the tutee what they think as well.
- You might need to go back to *read bits* of the book *again* at any time to check on things or answer questions. When you do, you might want to read the difficult bit TO the tutee, so they can think about it.
- When you are stuck trying to think of a question quickly, *"How do you know that?"* is often a good one.
- When you are reading a longer book, you might find the tutee has trouble *remembering* everything, even if they did understand it in the first place. If they don't remember, it does not always mean they never did *understand*.
- You might find tutees remember the beginning or end of a book better than the middle— but they do need to think about the middle as well!
- In the "After Reading" Stage when you are finding the main ideas or "Summarising", and choose to write down some keywords and/or write a summary for your classmates, it is usually *easier* if the *tutor does any writing*—but the tutor must not do all the thinking!
- In the "After Reading" Stage when you are doing "Self-Assessment", this is a good time to really *praise* each other—AGAIN!

Differentiation and Progression: Levels of Prompt Sheet

As we have noted, the 13 Activities are supported by prompt sheets, available in four differentiated Levels of complexity and difficulty, to suit different pairs and provide developmental progression. Some teachers differentiate these levels further, which is easily done as the materials are freely available as electronic files for adaptation and customisation as required (see Resources section below).

The 13 example questions listed in Box 18.1 constitute the whole content of the Level 1 question prompt sheet. For the training sessions and for subsequent regular sessions, all pairs start with a Level 1 Prompt Sheet.

As pairs progress at different rates in subsequent sessions, Level 2, 3 and 4 Prompt sheets can be issued to particular pairs as judged appropriate. Level 2 is intended to be a relatively small step from Level 1 (to encourage all concerned), so all pairs should eventually progress to Level 2. However, progression to Levels 3 and 4 will be much more dependent upon the different abilities of individual pairs. The Levels are intended to enable the project organiser to differentiate and individualise the thinking activities for different pairs progressively, adding layers of complexity and sophistication bit by bit, without making too much work.

To exemplify this progression, it is worth comparing the prompt questions at each Level for one Activity, namely Prediction (see Box 18.3).

Box 18.4   Prediction activity at levels 1, 2, 3 and 4

Level 1

"What might happen next?"

Level 2

"What might happen next?" (Prediction)

- What do you think might happen next?
- What might make this happen? How likely is this?
- Can you imagine or picture in your head what it would look like?
- Did the book end as you expected? How else might it have ended?

Level 3

"What might happen next?" (Prediction)

- What do the people in the book want or expect to happen next?
- What have you learnt about them which helps you to guess what they might do next?
- What do you think might happen next?
- How likely is this?
- What might cause this to happen?
- Might it depend on something else happening? What?
- Can you imagine or picture in your head what it would look like?
- Did the book end or conclude as you expected?
- How else might it have ended?

Level 4

"What might happen next?" (Prediction, Inference and Deduction)

- What do the people in the book want or expect to happen next? (Intentionality)
- What have you learnt about them which helps you to guess what they might do next? (Characterisation)
- What do *you* think might happen next? (Prediction)
- How likely is this? (Probability, Uncertainty)
- What might cause this to happen? (Causality)
- One cause or more? (Multiple, Complex, Interdependent Causality)
- How would you know what had really caused it? (Evidence)
- Might it depend on something else happening? What? (Conditionality)
- Will it *only* happen if something else happens?
- One thing or more than one? (Multiple, Complex, Interdependent Conditionality)
- Might there be a biggest or major cause? (Critical Factor or Incident)
- If this doesn't happens, what else might? (Alternatives)
- Can you imagine or picture in your head what it would look like? (Visual Imagery)
- Did the book end or conclude as you expected?
- How else might it have ended?

Thanks to the four differentiated levels of prompts, young and less able readers can participate, but the top level is certainly applicable to higher ability and age ranges. The Level 4 version of the questions is obviously very elaborate and over-inclusive—indeed, perhaps better suited to high school or even college students. However, some very able primary school pupils might prove able to handle it. At all levels, the intellectual strain on the tutor is quite considerable. Indeed, among both researchers and practitioners, there is now more interest in the impact of being a tutor than on the value of being a tutee.

ORGANISING PT IN THE CLASSROOM

Same-age within-class peer tutoring is easier to organise, but tends to lack the nurturing quality and wider effects on school ethos which characterise cross-age tutoring. In either format, pairs are matched to sustain a similar differential in reading ability in all pairs—matching the most able tutor with the most able tutee, and so on.

Paired Reading training should be carried out in the way described in detail in Topping (1995, 2001a). This typically takes about one hour or so.

PR should continue only for two to three weeks until pairs become fluent with the method, before moving on to PT. Some pairs (and especially peer tutors) find PT much more challenging than PR, and want to return to the easy, comfortable, flowing routine of PR, which does not unduly stretch their comfort zone. Diane Halpern (1998) addressed the issues involved in teaching critical thinking to transfer across domains, and from institutions of learning into the workplace. She proposed a four-part model for teaching and learning thinking skills. The first (and arguably most important) of these was the dispositional component, to prepare learners for the effort of cognitive challenge. The pairs should be conditioned from the outset to view PR as a transitional stage to PT, which will involve some brain strain. "Market" PT to students as a maturational progression from PR—a more "grown-up" thing to do. The PR/PT transition is also a good point to re-match some pairs where this is considered desirable.

Paired Thinking training also takes about one hour, and should be carried out in the way described in detail in Topping (2001a). As with all paired learning methods, train tutors and tutees together. The teacher first talks the pairs through the Level 1 prompt sheet and the most important of the Tips for Tutors, then spends 10 minutes (or so) reading a short book or self-explanatory chapter to all the pairs, telling them that they will later be practising "Paired Thinking" on the book.

The teacher then pretends to be a tutor in relation to the book—model asking some of the questions from the Level 1 prompt sheet, treating the whole training group as your "tutees". Solicit answers from any tutor or tutee—from as many different participants as will offer answers. Obviously it is difficult to demonstrate the "Before" questions on a book you have just unilaterally chosen to read to the whole group, but do the best you can.

Then change roles. You play the part of a tutee, and encourage all the participants to pretend to be your tutor and to ask you some of the questions. They should have their Level 1 prompt sheets to hand to help them. If you have a colleague present in support, they can act as a stooge "tutee" in the audience and fill in any gaps in the conversation.

Tell the pairs they will start doing Paired Thinking for themselves on whatever book they choose at their next session together. If you feel this is too much for your children to absorb in the training format outlined above, you might think about introducing the "Stages" on different days in sequence—cover "Before Reading" first, then "During Reading" another day a little later, then "After Reading" a day or two later still.

The minimal training will almost certainly be too brief to generate high-quality practice in all pairs—further training and/or coaching is likely to be needed, especially with younger and less able tutors, and perhaps especially with non-fiction books. Issues that should be addressed in more detailed onward training include:

• What exactly might all the prompt questions mean?
• When do you fit in the questions without breaking the flow?
• How exactly do you "prompt by asking another question"?
• How does the tutor judge if a question is too difficult for their tutee?

The students will certainly offer some interesting suggestions in response to these questions—and some of them might be practical.

As with PR, frequency of contact for PT should be three times per week for a minimum of 20 minutes (preferably spread Monday, Wednesday, Friday), for at least the first four to six weeks. This initial intensity is necessary to establish good quality implementation, give the professional teacher sufficient opportunity to monitor closely and fine tune the process in individual pairs, and promote fluency and automaticity in technique (which will, however, always remain somewhat effort-ful). After this initial period, teachers may flexibly stipulate an intensity which seems viable in the long run without risk of boredom or curriculum displacement.

Finding time and space within the National Literacy Hour (in England) or other local curricular requirements and demands is never easy. Fortunately, PR+PT very much lend themselves to double (and indeed multiple) counting. Such projects in-volve reading, thinking, language, communication, meta-cognition, learning about different learning styles, social skills, citizenship and other aspects of personal and social education—all at the same time. Even within the National Literacy Hour, any methods which are evidence-based and demonstrably effective may be used. As PR is considerably better researched than the prescribed components of the National Literacy Hour, teachers should feel confident in taking their own thought-ful, evidence-based and justifiable educational decisions.

Regular, frequent and reliable monitoring of the PT process in operation is essential, and planning must ensure that this can be easily and consistently delivered and sustained over time. When monitoring peer-tutored Paired Thinking sessions, the project organiser's first task is always to check which of the tutors and which of the tutees is absent. Members of incomplete pairs can be re-matched, and you might have standby tutors, as in Paired Reading. However, you will need to think about how re-matching might work if the original tutor is away from school and you have a "supply" tutor working with the tutee—who will be completely reliant on the tutee's interpretation of the book because they probably will not have read it themselves.

In a peer tutoring project, the project organiser must subsequently circulate to see how the pairs are coping. If a parent and child are doing Paired Thinking at home, it is just as important that the parent and child have access to support, monitoring and troubleshooting from school or other appropriate source. You might wish to design a "Paired Thinking Home–School Diary" based on the PR diary (see Resources section). Reassure pairs that "taking more time so they can think better" is OK, and indeed encouraged—provided they are actually talking about something relevant to their reading. Your observations while monitoring will indicate when each pair is ready to move on to the next Level.

EVALUATION OF PT

The power of the PR component of this programme has already been proven with-out question. Measuring improvements in thinking skills without confounding with many other variables is difficult. PT necessitates slower progress through books than PR, because much more time is spent in Socratic discussion, so crude reading ages might not be expected to rise so much. However, McKinstery and Topping (in press 2002) deployed the technique on a cross-age tutoring basis in a high school, and found remarkable increases in scores on reading tests for the tutees, far beyond any normal expectations. Both staff and pupils gave positive evalua-tions of the process and outcomes. In terms of affective gains, tutors appeared to gain more from the implementation than tutees. Both tutors and staff thought that there had been a positive effect on the thinking skills of both tutors and tutees.

A criterion-referenced test of thinking skills was devised by Topping and Bryce (submitted for publication 2002), and applied on a pre–post basis to cross-age tutoring in one primary school. One group started with PR then switched to PT six weeks after, while another group continued with PR throughout. The PT tutees showed significantly greater gains in thinking skills than the PR-only group, although this was not true for the tutors. Further research is now in hand, involving a more sensitive test of thinking skills and more detailed analysis of the process of implementation, actual tutoring behaviours, and the development of meta-cognitive skills.

A number of schools are currently experimenting with family involvement in Paired Thinking at home, and these results are awaited with interest.

PAIRED THINKING AND SPECIFIC LEARNING DIFFICULTIES

Imagine this pairing:

> *The Tutor*: Jane—a model of sweet-natured middle-class conformity and seeming on the surface to be one of the best readers in the class. Looked at more closely, the truth is that she is rather pedestrian, frankly not all that bright, and decodes well but does not process what she reads at all deeply—perhaps "overachieving" owing to massive support at home.

> *The Tutee*: Richard—from a fairly chaotic background, but diagnosed early as a classic case of specific learning difficulty; he is verbally very able both receptively and expressively, creative and original, but reads only with great difficulty, cannot concentrate on anything for very long and always seems disorganised.

Put together, this pair would form a whole brain of enormous power, and through the PR+PT process could not only stretch themselves, but also enjoy a flow experience, perhaps for the first time. Think about it, perhaps with a colleague. Paired Thinking might also be used in other ways, although these have not been trialled at the time of writing.

So why do the pair have to actually read the book together? With some organisational changes, this might not be necessary. Remember that Paired Reading is a cross-ability method—the tutor has to be somewhat more able at reading than the tutee. This has the advantage that the tutee is enabled to access more challenging books. However, you could also try operating Paired Thinking in same-ability pairs, requiring each pair to agree on a book both were able to read independently, then reading that book independently. The pair could meet Before reading to explore the questions for that Stage, meet at intervals During their independent reading of the book (perhaps when both had completed each chapter) to explore the questions for that Stage, and meet After the whole book had been read independently to explore the questions for that Stage. The role of tutor could reciprocate from stage to stage, or from book to book. Consider with what frequency roles should reciprocate in the pair—per book, per session, per page?

Cross-ability reciprocal role PT questioning might also be possible even when the members of a pair are of different reading ability, by using books available in two levels of readability (known as Hi-Lo books in the US). Each partner would read a version of the text independently at their own level, then meet for Paired Thinking.

Another possibility is to mix same-ability and cross-ability matching within the same class or group using PR+PT. You might choose cross-ability matching with some of your weakest students as tutees (tutored by average students), and same-ability matching with some of your most able students, but this degree of complexity is perhaps best left until you have more experience. For further information about peer assisted learning across the curriculum, see Topping and Ehly (1998) and Topping (2000, 2001b).

REFERENCES

Adey, P. & Shayer, M. (1994) *Really Raising Standards: Cognitive Intervention and Academic Achievement*. London & New York: Routledge.

Bangert-Drowns, R. L. & Bankert, E. (1990) *Meta-analysis of effects of explicit instruction for critical thinking*. (ERIC Document Reproduction Service No. ED 328 614).

Blagg, N. (1991) *Can We Teach Intelligence?: A Comprehensive Evaluation of Feuerstein's Instrumental Enrichment Programme*. London: Lawrence Erlbaum Associates.

Bowers, D. (1991) *Using peer tutoring as a form of individualized instruction for the at risk students in a regular classroom*. Fort Lauderdale, FL: Nova University. (ERIC Document Reproduction Service No. ED 331 631).

Brooks, G., Flanagan, N., Henkhuzens, Z. & Hutchison, D. (1998) *What Works for Slow Readers? The Effectiveness of Early Intervention Schemes*. Slough: National Foundation for Educational Research.

Brown, R., Pressley, M., Van Meter, P. & Schuder, T. (1996) A quasi-experimental validation of Transactional Strategies Instruction with low-achieving second-grade readers. *Journal of Educational Psychology, 88*, 18–37.

Coles, M. J. & Robinson, W. D. (Eds) (1991) *Teaching Thinking: A Survey of Programmes in Education*. London: Bristol Classical Press.

DeBono, E. (1990) *Lateral Thinking: Creativity Step-by-Step* (Reissue edition). London & New York: Harper Collins.

Fisher, R. (1990) *Teaching Children to Think*. Oxford: Blackwell.

Fuchs, L. S., Fuchs, D., Kazdan, S. & Allen, S. (1999) Effects of peer-assisted learning strategies in reading with and without training in elaborated help giving. *Elementary School Journal, 99*, 201–220.

Garcia-Moriyon, F., Colom, R., Lora, S., Rivas, M. & Traver, V. (2000) Evaluation of Philosophy for Children: A program of learning thinking skills. *Psicothema, 12*, 567–571.

Halpern, D. F. (1998) Teaching critical thinking for transfer across domains: dispositions, skills, structure training, and metacognitive monitoring. *American Psychologist, 53*(4), 449–455.

King, A. (1997) ASK your partner to think-TEL WHY: A model of transactive peer tutoring for scaffolding higher-level complex learning. *Educational Psychologist, 32*, 221–235.

King, A. (1999) Discourse patterns for mediating peer learning. In O'Donnell, A. M. & King, A. (Eds), *Cognitive Perspectives on Peer Learning*. Mahwah, NJ & London: Lawrence Erlbaum Associates.

King, A., Staffieri, A. & Adelgais, A. (1998) Effects of structuring tutorial interaction to scaffold peer learning. *Journal of Educational Psychology, 90*(1), 134–152.

Klingner, J. K. & Vaughn, S. (1999) Promoting reading comprehension, content learning, and English acquisition through Collaborative Strategic Reading (CSR). *The Reading Teacher, 52*(7), 738–747.

Lim, T. K. (1995) An approach to the evaluation of the Philosophy for Children program. *Journal of Cognitive Education, 4*(2), 89–101.

Lipman, M. (1984) The cultivation of reasoning through philosophy. *Educational Leadership, 42*(2), 51–56.

McGuinness, C. (1999) *From thinking skills to thinking classrooms: A review and evaluation of approaches for developing pupils' thinking* (Research Report No. 115). London: The Stationery Office (for the Department for Education and Employment).

McKinstery, J. & Topping, K. J. (2002) *Cross-age peer tutoring of thinking skills in the high school.* Educational Psychology in Practice (in Press).

Mastropieri, M. A., & Scruggs, T. (2000) 'Can middle school students with serious reading difficulties help each other and learn anything? Qualitative and quantitative outcomes of a peer tutoring investigation'. Paper presented at the annual meeting of the American Educational Research Association (New Orleans, LA, 24–28 April 2000).

Nickerson, R. S. (1988) On improving thinking through instruction. *Review of Research in Education, 15*, 3–57.

Niklasson, J., Ohlsson, R. & Ringborg, M. (1996) Evaluating Philosophy for Children. *Thinking: The Journal of Philosophy for Children, 12*(4), 17–23.

Nisbet, J. & Davies, P. (1990) The curriculum redefined: Learning to think—thinking to learn. *Research Papers in Education, 5*, 49–72.

Palincsar, A. S. & Brown, A. L. (1988) Teaching and practising thinking skills to promote comprehension in the context of group problem solving. *Remedial and Special Education (RASE), 9*(1), 53–59.

Perkins, D. N. & Grotzer, T. A. (1997) Teaching intelligence. *American Psychologist, 52*(10), 1125–1153.

Powell, S. (1987) Improving critical thinking: A review. *Educational Psychology, 7*(3), 169–185.

Raths, L. E., Jonas, A., Rothstein, A. & Wasserman, S. (1967) *Teaching for Thinking: Theory and Application.* Columbus, OH: Charles E. Merrill.

Rand, Y., Mintzker, R., Hoffmann, M. B. & Friedlender, Y. (1981) The Instrumental Enrichment programme: Immediate and long-term effects. In Mittler, P. (Ed.), *Frontiers of Knowledge: Mental Retardation.* Volume 1. Baltimore: University Park Press.

Rosenshine, B. & Meister, C. (1994) Reciprocal teaching: A review of the research. *Review of Educational Research, 64*(4), 479–530.

Rosenshine, B., Meister, C. & Chapman, S. (1996) Teaching students to generate questions: A review of intervention studies. *Review of Educational Research, 66*(2), 181–221.

Savell, J. M., Twohig, P. T. & Rachford, D. L. (1986) Empirical status of Feuerstein's 'Instrumental Enrichment' technique as a method of teaching thinking skills. *Review of Educational Research, 56*(4), 381–409.

Simmons, D., Fuchs, D., Fuchs, L. S., Pate, J. & Mathes, P. (1994) Importance of instructional complexity and role reciprocity to classwide peer tutoring. *Learning Disabilities Research and Practice, 9*, 203–212.

Shayer, M. & Beasley, F. (1987) Does Instrumental Enrichment work? *British Educational Research Journal, 13*, 101–119.

Topping, K. J. (1995) *Paired Reading, Spelling and Writing: The Handbook for Teachers and Parents.* (www.dundee.ac.uk/psychology/kjtopping/preading.html). London & New York: Cassell.

Topping, K. J. (2000) *Tutoring by Peers, Family and Volunteers.* Geneva: International Bureau of Education, United Nations Educational, Scientific and Cultural Organisation (UNESCO). Also available online at: www.ibe.unesco.org/International/Publications/EducationalPractices/prachome.htm [31 December 2001] (Also in translation in Chinese and Spanish).

Topping, K. J. (2001a) *Thinking, Reading, Writing: A Practical Guide to Paired Learning with Peers, Parents & Volunteers* (www.dundee.ac.uk/psychology/TRW). New York & London: Continuum International.

Topping, K. J. (2001b) *Peer Assisted Learning: A Practical Guide for Teachers.* (www.dundee.ac.uk/psychology/kjtopping/plearning.html) Cambridge, MA: Brookline Books.

Topping, K. J. & Bryce, A. (2002) Cross-age peer tutoring of reading and thinking in the primary school: A *Controlled Study of Influence on Thinking Skills.* Paper submitted for publication.

Topping, K. J. & Ehly, S. (Eds) (1998) *Peer Assisted Learning.* Mahwah, NJ & London, UK: Lawrence Erlbaum.

Topping, K. J. & Hogan, J. (1999*) Read On: Paired Reading and Thinking Video Resource Pack,* second edition 2002. London: BP Educational Services (www.bpes.com/).

Topping, K. J. & Lindsay, G. A. (1992) Paired Reading: A review of the literature. *Research Papers in Education, 7*(3), 199–246.

Topping, K. J. & Whiteley, M. (1990) Participant evaluation of parent-tutored and peer-tutored projects in reading. *Educational Research, 32*(1), 14–32.

Yuill, N. & Oakhill, J. (1988) Effects of inference awareness training on poor reading comprehension. *Applied Cognitive Psychology, 2,* 33–45.

Chapter 19

METACOGNITION AND LITERACY

David Wray

INTRODUCTION

> We often find pupils following instructions or performing tasks without wondering
> why they are doing what they are doing. They seldom question themselves about
> their own learning strategies or evaluate the efficiency of their performance. Some
> children virtually have no idea what they should do when they confront a problem
> and are unable to explain their strategies of decision making. There is much evidence,
> however, to demonstrate that those who perform well on complex cognitive tasks,
> who are flexible and perserverant in problem solving, who consciously apply their
> intellectual skills, are those who possess poorly developed metacognitive abilities.
> Costa (1985)

When we open a novel, unfold a letter from a friend or spread the pages of a
newspaper, we usually experience the reading process as automatic and almost
effortless. Most researchers into the reading process would agree that when skilled
readers read familiar material written in ordinary language, for relaxation or simple
information-gathering, we perform the process of deriving meaning from the text
on the page at a level below the threshold of consciousness. We recognise words
on the page almost instantly without consciously thinking about how to recognise
them, we follow the train of meaning communicated by those words with little
conscious attention to what is happening. Reading is automatic.

But what happens when we come across a word, or a phrase, or an idea, that for
some reason disrupts this easy flow of reading? What about when the language
of the text is no longer transparent? When something just doesn't seem to fit? If
you have read the quotation which began this chapter, you should have experienced just such a moment when you reached the fourth to last word. "*Poorly
developed metacognitive abilities?*" you might have queried: "Surely it should be
'well developed'."

Dyslexia and Literacy: Theory and Practice. Edited by Gavin Reid and Janice Wearmouth.
© 2002 John Wiley & Sons, Ltd.

Being able to do something to get back into the flow of reading during such moments of uncertainty means having the capacity to self-monitor your own understanding of reading in order to spot and then respond to a difficulty. Reading theorists refer to this capacity as "metacognition". In the language I shall use in this chapter, you have just had a metacognitive experience, and your comprehension monitoring has kicked into action. These terms are probably unfamiliar to many people, yet the processes to which they refer have been increasingly demonstrated to be of special importance in intellectual development and in the operation of many intellectual activities, in particular those of literacy. This chapter will explore the areas of metacognition and literacy, focusing in particular upon the roles of comprehension monitoring in reading and of metacognition in writing. I will then briefly review some of the practical ways in which teachers might respond to these insights by exploring some possible teaching strategies to develop metacognitive approaches to literacy processes.

METACOGNITION AND COMPREHENSION MONITORING

Vygotsky suggested (1962) that there are two stages in the development of knowledge: firstly, its automatic unconscious acquisition (we learn things or how to do things, but do not know that we know these things), and secondly, a gradual increase in active conscious control over that knowledge (we begin to know what we know and that there is more that we do not know). This distinction is essentially the difference between the cognitive and metacognitive aspects of knowledge and thought. The term metacognition is used to refer to the deliberate, conscious control of one's own cognitive actions (Brown, 1980), that is, cognition about cognition: thinking about thinking.

There is a hierarchical relationship between the terms "metacognition" and "comprehension monitoring" (Baker & Brown, 1984). "Metacognition" can be seen as the wider concept, applying to knowledge about cognition in general. "Comprehension monitoring" is seen as applying mainly to the comprehension of connected discourse, which may, of course, involve either reading or listening. In thinking about this topic the following kinds of questions tend to get asked (Wagoner, 1983): What do readers know about their own comprehension, that is, what they comprehend and how they comprehend? Are they aware of when they comprehend adequately and when they do not? How do readers decide when their comprehension is adequate? What kinds of strategies do readers use when they realise they do not comprehend what they read in order to compensate for this? Some fairly clear answers to these questions have emerged from research, and they are answers with important implications for teachers of reading.

An analysis of the operation of comprehension monitoring during the reading process must begin with a description of what this process involves. Good reading has been described as follows: "A good reader proceeds smoothly and quickly as long as his understanding of the material is complete. But as soon as he senses that he has missed an idea, that the track has been lost, he brings smooth progress to a blinding halt. Advancing more slowly, he seeks clarification in the subsequent material, examining it for the light it can throw on the earlier trouble spot. If still dissatisfied with his grasp, he returns to the point where the difficulty began and rereads the section more carefully. He probes and analyses phrases and sentences for their exact meaning; he tries to visualise abstruse descriptions; and through a series of approximations, deductions, and corrections he translates scientific and technical terms into concrete examples." (Whimbey, 1975, p. 91).

While it is, of course, true that all readers do not follow precisely this sequence of actions, most theories of reading have suggested similarly strategic models for the comprehension process. Reading for meaning therefore inevitably involves the metacognitive activity of comprehension monitoring, which entails keeping track of the success with which one's comprehension is proceeding, ensuring that the process continues smoothly and taking remedial action if necessary. It thus involves the use of what have been called "debugging" skills (Brown, 1980).

Although mature readers typically engage in comprehension monitoring as they read for meaning, it is usually not a conscious experience. Brown (1980) distinguishes between an automatic and debugging state. Skilled readers, she argues, tend to proceed on automatic pilot until a "triggering event" alerts them to a failure or problem in their comprehension. When alerted in this way they must slow down and devote extra effort in mental processing to the area that is causing the problem. They employ debugging devices and strategies, all of which demand extra time and mental effort. Anderson (1980) suggests that efficient readers need not devote constant attention to evaluating their own understanding and he suggests the existence of an "automated monitoring mechanism" which "renders the clicks of comprehension and clunks of comprehension failure".

The events which trigger such action may vary widely. One common triggering event is the realisation that an expectation held about a text has not been confirmed by actual experience of the text. For example, in reading a sentence such as: "The old man the boats", the fourth and fifth words will probably cause a revision of the reader's sense of understanding and therefore take longer to process. Another triggering event is the meeting of unfamiliar ideas at too rapid a frequency for the reader to maintain a tolerance for the subsequent lack of understanding. The usual reader reaction to this is to slow down the rate of processing, devoting time and effort to the task of sorting out the failure in comprehension. The reader enters a deliberate, "aware" state quite distinct from the automatic pilot state, and the smooth flow of reading abruptly changes. (Baker & Brown, 1984).

Realising that one has failed to understand is only part of comprehension monitoring; one must also know what to do when such failures occur. This involves the making of a number of strategic decisions. The first of these is simply to decide whether or not remedial action is required. This seems to depend largely upon the reader's purposes for reading (Alessi et al., 1979). For example, if a reader's purpose is to locate a specific piece of information, a lack of understanding of the surrounding text will not usually trigger any remedial action. On the other hand, if the purpose is to understand a detailed argument, then practically any uncertainty will spark off extra mental activity.

In the event of a decision to take action, there are a number of options available. The reader may simply store the confusion in memory as an unanswered question (Anderson, 1980) in the hope that the author will subsequently provide sufficient clarification to enable its resolution, or the reader may decide to take action immediately, which may involve rereading, jumping ahead in the text, consulting a dictionary or knowledgeable person, or a number of other strategies (Baker & Brown, 1984).

Several studies of comprehension monitoring in action have been conducted. These have found that, in general, skilled readers evaluate their own understanding during the actual process of reading. If they encounter a confusion they give extra time to studying it and they reread previous sentences in an effort to clarify their understanding. They also seem to be prepared to make allowances for the fact that the problem might lie in the text rather than in them. This comprehension monitoring behaviour implies an active approach to gaining understanding from texts.

Research studies have also examined comprehension monitoring in younger and less able readers, and there has been a remarkable consistency in their findings. Garner (1987, p. 59) sums these up well:

> The convergent findings from recent research can be summarised: Young children and poor readers are not nearly as adept as older children/adults and good readers, respectively, in engaging in planful activities either to make cognitive progress or to monitor it. Younger, less proficient learners are not nearly as 'resourceful' in completing a variety of reading and studying tasks important in academic settings.

It appears that "planful, strategic behaviour" (Brown, 1978, p. 457) in the face of the kind of reading tasks likely to be encountered in school learning does not develop until relatively late in children's school careers, and for some children, those who find reading difficult, this may be very late indeed. This is important because this kind of awareness is an essential ingredient in success in school. "Part of being a good pupil is learning to be aware of the state of one's mind and the degree of one's understanding. The good pupil may be one who often says that he does not understand, simply because he keeps a constant check on his understanding. The poor pupil, who does not, so to speak, watch himself trying to understand, does not know most of the time whether he understands or not. Thus the problem is not to get pupils to ask us what they don't know; the problem is to make them aware of the difference between what they know and what they don't." (Holt, 1969, p. 23).

METACOGNITION AND WRITING

It is probably true to say that, of all the processes of literacy and language, writing is the most self-evidently metacognitive. The essence of the act of writing is the opportunity it affords us to put distance between ourselves and our thoughts. By expressing these thoughts in a visible way which we can subsequently rethink, revise and redraft, we are allowed, indeed forced, to reflect upon our own thinking. Alongside this reflection comes an enhancement in the degree to which we can be conscious of these thought processes and thus an enhancement in our potential control of them. As Smith (1982) has argued, "Writing separates our ideas from ourselves in a way that is easiest for us to examine, explore and develop" (p.15).

The model of the writing process that has emerged from an increasing volume of research suggests that it is made up of a number of simultaneously operating and recursive processes, e.g. planning, composition, transcription, revision, etc. If this is so, then the mechanisms whereby these processes are controlled and co-ordinated in the writer are of some importance. What have been termed "executive control processes" (Raphael et al., 1989) have become a focus of interest precisely because they are a means of linking together diverse and complex component processes.

One of the main problems in teasing out the operation of executive control processes in writing is that it all seems so obvious. It is difficult to imagine writers with any degree of skill who are not continuously applying what they know about the writing process, about the structures of various text types, about purposes for writing, and about audiences, as they meld together a complex range of writing strategies and regulate their use of these strategies. However, while this is true of skilled writers, it is not so obviously true of writers who are less skilled, that is, children learning to write, or children who struggle in writing. It may be that one of the chief aims of instruction in writing should be to develop these executive control processes.

What does this metacognitive knowledge consist of? In many ways this parallels the metacognitive knowledge utilised in the process of reading comprehension (cf. Garner, 1987), which can be classified according to the dimensions of personal, task and strategy knowledge. I shall describe these three focal points of knowledge with reference to myself as a writer, although it is obvious, of course, that all writers are different.

Knowledge of Person

As a relatively experienced writer I know a good deal about how I write and the conditions which help and hinder this. I know, for example, that I write best, in the sense of committing words to paper, when I have a deadline that is looming, but that if that deadline becomes too pressing my writing performance deteriorates. I also know that in the long stretch of time between firming up an idea for writing and actually beginning to type text into the word-processor, I am engaged in what I might term invisible writing behaviour. I am testing out ideas, sequences, starting and finishing points in my mind; I am reading others' writing and assimilating their ideas to my own map of the territory I want to cover, or radically changing that map to accommodate these ideas; I am talking, and arguing, about the ideas I will write about, with my wife, my colleagues, my students—in fact, anyone who might be remotely interested. I know that all these things are a normal part of writing for me and I get concerned if they do not seem to be happening for any reason. I know also that when I begin to use the word-processor, however carefully I think I have worked out my map for this piece of writing, the act of writing itself will carry me off into new lines of thought and usually produce a much better end-product.

Knowledge of Task

The majority of writing I do tends to be similar in genre, that is, mostly expository prose and, occasionally, argument. Because I do a lot of this I know a good deal about how this kind of prose "works": that is, I know about structuring it to make it as accessible as possible to the reader; I know about the importance of erecting "signposts" in writing so the reader will be offered assistance through the piece; I know roughly who the likely audience will be for each of the pieces I write. My knowledge about other writing tasks is not so extensive. My experience, for example, of writing fiction has been very limited and unsuccessful, probably precisely because I have no clear, explicit understanding of the way such text "works".

Knowledge of Process

Being a student of writing as well as a writer, I am in the very privileged position of knowing a fair amount about the process of writing. The major effect of this, I am sure, is to reassure me that the processes I go through as I write, described above, are entirely normal and will, in the end, produce the right results. Because of this, when I encounter a particularly trying time in my writing, I do not panic as I once might have done but recognise the signs of normality and relax. (N.B. This does not always work!)

These three areas of knowledge can enable me to operate some executive control over writing, control which allows me to check my own progress, choose from alternative strategies, change direction as I proceed and make an evaluation of the emerging and completed product (Englert & Raphael, 1988). This knowledge can, however, only operate in this way if it is activated during the writing process. It is quite possible, as Paris (1986) suggests, to imagine a situation in which writers might have ample knowledge about themselves, the writing task and process, yet still fail to implement executive control because they did not recognise the particular situations in which they were writing as appropriate for particular actions.

In order, therefore, to develop children's executive control over writing, teachers need to ensure that they are given adequate opportunities to acquire the requisite knowledge about themselves as writers, about the writing process and about the demands of particular writing tasks, including textual structures. They also need to ensure that this knowledge develops beyond simply knowing that certain things can be done in writing to knowing how they can be done, and, further, to knowing when and why they should be done.

Of course, the process of establishing instructional aims in terms of metacognitive knowledge about writing is not as simple as stating the knowledge which skilled writers need. It may be that there are limitations on the extent to which young children are capable of mastering and implementing this knowledge. Such limitations might be a function of age and maturation or they might be a product of variable skill. One account of the differences between novice and expert writers has been that provided by Bereiter and Scardamalia (1987). From their own research and that of others, they affirm that studies of expert writers thinking aloud while writing provide plenty of evidence of reflective activity (Flower & Hayes, 1980, 1981). These writers continually elaborate and reformulate their writing purposes and their plans for achieving these purposes, critically examine and revise their writing decisions, anticipate potential difficulties, make judgements and reconciliations between competing ideas, and show an alertness to the needs of their potential and actual readership.

Such indications seem to be almost entirely absent from the think-alouds of writers of school age. The explanation suggested for this is that these writers are taking different approaches to the process of writing. Bereiter and Scardamalia claim that the procedure which novice writers follow (which they refer to as "knowledge telling") is, in fact, a linear, non-reflective process, which consists, basically, of deciding what the topic is and then writing everything they know about it.

Expert writers, on the other hand, are more likely to have in mind several alternative ways of handling their writing task and their writing consists not only of expressing what they wish to say, but also of actually working this out as they write. This "knowledge transforming" has been described by a variety of professional writers.

Other writers and researchers have pointed to some other differences between the operation of metacognition in the writing of different groups. Englert and Raphael (1988), for example, suggest that pupils with learning difficulties tend to lack the metacognitive control that would enable them to implement and regulate a range of learning strategies. They seem, for example, to be less successful in regulating their textual understanding and fail to monitor or correct potential confusions as they read others' texts and produce texts themselves for others to read. This lack of ability to detect problems and to imagine the confusion which readers of their compositions may experience prevents them from successfully rereading, monitoring and revising these texts.

Fitzgerald (1987) suggests that novice writers often lack the ability to read their own writing from the perspective of another reader. Research findings on this are, however, mixed. Bartlett (1982) found that elementary school children spotted more problems and revised to a much greater extent when they worked with texts which had been written by others than when working on their own texts, which suggests that egocentrism had contributed to the breakdown in their revision processes. Revision was considerably easier when the children had no personal ownership of the texts they revised.

On the whole, therefore, it does seen that younger and less experienced writers are less able to operate metacognitively in their writing than expert writers. Indeed, it even begins to appear that it may be the level of awareness of the writing process that is itself responsible for the difference between expertise and lack of expertise in writing.

DEVELOPING META-LITERACY

There are several teaching implications arising from research in this area. Chief among these is the proposition that teachers who wish to enable their children to develop their levels of awareness of the reading or writing processes do not simply have to wait for these children to get older and mature into more self-aware strategies. There are positive approaches which can be adopted, and research results suggest strongly that when potential problems in the operation of executive processes are minimised through supportive teacher behaviour, children tend to perform metacognitive operations such as comprehension (Palincsar & Brown, 1984) and revision (Fitzgerald, 1987) at a much higher level.

One way of offering such support is to try to ensure that the literacy experience provided for children is always meaningful and purposeful from their points of view. A number of studies have demonstrated positive effects from this approach, including Robinson et al. (1990), who found that young children can develop an awareness of audience in writing when they are engaged in authentic written dialogues with other writers. Bereiter and Scardamalia (1987) provide a possible explanation for this with their concept of children's "conditional competence" (p. 90), which suggests that children are capable of performing high-level mental activities when the task is of intrinsic worth to them. They do, however, introduce a caveat with their argument that successful writers are in fact those who are able to make tasks meaningful for themselves—this is part of the reason why they are good writers. Therefore, they claim, the teacher's provision of the "meaningful task" is only part of the solution. Of wider importance is the general prevalence of a knowledge-telling strategy in education which they see as part of a general problem of the lack of promotion of "intentional cognition . . . the setting and deliberate pursuit of cognitive goals" (p. 361). Children's awareness of their own thought processes, in writing and in reading, would be central to such intentional cognition.

Teacher Modelling

Several teaching strategies have been suggested as beneficial in developing children's abilities to monitor their own reading and writing. One relatively simple strategy with some history of success is that of teacher modelling. Tonjes (1988) discusses metacognitive modelling as a way of teachers demonstrating to children the monitoring strategies they use in their own reading, and Duffy et al. (1988) similarly discuss the idea of the teacher modelling mental processes to children. They argue that teachers using this approach should concentrate upon transferring metacognitive control from themselves to their children and should model mental processes—what they think as they read or write—rather than simply procedures—what they do. Only in this way, they suggest, can children learn strategies which they can apply across a range of situations rather than which are limited to the context in which they were encountered. This strategy is now familiar to most teachers as shared reading, but it is important to note that the real benefits of the approach are derived not just from a teacher reading aloud to a group of learners, but from his/her thinking aloud at the same time.

Shared writing is also a powerful teaching strategy and involves much more than just writing down what children say, acting as competent secretary to their authors. Shared writing provides teachers opportunities to:

- work with the whole class, to model, explore and discuss the decisions that writers make when they are writing
- make links between reading and writing explicit
- demonstrate how writers use language to achieve particular effects
- remove temporarily some of problems of orchestrating writing skills by taking on the burden of some aspects, for example, spelling and handwriting, thereby enabling the children to focus exclusively on how composition works
- focus on particular aspects of the writing process, such as planning, composing, revising or editing
- scaffold children in the use of appropriate technical language to discuss what writers do and think.

Think Alouds

Another apparently beneficial strategy is that of children being taught to ask themselves questions as they read. Miller (1985) reports on a study in which 8- to 10-year-olds were explicitly taught a self-questioning procedure to accompany their reading. These learners were better able to identify inconsistencies and errors in texts (that is, monitor their comprehension) than other children who were directly told to look for these inconsistencies. The self-questioning procedure these children were trained to apply consisted of the following questions, which they had to ask themselves as they read:

1. First, I am going to decide if this story has any problems in it, like if one sentence says one thing and another sentence says something different or opposite.
2. Second, as I read I will ask myself, "Is there anything wrong with the story?"
3. Third, I will read two sentences and stop and ask if anything is wrong.
4. Fourth, so far, so good, I am doing a great job. Now I will read the whole story and decide if there are any problems in the whole story.
5. Did I find any problems in this story?

Such prompting procedures have also been found to work well in developing writing. Bereiter and Scardamalia (1987) provide evidence of the usefulness of what they call "procedural facilitation", in which they include the use of prompt cards to suggest questions to pupils engaged in writing. Prompt cards might contain questions such as:

- An idea I haven't considered yet is . . .
- My own feelings about this are . . .

Prompts like these are a feature of the approach to scaffolding writing through writing frames (Wray & Lewis, 1997) and seem to enable learners of all levels of ability to extend their writing coherently. Important for the purpose of this chapter is that they work through generating reflection in the pupil writers, that is, metacognition.

Linked to the use of prompting procedures is the encouragement of pupil think alouds. Instruction that entails pupils themselves thinking aloud about their reading processes has been shown to be effective at improving comprehension. A study by Bereiter and Bird (1985) showed that pupils who were asked to think aloud while reading had better comprehension than pupils who were not taught to do this, according to a question and answer comprehension test. A compelling study by Silven and Vauras (1992) demonstrated that pupils who were prompted to think aloud as part of their comprehension training were better at summarising information in a text than pupils whose training did not include think aloud.

Several researchers have theorised about why pupil think aloud is effective at improving comprehension. One popular theory is that getting pupils to think aloud decreases their impulsivity (Meichebaum & Asnarow, 1979). Rather than jumping to conclusions about text meaning or moving ahead in the text without having sufficiently understood what had already been read, think aloud may lead to more thoughtful, strategic reading. A study conducted with 9-year-old pupils provides some empirical support for this. Baumann and his colleagues found that training in think aloud improved children's ability to monitor their comprehension while reading (Baumann, et al., 1993). Children trained to think aloud as they used several comprehension strategies were better than a comparison group at detecting errors in passages, responding to a questionnaire about comprehension monitoring, and completing cloze items. One pupil trained in think aloud explained, "When I read I think, is this making sense? I might . . . ask questions about the story and reread or retell the story . . . " This and other pupils' comments suggested a thoughtful, strategic approach to reading through think aloud.

Reciprocal Teaching

Reciprocal teaching was developed by Palincsar and Brown (1984) with the aim of helping pupils from 6 years onwards to improving their understanding when reading. Reciprocal teaching is best represented as a dialogue between teachers and pupils in which participants take turns assuming the role of teacher. It is interactive, supported instruction in which the teacher or peer leads a group of pupils as they talk their way through a text to understand it. As they work together, group members monitor their understanding by stopping at regular intervals to ask questions, summarise, predict and clarify what they have read.

Each of these activities has a cognitive and a metacognitive dimension, in that not only are the children working upon their comprehension of the texts (comprehension fostering) but they are also having to reflect upon the extent of their comprehension (comprehension monitoring).

The reciprocal teaching procedure involves an interactive "game" between the teacher and the learners in which each takes it in turns to lead a dialogue about a particular section of text. The "teacher" for each section first asks a question, then summarises, then clarifies and predicts as appropriate. The real teacher models each of these activities, and the role played by the children is gradually expanded as time goes on from mostly pupil to mostly teacher.

Palincsar and Brown (1984) tested this procedure on a group of 11-year-olds with reading difficulties. These children did initially experience some difficulties in taking over the role of teacher and needed a lot of help in verbalising during summarising, questioning, clarifying and predicting. They did eventually, however, become much more accomplished leaders of the comprehension dialogues and showed a very significant improvement on tests of reading comprehension, an improvement which seemed to generalise to other classroom activities and did not fade away after the completion of the research project. Palincsar and Brown attributed the success of their training programme to the reciprocal teaching procedure, suggesting that it involved extensive modelling of comprehension fostering and monitoring strategies that are usually difficult to detect in expert readers, and that it forced children to take part in dialogues about their understanding, even if at a non-expert level.

Reciprocal teaching has been extensively researched since the mid-1980s and results have generally been very positive. For example, Rosenshine and Meister (1994) documented the positive gains made by reciprocally taught pupils on experimenter-designed tests of expository reading, and Alfassi (1998) also reported the effectiveness of reciprocal teaching with suburban high-school pupils who were at least two years below grade level in comprehension. After 22 days of reciprocal reading, these pupils scored significantly higher than did pupils receiving traditional reading skills instruction, whose scores remained virtually unchanged.

CONCLUSION

Although there are several caveats to be made about the quality of the research evidence, in particular about the methods typically used to ascertain children's use of metacognition in reading or writing performance, it does seem to be likely that developing pupils' metacognition may be one possible way forward in developing their literacy. This seems to be particularly true for pupils who are struggling with literacy. It may be that a key to enhancing children's abilities in literacy is to develop their abilities to be more "aware" of their literacy processes.

If this is the case, then teachers need to consider carefully how they will set about doing this. Although, again, the research evidence is as yet incomplete, there do seem to be several teaching strategies that might be beneficial in this area. Reciprocal teaching has certainly created a great deal of interest, especially among teachers of children with reading problems (for example, McGowan & Bell, 1993), and this procedure currently seems to offer the greatest hope in terms of a well-founded, systematic approach to teaching. Its components, however, such as teacher modelling, encouraging self-questioning and explicit discussion of literacy processes, are all beneficial teaching activities in their own rights. The teaching of literacy would undoubtedly benefit from wider use of such approaches.

REFERENCES

Alessi, S., Anderson, T. & Goetz, E. (1979). An investigation of lookbacks during studying. *Discourse Processes*, 2, 197–212.

Alfassi, M. (1998). Reading for meaning: the efficacy of reciprocal teaching in fostering reading comprehension in high school students in remedial reading classes. *American Educational Research Journal*, 35(2), 309–332.

Anderson, T. (1980). Study strategies and adjunct aids. In Spiro, R., Bruce, B. & Brewer, W. (Eds) *Theoretical Issues in Reading Comprehension*. Hillsdale, NJ: Erlbaum.

Baker, L. & Brown, A. (1984). Metacognitive skills and reading. In Pearson, D. (Ed) *Handbook of Reading Research*. New York: Longman.

Bartlett, E. (1982). Learning to revise. In Nystrand, M. (Ed) *What Writers Know*. New York: Academic Press.

Baumann, J. F., Jones, L. A. & Seifert-Kessell, N. (1993). Using think alouds to enhance children's comprehension monitoring abilities. *The Reading Teacher*, 47, 183–194.

Bereiter, C. & Bird, M. (1985). Use of thinking aloud in identification and teaching of reading comprehension strategies. *Cognition and Instruction*, 2, 131–156.

Bereiter, C. & Scardamalia, M. (1987). *The Psychology of Written Composition*. Hillsdale, NJ: Lawrence Erlbaum.

Brown, A. (1978). Knowing when, where and how to remember: a problem of metacognition. In Glaser, R. (Ed) *Advances in Instructional Psychology*. Hillsdale, NJ: Erlbaum.

Brown, A. (1980). Metacognitive development and reading. In Spiro, R., Bruce, B. & Brewer, W. (Eds) *Theoretical Issues in Reading Comprehension*. Hillsdale, NJ: Erlbaum.

Costa, A. L. (1985). Teaching for, of, and about thinking. In Costa, A. L. (Ed.) *Developing Minds*. Alexandria, VA: Association for Supervision and Curriculum Development, 20–23.

Duffy, G., Roehler, L. & Herrmann, B. (1988). Modelling mental processes helps poor readers become strategic readers. *The Reading Teacher* 41(8), 762–767.

Englert, C. & Raphael, T. (1988). Constructing well-formed prose: process, structure and metacognitive knowledge. *Exceptional Children*, 54(6), 513–520.

Fitzgerald, J. (1987). Research on revision in writing. *Review of Educational Research*, 57(4), 481–506.

Flower, L. & Hayes, J. (1980). The cognition of discovery: defining a rhetorical problem. *College Composition and Communication*, 31, 21–32.

Flower, L. & Hayes, J. (1981). A cognitive process theory of writing. *College Composition and Communication*, 32, 365–387.

Garner, R. (1987). *Metacognition and Reading Comprehension*. Norwood, NJ: Ablex.

Holt, J. (1969). *How Children Fail*. Harmondsworth: Penguin.

McGowan, J. & Bell, G. (1993). *Learning difficulties and classroom support: Reciprocal teaching* (Primary English Notes 90). Newtown, New South Wales: PETA.

Meichebaum, D. & Asnarow, J. (1979). Cognitive behavior modification and metacognitive development: Implications for the classroom. In Kendall, P. & Hollon, S. (Eds) *Cognitive Behavioral Interventions: Theory Research and Procedures*. New York: Academic Press, 11–35.

Miller, G. (1985). The effects of general and specific self-instruction training on children's comprehension monitoring performances during reading. *Reading Research Quarterly*, 20(5), 616–628.

Palincsar, A. & Brown, A. (1984). Reciprocal teaching of comprehension-fostering and comprehension-monitoring activities. *Cognition and Instruction*, 1(2), 117–175.

Paris, S. (1986). Teaching children to guide their reading and learning. In Raphael, T. (Ed) *The Contexts of School-based Literacy*. New York: Random House.

Raphael, T., Englert, C. & Kirschner, B. (1989). Students' metacognitive knowledge about writing. *Research in the Teaching of English*, 23(4), 343–379.

Robinson, A., Crawford, L. & Hall, N. (1990). *Some Day You Will No All About Me*. London: Mary Glasgow.

Rosenshine, B. & Meister, C. (1994). Reciprocal teaching: A review of the research. *Review of Educational Research*, 64, 479–530.

Silven, M. & Vauras, M. (1992). Improving reading through thinking aloud. *Learning and Instruction*, 2(2), 69–88.

Smith, F. (1982). *Writing and the Writer*. London: Heinemann.

Tonjes, M. (1988). Metacognitive modelling and glossing: two powerful ways to teach self responsibility. In Anderson, C. (Ed) *Reading: The abc and Beyond*. Basingstoke: Macmillan.

Vygotsky, L. (1962). *Thought and Language*. Cambridge, MA: MIT Press.

Wagoner, S. (1983). Comprehension monitoring: what it is and what we know about it. *Reading Research Quarterly*, 18, 328–346.

Whimbey, A. (1975). *Intelligence can be taught*. New York: Dutton.

Wray, D. & Lewis, M. (1997). *Extending Literacy*. London: Routledge.

Chapter 20

CRITICAL LITERACY AND ACCESS TO THE LEXICON

George Hunt

INTRODUCTION

In much of the literature on dyslexia and on reading acquisition in general, there is an implicit view that the *sine qua non* of reading is the rapid recognition of single words, a process often referred to as "access to the lexicon". Adams (1990) for example, concludes that children need to be familiar with 80–90% of the words on a page before they can be expected to read it. Furthermore, there is a growing consensus in this literature that the best way to help disadvantaged readers to gain access to the lexicon is to provide training aimed at remediating phonological or visual deficits that prevent the reader from deriving the pronunciation and meaning of printed words (Klein & McMullen 2000).

This approach is supported both by common-sense conceptualisations of reading, and by research into the reading process. Intuition tells us that the input modality of most forms of reading is visual; its output, at least in the early stages of learning to read, is a phonological recoding of the print. The majority of studies of what skilled readers actually do while reading emphasise the role of both phonological processing and its relationship with orthographic awareness; that is to say, knowledge of letters, letter patterns and the sequential dependencies between them (Carr, 2000).

Although there is still controversy about whether, in instructional settings, relationships between the visual and the phonological should be taught at the level of phoneme, onset and rime or word, and about what emphasis should be given to text meaning during this process, much recent research has suggested that systematic attention to teaching these relationships is vital (Levy, 2000; Lovett, 2000).

Dyslexia and Literacy: Theory and Practice. Edited by Gavin Reid and Janice Wearmouth.
© 2002 John Wiley & Sons, Ltd.

However, there are dangers in using findings about what skilled readers do in order to draw direct implications about instructional practices for non-readers. In the 1970s, for example, Goodman (1970) used the evidence from miscue analyses conducted on competent readers to argue that effective and efficient reading is driven more by cognition than graphophonic processes. He speculated that the fluent reader "samples the print", using just enough visual information to confirm hypotheses derived from context. This top-down model of reading persuaded some educators (most influentially Smith 1972, 1982) to advocate downgrading the teaching of graphophonic relationships in favour of inducting non-readers into what Goodman had termed a "psycholinguistic guessing game". Thus, inexperienced readers confronted with an unfamiliar word were discouraged from sounding the word out, and instead persuaded to guess what would make sense in the context.

Developments in eye movement research and on the strategies used by good and poor readers now suggest that fluent readers do fixate on virtually every word in the texts that they read, and that reliance on context is more characteristic of poor readers who use guesswork to compensate for inefficient word recognition (Stanovich & Stanovich, 1995). These developments in knowledge about skilled reading behaviour have been used as arguments against teaching children to focus on the meaning of what they read, to the extent, in some instructional programmes, of delaying whole text experience, or even the teaching of sight vocabulary, until the alphabetic principle is firmly in place and children are able to recognise a number of CVC words in isolation (McGuinness, 1998).

Both the advocacy of a psycholinguistic guessing game approach at the expense of developing graphophonic skills, and the advocacy of graphophonic skills at the expense of whole text experience, demonstrate what seems to be an overconfident and unnecessarily exclusivist application of research to instruction. Although Goodman's view of the reading process overemphasised the role of context, it is clear that using context is one very useful aspect of reading, providing support for the beginner reader's processing of text while word recognition skills develop (Juel, 1995; Levy, 2000). The instructional implications of stressing context (rich experience of natural language books; discussion of stories and their links to real life; encouragement of active comprehension strategies) gave both learners and teachers a richer vision of literacy than that offered in code-based reading schemes. The evidence that has accumulated about the importance of word recognition should act as a useful counterpoise to this holistic vision, reminding learners and teachers that text-level discussion needs to be accompanied by the teaching of graphophonic skills, but it would be unfortunate if the assumption was made that because skilled readers process every word and letter on the page, learners should be taught to read by getting them to do the same thing to the exclusion or marginalisation of authentic reading practices (Juel, 1995).

A significant problem encountered by programmes aimed at automatic word recognition is that of transferring the sublexical skills acquired through the programme into the real-life reading activity. For example, Lovett (2000) cites research indicating that intensive phonological awareness training leads to enhanced skill in reading nonwords and doing phonological awareness tasks, but does not lead in any straightforward manner to enhanced comprehension or even real-word identification. Though Stanovich and Stanovich (1995) cite research that does indicate transfer, many reading authorities continue to argue that a heavy instructional emphasis on decoding provides the recipient with distorted and potentially demotivating demonstrations of what reading is for (Cambourne, 2001).

Even advocates of the primacy of teaching graphophonic skills concede that the ultimate purpose of reading is not word recognition but the ability to derive meaning from print (Stanovich & Stanovich, 1995). This requires not just decoding, but the ability to visualise, interpret, self-correct, argue and make life-to-text links. Being literate also involves participating in a range of text-centred social practices (Heath, 1983). It involves engagement with books and other types of print and electronic media for a variety of information and entertainment purposes, and interaction with other readers and writers. Furthermore, these literacy practices are shaped by constantly evolving cultural conventions about what it is appropriate to do with reading and writing in particular contexts (Street, 1993).

For example, a recent informal survey of literacy practices in an English primary classroom, in which teachers, pupils, students and assistants were asked to list the types of reading, writing and associated discussions that they had engaged in recently, disclosed the following range of practices:

- acquiring and practising in-group vocabulary (e.g. from the Harry Potter series)
- completing and asking for help with crosswords and other word puzzles
- collecting jokes
- consulting magazines in order to collect recipes, advice, gossip
- discussing and criticising environmental print, such as deliberately provocative or misspelt advertising
- discussing popular stories and predicting what will happen next (e.g. from the His Dark Materials trilogy)
- disputing texts by, for example, making fun of particular newspaper columnists or sports reports
- exchanging website addresses
- filling in pupil assessment forms
- filling in special offer forms
- writing and forwarding emails (including language play elements such as emoticons, and group-orientated products such as chain letters, petitions, circulated joke sets)
- marking and annotating children's work
- pooling interpretations of hand-outs and assignment briefs
- reading and writing graffiti
- sharing cartoons
- texting cell-phone messages that often involve language play, telegraphic spelling or the use of predictive text
- trading literary products (such as Goosebumps titles and Pokemon cards)
- trying to interpret instructions for domestic appliances
- writing and circulating private notes

- writing and pooling interpretations of lecture notes
- writing notes for noticeboards
- writing out and parodying pop song lyrics.

It is interesting that some of these practices, such as using predictive text, rely on a subtle fusion of lexical and semantic skills that are not explicitly taught by the school. Others, such as the use of graffiti and the circulation of messages in class, would no doubt be forbidden by the school. Moreover, there is anecdotal evidence that some of these practices are engaged in autonomously and enthusiastically by pupils who have been classified by conventional assessment measures as having literacy difficulties. This confirms ethnographic studies of reading in a variety of cultures which show that "sub-rosa" literacies are often practised by groups and individuals deemed to be illiterate or "at risk" by those who administer the official form of literacy within that culture (Gilmore 1986). A strong formulation of this contrast denies that the essential divide is between the literate and the illiterate; "the divide is rather between those whose literacy is recognised in school and those whose literacy is not" (Moss et al., 2000).

One consequence of this is that teachers should be aware that pupils with reading difficulties, as well as being objects of attempts to inculcate them into the institutional model of literacy, might well also operate as agents within these networks of vernacular literacies. Although it would be simplistic to assume that bridges can easily be built between literacies (see Moss et al., 2000 for a discussion of this issue) enhanced awareness of the range of literacy practices that pupils engage in could give a more optimistic view of their capabilities than one grounded in potentially self-fulfilling assumptions about cognitive or social deficits (Gilmore, 1986; Cambourne, 2001).

Another consequence is the need for teachers to recognise the sheer volume and diversity of the orthographic stimuli to which learners are subjected (and to which they contribute) in daily life. Luke, in a recent unpublished address to the International Reading Association's 18th world conference in Auckland, New Zealand, described today's young readers as surfers of an ocean of signs: "post-modern childhood involves the navigation of an endless sea of texts". Whether or not children can recognise the actual words of these texts rapidly and automatically, they will be affected by the social and commercial pressures that they exert. It is therefore necessary that, alongside measures aimed at establishing word recognition, learners with reading difficulties should be helped to develop a critical approach to the texts which shape their lives. Moreover, I would argue that the types of text encounters that critical literacy involves could provide supportive, motivating contexts for these learners to begin to acquire access to the lexicon.

WHAT IS CRITICAL LITERACY?

A common-sense view of literacy says that a person can read if he or she is able to recode graphic signals into the spoken words that they represent. A broader view demands that the reader must be able to comprehend the meanings encoded by the author of the text, including those which are not explicitly stated by the writer, but arrived at by inference on the part of the reader. Adding a responsive element to this, we can also demand that the reader be capable of relating the author's meanings to his or her own experiences, making evaluative judgements about such aspects as veracity, relevance and quality of expression. However, this still assumes an unproblematic textual encounter between an autonomous reader and an autonomous writer, the former replicating or reconstructing the meanings encoded by the latter, and both of them using skills which are ideologically neutral.

"Critical literacy" is a term which is used to subsume a number of instructional approaches which challenge assumptions that texts can ever convey "objective meanings" or that literacy is an ideologically neutral tool. It asserts that both readers and writers approach texts in ways that are conditioned by such factors as purpose, power relations, gender and historical period. These factors are expressed through a variety of rhetorical devices (such as vocabulary and grammatical structure choices) and by the writer's selection of which voices and positions to express and which to omit. These influences can be seen at their most obvious in material such as newspaper reporting, polemical literature and advertising, but it is a tenet of the critical literacy movement that *all* texts are structured to serve some interests rather than others. Traditional stories carry messages about the proper conduct of individuals and groups towards each other within specific social settings; historical texts recount events from privileged and contestable viewpoints; research literature selects information that favours one position at the expense of another; and, as Luke et al. point out (2001, p113) "even a medicine bottle label features particular values and positions—a possible world where the reader (as prospective purchaser, medicine consumer and 'patient') is constructed and located."

The implication for teachers is that they need to do more than simply train pupils to become skilled decoders. Luke and Freebody (1997) point out that decoding *is* an essential part of the reading process, but it is only one aspect of a set of sociocultural practices that also encompasses text participation (working out what the text means), text use (knowing how to use the text in the immediate context) and text analysis (recognising how the text has been constructed to produce specific effects on the reader). In order to become independent, readers need to be explicitly aware of these dimensions, questioning the choices and assumptions that underlie the writer's words. Literacy is seen not as a neutral set of skills, but as a social practice which is not necessarily empowering unless it is informed by critical awareness; "being able to construct and make meaning from text may appear empowering, but in fact may open one to multiple channels of misinformation and exploitation. You may just become literate enough to get yourself badly into debt, exploited and locked out." (Luke, cited in Fehring & Green, 2001, p8)

In the classroom, it is clear that texts can limit rather than liberate both teachers and students. Teachers can be bound by prescriptive curricula, their professionalism constricted by the use of mandatory booklists and guidelines; these texts also constrain the world view of the student, and may serve to limit literacy practices to the filling in of worksheets or other types of set responses.

The goal of literacy teaching is therefore the empowerment of the reader. Critical literacy teachers approach this goal in various ways (see Fairclough, 1992 and Fehring & Green, 2001 for accounts of theoretical groundwork and practical implications) but the following characteristics are common:

- a recognition that texts are constructed in specific ways in order to influence the reader
- an emphasis on collaborative investigation of texts, rather than on individual reconstruction through reading aloud, comprehension exercises or appreciative response
- encouragement of multiple interpretations rather than a quest for definitive meaning
- problematisation of a range of texts, from literary classics to such ephemera as magazines, junk-mail and advertising media
- a commitment to social action; for example, by writing in support of or against disputed texts, contacting authors and publishers, creating alternative versions, engaging in further research about issues raised.

Luke et al. (2001, p116) suggest the following framework of questions to structure critical investigations:

1. What is the topic?
2. How is it being presented? What themes and discourses are being used?
3. Who is writing to whom? Whose voices and positions are being expressed?
4. Whose voices and positions are not being expressed?
5. What is the text trying to do to you?
6. What other ways are there of writing about the topic?
7. What wasn't said about the topic? Why?

Critical literacy projects using this type of framework have been conducted with learners from a range of ages working on a wide variety of text types: O'Brien (1990) worked with 5–7-year-olds on analysing junk mail, raising their awareness of gender and age stereotyping by examining Mothers' Day catalogues; Kempe (2001) showed how junior-school children could make critical responses to the values underlying both traditional stories from old reading schemes, and updated fairy tales; Alvermann and Hagood (2000) encouraged high-school students to reflect on their own fandom by examining rock-song lyrics and websites; Mellor and Patterson (2000) engaged high-school students in discussions of the historical conditions underlying depictions of gender and ethnicity in Shakespeare's plays.

What is most promising about such activities for pupils with reading difficulties is that they provide rich contexts for the supported reading, and frequent revisiting, of texts which have relevance to the pupils' everyday lives. Although rapid word recognition may be the *sine qua non* of the autonomous literacy that is valued by schools, it is not the *sine qua non* for involving learners of all levels of attainment in critical discussions around such texts, and in cooperative writing as a response to the issues raised in discussion.

The essence of critical literacy education is its cooperative and dialogic nature. The objective is not to articulate exactly what the author "meant" by this use of language, but to examine the possibilities and implications. This mirrors the literate behaviour of the learner's culture (in which people customarily argue and negotiate over printed messages of all kinds, from instructions for domestic appliances to research papers and political manifestoes) while at the same time providing opportunities to develop more incisive awareness of specific uses of vocabulary, grammar and overall "texture". The social set-up of the critical literacy classroom involves collaborative whole-class or small-group work that encourages the pooling of ideas and the joint composition of responses. An emphasis on interactive oral work around shared text enables learners whose listening comprehension is in advance of their decoding ability to participate as equals. Mixed ability cooperative groups allow readers to observe and participate in demonstrations of active literacy. In Vygotskyan terms, this provides a zone of proximal development in which literacy novices interact with their more able peers, sharing others' reading practices and extending their own.

Skidmore (2000), for example, assesses a discussion between five primary school children, two of whom are on the school's register of special educational needs, who have cooperatively read a story called "Blue Riding Hood" (Hunt, 1995) a version of the traditional fairy tale rewritten to undermine readers' expectations of stereotypical roles. The participants have been asked to put the characters in the story in order of blame, and to justify their ranking to each other (a task reminiscent of the viewer-as-juror element of TV programmes like *Survival* and *Big Brother*). After analysing ways in which the task elicits child-to-child contingent exchanges, involving more speculative thinking than would have been allowed by a more convergent task, Skidmore concludes:

> I would suggest that the educational significance of the features of the talk is that they constitute a joint exercise in problem solving which has the potential to act as a model for the development of the students' autonomous literacy practices: by pooling their thinking and making it public, they are also encouraged to make it more explicit, and to open it up to modification through considering other points of view, with the result that they attain a richer understanding of the story collectively than they would be likely to achieve individually. (Skidmore, 2000, p293)

As well as the potential for developing critical understanding, it is possible that such discussions may provide opportunities for non-readers to acquire the word-level skills that they need for fluent reading. Critical literacy investigations often involve repeated readings of short, high-impact texts, highlighting key vocabulary and phrases. As Levy (2000) points out, such rereading has been shown to have benefits for both word recognition and comprehension. These investigations also feature response activities in which pupils cooperatively compose texts through shared writing, a practice in which the group's oral composition is written down by a teacher or other person more competent in transcriptional skills. The scribe usually uses a flip chart or other large writing surface in order to emphasise the collaborative nature of the writing process, to demonstrate such aspects of the process as spelling and punctuation, and to facilitate the reading and redrafting of the emerging text. Clearly, there are opportunities here for scaffolded and vivid demonstrations of a range of skills.

ACCESS TO CRITICAL LITERACY WITHIN THE
NATIONAL LITERACY STRATEGY

Most traditional curricula assume that the capabilities that readers need to bring to texts can be broken down into hierarchies of subskills that need to be learned sequentially. Such taxonomies of skills usually position word recognition through graphophonic processing as the foundation skill which has to be firmly in place before "more sophisticated" capabilities can be learned or taught. Comprehension, for example, is often seen as a higher-order process that has to wait upon the automaticity of word-level processing:

> To accomplish [skilled reading performance] pathways must be automatic or activated in response to sensory inputs without requiring conscious attention. Automaticity frees cognitive resources for the more difficult task of integration and comprehension. If attention and effort are devoted to low level processes, like decoding the pronunciation of a letter string, there may be insufficient resources to execute processes needed for comprehension. (Klein & McMullen, 2000, p3).

While this argument might make intuitive sense if we envisage the lone reader striving towards independence in reconstructing the autonomous author's message, it does not necessarily hold for a learner in a social setting sharing a text with other learners. A key claim made by critical literacy advocates is that readers of any age or attainment level have both the entitlement and the ability to become analysts of text. Comber (2001), for example, makes the following point:

> I want to question any suggestion that critical literacy is a developmental attainment rather than social practice which may be excluded or deliberately included in early literacy curriculum. . . . In the early years of schooling, students learn what it means to read and write successfully in terms of school practices. They need opportunities to take on this text analysis role from the start, as a part of how our culture defines literacy, not as a special curriculum in the later years of schooling or in media studies.
> (Comber, 2001, pp 92–93)

In practical terms, text analysis for those pupils who cannot yet read words independently takes place orally, in the presence of a text which is read by the teacher or more competent peers. The less able reader accesses the meaning of text through listening comprehension, supported by shared reading.

The hierarchical model of reading skills isolates disadvantaged readers from such investigations, even in curricula which acknowledge the importance of critical literacy. In the National Literacy Strategy for England (DfEE, 1998) for example, although work at word, sentence and text levels is prescribed for all ages, it is explicitly stated that younger pupils need a preponderance of word-level work; critical awareness is postponed until this is "secure". The text-level objectives in the early years are mainly concerned with learning about the anatomy of fiction and non-fiction and its associated terminology. It is not until year 1 term 3 (the sixth term of formal schooling for children who have been through a reception year) that the curriculum prescribes that children should begin to express preferences "and give reasons".

From the end of year 4 onwards, the NLS begins to stipulate investigations which are conducive to the development of critical literacy (see Table 20.1), but

Table 20.1   Aspects of critical thinking in the NLS text-level work

Year 4 Term 3	to identify social moral or cultural issues in stories
	to write critically about an issue or dilemma raised in a story
	to read compare and evaluate examples of arguments and discussions, e.g. letters to press, articles, discussion of issues in books
	from examples of persuasive writing, to investigate how style and vocabulary are used to convince the intended reader
	to evaluate advertisements for their impact appeal and honesty, focusing in particular on how information about the product is presented: exaggerated claims, tactics for grabbing attention, linguistic devices
Year 5 Term 2	to evaluate texts critically by comparing how different sources treat the same information
Year 5 Term 3	to investigate a range of texts from different cultures, considering patterns of relationships, social customs, attitudes and beliefs; identify these features by reference to the text; consider and evaluate these features in relation to their own experience.
	to read and evaluate letters e.g. from newspapers, magazines, intended to inform, protest, complain, persuade, considering . . . how language is used, e.g. to gain attention, respect, manipulate
	to read other examples e.g. newspaper comment, headlines, adverts, fliers. Compare writing which informs and persuades, considering, e.g. the deliberate use of ambiguity, half truth, bias; how opinion can be disguised to seem like fact
	to select and evaluate a range of texts, in print or other media, for persuasiveness, clarity, quality of information
	from reading, to collect and investigate use of persuasive devices: e.g. words and phrases . . . rhetorical questions . . . pandering, condescension, concession etc.; . . . deliberate ambiguities
	to write a commentary on paper or screen (e.g. as a news editorial, leaflet) setting out and justifying a personal view; to use structures from reading to set out and link points . . .
Year 6 Term 1	to set out in note form an argument to persuade others of a point of view
	to comment critically on the language style, success of examples of non-fiction such as periodicals, reviews, reports, leaflets
	to recognise how arguments are constructed to be effective
Year 6 Term 2	to identify the features of balanced written arguments
	to write a balanced report of a controversial issue

several points of reservation need to be made in relation to this. Firstly, critical literacy is anatomised into sub-skill objectives which are then positioned piecemeal into the later years of primary schooling, clearly implying that they are indeed seen as "developmental attainments" rather than entitlements for all readers; secondly, they form only small, scattered parts of the text-level curriculum, isolated within stipulated terms rather than forming a unified and unifying strand braided through the whole of the child's literacy experiences; thirdly, they do not explicitly address issues of language and power: rather, they focus on rhetorical features to be identified and imitated. This approach avoids both confronting the ways in which the text constructs the reader, and encouraging direct response.

Another serious reservation relates to the question of access to this part of the curriculum for pupils with reading difficulties. The NLS documents stress the inclusivity of the strategy, and much of the stipulated teaching involves whole-class reading, writing and discussion. Recent additions to the strategy documents provide potentially useful guidance on supporting pupils with specific learning difficulties within these whole-class activities (DfEE, 2000). However, the strategy is tied to a programme of quantitative target setting against which the performance of schools will be measured, then rewarded or punished. In an attempt to meet these targets, pupils who are deemed to be underachieving are commonly withdrawn from their classes and given parallel teaching through an Additional Literacy Support programme which focuses largely on phonic skills and tightly controlled reading and writing activities, set out in highly prescriptive manuals, and featuring scripted interactions and contrived texts (DfEE, 1999). Although this programme is neither designed for nor aimed at pupils with specific learning difficulties, schools under pressure to provide "remediation" for such pupils have often resorted to including these children in "low ability" sets which work through the ALS programme or similar types of material. They are therefore isolated from even the attenuated and fragmented version of critical literacy offered by the mainstream curriculum, as well as being exposed to the demotivating effects attendant upon setting (Sukhnandon & Lee, 1999).

Thus, even when critical literacy is at given at least lip service within the curriculum, the disadvantaged reader is denied access to it. This pattern is not confined to pupils working within the geographical and historical constraints of the English National Literacy Strategy. In an evaluation of instructional support programmes in the USA, Walmsley and Allington (1995) conclude that:

> Poor readers have historically experienced a curriculum quite different from that experienced by better readers . . . Low-achieving readers are more likely to be asked to read aloud than silently, to have their attention focused on word recognition rather than comprehension, to spend more time working alone on low level worksheets than on reading authentic texts, and to experience more fragmentation in their instructional activities. (Walmsley & Allington, 1995, p29)

What we have here is an instance of what Stanovich (1985), in a different context, referred to as Matthew effects (from the Gospel of St Matthew, 25:29) whereby the rich get richer and the poor get poorer: the pupils who most need extensive, active engagement in talk about the uses and abuses of literacy are instead channelled into regimes where such talk is endlessly deferred.

CONCLUSION

The claims that are made by critical literacy are large ones, and are based on qualitative evaluations of small case studies rather than quantitative measures of improved reading performance. It is therefore hardly surprising that some reading authorities from the positivist tradition have reacted with impatience to these claims. Gough (1995), for example, argues trenchantly that literacy is neither social, nor political, nor any more relative than any other experience, and that to argue otherwise is "errant, if not pernicious nonsense" (p84).

Perhaps critical literacy approaches would receive a better welcome if it were conceded that they do not obviate the need for word-level instruction, including attention to both visual-orthographic links and metacognitive strategies aimed at ensuring transfer. Peer discussion of sociocultural issues in texts does not make the need for fluent, independent reading go away, and fluent independent reading depends on automatic word recognition, which depends in turn on orthographic and phonological processing. But, as Luke (unpublished) argues, this "provides only 25% of the toolkit". Critical literacy is necessary to demonstrate the uses and abuses of literacy, and to make readers into perceptive consumers and producers of texts.

What is needed is more research into how effective critical literacy approaches are. Do pupils who are involved in critical literacy investigations derive more benefit from parallel word-level instruction than those who are not so involved? If so, is this due to greater exposure to text or to the nature of the investigations? Do shared reading, writing and discussion really provide access to the lexicon for disadvantaged readers? If so, is such access measurably better for those students whose investigations are guided by the framework of questions alluded to above? These are questions which lend themselves to empirical, and critical, inquiry.

REFERENCES

Adams, M.J. (1990) *Beginning to Read*. Cambridge, MA: MIT Press.

Alvermann, D.E. & Hagood, M.C. (2000) Fandom and critical media literacy. *Journal of Adolescent and Adult Literacy*, 43 (5), 436–446.

Cambourne, B. (2001) Why do some students fail to learn to read? Ockham's razor and the conditions of learning. *The Reading Teacher*, 54 (8), 784–786.

Carr, T.H. (1999) Trying to understand reading and dyslexia: mental chronometry, individual differences, cognitive neuroscience and the impact of instruction as converging sources of evidence. In R. M. Klein & P. McMullen (Eds) *Converging Methods for Understanding Reading and Dyslexia*. Cambridge, MA: MIT Press.

Comber, B. (2001) Classroom explorations in critical literacy. In H. Fehring & P. Green (Eds) *Critical Literacy*. Newark, DE: International Reading Association.

DES (1975) *A Language for Life*. London: HMSO.

DES (1989) *English for Ages 5–16*. London: HMSO.

DfEE (1998) *The National Literacy Strategy Programme of Objectives*. London: HMSO.

DfEE (1999) *Additional Literacy Support*. London: HMSO.

DfEE (2000) *Supporting Pupils with Special Educational Needs in the Literacy Hour*. London: HMSO.

Fairclough, N. (1989) *Language and Power*. London: Longman.

Gilmore, P. (198b) Sub-rosa literacy: Peers, play, and ownership in literacy acquisition. In B. Schieffelin & P. Gilmore (Eds) *The Acquisition of Literacy: Ethnographic Perspectives*. Ed. Greenwich, CT: Ablex, 155–168.

Goodman, K. (1967) Reading: a psycolinguistic guessing game. In R. Wardhaugh, *Reading: A Psycholinguistic Perspective*. New York: Harcourt, Brace and Wortld Inc.

Gough, P.B. (1995) The new literacy: caveat emptor. *Journal of Research in Reading*, 18(2), 79–86.

Heath, S.B. (1983) *Ways with Words*. Cambridge: Cambridge University Press.

Hunt, G. (1995) *Curriculum Bank: Reading*. Leamington Spa, UK: Scholastic.

Juel, C. (1995) The messenger may be wrong, but the message may be right. *The Journal of Research in Reading*, 18(2).

Klein, R.M. & McMullen, P. (1999) *Converging Methods for Understanding Reading and Dyslexia*. Cambridge, MA: MIT Press.

Levy, B.A. (1999) Whole words, segments and meanings: approaches to reading education. In R. M. Klein & P. McMullen (Eds) *Converging Methods for Understanding Reading and Dyslexia*. Cambridge, MA: MIT Press.

Lovett, M.W. (1999) Defining and remediating the core deficits of developmental dyslexia: lessons from remedial outcome research with reading disabled children. In R. M. Klein & P. McMullen (Eds) *Converging Methods for Understanding Reading and Dyslexia*. Cambridge, MA: MIT Press.

Luke, A. & Freebody, P. (1999) Further notes on the four resources model. *Reading Online*, http://www.readingonline.org/research/lukefreebody.html.

Luke, A., O'Brian, J. & Comber, B. (2001) Making community texts objects of study. In H. Fehring, & P. Green, (Eds) *Critical Literacy*. Newark, DE: International Reading Association.

McGuinness, D. (1998) *Why Children Can't Read*: London: Penguin.

Mellor, B. & Patterson, A. (2000) Critical practice: Teaching "Shakespeare". *Journal of Adolescent & Adult Literacy*. 43(6), 508–518.

Moss, G., Maybin, J. & Street, B. (2000) Literacy and the social organisation of knowledge inside and outside school. *Virtual Seminar 2*, International Association of Applied Linguistics, http://www.education.leeds.ac.uk/AILA/virtsem2.mos.

Qualifications and Curriculum Authority (2000) *Language for Learning in Key Stage 3*. London: QCA.

Skidmore, D. (2000) From pedagogical dialogue to dialogic pedagogy. *Language in Education*, 14, 4.

Smith, F. (1971) *Understanding Reading*. London: Holt, Rhinehart and Winston.

Stanovich, K. & Stanovich, P. (1995) How research might inform the debate about early reading acquisition. *Journal of Research in Reading*, 18(2), 87–105.

Stanovich, K. (1986) Matthew effects in reading: some consequences of individual differences in the acquisition of literacy. *Reading Research Quarterly*, 360–406.

Street, B. V. (1993). *Cross-cultural Approaches to Literacy*. New York: Cambridge University Press.

Sukhnandon, L. & Lee, B. (1999) *Streaming, Setting and Grouping by Ability: A Review of the Literature*. Slough, UK: NFER.

Walmsley, S.A. & Allington, R.L. (1995) Redefining and reforming instructional support programs for at-risk students. In R. L. Allington & S. A. Walmsley (Eds) *No Quick Fix: Rethinking Literacy Programs in America's Elementary Schools*. Newark, DE: International Reading Association.

Chapter 21

CHANGING DEFINITIONS AND CONCEPTS OF LITERACY: IMPLICATIONS FOR PEDAGOGY AND RESEARCH

Fidelma Healy Eames

INTRODUCTION

This chapter discusses changing definitions and concepts of literacy as we embark on the twenty-first century and proposes critical literacy as the overarching concept within which literacy abilities, processes and concepts belong. Implications for practice are outlined.

Over the years, a challenge for literacy educators has been discerning between the disparate views proposed about literacy and the attempts to polarise the teaching community about the benefits of some approaches over others. What is definite, though, is that literacy practices in formal education have yielded useful information about the importance of a definition of literacy. Au and Raphael (2000) illustrate that, as definitions of literacy have changed, so have the curriculum, instruction, and assessments associated with them (p. 150). They cite the example of Michigan State in the 1980s, when, following a redefinition of reading from fluent print decoding to an interactive process emphasising comprehension, major changes followed in English language arts' standards that tested higher levels of comprehension and writing in response to text. Another example by Morrow et al. (1999) implies a definition of exemplary literacy instruction as balanced literacy instruction where "children are exposed both to direct, explicit instruction for skill development" and "to the experiences that encourage social collaboration and constructive problem solving associated with an integrated language arts approach" (p. 474). These examples highlight

Dyslexia and Literacy: Theory and Practice. Edited by Gavin Reid and Janice Wearmouth.
© 2002 John Wiley & Sons, Ltd.

the responsibility educators, policy-makers and researchers have when defining literacy.

Since definitions potentially drive both the curriculum and what counts as progress towards becoming literate, then how we define and interpret literacy is crucial to the education programmes we provide for our pupils and the assessments they subsequently take. Above all, literacy education must relate to our children's lives—it must be real. By this is meant that it needs to reflect the pluralistic contexts in which children live. This assumption has implications for philosophies of teaching and for the methodologies and materials used to support these philosophies. Hence the need for a broad definition of literacy to reflect and embrace the cultural and linguistic diversities we increasingly meet in the classroom—a concept which intends to confer "ownership" of language to the learners, appropriate to the context. Inherent dangers include, for example, interpretations of the narrow range of literacy skills measured by standardised tests (e.g. MICRA-T: Ireland) which can imply a narrow definition of literacy and result in reducing literacy teaching to a limited set of isolated skills, unrelated to learner interest. To counteract this Au and Raphael (2000) recommend that the ultimate emphasis must be on critical literacy and higher-order thinking (p. 151). Engagement in critical literacy processes respects and empowers learners and supports Freire and Macedo's (1987) hopes for a society that is capable of "reading and (re)writing the world".

FACTORS INFLUENCING LITERACY

The concept of literacy "never seems to stand still" (Bruce, 1997). Changing demands for literacy (see Snow & Burns, 1998) indicate that our understanding of literacy is time-specific. As society changes, literacy changes in response. A wide variety of factors influence literacy at any point. For example, factors such as the complexities of technology, the uncertainty about accuracy of information (Cunningham, 2000), global economic competition and public policy initiatives (Leu & Kinzer, 2000) are cited in the literature. Mosenthal (1993) stresses the interwoven nature of politics with literacy, in that literacy is frequently defined in terms of agenda-setting and agenda-implementing endeavours. These examples give a flavour of how changing, responsive and contextual a concept literacy is. As society changes, our interpretations of spoken, written and viewed language are internalised against a different backdrop. We constantly integrate and process new knowledge in context-specific ways against our background knowledge and experience. Although much of this engagement with knowledge may be at an unconscious level, these changes influence our means of expression and representation. Freire's (1987) evaluation of the social and political world is that our "reading of the world" and possible "(re)writing" of it is changed through our literacy processes. This dynamic perspective on the fundamental value of literacy as an agent of change is central to the notion of citizenship and being "enabled to participate in society" (Healy Eames, 1999).

A crucial starting point, therefore, is the presentation of a dual perspective on the capacity of literacy: (i) as a concept changing in response to social construction and (ii) as an agent of change, which is elaborated on in the next section.

DEFINITIONS OF LITERACY

Definitions of literacy have changed over the years. Lower-level definitions have emphasised literacy as the ability to read, write and decode print (e.g. those proposed by UNESCO, in the 1950s). These definitions depict literacy as an upskilling concept in a culture-free context. Alternatively, higher-level definitions link the purposes of oral language, reading, writing and viewing to a capacity to reflect on the literacy engagement and make decisions resulting in greater personal autonomy and community participation (see Hall, 1998; Healy Eames, 1999; Hodges, 1999; Larsen & Williams, 1999). This latter perspective views literacy as a powerful change agent within the embedded context of culture and society.

In terms of trying to make sense of what comprises being literate, it is noteworthy that oral cultures were considered illiterate (see Mgydal-Ring, 2000) whereas oral cultures plus print were considered literate. So the symbol of the book and being enabled to interpret the written word are critical factors. Exploring this assumption in pedagogy terms may be interpreted as follows:

1. Oral culture + decoding of print = learning to read (a basic literacy).
2. Oral culture + print + use of critical thinking processes = reading to learn (literacy).
3. Literacy + metacognition = critical literacy (understanding evolves in course of chapter).

The conclusion arrived at here is that literacy equates with learning.

Interestingly, the recently revised English Language Curriculum (NCCA, 1999: Ireland) proposes that reading involves both learning to read and reading to learn. The application of a narrow understanding of the concept of literacy as "learning to read" has been a feature of many learning support programmes for pupils with learning difficulties, including dyslexia. In Ireland many of these pupils are 8 years old or more, when the focus should normally be moving to "reading to learn" (see Healy Eames, 2001). This case study reported on four dyslexic pupils whose interests reflect a need to "read for learning about their interests" and writing that is purposeful (e.g. writing to friend, Declan; writing to local newspaper about a controversial aspect of Olympics; writing about their favourite topics as opposed to writing on topics decided by teacher only, in which they reported having no interest). While there were obvious difficulties with written text production, they considered it worth the effort when motivated by the nature of the task.

Higher-order definitions of literacy are useful in terms of challenging how prominent definitions are framed in recent studies. For example, reading is regularly cited as the central component in most literacy definitions (see Martin & Morgan, 1994; Morgan et al., 1997) and, of course, reading is fundamental to being literate (Blair, 1998). None the less, it is important to express caution with the notion that literacy equates solely with reading. One can argue that this is dependent on an understanding of the term "reading" and, depending on the particular aspect under discussion, reading and literacy may be synonymous. Instead, a preference for terms such as "Reading Literacy" (Campbell et al., 2001) when discussing the relevance of reading to literacy is favoured. According to Campbell et al., (2001), "reading literacy", in addition to other abilities, is "directly related to the reasons why people read". This may be an even broader view than some may share about the meaning of reading. The second marker, therefore, that this paper proposes is that literacy is broader than reading alone. The next section describes the complexity of literacy.

THE LITERACY JOURNEY

The journey to becoming literate is complex. Key learning interactions and experiences are operational at two levels—"individual and societal" (Campbell et al., 2001). I have represented this complexity in Table 21.1.

Table 21.1 shows that a concept is broader than a literacy process or any single ability. It asserts that

- Literacy is more than "reading". It involves the integration of oral language, writing and viewing abilities as well.
- Being "literate" enlists a broad range of processes and contexts.

Because literacy comprises different abilities (i.e. reading, writing, oral language, and viewing) which implies the need for the activation of single/combined literacy processes (e.g. constructing meaning, reflection, expressing thought), different literacy abilities are operationalised and a wide range of processes may be activated across a range of social contexts. These abilities and processes are visible in a real way through their application in different contexts (e.g. media/political world), in specific subject areas (e.g. mathematics, computing) or communites (e.g, middle class, low SES, travelling). Each community, setting or subject draws on literacy for its own specific purposes. This is how a literacy concept is actualised (see contexts/concepts in Table 21.1). Thus, literacy is context-specific in that it provides the actor with the language to function within a given context. Literacy concepts represent the language that makes sense in a specific community (e.g. the sound bites of the media culture) or workplace setting (e.g. computer speak/applications in an IT environment). The literate community is made up of many sub-groups with their own particular literacy/ies. For a fulfilled existence, an individual is likely to engage in a variety of literacies between the home, the workplace and those related to their own interests. The more literate a person is, the more capable s/he is to deal with information change and representation (e.g. in a technological age). Hence, there is an absolute necessity to be equipped with fundamental literacy processes and abilities which are transferable across a range of settings.

FOCUS ON WRITING

Table 21.1 reveals that writing engages the pupil in many literacy-based processes, from initial expression of (unstructured) thought to the refined ideas that appear in a final draft. Pupils come to writing with a range of prior experiences and preconceived ideas. Many pupils, especially dyslexic pupils, view writing as hard work. While few mature writers would contest this view, none the less for

Table 21.1   Literacy taxonomy

Critical literacy, *the overarching concept of socially constructed literacies*		
Literacy abilities	Literacy processes[a]	Multiple literacies: concepts and contexts: *"the language of a specific community, setting or subject"*
Oral language	• Talk and discussion • Listening • Social collaboration • Expressing enjoyment and imagination	• **Cultural literacy:** *Communities have uniquely different capacities to express and support literacy* • ***Mathematical literacy:*** *Understanding the language of maths (e.g. maths texts)*
Reading	• Decoding • Engagement with text • Constructing meaning • Responding to and reflecting on text • Enjoying reading • Reading for different purposes	• **Economic literacy:** *Language of the market place* • **Media literacy:** *The language of the media world (e.g. sound bite culture)* • **Computer Literacy:** *Computer "speak" and application*
Writing	• Expressing thought, constructing ideas • Exploring different forms of writing for different purposes and audiences • Sharing/enjoying writing • Reflecting on writing • Formulating new ideas • Revising, editing and publishing writing	• **Political Literacy:** *The language of getting things done in the power arena*
Viewing /ICT	• Using ICT as a multimedia tool for the processes listed above • Accessing information • Exploring e. forms of text (e.g. hypertext) • Posting electronic texts on the Internet • Producing multimodal texts (Kress, 2000)	

[a] *The list of literacy processes outlined here is only a sample of the types of processes involved in becoming literate.*

writing to be a meaningful exercise it is vital that pupils associate enjoyment with writing.

There are ways that writing can be made more meaningful, for example by engaging pupils in

• themes related to their interests
• a range of writing forms for a variety of different purposes.

Too much emphasis has been placed on narrative, essay-type writing at the senior end of primary school. Pupils need to experience poetry, interactive writing as an introduction to drama, report/persuasive writing and letter-writing, as well as narrative. Self-chosen texts are an important option to build into literacy programmes. Knowing the pupil makes it possible to link the writing task to their own interests and purposes. Knowing the pupil well is demanding on teacher time. However, with dyslexic pupils it is a primary premise of good instruction to know the pupils' preferred learning styles (Reid, 1998) and conditions.

In Healy Eames (2001) these findings were noted in relation to the literacy-learning of four dyslexic boys (10–12 years):

- Each pupil has a range of specific interests. They would like reading and writing-related tasks to be linked to their interests.
- Because writing is hard work for them, they need to be goal-oriented and motivated. They would like writing to be purposeful and serve real communicative functions (e.g. writing to a newspaper to complain about the attitude of a journalist to the Para-Olympics was mentioned by Alan, mildly dyslexic, as an interesting writing task). All four confirmed that they are not motivated by busy, meaningless writing tasks.
- They each have different reading and writing needs. Importantly, interviews with these pupils reveal that they have a good sense of the help they need.
- Writing is difficult for a variety of reasons—spelling features highly. Their comments reveal that they need strategies to overcome this (e.g. self-monitoring strategies, banks of commonly used words, editing sheets, memory techniques).
- Regardless of skill level, their attitudes to literacy are indicators of the degree to which they are willing to persist with literacy-based tasks. For example, Michael (rated "severe") was more excited about his need to learn to write than Alan (rated "mild"). Alan (12 years) had internalised negative messages about his competence. Consequently his confidence had been badly shaken.

Dyslexic pupils: Writing and Metacognition

Informal conversations with class teachers yielded little evidence of dyslexic pupils' use of metacognitive strategies. In mainstream classes the boys frequently displayed lack of interest, opting out and diversion tactics. Yet in one-to-one review/revision exercises with these four pupils about their written drafts, there was increased evidence that they knew a lot about writing. On the whole they showed that they could conduct major and minor revisions (Graves, 1983). Although full of common errors (e.g. mispellings, omissions, substitutions, reversals, lack of punctuation), they could read their written pieces with little, if any, difficulty. Examples of revisions, when asked for by the researcher, included being able to locate errors and make substantial attempts at correcting them; making valid attempts at ways in which a sentence could read better; being aware of mis-spelling patterns they repeated (e.g. writing "but" as "put"; spelling "school" in three different ways in a short passage); identifying unfinished sentences. All of these revisions are really "major" ones where dyslexic pupils are concerned. It was exciting to see these pupils apply self-correction strategies, evaluate their own writing and make suggestions for improvement. The four boys displayed strategies fairly consistent with the degree of their learning disability—mild, moderate, severe. The key learning here is that teachers need to show pupils how to monitor their own work in progress as they don't do this automatically. When Ronan (rated "moderate") was asked why he hadn't re-read his piece and conducted the review exercise by himself, he shrugged his shoulders as if to indicate he didn't know it was relevant. It was apparent that he was learning. With enough practice in the one-to-one/small-group context it is likely that he would learn to apply this practice habitually. The more pupils monitor their own work and employ metacognitive strategies such as these, the more they are likely to take responsibility for their own learning (Reid, 1998). Certainly, learning to re-read and monitor their own work is a vital strategy for dyslexic pupils.

These findings have implications for teacher education and practice. Teachers need to:

- talk to pupils before designing and implementing programmes of work, to establish pupils' interests, preferred learning styles and conditions
- know how to facilitate writers on the journey from initial to final draft
- understand that the writing task will not be completed in one sitting
- facilitate interim sessions, mid-process, where writers have an opportunity to reflect on what they have written, to discuss it, to share it and to self-monitor their work in progress
- engage in these practices habitually until they become part of pupils' normal practice.

Writing gains have been reported when pupils engage in these processes (see NAEP, 1996; Healy Eames, 1999). These practices benefit all pupils on their journey to becoming literate (Graves, 1994; Levy & Ransdell, 1996).

CRITICAL LITERACY

Literacy emerges as a complex, organic phenomenon. It is a seamless language which enables us to collaborate socially, and which facilitates our "constructive, reflective" (PIRLS, 2001) interactions with the world. This interpretation borders closely on what Hall (1998) terms *critical literacy*. Critical literacy she describes as "coming to understand that one's own literacy practices and one's responses to texts are not only individual and personal but are socially constructed" (pp. 161–162). Practices of this nature allow readers to express their understanding and adjust their approach (Morgan et al., 2001), an outcome of metacognition (Reid, 1998). Table 21.1 places critical literacy at the highest stage of the literacy hierarchy, the overarching concept transforming multiple literacy concepts and contexts.

Table 21.2   A description of how literacy abilities and processes interact

Literacy ability	Literacy process	Description of engagement
Reading (Silent/oral)	Constructing meaning (CT)	Meanings are made when purposes are achieved during interaction of reader and text
Oral language	Discussion of text (CT)	Listening and responding to other(s), as a result of operating on new layers of thinking
Writing	Formulating thoughts and ideas through medium of writing (CT)	Discussing/Evaluating one's reading through writing helps reach wider audiences
Viewing/ ICT	May involve a combination of processes listed above but using electronic means	Discussing a text through electronic viewing may be facilitated differently (e.g. through hypertext)

CT = involves critical thinking

Literacy Abilities and Processes

As indicated earlier, to appreciate the complexity of literacy and the relatedness of the concept within and across social contexts, a sound basis in the literacy abilities of oral language, reading, writing, and viewing is essential. Table 21.2 identifies examples of the interactions between literacy abilities and processes when a learner and text interact through different media.

Table 21.2 shows that literacy is facilitated when different abilities and processes are engaged. Each of the literacy abilities requires the activation of a critical thinking process(es) to produce a literacy outcome. Figure 21.1 shows one example of the literacy continuum in action.

The ability to write interacts with the process of revising writing (requiring critical thinking and evaluation) for the specific purpose of producing a substantive, clear piece of work (i.e. written report), a product of higher-level functioning. Awareness

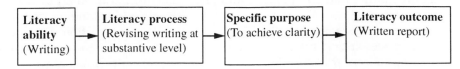

Figure 21.1   Literacy continuum in action

of audience for the written piece will help the writer to be more focused still. Thus, it is the interaction between the literacy ability and the literacy process(es) for a particular purpose that produces literacy in a specific context.

There are other concerns influencing literacy definitions and practices namely, attitudes to technology, assessment and construction of tests.

LITERACY IN THE TECHNOLOGICAL AGE

The way pupils receive messages is complex and has direct implications for teaching. In this section some of the challenges and benefits new technologies present for educators are explored.

Children grow up today in a very visual world, made up of TV, flashing lights, billboard advertising, and laterally, computer technology. Text, too, is becoming more visual. The structure of written informational texts is shifting to include richer visual and graphic displays, what Kress (2000) referred to as multi-modal texts. This expansion of formats and sources for information and ideas creates new challenges for readers, and since much of this reading is now done in new technological formats, readers need to learn new ways to evaluate texts and to combine ideas across several texts (Ogle, 2001). Interestingly, while technology may have caught many teachers unaware, children and adolescents appear quite capable and ready to embrace it.

Technology simultaneously presents two challenges for educators. It adds new possibilities for the exploration of literacy in critical ways and it challenges the more traditional view of literacy emerging from the printed page. Reinking (1995) believes that forms of electronic reading and writing are leading to profound changes in how we approach reading and writing tasks, how we communicate and disseminate information, and how we think about the teaching and learning of literacy (p. 152). Table 21.1 outlines some of the shared processes involved in using technology for literacy ends. Of course, underpinning all of this are the attitudes and readiness of the educators—they are key to the change process. Unless teachers are open to learning in the first instance, it is unlikely that they will be open to presenting and discussing these technologies in the classroom. In Ireland, addressing this challenge has begun through the introduction of training in ICT for all teachers. However, the degree to which teachers feel confident in working with these technologies in the classroom has not yet been evaluated.

Internationally, it is the view of many researchers that technology be recognised as an aspect of literacy to be included in pedagogy (e.g. Davis, 1991; Labbo, 1996; The New London Group, 1996; Scollon & Scollon, 1984; Talley, 1994). For example, in a study by Smith (2001) on multiple story book literacy (i.e. CD-ROM storybook), she details seven distinct literacy episodes of interaction which took place when the story was viewed and read from the computer screen by mother and child, namely: episodes involving artifacts (e.g. learning to use mouse, clicking and turning page); interaction with print; reading strategies; word meaning; story text; illustrations and hypertext; and episodes involving sharing and negotiating the routine. The visual appeal of the story on screen is an added incentive for engagement.

Computer-based learning approaches benefit many pupils. Visual strengths are apparent in many dyslexic pupils, and they appear especially to gain from the multisensory approach which the computer affords them (see Reid, 1998; Singleton, 1996; Healy Eames, 2001). In Healy Eames' study, a preference for computer-based literacy approaches was recognised by dyslexic pupils and their parents, but not maximised by teachers. This important support must not be overlooked. Contrary to one's initial hunch that a broader concept of literacy may be more difficult for dyslexic pupils (reading and writing to learn for one's own purposes), rather it seems that it may indeed be a motivating factor for them to try harder and to spend the time engaged in "overlearning" in order to achieve their own goals. Computer-based approaches seem to facilitate their learning more easily. It may be that they overcome their difficulties when they have more senses engaged simultaneously. One Special Reading Teacher of dyslexic pupils reported that "pupils choose to do computer-based literacy and Maths work over anything else" (Healy Eames, 2001). Critically, in this instance, how the pupils are supported requires understanding on the part of the teacher.

In a unique way, technology has the potential of exploring the concept of the "global village" and promoting multiple voices and perspectives. Luke (2001) welcomes the opportunity technology offers us to embrace multi-literacies. Understanding and appreciating multi-literacies requires much debate—interaction, dialogue and reflection between individuals. Herein lies a paradox. The oral culture which on its own is considered illiterate is likely to be the catalyst for critical literacy in the age of technology. It is through the discursive aspects of technology (e.g. e-mails, the chat/news groups) that knowledge can reach higher understandings. In the right hands, technology may indeed have the capacity to facilitate "knowledge as power".

MEASURING LITERACY PERFORMANCE

Successive studies have classified literacy performance according to various levels of interaction between individual competency and social demands (see Martin & Morgan, 1994; Morgan et al., 1997). Levels of literacy required for social functioning have varied across cultures and across time within the same culture. Today literacy is understood as a continuum, anchored at the bottom by illiteracy (Hodges, 1999, pp. 18–19). Attempts to define literacy have led to terms such as *functional literacy* (used by UNESCO in the 1950s), *marginal literacy*, *survival literacy* and *semi-literacy*. Snow and Burns (1998), in *Preventing Reading Difficulties in Young Children*, state that current difficulties in reading largely originate from rising demands for literacy, not from declining absolute levels of literacy. This report notes that in a technological society, the demands for higher literacy are ever increasing, creating more grievous consequences for those who fall short. The educational community needs to be aware that these higher demands may be unrealistic at certain developmental stages. Moves of this nature need to be carefully monitored. While endorsing the argument in favour of a holistic definition of literacy, it is vital within this working definition to discern between what is essential, desirable or superior, so we can be reasonable in our expectations of pupils' literacy performances and not overdriven by market forces. It is in the use of tests or assessments which may subsequently be interpreted inappropriately that the balance between the breadth of literacy and competency definition may be lost. Clearly, it is not easy to strike a correct balance that will meet all circumstances, and the rigours of time and thought need to be carefully applied. After all, it is on the young person(s) that we are imposing our standards. Because tests are widely accepted by educators and policy-makers for resource-provision decisions (see DES circular, 1999), it is important that we strive for an accurate and fair assessment of pupils' performance. The use of multiple assessment tools is certainly fairer than using the results of one standardised test. Notwithstanding this argument, the reasonableness of any assessment tool can only be evaluated against the definition of literacy which was used to frame it.

Criticism of Literacy Studies

As a measure of pupil literacy, in addition to reading, writing assessments need to be inbuilt on a more comprehensive scale. While acknowledging the reciprocal nature of reading and writing, it is unwise to presume that teachers place the same emphasis on writing in the curriculum if pupils are never assessed in this medium at a substantive level. Indeed, it may be argued that writing is greater evidence of literacy since it is the ability to produce and manipulate print for one's own purposes. Similar to the approach used in Campbell et al. (2001) in the area of "reading literacy", and in the interests of equity (see Au & Raphael, 2000), this chapter recommends an assessment of "writing literacy" as a means to achieving a more comprehensive, holistic measure of literacy. Of course, the type of writing assessed will need to be based on pupils' main purposes for writing at their particular stage of development. Broadly, a writing assessment needs to include a number of forms which aim to capture an individual's competencies when writing for specific purposes. In particular, there needs to be room for written text of a continuous, discursive nature wherein the writer will have an opportunity to demonstrate their thinking skills (see Healy Eames, 1999).

CHALLENGES FOR LITERACY EDUCATORS

The field of literacy presents a wide range of challenges for literacy educators. Au and Raphael single out one which merits particular mention. They make a strong case for supporting diverse students' engagement with both age-appropriate and reading-level appropriate materials:

> Teaching reading carries with it two obligations. On the one hand, we must make sure that all students are taught at an instructional level, within their zone of proximal development so that they make appropriate progress each year. On the other hand, regardless of reading level, we must engage students of every age in critical thinking using age-appropriate materials. (Au & Raphael, 2000, p. 152)

This practice needs to be encouraged for all, but especially for the literacy-challenged pupils so that pupils' attention is captured in order to "enable them to become powerful communicators, capable of analysing and presenting messages using a combination of written text and visual images" (p. 151). Motivation would appear to be a critical factor. In Healy Eames (2001), despite dyslexic pupils' difficulties with written language, they reported interest in reading about their own interests (e.g. car magazines, greyhounds, history, war), listening to read-alouds and being involved in paired reading of fiction texts. Practices which emerge from the pupils' life experiences (e.g. Language Experience Approach, Writing process) and which embrace multiple texts in context are more likely to promote critical literacy and confer "ownership" on the students about the function of their literacy learning capabilities.

SUMMARY

Literacy is an important construct at the macro/context level and the micro/individual level. It is a broad concept that is time- and context-specific. An agent of change, literacy is broader than reading alone. Subject to a wide range of influences, in particular, technological change has challenged our understandings of literacy in recent times. Overall, the literature reveals a picture of literacy as a socially constructed phenomenon within the embedded cultural context (Vygotsky, 1978; Bruner, 1986).

Pedagogically, literacy teaching needs to be real in order to embrace the diversities of pupils' experiences and it needs to be broad in order to challenge them to be tolerant of the multiple perspectives that exist in a pluralistic society. This needs to be reflected in the range of classroom texts and literature in use in the classroom. Assessment needs genuinely to reflect and capture this broad view of teaching. The pre-service and in-service literacy education of teachers is key to supporting this reconceptualisation of literacy.

With dyslexic pupils in mind, teachers need to learn to observe and listen to what such pupils are saying about their interests, learning styles and preferred conditions, in order to make suitable decisions for literacy teaching.

Implications

These deliberations give rise to a number of key implications for practice.

- The importance of the formulation of a broad definition of literacy which stresses higher-order functions and critical thinking—the conduit of critical literacy. This is a recognition that literacy is more than a single ability or process, but rather the symbiotic interaction of abilities and processes for specific purposes.
- The need for well thought out instructional programmes which reflect a broad definition of literacy, and which are responsive to pupils' interests and preferred learning styles. A balanced view of literacy education needs to include

direct, systematic and constructivist approaches to learning and literacy where the teacher is the key agent. Programmes should emphasise a range of active, reflective methodologies which engage metacognitive processes (Reid, 1998).

- The benefits of advances in technology to literacy education, including learning difficulties and dyslexia, need to continue to be explored from research and practice perspectives.
- Assessments need to be framed against the background of a broad concept of literacy and not just a narrow range of skills which can undermine effective teaching. Writing assessments, while difficult and time-consuming, need to be more effectively included in literacy assessments.
- Teaching materials and literature should reflect philosophies of teaching and need to be both age- and reading-level appropriate.
- Ongoing professional development for teachers needs to be supported and encouraged as part of education policy. Forums are needed where teachers are engaged in collaborative settings to debate and formulate their own definitions of literacy, and to engage in conversations and decision-making about best practice, pupil performance, and programme design.
- Informed educators and researchers need to work closely with policy-makers to inform political agendas about the implications of changing concepts and definitions of literacy. The merits and pitfalls of practices such as high stakes assessment (US) and the Literacy Hour (UK) need to be carefully considered.
- There needs to be an acknowledgement that practitioners are more likely to be concerned with the broad literacy picture whereas researchers may be exploring a single aspect of literacy which contributes to the overall picture. Because this is likely to be so, it is important that when researchers write they contextualise their findings against the background of the broader teaching context.

Directions for Research

It is fitting to end this chapter, and indeed this book, on dyslexia and literacy, with the view that studies which explore the relationships between emotions, environment and literacy performance are needed. Supportive classroom environments and pupil–teacher relationships leading to healthy pupil self-esteems contribute immensely to positive literacy experiences and performance in the classroom (Hagtvet, 2001; Berg & Lick, Dudelange School Project, 2001). This can be a constructive way forward for research and practice.

REFERENCES

Au, K.H. & Raphael, T.E. (2000). Equity and literacy in the next millennium. *Reading Research Quarterly*, 35(1), 143–159.
Berg, C. & Lick, P. (2001). "Schools Where Literacy Thrives: Emotional Situation and Literacy Achievement in the Dudelange School Project". Paper presented at 12th European Conference on Reading, Dublin, Ireland, 1–4 July 2001.

Blair, T. (1998). Achieving a balanced literacy programme: making a distinction between goals and instructional techniques. In G. Shiel & U. NiDhalaigh (Eds), *Developing language and literacy: The role of the teacher. Reading Association of Ireland*, 46–54.

Bruce, B.(1997). Current issues and future directions. *Reading Research Quarterly*, 35(1), 1–2.

Bruner, J.S. (1986). *Actual Minds, Possible Worlds*. Cambridge, MA: MIT Press.

Campbell, J.R., Kelly, D.L., Mullis, I.V.S., Martin, M.O. & Sainsbury, M. (2001). *Framework and Specifications for PIRLS Assessment 2001* (2nd Edn). Boston, MA: PIRLS International Study Centre.

Cunningham, J.W. (2000). Snippets: How will literacy be defined? *Reading Research Quarterly*, 35(1), 49–50.

Davis, J. (1991). Emergent literacy in two educational settings: A traditional kindergarten classroom and a holistic computer intervention. *Reading Research Quarterly*, 36(2), 152–183.

Department of Education & Science (DES): Ireland. (1999). Circular 8/99, *Services of a Resource Teacher*.

Freire, P. & Macedo, D. (1987). Literacy: Reading the word and the world. *Reading Research Quarterly*, 35(1), 143–159.

Graves, D.H. (1983). *Writing: Teachers and Children at Work*. Portsmouth, NH: Heinemann.

Graves, D.H. (1994). *A Fresh Look at Writing*. Portsmouth, NH: Heinemann.

Hagtvet, B. (2001). *Early Literacy Stimulation in a Preventive Perspective*. Keynote address presented at 12th European Conference on Reading, Dublin, Ireland, 1–4 July 2001.

Hall, K. (1998). "Our nets define what we shall catch": Issues in English Assessment in England. In G. Shiel & U. NiDhalaigh (Eds), *Developing language and literacy: The role of the teacher. Reading Association of Ireland*, 153–167.

Healy Eames, F. (1999). "The Teaching of Writing in Irish primary schools: Instruction, Curriculum and Assessment". PhD. thesis, National University of Galway.

Healy Eames, F. (2001). "Dyslexia and literacy learning in educational disadvantaged settings: multiple perspectives". Papers presented at 12th European Conference on Reading, Dublin, Ireland, 1–4 July 2001; ESAI Conference, Limerick, Ireland, 6–8 September 2001.

Hodges, R.E. (1999). *What is Literacy? Selected Definitions and Essays from The Literacy Dictionary*. Delaware: International Reading Association.

Martin, M.O. & Morgan, M. (1994). *Reading Literacy in Irish Schools: A Comparative Analysis. Irish Journal of Education*, vol. 28. Dublin: Educational Research Centre.

Kress, G. (2000). "Writing in the Context of Multi-modal Communication". Paper presented at International Reading Conference, Dublin, 29 September 2000.

Labbo, L. (1996). A semiotic analysis of young children's symbol making in a classroom computer center. *Reading Research Quarterly*, 36(2), 152–183.

Larsen, S.M. & Williams, K.A. (Eds.) (1999). *The Balanced Reading Program: Helping All Students Achieve Success*. Delaware: International Reading Association.

Levy, C.M., & Ransdell, S. (Eds.) (1996). *The Science of Writing: Theories, Methods, Individual Differences and Applications*. NJ: Erlbaum.

Leu, J.L. & Kinzer, K.K. (2000). The convergence of literacy instruction with networked technologies for information and communication. *Reading Research Quarterly*, 35(1), 88–105.

Luke, A. (2001). Talking about teaching. *Reading Today: Newspaper of the International Reading Association*, 18(6), 18–19.

Morgan, M., Hickey, B. & Kellaghan, T. (1997). *International Adult Literacy Survey (IALS): Results for Ireland*. Dublin: Stationery Office.

Morrow, L.M., Tracey, D.H, Woo, D.G. & Pressley, M. (1999). Characteristics of exemplary first-grade literacy instruction. *Reading Teacher Journal*, 52(5), 462–476.

Mosenthal, P.B. (1993). Understanding agenda setting in reading research. *Reading Research Quarterly*, 35(1), 54–56.

Mygdal-Ring, M. (2000). Literacy as a resiliency factor in Samoans. In I. Austad and E. Tosdal Lyssand (Eds.), *Literacy—Challenges for the New Millennium* (pp. 213–224). Stavanger: Centre for Reading Research.

NAEP (1996). *The Nation's Report Card: NAEP Facts*. Washington, DC: US Department of Education. National Assessment of Educational Progress. Office of Educational Research and Improvement.

National Council for Curriculum and Assessment (NCCA) (1999). *Curriculum for Primary Schools: English Language*. Dublin: NCCA.

Ogle, D.M. (2001). 'Reading in the 21st century: Challenges and possibilities'. Keynote address presented at 12th European Conference on Reading, Dublin, Ireland, 1–4 July 2001.

Reid., G. (1998). *Dyslexia, A Practitioner's Handbook*, Second Edition. Chichester: Wiley.

Reinking, D. (1995). Reading and writing with computers: Literacy research in a post-typographic world. *Reading Research Quarterly*, 35(1), 143–159.

Scollon, S. & Scollon, R. (1984). Run Trilogy: Can Tommy read? In *Reading Research Quarterly*, 36(2), 152–183.

Singleton, C.H. (1996). Computerised screening for dyslexia. In G. Reid (Ed.), *Dimensions of Dyslexia, Vol. 1, Assessment, Teaching and the Curriculum*. Edinburgh: Moray House Publications.

Smith, C.R. (2001). Click and turn the page. An exploration of multiple storybook literacy. *Reading Research Quarterly*. 36(2), 152–183.

Snow, C.E. & Burns, M.S. (1998). *Preventing Reading Difficulties in Young Children*. Committee on the Prevention of Reading Difficulties in Young Children. Washington, DC: National Academy Press.

Talley, S. (1994). The effects of a CD-ROM computer storybook program on Head Start children's emergent literacy. *Reading Research Quarterly*, 36(2), 152–183.

The New London Group. (1996). A pedagogy of multiliteracies: Designing social futures. *Harvard Educational Review*, 66, 60–92.

Vygotsky, L.S. (1978). *Mind in Society: The Development of Higher Psychological Processes*. Cambridge, MA: Harvard University Press.

INDEX

Lightning Source UK Ltd.
Milton Keynes UK
UKOW020604020512

191840UK00003B/26/P

9 780471 486343